Beyond Phenomenology

Rethinking the Study of Religion

Gavin Flood

CASSELL

London and New York

Cassell
Wellington House, 125 Strand, London WC2R 0BB
370 Lexington Avenue, New York, NY 10017–6550

First published 1999

British Library Cataloguing in Publication Data
A catalogue record for this book is available from the British Library.
ISBN 0 304 70131 9 Hardback
       0 304 70570 5 Paperback

Library of Congress Cataloging-in-Publication Data
Flood, Gavin D., 1954–
      Beyond phenomenology: rethinking the study of religion/Gavin Flood.
          p.   cm.
      Includes bibliographical references and index.
      ISBN 0–304–70131–9 (hardcover).—ISBN 0–304–70570–5 (paperback)
          1. Religion—Study and teaching. 2. Religion—Methodology.
      I. Title.
      BL41.F57   1999
      200'.71–dc21   99–12544
                                                                        CIP

Typeset by York House Typographic
Printed and bound in Great Britain by Biddles Ltd, Guildford and King's Lynn

Contents

Acknowledgements

Although the formation of this book was accomplished within a comparatively short span of time, its roots go back many years, particularly to lively discussions with fellow postgraduate students at Lancaster University, which provided an excellent research culture, and to the stimulating classes of Professor John Bowker and Professor Paul Heelas who raised many of the issues this book grapples with. Since that time my thoughts have been clarified in dialogues with others, among whom I would particularly like to thank Dr Fiona Bowie of the University of Wales, Lampeter, who raised with me the issue of feminist scholarship; Dr Rich Freeman of the University of Michigan who infected me with his contagious enthusiasm for a certain kind of linguistic anthropology; and Professor Richard Roberts of Lancaster University, who drew my attention to the need for the author's presence and commented on a draft of chapter one. Dr Sophie Gilliat of the University of Exeter also commented on an early draft of the first chapter and my thanks to her. I would like to thank Dr Robert Segal of Lancaster University for his extremely helpful comments on part of the manuscript and for drawing my attention to problematic areas in the philosophy of science. Dr Russell McCutcheon of Southwestern Missouri State University, who suggested an amended title, commented very usefully on a draft of the entire manuscript, as did the critical, but again useful, anonymous reader's report. Dr Oliver Davies has been an excellent 'dialogue partner' and (if he reads it!) will recognize conversations we have had in its pages. Another dialogue partner, Luke Hopkins – who will perhaps resist the shift from consciousness to utterance – has also provided many rich conversations over the years. Lastly I should like to thank my mother who in 1974 gave me a copy of Borges' collected poems; the 'other tiger' has been with me ever since.

Permission to reprint the following is gratefully acknowledged: nine lines (p. 145) from 'The Other Tiger' translated by Norman Thomas di Giovanni in *Jorge Luis Borges: Selected Poems 1923–1967* edited by Norman Thomas di Giovanni (Allen Lane The Penguin Press, 1972) translations copyright © 1968, 1969, 1970, 1971, 1972, 1985 by Emecé Editores S.A. & Norman di Giovanni. Reproduced by permission of Penguin Books Ltd.

For Professor John Bowker

ममाचार्येभ्यो नमः

'But I hear *voices* in everything and dialogic relations among them.'
(Bakhtin, *Speech Genres and Other Late Essays*)

Introduction: the relevance of metatheory

In his famous *Mimesis*, Eric Auerbach opens his text by contrasting the story of Odysseus' scar with the biblical narrative of Abraham and Isaac. In Homer's story the old nurse Euryclea recognizes the hero returned to Ithaca disguised as a beggar by the scar on his thigh. We are told every detail of how Odysseus restrains the joy of the old woman as well as how he obtained the scar. The narrative is clear, within a well-ordered temporal frame in which nothing is hidden, where all is visible and illuminated. This contrasts starkly with the biblical narrative of God commanding Abraham to sacrifice his son Isaac which he obeys, only to be restrained by God at the last minute. Here we are told very little, only the bare necessity to illumine the narrative with all else kept in obscurity.[1] Auerbach takes these as narratives representing the Greek and Jewish traditions, the one emphasizing light and clarity with nothing left unsaid, the other emphasizing darkness and things hidden, outside of conscious awareness.

The contrast in these narratives in our own time might be taken to represent the Enlightenment desire for clarity, truth and temporal order, which is questioned by postmodernity in which there is temporal rupture, resistance to closure, and an emphasis on ambivalence and hybridity, with things remaining obscure. The present book is written at a time when these two positions, one might say powers, have argued over the contested ground of truth and knowledge, and at a time when the humanities and social sciences have gone through, and are going through, a process of self-reflection and a questioning of their presuppositions and horizons of possibility. This book attempts to locate the academic study of religion within this contested arena of meaning

1

and explanation, aligning issues in the study of religion with issues in other fields of cultural inquiry. While not abandoning the importance of reason and clarity, the book does wish to absorb into the academic study of religion ideas of indeterminism, the situated nature of inquiry and its dialogical nature, and the importance of a reflexive or met-atheoretical discourse about religious studies.

Such a reflexive discourse has not been absent and there have been, at times, heated debates about the purpose and methods of the academic study of religion and whether the term 'religion' itself is a category that has significance outside a particular history in the West. I hold the view that the academic study of religions is an important, viable endeavour that can be examined within the subject area of 'religious studies', but that must draw upon other disciplines because 'religion' cannot be separated from historical, social and cultural contexts. To the question 'then why not simply study religion within anthropology, philology, politics, history or sociology?' I would answer, because religions are certain kinds of value-laden narrative and action that can be distinguished from other kinds of cultural forms (going to church is different from going to the supermarket) but which are only given life within specific cultures. But this is not to present a picture of religion as a category outside of history and narrative. Indeed, there can be no discourse of religion outside of specific cultures (even globalized culture is specific in its historical occurrence). Conversely, while some kinds of cultural expression can be identified as religious in contrast to cultural forms that are not, there are also 'religious' dimensions to many aspects of culture (such as football or running). Nor do I hold to the view that religion can simply be reduced to politics. While it is integral to any understanding of religion, there are forms of religion resistant to political power (such as the survival of traditions in the face of political oppression or simply wider cultural indifference) and questions addressed by religions that resist erosion by the course of history. Questions about meaning and purpose arguably arise in varied cultures and histories, which itself poses the question of whether there is a common human nature.

Metatheory, theory and practice

But there are two problems with the present state of religious studies. First, while the academic study of religions has largely moved away

2

from essentialist understandings that religion has some common, per-haps transcendent, essence, it has only begun to take seriously the claim that religion cannot be abstracted from its cultural matrices. Courses on 'world religions' still present these constructed entities as if they are in some timeless realm (perhaps a realm of pure doctrine) outside of wider cultural patterns and history (especially colonial history, the relation between religion and capitalism, and recently globalization). This is markedly true of 'eastern' traditions that absorb the West's projections, but also true, though to a lesser extent, of Christianity. This can sometimes be linked to an often hidden, totalizing claim about the 'spiritual unity' of these traditions, itself developing out of liberal Protestantism. To address this issue the academic study of religion needs to examine religions within their political, cultural and social contexts. This kind of work is being done in other disciplines, the reading of 'literature' alongside other kinds of writing, for example; I am thinking particularly of the new historicism and Stephen Green-blatt's work on Shakespeare and the Renaissance. We need much closer attention to religious texts being read alongside political documents, and questions asked concerning the constraints operative upon the text, the pervasiveness of social agency within them, and questions of resistance and compliance. This book does not directly engage with this problem which is best done in the context of specific regional studies.

The second problem, that this book does seek to address, is the need for the academic study of religions to engage much more with wider debates in the social sciences and humanities and to develop a rigorous metatheoretical discourse. This problem is directly related to the first in so far as the construction of 'world religions' is underpinned by a certain kind of theorizing whose roots are in the Enlightenment and which seeks universals. The ability to abstract the world religions from history and to see them as in some sense equal (though often not equal to Christianity with which they have been set in contrast), might itself be seen as part of the modernist idea of progress towards a clearer future in the academy, emerging, as Blumenberg reminds us, from a developmental process governed by scientific method.[2] Abstracting the world religions and presenting them as 'objects' of study is part of this progress whose scientific method, it is claimed, generates accurate, objective knowledge. Within the borders of its own field, religious studies needs to examine these kinds of questionable assumptions and to look at the ways in which its categories have been formed and its knowledges constructed.

3

There has been a decided lack of enthusiasm for metatheory within the subject area and this book hopes to contribute to redressing this imbalance. Moccasin walking or empathy does not provide a sufficiently rigorous theoretical basis on which to build an academic discipline. Indeed, within the academic study of religion there has been a strong antitheoretical tendency and a resistance to metatheoretical discourse. This antitheoretical tendency has rather sought to foster a pragmatic approach to 'world religions', that might use phenomenology or a 'toolbox' method. On this line of thinking what is important are the 'data' and the illumination of the data, by any methods that are to hand. The antitheorist simply claims that world religions are historical realities that demand 'our' understanding (for 'we' who stand outside of them) and all that is required is fellow-feeling and empathy. For the antitheorists, who might situate themselves within the phenomenology of religion, religious data are transparent as 'religious'. But this is to beg questions not only about the nature of these 'religious data' but also about the nature of the inquiry that is taking place: why is it taking place and who is doing the inquiring?

There are two potential criticisms of the present project from the antitheorists that I wish to pre-empt. The first is that a meta-theoretical discourse is irrelevant to practice; there can be metatheory until the cows come home but in the end, so what? The second is that the discussion of issues and thinkers highly relevant to metatheory within the general areas of the philosophy of social science, literary theory and anthropology, is irrelevant to the academic study of religion; that the links between these disciplines and religious studies are tenuous at best. In response to these potential criticisms I would wish to argue that metatheory *does* matter because it affects theory, questions the apparent transparency of practice and data, and even that the institutional future of the study of religions depends upon it. If the antitheorists win the day then religious studies will be marginalized at intellectual levels, will not be taken seriously by other disciplines, and will, in the end, lose out in the all too important institutional competition for limited funds. Metatheory provides a rigour at the level of discourse, interfaces with other disciplines and so integrates religious studies into the wider academy, and the only way a discipline can develop is through reflexive critique.

In relation to sociology Ritzer has defined metatheory as 'the systematic study of the underlying structure of sociological theory'.[3] We can replace 'sociological theory' with 'theory of religions' and add the 'practice of the academic study of religions' to express what I intend by the term 'metatheory'. Metatheory in the academic study of religions is critical reflection upon theory and practice. Through metatheoretical analysis we can attempt to unravel the underlying assumptions inherent in any research programme and to critically comment upon them; a metatheoretical perspective is a critical perspective. It involves deconstruction in the analysis or rereading of texts that are its object. In contrast to the antitheorist, the metatheorist would argue that data are not transparent and that the fault-lines and tensions within a research programme can be brought into the open; a metatheoretical perspective is therefore a reflexive perspective. If, as Ritzer claims, metatheory is coming of age in sociology, it has hardly been born in religious studies. This is partly because there is as yet no critical mass of metatheorists within the subject area, as there is in sociology, but also more importantly because, with the exception of some university departments, there is a strongly antitheoretical tendency. There is comparatively little work done on the paradigms operative within the study of religions, an unquestioning use of methods developed long ago and, although with notable exceptions, a suspicion of any metatheoretical perspective. But before developing a metatheoretical perspective, let me here briefly illustrate the importance of metatheory in relation to religious studies and its practice, through an example from Eliade.

Taking a passage almost at random from the Eliade *œuvre*, we read in *The Myth of the Eternal Return*:

> Every ritual has a divine model, an archetype; this fact is well enough known for us to confine ourselves to recalling a few examples. 'We must do what the gods did in the beginning' (*Śatapatha Brāhmaṇa*, VII, 2, 1, 4). 'This the gods did; thus men do' (*Taittiriya Brāhmaṇa*, I, 5, 9, 4). This Indian adage summarizes all the theory underlying rituals in all countries. We find the theory among so-called primitive peoples no less than we do in developed cultures.[4]

This passage implicitly contains his theory of hierophany, that religious forms manifest the 'sacred', and the theory that ritual recapitulates myths of origin and, indeed, that the origins of ritual are in myth. But the theory of hierophany is itself questionable from a cultural materialist perspective and based on an implicit theological and ahistorical understanding of religion; an understanding that sees religion as transcending history. Eliade's statements about ritual in the

5

Indian context are particularly open to criticism, for example from Staal's perspective of Vedic ritual as having syntax but no semantics, structure but no meaning, or from, say, a Girardian perspective that sacrifice is a kind of safety valve that channels a society's violence. That every ritual 'has a divine model' is far from clear and is unreflexively assumed.

The critique of Eliade (not to mention his defence) is by now well established. It is not my intention to score points through criticizing him – indeed, he remains a giant figure in the academic study of religion – but merely to point to the relevance of metatheory. A metatheoretical critique of Eliade would not necessarily present an alternative theory of ritual, but would bring out Eliade's implicit assumptions about the foundational basis of knowledge about religion and contextualize his readings of religion within a specific social, historical and, indeed, political time-frame. Not to mention the personal trajectory of his astonishing career and his existential encounter with the 'terror of history' that stands opposed to the ahistorical sacred, a metatheoretical analysis would examine what McCutcheon has called the 'politics of nostalgia' in the context of mid-twentieth-century politics and wider historical framework.[5]

Metatheory is therefore very important within the study of religion, not only because its antifoundationalism reveals what lies hidden, but especially because what is hidden has immediate consequences at the level of praxis. This can be illustrated, most importantly, in religious studies pedagogy. Metatheory directly affects what goes on in the classroom from the university to the primary school. The teaching of religion, or rather about religion, largely follows from the work of the phenomenologists such as Eliade. For them, religion is a category that stands outside of history and socio-political structures, and is presented as a *sui generis* phenomenon, beyond other social and historical concerns. Many introductory textbooks to world religions used in tertiary education – let alone in secondary education – reflect this bias as McCutcheon has shown.[6] In such texts there is a general absence of theoretical and critical considerations and an assumption about the nature of religion as having a common essence variously manifested. McCutcheon offers numerous examples of such implicit assumptions in text books. For example, he cites Karen Armstrong's *History of God*, who can still write in 1993 that her study of the history of religion 'has revealed that human beings are spiritual animals . . . Men and women started to worship gods as soon as they became recognizably human.'[7] Such sentiments reflect a precritical approach to the study of religions and reflect implicit assumptions generated through 'world religions' scholarship.

There is nothing inherently wrong with assumptions, they are the inevitable historical contingencies within which we all operate. Indeed, as Gadamer has argued, 'prejudice' is a precondition for understanding. But metatheoretical considerations can make us aware of the importance of assumptions in theory formation or, in the case of phenomenology, a proclaimed renunciation of theory. The importance and relevance of metatheory can be seen in the necessity to deconstruct implicit assumptions about the nature of religion and its place, for such assumptions impact upon the classroom and so upon the wider society. Metatheory is important because it questions the contexts of inquiry, the nature of inquiry, and the kinds of interests represented in inquiry. Rather than a merely notional, objective description that engenders a kind of passive reception in the minds of students and children in the classroom, metatheory promotes questioning, critique and analysis, that, in my opinion, are educational ideals that should be fostered. Against the passive, notionally objective description of the antitheorist, the metatheorist promotes an active, perspectival, questioning of the ground of practice and the theory that underlies it.

Anticipating my argument, the kind of metatheory I wish to promote can be characterized as dialogical. Although the present text is a metatheoretical consideration, and there is little systematic discussion of concrete examples, it does have practical consequences for the study of religion. The phenomenology of religion, I argue, contains implicit assumptions about an ahistorical subjectivity – it entails a philosophy of consciousness – that is inevitably imported into practice, whereas the dialogical model I wish to support entails a philosophy of the sign. This means that rather than subjectivity (belief, cognition, inner states and religious experience) language and culture, the realm of signs become the locus of inquiry. Phenomenological description contains hidden assumptions about subjectivity and transtemporal objects, but focusing on language emphasizes the dialogical and situated nature of inquiry, that fosters rigour in analysis, reflexivity, and critique. For example, a phenomenological account of a Hindu ritual offering 108 pots of sanctified water to Gaṇeśa, will simply describe the pots and the actions of the participants in a way that assumes a detached objectivism. A dialogical account will assume the presence of the researcher, will be explicit about the research questions brought to bear upon the situation, and will focus on the analysis of language-as-performance in relation to action within a historically circumscribed horizon. Similarly, a dialogical reading of the New Testament might focus on the text as a literary document and upon the differing historical contingencies that produced both it and its reader. A dialogical account would therefore need to bring to the material different levels of narrative and its analysis.

This is not simply 'conversation' or a sharing of affective bonds that the term 'dialogue' might imply, but is 'critical conversation' – or even argument – that brings different kinds of analysis to bear. But unlike objectivist studies, it has implications for a wider interconnectedness in recognizing that inquirer and inquired-into are within a framework where discourse is possible. I hesitate to use the term 'common' framework, but certainly a dialogical model implies that researcher and researched are co-partners in dialogue, that they can share speech genres, that understanding is possible (though not necessarily translation), and that this occurs within an increasingly 'global ecumene', to use Ulf Hannerz' phrase.[8] Yet a dialogical model must also emphasize difference, particularity, and the non-closure of research. Such a model moves away from a postulated universalism and objectivism towards the sharpening of difference and clarification of discourse.

Lastly, metatheory is important because of the increasingly fragmented nature of the academic study of religion. As I will argue, if there is an extension of the liberal humanism of the academy to embrace the scholarship of feminism, postmodernity, gay criticism, or even religious scholarship, then metatheory becomes indispensable for the coherence of any discipline. If the study of religions is to become a critical study that interfaces with related disciplines and includes within it multiple theoretical positions and approaches from feminism to Islamic scholarship, then metatheory is the only ground where these approaches can meet. Metatheory provides the only possibility of shared discourse. The contribution to this discourse offered here is an argument for a dialogical approach set against the objectivism of phenomenology.

Setting the parameters

The most important paradigm in the academic study of religions has been phenomenology. Through the adoption of its method religious

8

studies hoped to reach an objective, unbiased, empathetic understanding of religions that moved away from the traditional Christian attitude to other religions either as wrong, or as pale reflections of its truth. In this sense the phenomenology of religion offered a welcome antidote to theological dogmatism and opened the way for the West to encounter other horizons of possibility. But the objectivism of the phenomeno-logical research programme can be brought into question from the perspective of postmodern indeterminism, and an argument presented that the understanding and/or explanation of religion is always histor-ically contingent; knowledge is always produced from a social base, though this base is rendered invisible by objectivist science. This histor-ical contingency entails a dialogical relationship between the object tradition and the method, between the researcher and the researched. Awareness of historical contingency means that a research programme is reflexive in the sense that interacting or conversing with its 'object' will also illumine its own context, its own assumptions and its own theory of method (or methodology). It is primarily the problem of phenomenology in the context of religion that the present study exam-ines. While not underestimating the force and importance of phenomenology, this book seeks to develop a critique of it broadly from the perspective of a hermeneutic or narrativist tradition (particularly the work of Ricoeur) and dialogism (particularly the work of Bakhtin and the Bakhtin school). Indeed, Husserl, Ricoeur and Bakhtin, so very different, are enormous figures always in the background of this study.

In many ways, the contrast that underpins this book between phenomenology on the one hand and hermeneutics and dialogism on the other, is a contemporary recapitulation of a distinction between the philosophy of consciousness (*Subjektphilosophie*) and the philoso-phy of the sign. The tradition of the philosophy of consciousness can be traced from Descartes, and beyond him to Greek thought, but it especially developed within German idealism of the late Enlight-enment and early Romanticism. Here it is associated with the work of Fichte who claimed that the intelligibility of the world only follows from the 'I' as the absolute ground of knowledge; the 'I' cannot itself rest on some other certainty.[9] This concept is foundational in German philosophy and, although he criticized Fichte, has echoes in Kant's idea of the transcendental unity of apperception. For Kant the intelli-gible, autonomous self is distinct from the world governed by laws. This philosophy of consciousness – the 'I' as the absolute ground of knowledge – can be traced through to Husserl who continues the transcendental inquiry of Kant and Fichte,[10] in his development of Descartes's subjectivity or 'I think' (*cogito*). From Husserl the assumption of the transcendental 'I' as the absolute ground of certainty enters the phenomenology of religion, as I hope to show.

In contrast to the philosophy of consciousness, the philosophy of the sign, that communication and systems of signification are more important than subjectivity in understanding society and culture, develops with the hermeneutical tradition from Luther and the Reformation, eventually to Schliermacher, Dilthey, Gadamer and Ricoeur. Here interpretation as a transindividual, historical activity takes precedence over subjectivity and consciousness. In contrast to Husserl, Dilthey's grounding of the human sciences is a shift, in the words of Gadamer, 'from the structure of coherence in an individual's experience to *historical coherence*, which is *not experienced by an individual at all*'.[11] The philosophy of consciousness is critiqued from this perspective of historical contingency and the self as a self-in-relation to others: communication and intersubjectivity take precedence over subjectivity as the basis of epistemology and analysis, and interpretation takes precedence over ontology. This move from ontology to hermeneutics, from subjectivity to communication is further enhanced by the development of the semiotics of Saussure and Peirce, and from them the structuralists and the Russian formalists. While it is the consciousness tradition that has been most important in German thought, the seeds of structuralism are nevertheless also found there in Jacobi's idea of knowledge as the relation (the 'linked determinations') between elements within perception.[12] It might even be argued that the philosophy of consciousness and the philosophy of the sign are opposites that generate each other and there has been tension between them throughout the recent history of philosophy. In structuralist accounts, meaning is found not in any essential properties, but in the relations between elements of a signifying system, and so the philosophy of consciousness has no ground, and inquiry must begin from the sign. These developments in turn lead to the poststructuralist critique of structuralism (e.g. Kristeva and Bakthin's critique of the formalists) and the postmodern deconstruction of the philosophy of consciousness (e.g. Derrida's critique of Husserl). We might say that in response to structuralism, two currents developed, the one as postmodern deconstruction, a hypercritical account of modernism, suspicious of all claims to certainty and knowledge which tends to read knowledge as power, the other as dialogism with its links to hermeneutics and narrativism, that is suspicious of claims to objectivity and truth, but is fundamentally grounded in communication and acknowledges a self-in-relation.

Within the extremely broad purview of the philosophy of the sign we have cultural studies whose intellectual foundations can be found in dialogism and hermeneutics, but most importantly in the dialectical, social thought developing from Hegel to Marx and, in the twentieth century, into the critical theory of Adorno, Benjamin and Habermas, among others. In broad relation to this subject area we have feminist theory and postcolonial theory that offer sweeping critiques, though often indirectly, of the philosophy of consciousness. These are the broad parameters of the landscape within which the academic study of religions now finds itself.[13]

In the following pages I wish to present a metatheoretical discussion, locating religious studies within the landscape I have outlined here, by showing how its predominant paradigm, the phenomenology of religion, assumes a Husserlian philosophy of consciousness and how this can be criticized from the perspective of the philosophy of the sign. My basis for the critique of phenomenology and the ghost of essentialism in religious studies is provided by the dialogical tradition in relation to narrativism, and I argue for the demise of the ahistorical, philosophy of consciousness within the academic study of religions in favour a historically contingent philosophy of the sign. While this critique locates itself broadly within a hermeneutical tradition, an alternative critique could equally be launched from the perspective of critical theory and emancipatory praxis,[14] though this is a path I do not take for it is not the tradition I find myself standing within and I am sceptical of the *Aufklärung* engendered by an ideal speech situation. Some of this book is spent in describing the arguments and positions of those I would wish to refute. I do this both because I cannot assume the reader's familiarity with these arguments and because it clarifies the following critique. I must repeat that this book is not a theory of religion but a metatheoretical analysis of phenomenology and an argument for dialogism. Nor is the book about the relation of postmodernity to modernity. While there are clearly continuities between deconstruction and metatheory, and I certainly wish to absorb indeterminism into the study of religion, the book locates itself within a broadly hermeneutical tradition that recognizes a distinction between 'insiders' and 'outsiders' and does not read relationships within culture purely in terms of power. It does not locate itself within postmodernism as pure, political critique.

A summary of the book's argument can found in the first chapter, which is followed by two preliminary chapters setting the scene by examining the nature of the academic study of religion in relation to reductionism and non-reductionism. The direct encounter with phenomenology in which the main critique is developed is found in chapter four, and the remainder of the book develops the implications of that critique in terms of narrativism and dialogism, arguing for dialogical practice in chapter seven and the ethical entailments of a dialogical religious studies in chapter eight. The epilogue considers some of the implications of the position I defend for the future of the academic study of religions.

1. The other tiger

In Borges' poem 'The Other Tiger', he juxtaposes the tiger incessantly constructed in the imagination with that of the real tiger that paces the earth beyond the text and beyond imagination. In this portrayal of a search for the 'real' tiger we have a metaphor for the search for an 'objective' understanding of the human subject and world which has traditionally been the goal of the social sciences and humanities. This goal of objectivity beyond representation is however, like Borges' tiger, constantly deferred and constantly slips out of reach. This quest for the objective and the real, while having its roots in the ancient world, particularly developed from the seventeenth century in the West at least, and by the twentieth century became articulated in the natural sciences, on the one hand, and the social sciences which reflected the methods and procedures of the natural sciences, on the other. But the quest for objective knowledge through rational investigation has, primarily since Nietzsche but especially with the advent of postmodernism, become the subject of severe criticism. Like Borges' tiger made of symbols and shadows, knowledge and understanding have been seen largely as constructed in the imagination of the researcher, and the quest for an objective truth independent of language or a particular system of symbols, has been abandoned by many within the social sciences and humanities. Within literary studies, sociology, anthropology, and philosophy, and especially with the development of cultural studies, there has been a move away from the idea of understanding any objective truth towards relativism and perspectivalism; that objectivity is relative to the contexts of its occurrence and to perception.

At the same time as the move away from objectivism, has arisen the erosion of boundaries between disciplines and inter-disciplinary approaches developed which draw from a number of sources. While this is not necessarily related to the erosion of objectivity (indeed some disciplines that cross traditional boundaries, such as biochemistry, are strongly wedded to objectivity), it does point to new configurations within academic disciplines and the creation of new 'symbolic cultures', each with their own rules of coherence and patterns for establishing knowledge.[1] The interface between these symbolic cultures has become the focus of intense interest and has generated new ways of approaching human subjectivity and intersubjectivity. At a general level the present study is set at the interface between the broad areas of the philosophy of social science and religious studies. More specifically I see this work as being located at the confluence of the phenomenological tradition, on the one hand, and the narrativist and dialogical tradition on the other, with the general aims of re-examining some central methodological claims at the heart of the phenomenology of religion and to take seriously the intersubjective nature of research.

By phenomenological tradition I refer mainly to Husserl, who inherits the German tradition of a philosophy of consciousness from Kant and especially Fichte, and by the narrativist or dialogical tradition I refer to Ricoeur, Gadamer and Bakhtin/Voloshinov who inherit and advocate a philosophy of the sign. Given a construction of the human subject in terms of a philosophy of the sign, any research programme external to the traditions it is applied to will be in a dialogical relationship with those traditions. The central argument of this book runs as follows:

1. The phenomenology of religion which advocates a method of bracketing the ultimate status of research data, the creation of typologies or 'reduction to essences', and empathy, entails a phenomenology of consciousness. That is, this method inevitably brings with it Husserl's idea of a disembodied, disengaged consciousness or epistemic subject who has privileged access to knowledge.

2. The philosophy of consciousness entailed by the phenomenological method can be critiqued from the perspective of the philosophy of the sign. That is, the self is a sign-bearing agent embodied within social and historical contexts, within narratives, rather than a disengaged consciousness. This critique of the philosophy of consciousness is a critique of the phenomenology of religion.

14

3. The critique of phenomenology means the recognition of the interactive nature of research, which firstly entails the recognition of the centrality of narrative in any research programme, and secondly that all research programmes are dialogical, constructed in interaction between self and 'data' or subjects of research.

4. The dialogical nature of research places language, and particularly utterance, at the centre of inquiry and provides the tools for the analysis of religious utterance. The dialogical nature of research entails that it is impossible to get behind language and its reference systems.

5. The dialogical nature of research entails an ethic of practice which reflexively recognizes the contextual nature of research and its implicit values and is sensitive to the power relationship in any epistemology.

Contemporary religious studies

The academic study of religions, as with other human sciences, is concerned with questions of human meaning, subjectivity and inter-subjectivity. It implies a theoretical as well as an empirical discourse concerning the relationships between 'self', 'body', 'culture' and 'transcendence' and concerning wider political issues of the relation between 'self' and 'other', 'first world' and 'third world', 'world capital' and 'ecosystem', and between 'global' and 'local'. The inspiration behind this book partly comes from puzzlement at what sometimes appears to be marginal interest in a developed metatheoretical discourse within religious studies and partly from the discipline's general failure, with notable exceptions,[2] not only to engage with broader intellectual issues but also to *influence* wider debates. This book is intended to be a contribution to the literature which addresses the contemporary theoretical and philosophical issues concerning method in the study of religion, as well as the nature of religion itself, generated both by the interface between religious studies and other disciplines, and by developments within contemporary religion. The study of religion should, echoing a sentiment of Richard Roberts, be drawn back 'from the intellectual and affective periphery to a position nearer the centre of current concerns in social and cultural theory'.[3]

This general lack of engagement with contemporary theory in the

15

study of religions is partially accounted for by the use of the phenomenological method and the acceptance of the implicit distinction between theory and method, and partially on account of the lack of a strong, reflexive intellectual tradition within religious studies itself as Walter Capps has implied.[4] Taking 'theory' to mean both the Popperian sense of hypotheses open to falsification and to the interpretation of the socio-cultural world, the argument might be that religious studies has method but no theory because it does not attempt to impose theory upon data, but rather wishes to allow religious phenomena to reveal themselves. There has been, of course, a lively debate, as we shall see, about the reductionistic or non-reductionistic nature of the discipline and the status of the concept 'religion', but little sustained debate with wider epistemological problems concerning the status of knowledge and the place of theory in the construction of knowledge. While the origins of the science of religion can be found, as Preus has so marvellously shown, as far back as Jean Bodin,[5] it is in the nineteenth century that the term 'science of religion' is coined by Max Müller.[6] But while the antecedents of modern religious studies can be found before the Enlightenment, it is nevertheless to phenomenology generally and to Husserl in particular that religious studies as the phenomenology of religion owes three of its most central concepts: that of 'bracketing' (*epoché*) truth statements, the intuition of essences, and empathy. Although, as Ryba has shown,[7] philosophical phenomenology and the phenomenology of religion are distinct, nevertheless the phenemenology of religion adopts bracketing, the reduction to essences and empathy directly from philosophical phenomenology. Some of the most important thinkers in the phenomenology of religion, Kristensen, Van der Leeuw, Eliade and Ninian Smart for example, have adopted, or partly adopted, the method developed by Husserl.

Yet given the importance of Husserl in religious studies methodology, there has been little continued discussion with him.[8] There has been no development of the phenomenological method since its adaptation by Van der Leeuw within religious studies and indeed the concepts of *epoché* and *eidetic intuition* seem to have been deemed sufficient in the methodological *bricolage* of the subject. Yet outside of religious studies things have moved on considerably and the phenomenological tradition has offered critiques of Husserlian method and has set out in new directions, some of which engage with the wider cultural movement of postmodernism. I am therefore 'coming from' a desire to see religious studies claim a place within the contemporary study of culture and society and not to be marginalized at intellectual or theoretical levels. I am convinced that where theory is disavowed in the interests of objectivity, there theory is most rife, and while it may not at the present time be possible to generate theory out of the discipline of religious studies in itself, it certainly is possible to generate a metatheoretical discourse within the subject area by drawing upon other, related disciplines, and by putting other disciplines alongside religious studies, to generate, as it were, an alchemical reaction between them. This book therefore wishes to have a foot in two camps, within the academic study of religion and within the philosophy of social science, that itself interfaces with other disciplines, especially literary theory. But while the emphasis of the book is on metatheory and its relation to method, in looking at theory one must not forget its object 'religion', which is such a vital force in the contemporary world, and which has bearing upon culture, society, and economics, and above all on human subjectivity and meaning. While recognizing that a discussion of methodology cannot be divorced from a discussion of that to which method is applied, namely 'religion,' this study intends to address the problem of method at the level of discourse rather than in terms of the ways in which method has been applied to the history of religious change. It is not a theory of religion, but a metatheoretical consideration.

As a way in to a discussion of the nature of the study of religions, the present chapter will provide a background by looking at the foundations of the academic study of religion, namely theology and social science. First I will discuss the relation between theological language and the language of religious studies, looking at how both theology and religious studies are discourses and kinds of writing which are underpinned by practices sanctioned by wider social and historical contexts. This discussion will point to parallels between theological language and the language of religious studies. Secondly, against this backdrop, we will be in a position to see how the discourse of religious studies inherits objectivist values that have traditionally underpinned the social sciences. Thirdly, I suggest that a metatheoretical discourse can be developed that critically reflects upon these foundations by keying in to what can broadly be termed narrativist and dialogical theory. There are a number of directions in which to go here. For the purposes of the present chapter I shall draw upon the work of Bourdieu and Bakhtin to sketch one shape of what such a discourse might look like, and shall develop this model in later chapters by drawing further on the work of Bakhtin, but also using Ricoeur. The academic study of religions had the seeds of a metatheoretical discourse in its partial engagement with Husserl's phenomenology, but this discourse has been slow to develop, and I will suggest that a dialogical model can provide the impetus for both reflexive critique and for developing the practice and writing which is the study of religions.

Religious studies and theology

The establishing of religious studies departments in the USA and the UK during the decades following the Second World War,[9] marked an important shift in the study of religion away from theology – traditionally regarded as an insider discourse, in Anselm's terms echoing Augustine, of 'faith seeking understanding' – towards a 'non-confessional' approach which tried to treat religions as key dimensions of human culture which can be understood in ways akin to other disciplines' understandings of their objects; to sociology's understanding of 'society' or psychology's understanding of the 'mind'. While institutionally theology and religious studies often find themselves in close proximity as there are many combined theology and religious studies departments in European (though not American or Canadian) universities, many within religious studies have perceived the separation of religious studies from theology as a hard-won battle which has separated a confessional understanding of religion from a non-confessional, objective one.[10] Religious studies tended to define itself negatively against theology, seeing itself as a rational scientific discourse, aligned to objectivist science. There is a discernible process in the development of religious studies on the one hand rejecting theology, while at the same time ironically drawing on Protestant theological tradition in the use of Otto, and beyond him, Schliermacher, while on the other hand embracing Müller's idea that there can be a science of religion. I shall therefore begin the discussion by briefly exploring the relation between religious studies and theology in order to show that the ground has now changed and that old debates and antagonisms between theology and religious studies have been superseded by fresh debates in the wider academy.

I shall attempt to illumine the differences between theology and religious studies by arguing that these differences have been primarily about language, but that the language of contemporary, academic theology is closer to religious studies than to traditional theology understood as 'faith seeking understanding'. Although they have different histories, both academic theology and religious studies are kinds of writing *about* religion, with convergence and divergence, and both arise from the practice of rational method. While this might be obvious, it is not a trivial point and has consequences for the location of these disciplines within academic discourses generally. This discussion will necessarily take us down paths that will be explored in more detail in future chapters, but of which some foreknowledge will be necessary. Examining the nature of the languages of theology and the study of religion shows us the ways in which these disciplines are located within the overall pattern of academic disciplines, and illuminates the nature of the differences between them.

Theology and religious studies are both kinds of discourse expressed in writings about religion. In speaking about religious studies we are primarily speaking, on the one hand, of an institution within the education system given legitimacy by the wider social and historical context of its occurrence (or *place*) and, on the other, as certain kinds of *practice* which result in a *discourse* primarily expressed, modifying a phrase of de Certeau, as the 'writing of religion'. This is directly akin to de Certeau's understanding of history as comprising a practice (discipline) and its result (discourse).[11] The discourse of religious studies that results from the practices embedded within the educational institution (practices such as rational analysis, readings of texts, or fieldwork), characterizes itself in a number of ways, but above all as the proclaimed value-free exploration of religious meaning and institutions which comprise its 'subject matter' or 'object'. The language of this discourse, as we shall see, distinguishes itself from the object of its investigation and presents itself as detached from that which it studies: there is a rift between the writing of religion and religion as the object of that writing, and the clearer the rift the more objective the discourse is perceived to be.

This is what has traditionally separated religious studies from theology. Whereas religious studies is a kind of writing about religion in which there is a clear separation between the discourse and the object of the discourse, theology, on this view, is a kind of writing about religion in which there is no separation between the discourse and its object. Theology is a reflexive discourse, a discourse about something of which it is itself a part; the reflexive self-description of a religious tradition. On this view, the language of theology is a language which *expresses* religion whereas the language of religious studies is a language *about* religion.[12] Weston La Barre once criticized theology for being meaningless in that if God is unknowable then theology is a science without subject matter and theologians are ones who do not know *what* they are talking about.[13] But this is to miss the point that theological discourse only claims to refer to something outside of itself as part of its internal discussion. Claims about transcendence are only ever constituted within language which is the articulation of tradition; from one perspective theology is a discourse about itself. Indeed, theology in this sense can become an object of religious studies discourse. Conversely, theology can use or incorporate the data gathered by religious studies into itself.[14] The issue of the distinction between religious studies and theology is therefore about different kinds of discourse and about the kind of the language they employ. To make this clear let us briefly examine the nature of theological language.

The language of theology and rational analysis

Like other academic disciplines, Christian theology in the West is given legitimacy by the wider social context in which it is embedded, by the place of its occurrence, but unlike other disciplines is legitimized not only as part of the educational establishment, but is also a part of institutionalized religion. The practices which lead to theology, or the discourse (*logos*) about God (*theos*), have therefore developed directly from a wider and deeper historical basis than the more recent study of religions, and the nature of contemporary theological discourse has its roots and draws its inspiration from the history of its traditions. The nature of theological language is, of course, a vast topic with a complex history, but our purpose here is simply to take some general, central features of theological language in order to juxtapose this language with the language of religious studies.

Nicholas Lash, citing Anselm's distinctions between soliloquy and allocution, monologue and address, suggests that whereas philosophical discourse is concerned with monologue, theological discourse is concerned with dialogue.[15] While it is obviously the case that philosophy can be conceived as dialogue – or conversation as Rorty would argue[16] – within texts and between thinkers over the centuries, what Lash means is that in contrast to philosophical language theological language is the language of address. Theological language claims to address an 'other' beyond discourse, beyond the world, and beyond all predicates,[17] although this claim is only ever constituted with the language of theology itself. Philosophical language, by contrast, does not address a 'Thou' or anything beyond itself and in this sense is monological. Theological language, for Lash, is dialogical language. Indeed, the breakdown of the possibility of faith in a meaning beyond the world is a feature of modern philosophy that distinguishes it from theology. Philosophy on this view cannot be addressed to anything beyond the world and is necessarily atheistic. According to Simon Critchley, philosophy in the modern world is atheism 'arising out of the experience of nihilism'.[18]

This dialogical language of address to that which is other than the world is also the language of analogy, based on the analogy of the being of God with the being of the world. It is through analogy that an attempt is made to circumvent the problem at the heart of theological language, as Ferré has described echoing Anselm, that to speak of God in terms of human language is not to speak of God but to speak of worldly things drawn from human, transactional experience. But, on the other hand, if theological language is not about finite things then it becomes meaningless for human finitude; theological language as 'univocal' or 'equivocal' is caught between anthropomorphism and agnosticism. As Ferré says,

> the theist would seem compelled to choose between *univocal* language, which makes the object of his talk no longer 'God' because merely comparable to the rest of his experience, and *equivocal* language, which 'cleanses' the terms used in describing God entirely of any anthropomorphism but thereby forces the theist into a position of total agnosticism.[19]

Ferré describes a third way between these extremes; the logic of analogy, the abstraction of a characteristic from finite being applied to infinite being. Thus God can be described as a 'father', a 'king' or as 'love' – or, indeed, in the Indian traditions as 'mother' (*mātṛ*), 'old crone' (*kubjikā*) or 'child' (*bāla*) – although these are not without problem in that to understand the meaning of metaphor one has to understand the meaning of its primary and secondary terms, of both 'God' and 'king', or 'love' or whatever.[20] But while these are problems specific to theological language, theological language is not dissimilar to other forms of discourse in so far as analogy is pervasive. As Tracy says '(e)ach of us understands each other through analogy or not at all',[21] and the metaphorical space in which analogy occurs is at the heart of many if not all, at least Indo-European, languages.[22]

While theological language addresses analogically a 'Thou' beyond the world, in a more concrete sense it arises out of the practice of understanding revelation: revelation is the object and source of theological discourse, be it the Christian Bible, the Hindu Veda or the Moslem Qur'ān. Theological language, while centred on analogy, is the language of the interpretation of revelation and in this sense is an internalized discourse which does not refer to anything outside of itself. We can see this particularly clearly with Hindu theology where rival schools wrote commentaries on sacred texts offering alternative, often contradictory, readings concerning the key themes of knowledge, action, the nature of liberation and the relation of transcendence to the world. It is the place of revelation that distinguishes Hindu theology (astika) from its Buddhist counterpart (nāstika), although both share a common world and terminology about paths to understanding or shared discourse (vāda) and means of knowledge (pramāṇa). In this sense Buddhist and Hindu discourses are closer to each other than a Hindu theological discourse would be to a Christian one, exemplified, as Milbank observes, by the themes of creation, the Trinity, incarnation, christology and sacrament.[23]

So far, we have discussed the nature of theological language as traditionally understood, as a primary discourse about God and revelation. Contemporary theology, however, is an academic discipline which sits alongside biology, philosophy, history, religious studies and so on, within secular academic institutions as part of the liberal humanist, Western academy. Indeed, the question might be asked as to whether a discourse whose focus is on revelation has any place in a modern, secular university. In response to this question we must distinguish between two kinds of theological language, on the one hand theology as a primary discourse, on the other, as a secondary one.[24] Put simply, the former can be described in traditional terms of faith seeking understanding, of the language of analogy and of a discourse in Christianity about the Trinity, christology etc. The latter by contrast is a language about the primary discourse and is the subject of university degree programmes and indeed, much valuable research; but it is not theology in its primary and original sense. It is theology in this secondary sense, as the history of Christian theology, the history of a certain kind of analogical language, which is taught at universities and which often sits alongside religious studies at a pedagogical level within a single department. Theological language as a secondary discourse – or the history of theology – would not be dissimilar to the language of the religionist because at this level both the theologian and the religionist share a common practice of rational, critical analysis sanctioned by the wider society around them. Theology in this sense is not 'faith seeking understanding' but rather 'understanding "faith seeking understanding"' which is a particular form of the religionist's 'understanding religion'. In the sense of academic disciplines, both theology and religious studies stand outside of the narratives upon which they comment and of which they can offer critiques. Indeed, theology in this second sense only differs from a secular religious studies as concerns its 'object' tradition and in its historical trajectory. The degree to which personal religious agendas influence or should influence scholarship is an issue we shall return to presently. But at this point we need to make some general remarks about the process of rational analysis which characterizes, or rather is the practice which results in contemporary academic discourses.

The educative process in Western educational institutions, particularly since the Enlightenment, has been the transmission of a modality of thinking or practice characterized as the method of rational analysis.[25] This method of rational analysis, always founded upon narrative, entails the processes of the assimilation of material, the interpretation of material through the construction of appropriate hermeneutical paradigms and the critique of those paradigms. The method of rational analysis is a practice which is not limited in the scope of its inquiry and which generates a discourse characterized by openness and a critical distanciation from its object. This practice, however, does not occur in a kind of vacuum, but is communitarian and its practitioners have an investment in the maintenance of this rational community[26] of practitioners in open conversation. As such, the transmission of method therefore entails a dimension of power and implies the structural maintenance of certain social relationships (between teacher and student, between professor and lecturer, between government funding body and institution, or whatever). This transmission of rational analysis has, of course, been the subject of postmodern criticism of the Enlightenment project, although the practice of criticism which this critique presupposes is itself a part of the practice which it criticizes. While those who employ the practice of rational analysis might not agree with each other, all with investment in the 'academic community' in its widest sense share in this practice and its transmission.

But even though the method of rational analysis fosters discourses open to the otherness of the material at hand, this practice only ever occurs within specific cultural, historical or even biological and psychological contexts. These contexts constrain the method's field of operation. That is, the practice of method which results in a discourse always operates within a context; the human space and 'gendered location' in which analysis occurs.[27] All discourse is from a place. The objectivity which the practice of method proclaims is only ever reached, therefore, through intersubjectivity. This intersubjective agreement concerning the limits of a discourse, itself might be determined by deeper historical, social and economic forces. Thus intellectual concerns in the late twentieth century will be very different from those of the early twentieth century (although the practice of rational analysis might well be agreed to be the same). The context legitimates and allows the practice to develop which results in a discourse, or kind of language sharing common presuppositions. The content of theological and religionist investigation is deeply contingent upon wider social and cultural determinants and the content of a discourse will reflect the attitudes and ethos of the wider society in which that discourse takes place. But those discourses can also, most importantly, reflexively serve to critique the contexts of their occurrence.

The point I wish to come to is therefore that both the discourses of religious studies and of theology in its secondary and, most importantly, pedagogical sense as 'history of theology' are involved in the practice of method. Theology in a primary sense of 'faith seeking understanding' is nevertheless a critical discourse which assumes the processes of rational analysis, but within the context of 'religious' presuppositions. The Western discipline of theology is a kind of discourse whose language in a primary sense is concerned with rational reflection upon the themes of Christian revelation, while in a secondary sense is reflection upon that reflection which is the legitimate concern of secular institutions sanctioned by the wider social contexts of their occurrence. It is theology in the primary sense that religious studies has tried to distinguish itself from and this is because of the presuppositions underlying the respective discourses. The language of primary theology presupposes Christian revelation, whereas the language of religious studies presupposes the process of secularism, the language of social science and, ultimately, presupposes values derived from, or in reaction to, nineteenth-century positivism. Religious studies, in the end, comes from a tradition which places itself under the sign of reason and has placed religion under the sign of 'myth' and 'superstition'.

Postmodern theologies

While this is not the place to assess the importance of theology in the contemporary world, it is necessary to make some note of theology's responses to changes in academic discourse, particularly its responses to postmodernism. Theology can, claims Richard Roberts, either 'retreat ever more into the diminishing and fragmented redoubts of traditional religious discourse' or 'redefine in a comprehensive way the remit and tasks of divinity'.[28] Redefining divinity has been a task that evinces a range of theological responses, either agreeing with Habermas that the project of modernity is incomplete and introducing critical theory into their work (such as Helmut Peukert),[29] or by responding to liberal, universalizing theologies, on the one hand by simply reacting against liberal culture and against secularism, in a reactive retreat into traditional religious discourse,[30] and on the other by circumventing Enlightenment discourse through postmodernism and attempting to resituate theology within the contemporary, detraditionalized context. This postmodern trend, particularly articulated in the work of Mark Taylor, David Ford, David Griffin, Graham Ward, John Milbank, Richard Roberts, Oliver Davies and Jean Luc Marion, incorporates the 'postmodern turn' into theology, using the work, for example, of Levinas, Derrida and even Bataille, to address traditional problems and to reinvigorate Christian discourse with contemporary relevance. A discussion of this work is beyond the scope and purpose of the present text,[31] although it is highly relevant to religious studies, not only in an obvious sense as a discourse about religion, but for its critique of Enlightenment discourse. The postmodern turn in theology – in its primary sense – also allows for the possibility of a closer alignment with a theoretical discourse within religious studies, which is itself critical of the subject area's Enlightenment assumptions.

Part of the reaction against liberal theology has been the rejection of theological foundationalism; that religious propositions are open to rational assessment and that they somehow precede their expression in religious language and symbols. Lindbeck is in consonance with many religionists here when he claims that different religions produce divergent experiences, and that theological language shapes experience.[32] 'The proper way to determine what "God" signifies', he writes, 'is by examining how the word operates within religion and thereby shapes reality and experience rather than by first establishing its propositional or experiential meaning ... '[33] The narratives of tradition define or determine the experience of the claims of tradition. But nevertheless, Lindbeck still wishes to maintain a 'metanarrative realism' in which a Christian narrative is presented as a paradigm against which others (within Christianity) are measured and thereby, in Milbank's view, 'fails to arrive at a postmodern theology'.[34] Milbank, in contrast, wishes to develop a thoroughly postmodern theology which shows how secular reason itself develops out of theology, whose relativism allows the claims of Christianity to stand coherent within the bounds of tradition. Within this tradition others have developed positions that circumvent the modernist requirement of empirical or rational justification – such as Pickstock's account of the liturgy as the prime focus of meaning.[35]

Postmodern theological discourse has largely operated within the bounds of its own discipline, promoting a critique of secular reason; as there are no rational grounds outside of tradition from where to stand, it is quite legitimate, on this view, to promote a particular narrative above others. The critique of secular reason has also been expressed as a critique of religious studies and its Enlightenment assumptions. Garett Green, for example, has argued that as the academic study of religion begins to absorb the postmodern turn, the exclusion of certain theologians such as Karl Barth from the 'religious studies canon', while including other such as Tillich who are more in accord with a religious studies liberal agenda, is unjustified.[36] Indeed, there are no good reasons for *not* teaching about Barth's theory of religion within a religious studies programme, so long as Barth is set alongside Freud, Durkheim and so on. But nevertheless, while this is good practice at a pedagogical level, it is also the case that Barth is set within a quite distinct intellectual tradition – German Protestant theology – with its own internal problematics, whereas the thinkers lauded in the 'religious studies canon' are set within a historical tradition that contains its own secularist assumptions.

Given the postmodern critique of Enlightenment assumptions within liberal humanism that allows the development of critical theory, feminist theory, queer theory and so on, not only postmodernists, but liberal theologians or Christian scholars too have argued for the legitimacy of pursuing an openly religious, especially Christian, agenda. Along with Green, George Marsden has argued for the legitimacy of Christian informed scholarship in all disciplines within the publicly funded, secular university. In *The Outrageous Idea of Christian Scholarship*, Marsden argues that scholars who have a religious faith should reflect upon its intellectual implications for their work. As religious commitments are 'basic to the identities and social location of many if not most human beings, and academics routinely recognize such factors as having intellectual significance', then why should not religious factors be acknowledged and taken into account in public debate? Within mainstream academia there are, observes Marsden, 'Marxist, feminist, gay, postmodern, African-American, conservative, or liberal schools of thought', so why should not identifiable Christian (or indeed other religious schools) be represented?[37] Marsden criticizes the secular humanist assumption that religion is a wholly private affair that should not intervene in academic study or be part of a public arena of debate within the academy. So long as individuals or religious schools of thought agree to play the academic game and play by the rules of communication necessary for the exchange of ideas and genuine dialogue, then religions should have a legitimate voice – among all the other voices – within the academy.

This is a strong argument that, although uncomfortable for proponents of secular humanism, seems to follow from the logic of a position that would advocate, as I do, a plurality of voices within a secular academy. A Christian voice would become another in the contested ground of meaning, and a Christian critique of secularism and liberal assumptions would become another alongside feminist or Marxist critique. Which voices gain most influence and are heard above the others would become a matter not only of which institutions wield most power, but of what is sanctioned by the wider community. But it is not precisely clear – so long as scholars accept intersubjectively agreed academic standards, which means abiding by the procedures of method or rational analysis – that Christian scholarship in the majority of cases would be that different from 'secular' scholarship, as Marsden himself acknowledges. In some fields it might well be possible to develop subject areas along the lines that Marsden suggests. It is perfectly conceivable for there to be Islamic jurisprudence and feminist history taught within Western academic institutions which are driven by ideologies often critical of liberal humanism. Similarly, Christian literary studies would equally be conceivable, but could there be a Christian sociology of religion? While it might be possible for there to be a distinctively Christian view of religion (indeed, this is theology in the primary sense), it is not clear that there could be a specifically Christian social science, even though particular social scientists might be Christians, because social science has its own secular history. As Turner says, 'there is a basic logic and theory to the social sciences which cannot be subsumed under a particular ethnic or cultural or historical label.'[38] It is not precisely clear what a Christian or an Islamic social science would look like, or how it would differ from secular social science if it abides by the usual standards and procedures accepted by the academy. While the general point that an individual's beliefs and way of being in the world will inevitably influence their practice and fields of interest, and that these should be reflexively acknowledged, it is not clear that there could be a systematic research programme of Christian scholarship within the social sciences which contain implicit assumptions, critical of religion.

Even if we concede Marsden's point that there could be Christian scholarship in all areas of the academy, in the post-Christian world of the West the Christian scholarly voice would be a minority voice, unless there is radical change in the wider community which sanctions and pays for the academy. The call from liberal and postmodern Christianity for religious scholarship within the secular academic establishment is a long way from the objectivist aspirations of the early human sciences that modelled themselves on the hard sciences. Underpinning the language of religious studies, which sets it at a distance from the language of primary theology, have been assumptions about scientific objectivity and the superiority of external, reductionist explanations over insider accounts.

Social science and the study of religion

The quest for the third tiger, the objective reality beyond representation, beyond the text and beyond the practice which gives rise to it, has been a particularly strong motive behind both the natural and social sciences. Within the study of religion Samuel Preus has contrasted the 'reductionist' or 'naturalist' approach of the social sciences ('from Bodin to Freud') with the 'religious' approach of traditional ('primary'

28

in our sense) theology.[39] One might add to this a third approach – and the approach which is central to the discipline of religious studies – that claims not to be naturalistic nor yet religious, but claims to offer objective description of religion, namely the phenomenological (from Chantapie de Saussaye to Eliade). While these traditions are very different, both the naturalist and phenomenological have regarded themselves as 'scientific' in promoting the value of objectivity and that scientific method, although variously conceived by each, will result in the establishing of truth and of 'ideal types' which define particular patterns of religious thought and behaviour.

Both the phenomenologist Husserl and the sociologist Weber regarded their methods as objectivist science. Weber writes:

> The type of social science in which we are interested is an *empirical science* of concrete *reality* (*Wirklichkeitswissenschaft*). Our aim is the understanding of the characteristic uniqueness of the reality in which we move. We wish to understand on the one hand the relationships and cultural significance of individual events in their contemporary manifestations and on the other the causes of their being historically *so* and not *otherwise*.[40]

For Weber following in the post-Kantian tradition of Dilthey, Rickert and Simmel, 'understanding' (*Verstehen*) is the appropriate method of the social sciences for penetrating 'the reality that surrounds our lives', which arrives at an objective account of social history, albeit an objectivity constrained by culture and the conditions of its production. For Rickert the objectivity possible in historical investigation is legitimated by reference to objective values,[41] though for Weber this objectivity is always constrained by history and culture: science itself can change its standpoint and analytical apparatus as the 'light of the great cultural problems march on'.[42] Yet Weber would not wish to go down the road of complete relativism. To recognize that scientific method is contained within the limits of history is not to abnegate the possibility of understanding social change in an objective way and here Weber and Rickert are in agreement.

Husserl, similarly, regards his phenomenological method as scientific. In contradistinction to the 'unified science' (*Einheitswissenschaft*) of the Vienna Circle, which attempted to combine the human and hard sciences in a causal model based on physics,[43] Husserl distinguishes two distinct though related kinds of science. On the one hand there is science concerned with ideation or 'eidetic seeing' outside of experience (the eidetic sciences, including phenomenology), on the other a science of 'matters of fact' understood through experience. He writes:

> There are *pure eidetic sciences* such as pure logic, pure mathematics, and the pure theories of time, space, motion, and so forth. Throughout in every step of their thinking, they are pure of all positings of matters of fact; or equivalently: *in them no experience, as experience*, that is as a consciousness that seizes on or posits actuality, factual existence, *can assume the functioning of grounding* . . . It is quite otherwise in the case of the scientific *investigator of Nature*. He observes and experiments; that is he ascertains *factual existence* according to experience; *for him experience is a grounding act* which can never be substituted by a mere imagining . . . But for the *geometer* [for example] who explores not actualities but 'ideal possibilities', not predicatively formed actuality-complexes but predicatively formed eidetic affair complexes, *the ultimately grounding act* is not experience but rather *the seeing of essences*.[44]

We will explore Husserl's somewhat complex conception of scientific inquiry in a later chapter, but for the present I wish to indicate that Husserl understands science both in Weber's sense as the explanation of 'concrete reality' accessed through experience, and in the phenomenological sense of the intuition of essences at the ideational or eidetic level beyond experience and matters of fact. But while Weber would no doubt have found Husserl's distinction between the two kinds of science problematic in that the ideational world, on Husserl's account, would seem to be divorced from any social reality – a problem which Alfred Schutz sought to address[45] – both accept the idea of science as arriving at objectivity. For Weber such objectivity is the objectivity of social life and social forces functioning at a macro level (the level of structures and institutions). For Husserl objectivity is both that of 'matters of fact' as well as structures within consciousness constituted subjectively within individuals. Husserl's conception of science is therefore objective, yet an objectivity which is constituted subjectively within consciousness.

Religious studies has inherited both conceptions of science: on the one hand empirical investigation in which 'religion' is discovered within a spectrum of behaviours and ideologies constituting a social and cultural world, on the other the attempt to understand the 'essence' of religious meanings as constituted within consciousness, through Husserl's eidetic intuition (see chapter 4). Indeed, religious studies has identified the 'science of religion' with the 'phenomenology of religion'. Max Müller, who first coined the term 'science of religion', influenced by the positivism of his time, saw the possibility of a study of religion as 'an impartial and truly scientific comparison of all', analogous to the science of language.[46] The identification of the 'science of religion' with the 'phenomenology of religion' as the objective study of religion through ethnography and history, was made by Chantepie de la Saussaye who first coined the term in 1887, deriving it not of course from Husserl, but rather from the Hegelian tradition.[47] For him both 'science' and 'phenomenology' are objective and impartial. These two methodological streams within religious studies, although in tension with each other, the one seeking causal explanations of religion and the other aspiring to non-reductionist descriptions and interpretations, have both traditionally shared a common view of scientific objectivity. It is this objectivity that allows the science of religion to be identified with the phenomenology of religion, an identification that has changed little since its original conception, although perhaps with the added emphasis that, even though the science of religion is, as Ninian Smart says, 'aspectual, polymethodic, pluralist, and without clear boundaries', it nevertheless seeks 'to provide *explanations* regarding religious phenomena' and so to move beyond description.[48]

There are two important features or aspirations of hard, or phys-icalist scientific methods. One is the ability to explain a phenomenon, to offer causal explanations of how some state of affairs has come to be as it is, and the other is to offer predictions for the future; how, given specified constraints, a phenomenon will change. Although religious studies along with the social sciences and related humanities, has shared the value of scientific objectivity, that a neutral method arrives at a truth beyond representation, it has not succeeded in generating predictive theories about religion nor causal explanations (of the form 'the origin of x is y'). Causal explanations of religion have come from other disciplines, notably sociology, psychology and socio-biology. While recognizing some degree of autonomy for religion at the level of description, these disciplines have tried to provide causal explanations that function at a lower level; thus sociobiology would account for religion in terms of the genes. In contrast to causal explanations religious studies has offered phenomenological ones which try to interpret a meaning rather than to establish a cause, and which attempt neutral description and the gathering of data along with typological classifications. The study of religions therefore finds itself at an impasse. On the one hand maintaining the autonomy of religion in phenomenology is deeply problematic, for religion cannot be set outside of culture and history, on the other hand causal explanations have been unsuccessful in accounting for religions.

Thomas Lawson and Robert McCauley (who themselves do not seek to provide a causal account of religion) set up the problem in an interesting way. They make an initial distinction between a group of scholars of religious behaviour characterized by a 'terror of theory' due to an '[a]we in the presence of signals of transcendence' with those who do not abrogate theory but who think that scientific theory entails the 'derogation of the truth content of religious beliefs'.[49] The former are antitheoretical – and one might even add 'quasi-theological' in our primary sense – the latter are reductionist in a way which 'instils an unduly narrow view of scientific methods and urges an exclusively physicalist metaphysics'.[50] These two positions are related to, although not coextensive with, the phenomenological and social scientific traditions which we introduced above. Lawson and McCauley identify a third group of positions which believes in theory but advocates a wider understanding of scientific theory and method, in which the matter is far from settled as to what constitutes 'theory'. For the first group, notes Lawson and McCauley, method is a non-issue, for the second group the model of method has been settled by the physicalist sciences, but for the third group method and theory are live issues which are far from settled and it is this group which generates methodological debates and metatheoretical considerations.[51] It is within this third group that the present study is situated, in offering a dialogical contribution to a metatheoretical discourse, critical of the proclaimed objectivity of both hard and soft scientific method. This metatheoretical position understands that the cultural representations we call 'religions' are the products of signifying practices within a diversity of social contexts, as indeed are the practices which study those representations.

While both the social scientific and phenomenological currents within religious studies share the values of objectivity and that scientific method arrives at truth beyond representation, the reflexive trend in much social science has shown that there can be no neutral gathering of data, but rather that data are generated by method. In any investigation, the selection of material for analysis or even description, involves a reduction and selection – for otherwise the object of investigation would simply be itself – which entails a selection and occlusion of material. As Samuel observes, all theories and models are partial and imperfect, incorporating unjustified assumptions, partly already encoded in symbolic structures within language.[52] Any religious or cultural phenomenon selected for explanation or description is already interpreted in the very practice of description or analysis.

Bourdieu has referred to this as the 'synoptic illusion'; the inevitable simplification of complex phenomena into a single interpretative framework. He illustrates this with reference to structuralist use of the 'diagram' which oversimplifies complex, temporal relationships. The diagram, Bourdieu writes, creates relationships which do not exist in practice and which juxtapose 'in the simultaneity of a single space the complete series of the temporal oppositions applied successively by different agents at different time ... '[53] The data derived within religious studies are similarly subject to the synoptic illusion, but this can be treated as an inevitable constraint upon research as long as the method and its implicit assumptions are acknowledged. De Certeau has observed with regard to history, that the historical operation is a combination of place, practice and writing.[54] Similarly the academic study of religion is the product of practices (particularly rational analysis as outlined above) embedded within a social and historical context that produces the writing of religion: the data of religious studies are not innocently self-revealing.

Towards a metatheoretical discourse

So far I have suggested the need for a metatheoretical discourse within religious studies which both draws from and contributes to wider intellectual debates in the social sciences and humanities. As a way into the issues I have given a thumbnail sketch of how religious studies has distinguished itself from theology, and the relationship between the language of theology and the language of religious studies in the modern university context. I have also suggested that religious studies inherits a model of objectivity derived from both the social sciences and from phenomenology, and raised questions concerning the degree to which scientific method has access to a truth beyond representation. I wish to develop a position that allows for a reflexive critique which contributes to a metatheoretical discourse about the study of religions. This position can be broadly characterized as dialogical and draws from, and is situated within, a general hermeneutical and narrativist

33

discourse. In later chapters I shall elaborate this position in the context of developments within a post-Husserlian philosophy of social science, drawing on the work of Ricoeur, Bakhtin and linguistic anthropology.

For the remainder of the present chapter I wish to discuss three key terms that occur at various points of my exposition, namely 'dialogue', 'reflexivity' and 'critique'. Dialogue between researcher and object of research entails reflexivity, in which the social and cultural constraints of the research situation itself are highlighted, which in turn entails a distanciation that allows cultural critique to come into play. The term 'cultural critique' could theoretically incorporate a wide variety of discourses including critical theory, feminist theory, queer theory, postcolonial theory and genealogical analysis, or even religious perspectives as Marsden has argued. To allow these critical perspectives into religious studies would be to free-up the discipline considerably from a narrowly conceived objectivism and would enable religious studies to become a discourse that engages with wider, important issues and debates to which it has traditionally contributed little. But the incorporation of multi-disciplinary critiques into the study of religion also highlights the need for a developed metatheoretical discourse that can provide an anchor point for its multiple theoretical voices. The more theory and varieties of practice there are in the study of religions, the more the need for metatheory in order to form a common discourse in which various practitioners of the subject can speak with each other.

DIALOGUE

Let me begin this sketch with a quote from Donna Haraway:

> Above all, rational knowledge does not pretend to disengagement: to be from everywhere and so nowhere, to be free from interpretation, from being represented, to be fully self-contained or fully formalizable. Rational knowledge is a process of ongoing critical interpretation among 'fields' of interpreters and decoders. Rational knowledge is power-sensitive conversation.[55]

It is here that my understanding of a metatheoretical discourse of religious studies must begin. To see 'rational knowledge' as 'conversation' sensitive to context and sensitive to power relations both within its own discourse and within the 'object' of its investigation, is to maintain a position between the scientific objectivism of third-person accounts or explanation as the location of causes, on the one hand, and the subjectivism of first-person accounts on the other. Research within the many fields which comprise religious studies is in the end conversation with texts and persons. The researcher is entering into a dialogue with a text or person and herself becoming a part of an intersubjective and intertextual matrix in which all understanding – and explanation – arises. Understanding is always from a place, from a 'gendered location' to use a phrase of Lorraine Code,[56] and is legitimated by wider social forces. To develop method sensitive to context is to be open to the 'otherness' of the material or persons who are the 'object' of study and to recognize speaking and hearing subjects as the place of meaning.

The practice of conversation that gives rise to a context-sensitive discourse and writing, entails the recognition of 'many voices'. Mikhail Bakhtin, the 'founder' of dialogism – although he did not use the term – called this presence of many voices 'heteroglossia'; the presence in language of different (dominant and subservient, open and hidden, official and unofficial) discourses. He also means the trace of other utterances within any single utterance. All utterance assumes preceding utterances. Dialogue therefore involves the recognition that all utterance is intertextual and all encounters intersubjective. Such an approach to the inquiry into religions, that might be called 'dialogical reflexivity', becomes aware of the intertextual and intersubjective webs in which it is embedded, is sensitive to history, to language and to subjectivity. Furthermore dialogue is not agreement or consensus, but can be the clarification of difference; a clarification that will necessarily entail reflexivity in delineating the boundaries of a discourse against another's, which is also critique.

REFLEXIVITY

Without some degree of reflexivity any research is blind and without purpose. Reflexivity refers to the ability of a researcher, or indeed as a strategy embedded within method, to become aware of the contexts of research and the presuppositions of the research programme. In the succinct words of David Hufford: 'Scholars can study themselves. Scholarship can be an object of scholarship ... '[57] Reflexivity has become a central concept in the social sciences, an idea particularly developed by Pierre Bourdieu.[58] Although I do not generally draw on Bourdieu in the body of my text, it is worth presenting his understanding of reflexivity here, as he expresses the idea clearly and places it in the context of three modes of theoretical knowledge for understanding the social world. These three modes are the 'phenomenological', the 'objectivist' and the 'dialectical'. By 'phenomenological' Bourdieu means a mode of knowledge which makes explicit the 'primary experience of the social world', the world of daily commonsense transaction. This is the realm highlighted by and explored in the sociological phenomenology of Alfred Schutz, the student of Husserl, who described agents' experience of the social world and from which developed ethnomethodology. The primary experience of the social world is the realm of daily transaction and the realm of 'data' gathered in sociological analysis. By contrast the 'objectivist' mode constructs objective relations (e.g. linguistic and economic) 'which structure practice and representations of practice' in the social world. There is therefore a critical break in objectivist knowledge with the social world and with its 'self-evident' or 'natural' character. Another way of saying this might be that there is a rift between outsider accounts and insider experience and accounts of the social world, an idea that can be applied *mutatis mutandis* to religion and its study. The third kind of knowledge, the 'dialectical', aims at revealing the dialectical relations between objective structures to which the objectivist mode of knowledge gives access (economic, linguistic, etc.) and the structured dispositions in which those 'objective' structures are brought to light.[59] That is, there is a dialectical relation between the method, or structured dispositions, and the object, or objective structures, which give rise to this third kind of knowledge of the social world. The objective structures of sociological theory relate to the social world which in turn relates back to sociological theory.

This latter process concerning the relation of method to object is reflexive: the objectification of objectification in which there is a 'second break', namely with the objectivist mode of knowledge. While the objectivist mode of knowledge 'breaks' with the social world which is its object, this dialectical mode of knowledge 'breaks' with that objectivity. This is pure reflexivity. Bourdieu calls it 'participant objectivation'; a stepping back, not only from the object of study but from the act of objectification itself. He writes:

> Social science must not only, as objectivisms would have it, break with
> native experience but also, by a second break, call into question the
> presuppositions inherent in the position of the 'objective' observer who,
> seeking to interpret practices, tends to bring into the object the principles of
> his relation to the object ... [60]

This kind of critical reflexivity allows us to understand the limits of
method. Bourdieu goes on to say that such critical reflection on the
limits of theoretical understanding

> is not to discredit theoretical knowledge ... but rather to give it a solid
> basis by freeing it from the distortions arising from the epistemological and
> social conditions of its production ... (I)t aims simply to bring to light the
> theory of practice which theoretical knowledge implicitly applies and so to
> make possible a truly scientific knowledge of practice and of the practical
> mode of knowledge.[61]

So-called objective explanations produce a distorted picture of that
which they claim to represent. The limits of the objective and objectifying mode of knowledge need to be apprehended and a 'critical break'
made with that mode in order to appreciate the dialectical relationship
between the structured dispositions of the objectivist method and the
objective structures of the object. Reflexivity can create a critical
distance from theory formation and reveal the biases inherent within
any research programme. Applied to the sphere of religion, the intentionality of the method in relation to the intentionality of the object
(religion), needs to be appreciated for a deeper understanding of both
religion and of the ways it is approached by academic discourses. In a
way directly akin to Bourdieu's analysis of sociological theory formation, theory formation in the study of religions needs to be reflexive in
order to see how the structures and biases within theory relate to
religious practices and ideologies. This is, indeed, to reveal the dialogical nature between researcher or research programme and the
'objects' of research. As June O'Connor says, 'It's not enough to tell
me what you see. I want to know where you are standing as you see
and speak, and also why you stand there.'[62] The recognition of the
intentionality of method needs to be understood as a dialogical process
with the intentionality of its object.

Bourdieu's programme advocates a critical intersubjectivity; a dialogue not only between the method and its object, but between
methods or between inquirers. His three-fold procedure recognizes

research as intersubjective and critical encounter, as opposed to either a detached objectivity that ultimately distorts the relation between theory and data, or a mere 'celebration' or 'acceptance' of difference. This would also be advocacy of a critical intersubjectivity, a dialogue not only between the method and its object, but between methods or between inquirers. It is, in fact, an advocacy of Bakhtin's heteroglossia and a move away from a detached objectivism towards intersubjective, critical research in which the biases within a theory and method are appreciated as far as possible, as indeed the biases within an individual researcher. Indeed, a scholar's personal biography is highly relevant in this process and, as Bowie observes, the degree to which a particular paradigm is adopted is – at least partly – due to our personal history, as Nietzsche well knew.[63]

A concrete example may serve to illustrate what I mean. In the study of a Hindu ritual the process of method initially shows itself in description which might include emic understandings; secondly the researcher from the perspective of method relates description to paradigms external to the ritual (to sociological/psychological models, to historical explanations and so on); and lastly the researcher might undergo the reflexive task of bringing to light the interiority of method's own assumptions in showing, for example, how the ideal of a universal semantics in respect of Hindu ritual has been assumed, or how the 'objective' paradigms brought to bear on the material, themselves contain deep cultural assumptions about the nature of the self, about gender and about power relations. Reflexivity allows other perspectives such as post-colonial and feminist criticism to have a voice and generally legitimates the idea of cultural criticism. Through this kind of reflexive dialogism, method moves away from a façade of neutrality and objectivity towards a recognition of context, and a recognition of agency – that the researcher is a social actor in a socially legitimated activity, as are the people or community whom are the object of research. Dialogical reflexivity is the recognition of agency, an agency constrained by context but which can influence context.[64] This kind of reflexivity is criticism turned in on method and turned towards method's object.

CRITIQUE

The development of a dialogical approach allows place for cultural critique and the introduction of debates and issues which have traditionally been regarded as existing outside of the academic study of religions. For example, the problem of the degree to which social agents create their own futures or are constrained by social hierarchies is understood differently within the phenomenological and objectivist modes of knowledge described by Bourdieu. As he observes, the phenomenological approach as developed within ethnomethodology by Erving Goffman, regards the social world as the product of individuals' actions which produce hierarchy through deference and respect. On the other hand the objectivist mode, such as structuralism, emphasizes power relations and objective structures of domination which ultimately constrain social actors.[65] How one understands this complex issue is therefore not simply a matter of neutral scholarship but in the end has political implications (the former model tending to empower subjects, the latter tending to disempower them). This issue has direct bearing on the study of religions in many instances, the Hindu caste system for example. Do social actors create the system or are they powerlessly subjected to it? Or does it vary depending upon social actors within the hierarchical spectrum? While my own position would be, largely agreeing with Milner's excellent study,[66] that both positions are true, this is not something I wish to argue here, but merely wish to illustrate that modes of knowledge affect the result: the method to a large degree (but not wholly as I shall argue) determines the data.

A reflexive dialogical model that is aware of the limits of its own possibilities is inherently critical and aware of the narratives in which it is embedded. Critique allows a distanciation between self and other, self and self, and method and object, that is not objectivist, yet is critical of its own procedures, critical of the context of its occurrence, and even critical of the object of study. To take an extreme example, one which has been used by Ninian Smart, the phenomenological study of Nazism would entail the imaginative entering into the feelings and beliefs of those at the Nuremberg rallies, but this would not 'entail that we therefore approve of the values of Hitler and his followers'.[67] But a dialogical model would entail that our own values *vis à vis* the object of study, namely Nazism, would necessarily be brought to light and would inevitably be involved in evaluation. An ethical dimension would be integral and inevitable to the investigation, and an under-standing which claimed to exclude the ethical – and the place where the investigator stood – would arguably be no real understanding. This is not to argue for a kind of emotivism or distortion of objective historical constraints, but rather for an awareness not only of the object of study, but of the procedures and the context from where the study stems. It would also be to recognize the inevitably ethical nature of research. In understanding that there is no 'view from nowhere' to use Nagel's phrase,[68] reflexivity answers the questions by whom, for whom and for what reasons, and allows for criticism from the same place as well as from other places. Dialogism promotes a 'view from somewhere'. It has the potential to develop new perspectives and highlights the non-closure of explanation.

Summary

In this chapter I have introduced some of the key issues and indicated the directions we will travel towards. I have argued that the academic study of religion needs to engage more fully with wider theoretical debates within the social sciences and humanities and develop a much more acute self-awareness of its procedures and contexts of occur-rence. Since Husserl there have been few methodological developments within the subject area and I would argue that such lack of engagement with metatheoretical concerns has the effect of margin-alizing religious studies when it should be at the centre of contemporary debates about power, agency, and ideology. The aca-demic study of religions has potentially great contributions to make to debates, not only concerning contemporary religious change and the commodification of religious goods, but also concerning globaliza-tion, world capitalism, and environmental issues. To set the scene, this chapter has examined the relation of religious studies to theology and the social sciences, focusing particularly upon language and the con-texts in which these disciplines take place; has discussed the objectivist assumptions which inevitably 'creates a fiction, not a living creature, not one of those who wander on the earth'. Having described the first two tigers of the imagination and of representation, Borges concludes his poem:

We'll hunt for a third tiger now, but like

The others this one too will be a form
Of what I dream, a structure of words, and not
The flesh and bone tiger that beyond all myths
Paces the earth. I know these things quite well,
Yet nonetheless some force keeps drawing me
In this vague, unreasonable, and ancient quest,
And I go on pursuing through the hours
Another tiger, the beast not found in Verse.[69]

If the third tiger of Borges' poem, the objective, constantly deferred tiger, is always out of reach, then we are left with systems and arrangements of human language, and are left inevitably, but richly, with intertextuality and the intersubjectivities which are our fates to explore.

2. The idea of 'religion'

Writing on myth, Hans Blumenberg, distinguishing it from science, ideology and mysticism, speaks of myth's quality of *significance* (*Bedeutsamkeit*) as something which 'constitutes [the] satisfaction of intelligent expectation.'[1] This quality of significance as indicating not only intelligent expectation, but also something which demands our attention,[2] could equally be applied to 'religion', thereby pointing to a problematic at the heart of the inquiry into religion, namely whether it is a *sui generis* category resistant to explanation in terms of external factors (such as genetics). Indeed this has been the subject of intensive debate.[3] When speaking about 'religion' we are speaking about something which only exists among human populations (as far as we know) and is articulated in 'texts' and 'practices', and reconstituted in experience within human subjectivities, along with our intelligent (and not so intelligent) expectations. Like the term 'significance' itself, *religion* is resistant to definition, yet despite this problem there are forms of cultural life which are clearly identifiable as 'religion' in contrast to other cultural practices; we can, for example, distinguish between offering a flower to Krishna and cooking an evening meal. But there can be no privileged discourse of religion outside of culture.[4] The western category 'religion' is itself a product of the particular historical conditions of Enlightenment discourse[5] and elements in non-Western cultures identified as religious are similarly culturally embedded.[6] But even given the historicized nature of the category, religion is nevertheless important in the transformations of contemporary culture in the context of modernity/postmodernity. Religion has not died out in the modern world as secularization theory might have suggested, and in many areas, such as post-communist Russia and Eastern Europe, is, on the contrary, blossoming. Because of the changing nature of religion in the contemporary global world and the complex inter-relation between religion, social structure and politics, we need new ways of modelling religion which transcend the rather sterile distinctions between phenomenological and social scientific explanations, reductionism and non-reductionism, and tradition and secularization. New ways of imaging religion need to be located within the reflexively aware human sciences which recognize the importance of language, narrative, re-traditionalization, and contemporary expressions of religiosity.[7]

The present chapter discusses problems in the definition of religion and identifies three general groups of theorizing about religion. These three groups are first quasi-theological theory, developing from liberal Christian theology; secondly hermeneutic/phenomenological theory, developing from the hermeneutical tradition of Dilthey and from the phenomenological tradition of Husserl; and thirdly scientific reductionist theory, developing from objectivist trends in sociology and, particularly, cognitive anthropology and psychology. While the first and third of these types tends towards universalizing claims about the nature of religion, the second tends towards various forms of relativism. The position developed by the present book is broadly within the hermeneutical/phenomenological tradition and will critique the universalism of both quasi-theological theory and scientific reductionist theory from that perspective. The backdrop against which this discussion takes place is the shift in contemporary theoretical discourse from a philosophy of consciousness to a philosophy of the sign, of language and culture. The general point defended is that there can be no essentialist understanding of religion and that there is no discourse of religion outside of particular cultures.

Religion as a category

It has been notoriously difficult to arrive at a universally acceptable definition of religion and it seems that the task is doomed from the outset. Some scholars such as Melford Spiro have argued for the necessity of definitions, preferably explicit ones, which mark out the field to be investigated,[8] while others have claimed that the beginnings of an investigation do not need their object to be defined, that definitions come at the end.[9] Others have argued that we need an 'operational definition',[10] or at least that our pre-understanding of religion as it is applied to different spheres of human cultural experience needs to be brought into the open, while yet others have abjured the possibility of any definition. Of the various arguments and opinions on this matter there are broadly two orientations: a non-essentialist orientation which denies that a hard-edged definition can be arrived at, and an essentialist orientation which claims that a clearly defined concept can be achieved. Russell McCutcheon articulates this distinction as one between those who would argue that 'religion' cannot be reduced or explained in terms of human, historical categories and those who think it can be used in a taxonomic sense to describe and analyse portions of human behaviour and belief.[11] The present study is located within the latter camp, but in wishing to see the inquiry into religion grounded broadly in the human sciences, I am nevertheless distanced from naturalist theories that assume an objectivist and universalist understanding of social science.

It must be remembered that 'religion' is an emic, Western category, that originated in late antiquity and developed within Christianity as part of that tradition's self-understanding.[12] The origin of the term is in the Latin *religio* which Cicero took to be from *relegere*, 'to re-read', with the implication of 'tradition' as that which is 're-read' and so passed on; and with Lactantius from *religare*, 'to bind fast', with the implication of that which binds people to each other and to the gods in the Roman state. In both cases *religio*, as indeed 'religion', has the implication of a boundary, a limit or a horizon which is an ultimate constraint upon belief, values and behaviours. Although the early church distanced itself from the idea of the Christian faith as a 'religion', which Paul associated with 'false' Paganism,[13] by the seventh century, according to Ernst Feil's research, *religio* had come to refer to communities whose members (the *religiosi*) devoted their lives to the service of God. By Luther's time the term had come to have a more general designation as the source of truth[14] and with the Deists and the Enlightenment became the abstract category which we have inherited. Peter Harrison in an excellent study has shown how our modern concept of 'religion' (and therefore the roots of the scientific study of religion) originated with the Deists and developed during the Enlightenment out of a Lutheran tradition.[15] Sounding a note of caution, Ernst Feil has alerted us to the point that there is no continuous development from the category *religio* as meaning the 'careful and even fearful fulfilment of what man owes to God', to the Deist's, notably Herbert of Cherbury's, understanding of *religio* as embracing general principles 'which derive from universal truth itself and represent the truth that can be found by understanding and intellect'.[16] But while there may be no linear continuity from Luther to the Deists, what is significant, as Harrison argues, is that the abstract category 'religion' develops in tandem with the methods of reason designed to illuminate it.

Religion, on this line of reasoning, did not precede the methods of its enquiry, but rather the methods of investigation defined as well as explicated it.[17] The abstraction 'religion' – along with the abstractions 'culture', 'mysticism' and 'spirituality'[18] – originated in the context of the critique of Christianity in the Enlightenment and the rise of the modern individual, which has since become an etic category in being applied outside of Christianity. While it does not of course follow that the category cannot be applied outside of Christianity, it is nevertheless the case that it is difficult to translate the term into other (non-Western) languages.[19] There are difficulties and objections in extending the category to 'Judaism', 'Islam' or 'Hinduism', which thereby become part of a single unified field. Lash suggests that perhaps 'religion' has been a long moment in the history of Western thought which history is now moving beyond,[20] but that remains to be seen.

An important question here is whether the term 'religion' has semantic equivalents in other languages and cultures? Some, such as Michael Pye citing examples from Japan, have argued that there are such parallels,[21] while others, such as Frits Staal, would wish to restrict its use to the Western monotheisms.[22] But perhaps it is more fruitful to look at the problem the other way around. Are there English semantic equivalents of terms indigenous to another culture which denote certain kinds of discourse and practices concerned with social ethics, transcendence, narratives and ritual? As regards Hindu traditions, there are no direct English semantic equivalents for the technical terminologies which developed as part of those traditions self-descriptions, though a number of Sanskrit terms have some conceptual overlap with the category.

Although textual study of their particular uses would need to be undertaken, the terms *śāsana*, *mata*, *āgama* and *siddhānta*, might be loosely rendered as 'teaching'; *āmnaya* as 'tradition'; *darśana* as 'critical world-view' or 'philosophy'; *vāda* as 'discourse'; *śāstra* as 'science', 'discourse', or 'discipline'; and *marga* as 'way' or 'path'. The first four terms imply a revealed doctrine in a text or groups of texts (such as the

Tantras or Āgamas), initiation (*dīkṣā*) by a guru and a practice (*sād-hana*) which leads to the teaching's goal (*sādhya*). For example, in the tradition of Śaiva Siddhānta, a dualistic system which maintains an eternal distinction between the Lord (*pati*), self (*paśu*), and binding cosmos (*pāśa*), the practitioner (*sādhaka*) undergoes an initial initiation after which he has access to texts and binding rituals of the tradition, which is followed by the liberating initiation that ensures his final liberation at death from the cycle of reincarnation.[23] The terms *śāsana* and *mata* are used in Śaivism to denote 'revealed teachings' which facilitate the attaining of either liberation (*mokṣa*) or power (*siddhi*) through practice or observance (*vrata*). *Śāsana* and *mata* may have the implication that *pūjā* will be performed, the ritual propitiation of a deity through making an offering and receiving a blessing, though *pūjā* can function outside of the context of particular teachings. Not only does the structure of *pūjā* cut across doctrinal and textual boundaries, but, very significantly, a person might perform *pūjā* without adhering to any *mata*. The term *dharma* is often taken to be a Sanskrit equivalent of 'religion', a term which indicates the social virtues and might be translated as 'culture'. The terms *āmnaya*, and *śrotas*, imply a tradition or 'stream' flowing from revelation, and *paramparā* or *san-tāna*, the flow of teachings through the guru to disciple. Similarly *sampradāya* can refer in a synchronic sense to the teachings of a tradition or in a diachronic sense to the guru succession.

A picture emerges of traditions defining themselves against each other through time and developing terminologies which articulate their self-understanding. These terms imply tradition-specific narratives of origin and purpose along with practices and observances which constrain an individual's life from birth to death. Among this terminology there are common features encompassed by the term 'religion' but only at a superficial level. What does become clear is that once beyond a fairly general level, the concept 'religion' is of little use in illuminating these traditions for Western analytical purposes. The Sanskrit terminology is much richer than the English. Indeed, these brief examples show how language and concepts are deeply embedded within the contexts of their occurrence and the translation of these terms into European languages is difficult, if not impossible, because of the connotations of each. None of the Sanskrit terms I have listed could be a direct equivalent of the category 'religion', though some of the features within the semantic field of 'religion' are encompassed by them.

Binding narratives and behaviours

Given the relativization of the idea of religion, it could be argued that definitions of religion, as Leszek Kolakowski has suggested, are more or less arbitrary abstractions from a range of beliefs, emotions and behaviours selected by our interest.[24] But while there is truth in this, it is nevertheless also the case that there are objective constraints – traditions of narrative and ritual – upon the range of beliefs, emotions and behaviours selected. While acknowledging that religion is impossible to define in any definitive sense, different theories and studies do construct different definitions of religion that best suit their purposes. For the present study – influenced by the south-Asian traditions in my wish to emphasize language, communication and the narrative aspects of theory construction – I shall take 'religion' in Lactantius' sense of *religio* as 'that which binds'. I broadly understand religions to be *'value-laden narratives and behaviours that bind people to their objectives, to each other, and to non-empirical claims and beings'.*[25] Such a definition, strongly influenced by Bowker, indicates a conviction that religions are less about truth claims and more about identity, less about structures and more about texts, less about abstraction and more about tradition or that which is passed on (*Überlieferung*). Indeed, the idea of binding narratives and behaviours could equally be applied to 'politics', 'society', 'culture',[26] or 'ideology'. Indeed the concept of ideology in the sense of a group's 'world-view' or 'world-picture', would probably serve as an equivalent to 'religion'. The advantage of such a broad definition allows the incorporation of 'quasi-religious' dimensions of culture which might include crowd behaviour at a football match or New-Age managerial strategies, as well as secular ideologies and nationalism. Sometimes religion can be distinguished clearly from other types of text and practice such as 'religion' from 'politics' in many instances in the West (or a church liturgy from a fashion show) but at other times such claims and practices cannot be legitimately abstracted from other forms of cultural life, such as narratives of origin from exogamous moieties among the Bororo.[27] The problem is, of course, what is it that makes certain cultural narratives 'religious' and others not? And how can such elements be recognized without falling back on essentialism?

These are thorny questions which can be approached, I would argue, not through the rather empty task of attempting to arrive at impossible, universal definitions, but through taking religion as a soft category or a category with 'fuzzy edges' in Lakoff's sense.[28] Prototype theory, developed by Rosch[29] and later by Lakoff among others, maintains that it is not necessary to adhere to the Aristotelian model of categories which have necessary conditions of membership or shared properties. Categories can be conceptualized as not having rigid boundaries, but rather that there are degrees of category membership; some members of a category being more prototypical than others, though this does entail making judgements about the degree of proto-typicality. The degrees of membership of a category can be linked through family resemblance. This approach is certainly useful in looking at the category of 'Hinduism'.[30] The prototypical approach is adopted by Saler who supports the use of 'religion' but without hard and fast boundaries. In a very thorough discussion he points out that the term 'religion' is used in common parlance by millions of people, and while some scholars might wish to abandon the term, particularly in its application to non-Western cultures because those cultures do not have an expression or concept approximating to it, they must nevertheless 'confront its considerable powers among the millions who do employ it'.[31] Regarding Hinduism Bowker observes that Hindus are well aware of themselves as not being Muslim or Sikh, and that it is possible to specify constituent characteristics which allow for these distinctions. But it is not the case 'that *all* claimants to belonging must exhibit *all* the characteristics' and there will always be disputed boundaries, and debates about claims to adherence are 'a constant cause of disruption and schism in the religious case'.[32]

This means that the object of inquiry is recognized as being a construction based both on levels of constraint outside of method and on the specifications of any given research programme. In other words, we recognize religion when we see it, but must reflexively be aware that our recognition partially constructs it. In exercising constraint upon human life, religions identified as prototypical are concerned about human limits and the possibility of their transcendence or transformation. John Bowker notes that religions 'cluster around' those human limitations which are 'particularly intransigent or opa-que in nature' such as disease, earthquakes, madness, and, above all, death.[33] Limitation or constraint is here identical to Bakhtin's 'bound-ary' that circumscribes a life.[34] While many of these limitations, as Bowker observes, have been transcended through science and technol-ogy, many have not and religions continue to wrestle with them and to provide narratives whereby communities try to understand and cope with these events. This is not to fall back on essentialist definitions of religion as providing answers of 'ultimate concern', but it is to claim that religions focus upon central issues of human life and provide interpretations of birth, death, sexuality and drive. Indeed some religious narratives (though not all) claim to break through the boundary of death, and in this sense religious narratives can be distinguished from those of other human institutions, such as politics, though of course politics does address boundaries and some political narratives are utopian. Religion in this sense can be identified with the concept of ideology, though this too is not transparent and has been used in a number of ways within critical theory, both in a descriptive sense of systematically interconnected beliefs and conceptual schemes and in a pejorative (Marxist) sense of delusion or false consciousness.[35]

On this line of reasoning, religion cannot be given privilege outside of culture, but can be distinguished from other aspects of cultural life. The constraints operative upon the liturgy and the human limits which it addresses are evidently deeper in Western culture, having existed for a longer time, than those operative upon a fashion show which functions within different limits (such as gender, role models, and social power). One of the most important constraints affecting religion is language, in the sense that language can be seen to construct human experience. While it is beyond the scope of the present study to investigate here, linguistic anthropologists have argued that grammatical categories lead to different constructions of the world and to different ideologies. For example, nouns in Western languages are maximally referential and lead to referential theories of meaning which are then, mistakenly, taken to be universals.[36] Language is independent of a research programme and is a crucially important constraint upon religious narratives and behaviours which any theory of religion would need to focus upon (see below).

But while constraints upon religious narratives are in one sense objective and texts exist independently of research, these narratives are also partially constructed by the research programme itself. Religious narratives articulated in written and oral texts are the primary data of the human sciences. The constraints which result in the ordination of a Buddhist nun at a Buddhist monastery in the south of England are independent of research methods, but those methods nevertheless construct the 'data' through research questions and in the attempt to specify constraints. A research programme, that for example seeks to show how language in the nun's ordination not merely

49

reflects the social act, but generates it, selects data to corroborate the theory. Data are generated by the interaction of the theoretical paradigm with the material or objective constraints. The research programme – or more specifically the particular researcher – is therefore placed in a dialogical relationship with its/her 'object' – a tradition articulated in texts, forms of behaviour, personal biography or whatever – and the result of their interaction is the study, monograph, or course of lectures. As Bakhtin has observed, scholarship or research responds to and reproduces another's text in a second, framing text that comments, evaluates and so on.[37]

In recognizing constraints beyond scholarly representation (that is in the binding narratives and behaviours), this kind of dialogical model, focused on language and communication, avoids the implicit idealism of Baudrillard's *hyperreality* in which all we have are images of images,[38] yet also avoids the problems involved with the objectivism of Weberian, Marxist or empiricist social science in recognizing the importance of interest in any research programme. A general, non-specific view of the category 'religion', such as I am proposing, bypasses the problem of projecting the abstraction on to other cultures, for whatever the binding narratives and behaviours within a culture may be, whatever the traditions, communities and expressions of authenticity, they are the legitimate object of inquiry from the perspective of the academic study of religion; a perspective which nevertheless brings to the material paradigms external to it.

Two things are immediately striking about binding narratives and behaviours. First, they impact upon individual lives and are appropriated through language, learning and imitation within individual subjectivities; and secondly they function on a much broader scale of collective representations or traditions, transforming history and affecting the movement of entire peoples, political events and wars. These can be taken as two interrelated levels. On the one hand an agent is born into a particular community, brought up in its traditions, and can act upon them. On the other, those traditions or collective representations form the agent and constrain the degree to which she can act within the tradition and community. The social agent is always constrained by the power relations inherent within the traditions' structure, yet we must not forget that, historically, an untouchable could become a king.

These binding narratives and behaviours, articulated in texts and in specific uses of language which express the deepest values of a community, constitute religions. A way of unpacking this idea further is to map the distinction between narrative and behaviour onto a distinction in semiotics between systems of communication and systems of signification. Eco defines a communicative process as the passage of a signal from a source to a destination, an addresser to and addressee, though when it is a person who responds with interpretation, then the process is one of signification.[39] Everything within culture is a system of communication in this sense – indeed that is what culture in the broad sense is – and religions are communicative processes in so far as they convey information from a source (revelation, tradition, experience) to a human addressee. Religions convey through time narratives and behaviours that express values, yet are generally unintentionally communicative, in so far as most people in the world simply grow up in the tradition they are born into. Religions as systems of communication are concerned with the conveyance of culturally recognized, important information through the generations; information of binding significance for individual lives, which is articulated in linguistic forms, namely texts (and some would argue constructed by them), encoded in forms of behaviour (gesture, posture, body, symbol, ritual) and in material culture.[40] Such systems communicate intentional meanings through language, particularly through narratives of origin, purpose, and identity (called 'myth'), upon which doctrinal discourses are founded. So when speaking about religions we are usually speaking about such narratives and texts and the linked utterances within them (both written and aural).

Religion in late modernity

It might be objected that seeing religion in terms of binding narratives and behaviours may work in traditions with clearly demarcated boundaries, or in pre-modern cultures, but is not appropriate in cultural contexts without such clearly demarcated boundaries, such as the transformations of religion in the contemporary, postmodern or late modern world in which tradition and community have been shattered by the processes of 'detraditionalization' and a hidden community of communally isolated, 'authentic individuals' developed, alongside the reconstruction of tradition or 'retraditionalization'.[41] But, on the contrary, binding narratives and behaviours are as important as ever in the contemporary transformations of religion through

51

cyberspace, in paganism, in the New Age, in self-religions, and in the return to old forms in the reconstruction of tradition (or construction of tradition or process of 'retraditionalization'). While it is not the place to map these developments,[42] it is important to note that a number of mechanisms can be identified in these transformations in which the centrality of binding narratives and behaviours can be seen, notably in the forces of globalization and localization, in retraditionalization, and in the commodification of religion alongside other cultural signs,[43] all of which have consequences for the formation of theory and methodology.

Contemporary world religiosity has been fundamentally affected by the collapse of communism, the growth of global capitalism and the reinvigoration of Islam. Closely associated with global capitalism, the contemporary world is characterized by the dual processes of localization and globalization, both interrelated features of late modernity as Roland Robertson has convincingly argued.[44] These processes can be characterized by the fragmentation of culture on the one hand and by the homogenization of culture on the other, especially through commercialism and 'McDonaldization' in Ritzer's phrase. Both are constitutive of global reality in which communicative barriers have been broken down by technology and by peoples of the world in almost instantaneous communication with each other.[45] In Robertson's view globalization is a twofold process involving 'the universalization of particularism and the particularization of universalism',[46] making the world both a single place and a place of distinct identities. But there is no common model, each particular society producing its own version of a global order by creating its own national identity. Indeed the rejection of globalization by political and religious fundamentalisms is itself a form of globalization. Contemporary forms of religion inevitably respond to this process, on the one hand through focusing on global culture, such as new religions on the Internet, on the other through focusing on a particular sub-global culture and enforcing a local, social identity, as Beyer has shown.[47] An example here might be the loose amalgam of ideas and practices under the sign of 'the return of the Goddess' or even 'paganism' which is both hyperlinked to a global movement and is grounded in specific localities; the global movement being expressed through computer technology and the transcendence of nature in a noetic world-view, as Roberts has shown, the local with an earthbound, chthonic world-view.[48]

Associated with this process is secularization, or the retreat of religion from the public realm in the West, which, because of globalization, also occurs in non-Western cultures. However, secularization is not particularly useful in understanding postmodern religion; the demise of religion predicted by secularization theory has not occurred, although religion has been reformulated in private contexts and transformed in global culture. The withdrawal of religion to the private realm in global culture is also associated with the commodification of religion, with the processes of detraditionalization and retraditionalization, and differentiation and dedifferentiation, as Heelas has argued.[49] Religions and their modern constructions become products in the global market-place chosen by consumers; vast numbers of people, although mostly in the advanced capitalist countries, can elect to participate in the myths they choose and to be bound by narratives and behaviours selected from a range of possibilities.[50] Religious sensibilities in the West have become aestheticized and linked to a quest for ecstatic experience. Conversely, vast numbers of people are excluded from this 'free exchange' of religious commodities. For many untouched – or negatively affected – by modern technologies and globalization, religious traditions become identified with nationalisms and find articulation in nationalist politics, such as Hindu nationalism in India.[51] On the one hand there is move away from authority and tradition towards individualization, yet on the other there is a return to religious authority, tradition-maintenance and tradition-construction.[52] All these factors point to the importance of religion in modern, global culture and the consequent need in the social sciences for developing new ways of imaging and inquiring into religion that take into account both global and local dimensions.

These recent transformations of religion in global culture and the assertion of religions' particularity within a global context, present challenges to ways of imaging religion either in the quasi-theological terms of a common essence or in terms of a hard science such as cognitive psychology or sociobiology. Given that, as the sociology of religion has shown, religion must be located within the context of privatization and retraditionalization, as well as in the context of globalization and commodification, what theoretical models can account for it and what methods are required to inquire into it? Two recent responses to these questions have been the positing of a quasi-theological universalism and the reductionism of cognitive psychology. While I wish to defer a discussion of reductionism and non-reductionism for the next chapter, to indicate the directions in which I wish to push it is necessary here to give some account of these.

While both the non-reductive universalism that religions share a common essence stands completely opposed to the materialist argument that religion can be understood in terms of cognition, both types of theory share a limited view of language and its cultural embeddedness, and therefore both present inadequate accounts of religion. Both universalism and cognitive psychological explanations can be criticized from within the hermeneutical tradition, particularly from a dialogical perspective which, anticipating my argument of later chapters, places language, or rather its articulation in utterance, at the centre of inquiry. Both universalist and cognitive models override the particular narratives of particular religions, override the importance of language within particular cultures, and assume the epistemological privilege of explanation. For the remainder of the chapter I shall discuss quasi-theological and cognitive theories of religion in order to point to alternative research programmes that take seriously the particularity of religious languages, the particularity of narrative traditions, and the situated nature of inquiry.

Theological universalism

Perhaps the most sophisticated contemporary exponent of a quasi-theological theory of religion is by the liberal theologian John Hick, who has established his position in a number of publications, most clearly and eloquently articulated in *An Interpretation of Religion*.[53] While claiming to take seriously the cognitive and doctrinal claims of religious traditions, Hick argues that religions are different ways of responding to, and as paths for individuals to follow towards, an ultimate, transcendent reality he calls 'the Real'.[54] Thus the Moslem 'Allah', the Christian 'God' and the Hindu 'Brahman' are all terms for the same ultimate reality towards which the various paths we call world religions are climbing. Hick even identifies the Mahayana Buddhist *dharmakāya* as the 'Real'. In itself the Real is ineffable and transcendent, but humans respond to this reality through the world religions. Hick seeks to establish this claim through the following argument.

The universe is 'religiously ambiguous' in so far as it can be interpreted naturalistically or religiously: we experience the world in a range of different ways according to different dispositional states in which '(t)his all conscious experiencing is 'experiencing-as'.[55] Experiencing the world leads to three levels of interpretation or meaning: the physical, or environment of our survival; the ethical, or awareness of other humans beings and concomitant obligations towards them; and the religious, or ways of living in the world in accordance with religious meanings. Although religious meanings are diverse, we have a cognitive choice that Hick calls 'faith', between living in a world naturalistically interpreted and a religiously interpreted world. Neither of these can lay claim to greater rationality and both run the risk of being ultimately deluded, but a person who experiences life religiously is 'rationally entitled to trust that experience and to proceed to believe and to live on the basis of it'.[56] The argument that to view the world religiously is rational, next leads to the problem of religious plurality and the diversity and mutually exclusive claims of the traditions. Here Hick evokes Kant's distinction between the thing in itself and its appearances. The Real appears in the various forms of human interpretative and linguistic systems and it is only possible to respond to the Real within the different cultural ways of being human. Human experience of this transcendent Real is structured in the different traditions, either by the idea of a personal deity or a non-theistic, abstract absolute. Incompatible doctrinal schemes within diverse religious traditions – such as between reincarnation or not – cannot be resolved by human concepts and do not, therefore, threaten the overall hypothesis that religions are responses to the Real and that religious myths 'represent different phenomenal awareness of the same noumenal reality and evoke parallel salvific transformations of human life'.[57]

While Hick's account of the rationality of religious belief is well argued and the intentions behind such a thesis of religious pluralism and equality of claims to truth are no doubt worthy, there are problems with this approach. Segal has drawn our attention to these problems, particularly highlighting Hick's distinction between truth and rationality.[58] But the point I wish to focus on here is the issue of conflicting truth claims. Hick dismisses conflicting claims to truth on the grounds that these are of a kind which concern historical fact (an so can be potentially resolved), or which concern transhistorical fact (which cannot be established by historical and empirical evidence), or which concern the ultimate nature of the Real. Hick argues that 'transhistorical facts' should be recognized and difference regarding such 'facts' tolerated by different traditions. The answers to these questions are not yet known, and in the case of the Real, cannot be fully known.[59] But the problem here is that these doctrinal distinctions within religions are of vital importance and are central to many traditions' self-descriptions. For example, God as a trinity is a defining feature of Christian doctrine about God, and *nibbāna*, as a distant goal for a Theravāda Buddhist, cannot be reduced to an identical transcendent without doing violence to the specificity of the traditions. Specific traditions have specific goals. As John Clayton has argued, what is ultimate is tradition-specific and it does not follow that what one tradition conceives as an ultimate reality is the same as an ultimate reality conceived by another. The goals of religions are specific, they are 'different paths to different goals'. Clayton writes: 'The goal aimed at is as tradition-specific as the path taken. The goal is constituted as goal by the path chosen. It is the tradition followed that allows the practitioner to recognize the goal as goal.'[60]

This must surely be the case as the claims of traditions are completely embedded in the contexts and languages of their occurrence. To claim in a totalizing way that all traditions are paths leading to the same goal is to disclaim their uniqueness. For example, the ultimate goal of the monistic Śaiva is recognition (*pratyabhijñā*) of his identity with pure consciousness (*saṃvit*, *caitanya*) identified with Śiva. The goal of the sister tradition the Śaiva Siddhānta is to become equal to Śiva (*śivatulya*); to become *a* Śiva but not to lose one's distinct identity. There was rigorous debate between these two traditions and to suggest that they are simply both different ways of responding to the same ultimate reality is not to appreciate the historicity of tradition, nor the true nature of the difference between them in the theological sophistication of their positions. That they share a common ritual substrate is not to indicate a theological unity, though it does indicate the divergence between ritual and doctrine in these traditions.

Clayton has suggested that in Indian philosophical discourse – the *vāda* tradition – we have a model for understanding traditions which does not attempt to reduce the other to one's own, universalized emic category, but rather respects the boundaries of another discourse while simultaneously being aware of the boundaries of one's own. Clayton describes how the Indian *vāda* tradition originated in the methods of Vedic textual exegesis and developed into a public forum for debates between rival schools. Such debates had the effect of sharpening discourses and making the delineation between competing viewpoints and schools much clearer.[61] Clayton contrasts this Indian model with the Enlightenment model exemplified by Thomas Jefferson, which is inherited by Hick. For the Jeffersonian model, a given rationality transcends tradition-specific reasons, whereas in the Indian model it does not and reason constructs itself in public debate. For the Jeffersonian model the Other is not necessary for debate in a trans-tradition rationality, whereas in the Indian model both self and other are constructed in debate. Lastly, the Jeffersonian model seeks consensus whereas the aim of the Indian model is the clarification of difference.[62]

This is wholly in accord with the dialogical model I wish to develop in the coming chapters and which relates to Geertz' question regarding what we are doing when we study religion. One response might be that we are clarifying difference through intersubjective and intertextual engagement. This is to move away from the idea of a detached objectivity; a neutral place from which to examine the 'world religions' towards the idea that all knowledge is generated from a perspective and that the study of world religions is the intersubjective engagement of one mode of socially sanctioned discourse with another. Like the *vāda* tradition, such a perspectival intersubjectivity serves to reflexively clarify the research programme as well as the 'object' of research, which itself is another traditionally sanctioned discourse and set of practices. Rather than consensus, the project here is about the clarification of difference.

Religion and cognition

Opposed to theological universalism, as well as to the relativism implied in the *vāda* model, we have reductionist, materialist accounts of religion, which are nevertheless universalist. One of the most important trends in recent years has been the application of cognitive theory to religion. Cognitive anthropology is the discipline, or sub-discipline of cultural anthropology, which examines the place of cognition in human societies and which applies insights from linguistics to the wider field of culture.[63] Within the field of religion the work of Sperber,[64] Boyer,[65] and Lawson and McCauley[66] have done most to develop its application, while Scott Atran has worked on the influence of cognition on folk biological categories.[67] While it is not a uniform field, an important general claim of cognitive theory applied to culture is that certain abilities, responses and beliefs are activated or acquired independently of cultural transmission or tuition. People generate cultural expressions due to universal, cognitive processes. Culture comprises mental representations produced by individual minds which become disseminated within a population, some of which disappear quickly, while others are more stable. These stable representations – say myth or religion – are cognitive 'viruses' that diffuse contagiously through a community 'with little alteration over space or time because of their ability to fix onto a psychologically universal basis'.[68]

Cognitive theory generally holds culture to be a cognitive system: beliefs, values, forms of knowledge, and transactional skills exist within the minds or brains of members of a particular social group. In understanding culture two interacting variables are of key importance, the cognitive system and language. Universal cognitive structures, or 'schemata', are causally linked, located within memory, and organize our experience of events, actions, time and objects. Such a schema is a mental structure that controls relationships between concepts within a 'domain' and 'makes it possible to organize the comprehension of situations as well as expectations about them'.[69] As a schematic structure Boyer gives the example of 'car', a concept which contains implicit causal assumptions, such as engines, transmissions, and a chassis, each one of which 'provides a context in which the others are intelligible'.[70] Schematic structures are assumptions linked by strong causal connections that provide the basis for conceptual coherence. Alongside these cognitive schemata we have lexical items (namely, words) which articulate schemata. These schemata are in turn stimulated or activated by lexical items (thus the term 'car' will activate implicit causal assumptions). In other words, cognition is expressed in language and language activates cognitive schemes.

A strong form of the thesis that culture is caused by universal cognitive processes, would be that cognitive processes generate systems of belief completely independently of acculturation; while a weak form would be that cultural forms are constrained to some degree by universal cognitive processes. The weak form of the thesis is much less problematic than the strong form, in so far as few would deny the importance of cognition in human experience. I shall here review the work of Pascal Boyer, who presents a strong form of the thesis, with a view to arguing that while there may be innate cognitive responses particular to different areas of life – or domain-specific cognitive dispositions – the specificity of languages and cultural areas which provide the content for cognition shows that cognitive theory cannot give an adequate account of the historical and linguistic specificity of cultural formation. Furthermore, the presupposition of cognitive theory, namely an objectivist view of truth and of science, has itself been severely critiqued within the social sciences.

Boyer, developing the work of Sperber, in *The Naturalness of Religious Ideas* presents a cognitive theory which attempts to explain the formation of religious ideas by reference to universal cognitive processes and finally relates cognition to wider processes of biological evolution. Boyer attempts to explain the simple fact that people have religious ideas and have these ideas because others had them in previous generations. He attempts to present causal explanations for this by arguing that it is possible to understand how mental representations are transmitted and once this is done, we can then understand how religious ideas are transmitted and can explain religious representations. The recurrence of representations in diverse cultures are due to processes which are dependent upon universal cognitive processes. His rather complex argument can be summarized in the following terms.

Cognitive processes, particularly of categorization or classification, are causally related to religious representations. Categories can be understood either in classical Aristotelian terms in which a category has clearly defined boundaries that a concept is either within or without, or in terms of prototypes in which there are degrees of membership (as we have seen above), both of which, suggests Boyer, are operative in different circumstances. But what is important is that underlying both types of categorization are implicit theories that cause something to be attributed to a certain category. There are wider conceptual structures that constrain categorization. These constraints are of two kinds, schematic and non-schematic structures. Schematic structures are causally linked, whereas non-schematic ones are not linked by causal connections, but rather through the apprehension of similarity. An example of non-schematic assumptions cited by Boyer, though a difficult example not at first obvious, concerns the costs of running a small Japanese car as opposed to an American limousine, in which the connections between car and costs (that the one will be cheaper than the other) are merely inductive generalizations which are not causally linked.[71] A clearer example (though not used by Boyer) might be the Nuer's placing of birds and twins in the same 'sky' category. Such non-schematic assumptions (as between car and costs, birds and twins) are linked through induction and can be accounted for by induction theory which describes the way in which a cognitive system receives inputs from perception and memory, and then generates expectations and descriptions.[72] Non-schematic assumptions are generated in cognition from perception and memory which then control or determine expectation (and so reinforce certain perceptions).

Religious representations, claims Boyer, exist as non-schematic assumptions (assumptions such as birds are twins because of their multiple births), but which are nevertheless constrained by schematic assumptions (such as causation) which serve to strengthen those representations. The schemata, which function in everyday situations, constrain religious representations. He claims to establish this by showing how four repertoires of religious representations, that is, non-schematic assumptions, are constrained by schematic, namely causal, assumptions. These four are ontological assumptions, causal judgements, social categories and ritual episodes, and Boyer discusses evidence for each. Regarding the first, Boyer argues that ontological assumptions need not be culturally transmitted to be represented, but can rather develop spontaneously independently of tuition.[73] Ontological judgements contain intuitive assumptions which are precultural and constantly function in the representation of religious ideas.

For example, a tiger is within a category for which there is an immediate, intuitive acceptance of its existence, whereas religious representations, such as the Fang ancestor-ghosts, present challenges to natural ontologies. The tiger can be classified within a natural ontology, but Fang ancestor-ghosts cannot and so this idea threatens that ontology, while at the same time assuming the category. Because there are natural conceptual structures in which there can be ontological assumptions in specific domains (such as the natural world), this allows for the possibility of unnatural conceptual constructions and the violation of those domains. Supernatural beings, such as the Fang ancestor-ghosts cited by Boyer, on this account are an explicit violation of intuitive principles.[74] The non-schematic assumption of the ancestor-ghosts is constrained by the schematic assumption of the tigers. In other words, Boyer seems to be saying that because of the existence of cognitive processes in which entities are given ontological status in the natural world, not through cultural transmission or tuition but through immediate apprehension or intuition, then those same processes allow for the construction of religious ontologies through the violation of natural categories. The very violation of intuitive principles is constrained by those principles. This shows that there is therefore a universal intuitive understanding of basic onto-logical categories (and conversely of their violation). Boyer goes on to elaborate the ontological case in respect of the other three repertoires (causal judgements, social categories, ritual episodes).

The justification of this cognitive approach is that, according to Boyer, accounts of religion have been inadequate. He seeks to show this by arguing that first, theories of religion and explanations must choose between interpretation of religion in which interpretation 'seeks to give an intuitively satisfactory rendering of religious phenom-ena', and explanation which seeks to relate the general properties of religion 'to some general, explanatory principles'.[75] Choosing the explanatory route, the next choice is between understanding culture as a level of reality independent of individuals' minds, or not. If this latter is chosen then cognitive constraints must be regarded as relevant or irrelevant; if relevant, then one option is the development of hypoth-eses by cognitive anthropology which explain cultural formation by reference to the mind-brain. Such an approach can begin, argues Boyer, to show how religious knowledge differs from everyday knowl-edge structures.[76]

While there is admirable clarity in this kind of binary system of methodological choices, there are nevertheless fundamental problems with this kind of cognitive model. Indeed, it is far from clear among cognitive psychologists themselves that there are universal structures of cognition. But I shall confine my observations to whether culture is independent of individuals, and the degree to which cognition is relevant to culture and its explanation. I shall defer a discussion of the problem of distinguishing explanation from interpretation until the next chapter.

One of the assumptions of Boyer's argument is that culture does not exist with any degree of autonomy, independently of human brains; it is not 'a level of reality'. While it must of course be true that culture exists in the minds of individual social actors, it does not follow that culture does not operate with some degree of independence. The macro effects of culture through history cannot be accounted for in terms of individual cognition: there are systems of economics and historical processes such as globalization, which operate independently of cognition, even though they may be epiphenomena of whole populations of individual minds and actions. To explain the Russian revolution at the level of cognition is simply inadequate. Similarly, to explain the historical specificity of those cultural forms we call religions, it is not enough to simply examine cognition. Cognitive constraints are surely relevant, but culture, and most notably language, exist independently of cognition. Without a person being nurtured within a culture and language, individual cognition would not be stimulated or activated. So while we might accept the reciprocal relationship between schemata and the lexicon, without the lexicon the schemata would not begin to operate. While cognition might be a necessary condition for any one individual to experience the world, language and culture provide the content. As Geertz observed long ago, humans are completely entangled in where they are, who they are and what they believe; so entangled in a culture, as to be inseparable from it. He writes: 'men unmodified by customs of particular places do not in fact exist, have never existed, and most important, could not in the very nature of the case exist.'[77] Culture, on Geertz' view, is an essential condition of human existence and there could be no human nature independent of it.

This is not to decry the possibility of universals, but it is to claim that cognitive processes are not a sufficient explanation of cultural phenomena. While cognition is, of course, a necessary condition for experiencing the world, it is not a sufficient condition. Imitation learning could not occur without the psychological capacities for it, but the content of imitation – namely language and culture – exists independently of any particular cognitive system. Indeed, more important than cognition, the body itself is a necessary condition for experiencing the world. The body from conception is a cultural body, constrained by such factors as language and gender roles. The cognitivists certainly accept some degree of cultural independence in the sense of co-evolution; that while there are genetic constraints operative upon organisms, this genetic fitness can be mediated through cultural 'memes', to use Dawkins' phrase, or 'ideational units', in Boyer's phrase, which select or create environments best suited to successful gene replication.[78] But culture is not in one-to-one correspondence with the genes, as John Bowker has so forcefully argued,[79] though the question does remain as to what their relationship is. This huge topic is beyond the scope of the present enterprise, but the point

I am trying to make is that if culture is 'a level of reality', to use Boyer's phrase, that exists independently of cognition – which it does in the sense that it is transmitted through imitation learning – then cultural inquiry at its own level is important. If the study of religions is to avoid a phenomenological 'transcendentalism', on the one hand, or a reduction to the biological organism on the other, then it must take seriously the intersubjective realm of the cultural sign.[80] Cognitive theory cannot account for the difference between, say, belief in the necessity to appease supernatural beings in a Kerala Hindu temple, and the Buddhist's belief that meditation leads to *nirvāṇa*. This kind of account can only be achieved by the situated interaction of the inquirer or research programme with the particular domain.

Lastly, it is not clear that even if cognitive theory were to establish direct causal links between cognition or brain states and specific religious beliefs, that this would *explain* religious belief. That belief in the saving power of Christ or that the Buddha showed the way to the cessation of suffering, can be shown to have brain-state correlates, would not be an explanation. Such large questions of death and suffering confronted by religions, Blumenberg's 'significant expectations' of religious believers, simply could not be adequately explained by cognition (indeed it is unclear what *any* complete explanation of such questions would look like). This leads on to the point to be further discussed in chapter 3, that explanation cannot so easily be distinguished from interpretation.

Summary

The abstract category 'religion' which developed within the particular history of Western thought, has been taken since the Enlightenment to be universal. This, however, is problematic when 'religion', if defined in essentialist terms is applied to non-Western contexts. But rather than abandon the term, 'religion' is a word within language whose use is not determined by scholarship but by the wider linguistic community. Furthermore, if the category 'religion', as Russell McCutcheon has pointed out,[81] were to be replaced by another such as 'culture' or 'ideology', this would be simply to defer the problem of applying culture-specific meanings to a general level. For the purposes of the present study, I take religions to be binding narratives and behaviours within cultures: there is no discourse of religion outside of particular cultures. To say this is to place language at the centre of inquiry, both in terms of the narratives of particular traditions and in the language of ritual.

Theories about religion have fallen broadly into three categories: quasi-theological explanations, such as theological universalism; hermeneutical/phenomenological explanations or interpretations; and reductionist, scientific explanations such as those of cognitive anthropology. I have discussed briefly the theological universalist and cognitivist programmes, discussed problems with these strategies, and indicated some ways forward by introducing John Clayton's exposition of the *vāda* tradition in Indian philosophical disputation as a form of dialogical model. Both the theological universalist and the cognitivist seek to explain religious diversity by locating its cause, on the one hand, in the supernatural and, on the other, in cognitive processes. I have argued that both strategies do not take seriously the particularity of religious utterance and seek to diminish the importance of cultural, narrative transmission. Explanations or research programmes are always embedded within a particular social context and the inquirer is always in a dialogical relationship with the material at hand. In this sense explanations are inevitably interpretations based on different epistemological assumptions, themselves provided by the wider research culture. To this problem we will now turn.

3. Reductionism and research

The discussion of how religion is defined is not an empty or obscurantist debate for it bears directly upon the research strategies and practices which comprise the discipline of religious studies. Presuppositions inform the construction of the object of any discipline, and presuppositions about religion – or the inevitable pre-understanding of religion – determine to some extent the outcome of research. Eliade's idea of theophany, the manifestation of the sacred, has structured his research findings and is based on a pre-understanding or presupposition of religion as theophany. Similarly, Godelier's understanding of religion as ideology linking the symbolic system of a society with its modes of production entails Marxist presuppositions about the nature of religion. The definition and the explanation of religion are interdependent and different answers will be produced by different research programmes.

In the endeavour to understand religion we are presented with a number of research programmes and methods – psychological, sociological, phenomenological, anthropological, and so on – each of which claims leverage on the question of religion and its relation to human life and wider society. A research programme I take to be a coherent theoretical and methodological orientation which has a clear formulation of its aims, theoretical underpinnings, intersubjective criteria of adequacy, and method; all of which occur within a wider environment which sanctions the process. A research programme is a practice and its result or, to use de Certeau's terminology, a discipline and its discourse. There are of course, many rival research programmes and old programmes are superseded by new ones. This idea of a research programme was developed by Lakatos who maintains that research programmes, or theories, should be placed within wider

historical and social contexts and that it is these contexts that determine the success of a programme; whether it progresses or degenerates
by presenting *ad hoc* hypotheses in support of its central theses.[1] Rival
research programmes must therefore be seen in the contexts of their
development within a wider tradition, sanctioned by the society or
community in which they are embedded.[2] This dimension of reflexivity
in the sciences is crucial in placing any research programme in context
and in attempting to establish criteria of adequacy. It is also central in
regarding the question of reductionism and non-reductionism, for
while all research programmes are reductionist in some sense – otherwise the research programme would simply be a representation of the
totality of its object – they differ with regard to the type of reductionism and their implicit values and attitude towards objectivity.[3] The
present chapter will therefore focus on a fundamental problem under-
girding much discussion in the study of religions, namely the key issue
of reductionism and non-reductionism or, in the terms I shall use,
naturalism and non-naturalism.

Naturalism and non-naturalism

The distinction between the natural and social sciences has broadly
maintained that the natural sciences are concerned with causal explanation and the reduction of complex phenomena to a set of simpler
propositions or rules, while the social sciences have been concerned
with non-causal interpretations. Natural sciences are concerned with
objectification and a clear distinction between their object and method
or theory, social sciences are reflexive and non-reductionist, being a
part of what they study. This is, however, a rather crude characterization, for all research programmes must involve reductionism of one
kind or another – this is the case with theology as much as with
sociology. Rather than the tension in the study of religion being
between reductionist and non-reductionist approaches, a more accurate framing of the debate would be in terms of a tension between
naturalism and non-naturalism, in which naturalism performs very
radical kinds of reductionism absent from non-naturalist research
programmes. Naturalism can be taken in the general sense that potentially there is nothing that cannot be explained by the natural and
human sciences, a generally materialist view that entails a radical
reductionism.

66

On the one hand with naturalism there is an emphasis on causes, on the other with non-naturalism there is an emphasis on rules and meanings in the social world. The well-rehearsed debate about the nature of religion has in recent years revolved around this issue of naturalism as reductionism and non-naturalism as non-reductionism, a debate which itself is part of wider discussions over reductionism in the human sciences.[4] Naturalist explanations in the human sciences, modelled on the natural sciences, attempt to explain religion by reference to causes such as economics (in the case of Marxism), unconscious drives (in the case of psychoanalysis) or genetics (in the case of sociobiology) outside of social actors' power, while non-naturalist explanations – or more typically 'interpretations' – seek to understand religion on its own terms which take seriously insider accounts (in the case of phenomenology) or within a horizon of theological assumptions (in the case of theology). On the one hand religion is explained by the location of specifiable causes, on the other it is interpreted through understanding its rules and meanings. In taking insider accounts of actors seriously, much of social science – particularly the *Verstehen* tradition – has moved away from hard-edged naturalism and presents holistic rather than reductionist accounts; that a phenomenon is understood not through reduction, but through understanding the relationship between the part and the whole.[5] On the one hand reductionism tends towards the idea of a universally valid epistemology and cognition while on the other non-reductionism or holism tends towards three distinct but related concepts of relativism, particularity, and scepticism regarding any universally valid knowledge.

We can locate three types of reductionism in the academic study of religions that claim that their theories are universally valid across cultures: naturalist or materialist reductionism (that itself can be sub-divided into biological, sociological, and psychological reductionism); phenomenological reductionism that claims to reduce phenomena to universal essences; and theological reductionism that ultimately denies difference and reduces diversity to a single, totalizing, theological truth. Phenomenological reductionism would wish to defend elements within local narratives as expressions of universal essences, while theological reductionism would wish to maintain the universal validity of one particular narrative, even at the expense of a universal rationality. It is naturalist reductionism which is my concern in the present chapter. Opposed to these reductionisms we have cultural relativism,

recently exp . sed in the postmodernist position that resists the reduction of local narratives to universal truths standing outside of those
narratives. The cultural relativist celebrates difference and particularity, denies truth in any universalist sense, and in the end must
claim that all we have are competing narratives which gain ascendancy
through a will to power. This latter position denies that Enlightenment
rationalism has universal validity in contrast to naturalist reductionism that tends to deny the truth of narrative, that it reads as 'myth',
claiming universal, materialist truth.

The general position I wish to defend might be called a 'soft
relativism' or fallibilist position that accepts indeterminacy, that
knowledge about religion cannot be grounded on certainty, and that
this indeterminacy allows for a dialogical process in which the
research programme, through focusing on language, is constantly
open to the further possibilities of its dialogical object. Indeed, this is
a fairly moderate claim that Popper would have no problem with, as
science proceeds in a dialogical fashion through the falsification of
hypotheses. While this is to privilege hermeneutics over epistemology,
in Rorty's terms, it is not to argue for a cleavage between explanation
and interpretation, but to maintain that explanations are forms of
interpretation. But to arrive at this position in the context of research
programmes in religion, it is first necessary to pay attention to the
discussion of naturalist reductionism, for it is this position to which
the term 'reductionism' generally refers and that makes the strongest
claims about religion and from whence the critique of religion
comes.

Naturalism in the study of religion: Segal and Wiebe

The conflict in religious studies between naturalism and non-
naturalism is a debate between two different kinds of universalizing
claims, the naturalist and the phenomenological. The debate concerning how to study religions has revolved around on the one hand
'religionists' (such as Cumpsty) who claim that religion must be
understood on its own terms and cannot be explained by reference to
non-religious factors, and those (such as Segal and Wiebe) who
maintain that reductionism or naturalism is necessary for explanation.[6] Indeed it is largely thanks to the very important raising of the
issue by Segal and Wiebe that it has been so widely discussed. This

debate has been expressed and the positions laid out in sometimes heated exchanges in a number of journals.[7] Put bluntly, Robert Segal claims that religionists distrust the explanations of religion by social scientists because religionists wrongly think that these explanations ignore the believer's point of view and challenge the truth of religion. For the religionist, the believer's point of view is paramount; a stance that is an implicitly theological position which bolsters up the truth claims of religion. In a similar vein Wiebe claims that because of the emphasis on interpretation, religious studies is in danger of becoming open to theology which compromises its objectivist, scientific method. To maintain its academic credibility religious studies needs to maintain its 'positive episteme', i.e. its reductionism.[8] Furthermore, Wiebe makes the political point that proximity to theology at a methodological level opens the question as to who sets the agenda for the study of religion, the scholar-scientist or the scholar-devotee.[9] Both Wiebe and Segal make a strong case that any 'science of religion' must of necessity be reductionist and abjure theological explanations. This is because one dominant current leading to religious studies as the science of religion is the naturalist or reductionist one. These naturalist explanations tend to contain materialist assumptions about the nature of the world and about the mythic (i.e. false) nature of religious claims to transcendence.

In a general sense the aim of the naturalist programme in the study of religion is the explanation of belief or a religious ideology in terms of social, psychological or biological factors external to it.[10] This is the reduction of emic accounts to etic ones or the explanation of how and why a group of people should hold such views. Not necessarily, but often there is an implicit assumption that these views are erroneous. While naturalist accounts of religion – such as Freud's psychoanalytic account or Wilson's sociobiological account – are primarily concerned with the issue of the origin and function of religion (and not its truth), many naturalist accounts are also sceptical of religion's truth. If religion can be accounted for in terms of projection, as Segal observes, then this does not have bearing in itself on the truth of religion, but rather what would be significant is the extraordinariness that the projection corresponds to an independent truth.[11] That a 'sense of God' could be located to a specific gene formation does not refute the claim to God's existence, though it might, indeed, cast doubt upon it. The history of religions in many naturalist accounts (such as Freud's) is inevitably the history of error which must be explained in the light of

Enlightenment reason: a view that is behind traditional sociological and psychoanalytic studies of religion. This is indeed a stated aim of much reductionism and sociologists of religion have advocated a methodological atheism.[12] The science of religion in this reductionist sense, as Wiebe acknowledges,[13] is a development of Enlightenment rationalism in which the narratives of religion can be critiqued by reason: the universality and truth of *logos* critiques the local errors of *mythos* and in so doing reveals the lucid clarity of the truth of the procedures' materialist assumptions. These foundations, however, have been exposed to questioning in the context of critiques of rationalism or 'grand narratives', and can be brought into question on a number of accounts. The work of Segal and Wiebe have done most to discuss the issue of reductionism in the study of religions. It to Segal's clear arguments that I now turn.

Segal's claims about the non-reductionist nature of much that goes on within religious studies, as I understand them, can be summarized in the following points:

1. The view of religionists (non-reductionist scholars of religious studies) is characterized by the claim that the *religiosity* of religion must be explained in its own terms, it must be understood at its own level, and that the reduction of religion to other factors such as economics, society or psychology cannot explain religion because it misses the essential point of religion's religiosity.

2. Such a view is an attempt to defend religion against reductionism, which in explaining religion in terms of sociology, economics or whatever, implicitly critiques those truth claims that the religionist wishes to guard. His criticism can also hold true of the cultural relativist – the position identified by Segal with the Wittgenesteinian who holds that truth means internal coherence rather than correspondence to any external reality.[14]

3. There is an unbridgeable gap between the religionist's defence of religion with its implicit theological stance, and social scientific reductionism that both explains and interprets religion in other, verifiable terms.

4. To fend off attack from social science, the religionist attempts either to neutralize it by placing religion beyond the realm of its enquiry (see point 1) or by embracing contemporary social science which is sympathetic to believers' accounts.

Segal, in a number of publications, has developed an important critique of the 'religionist' approach, but while I share many of these concerns and am sympathetic to some of these claims, they are not without problem. The exemplum of the religionist for Segal is Mircea Eliade who clearly states in an oft-cited passage that religion must be understood at its own level – 'a religious phenomena will only be recognized as such if it is grasped at its own level ... if it studied *as* something religious.'[15] This is a good example of the resistance to the social scientific reductionism of which Segal speaks. But it is not clear that Eliade's position reflects a general attitude among religionists and whether Eliade does indeed have a theological agenda is the subject of debate.[16] But even in Eliade the resistance to reductionism is not a resistance to reductionism *per se*, but a resistance to a certain kind of reductionism, namely naturalism, that seeks to explain religion in non-religious terms. Eliade himself reduces the particularities of religious phenomena to an overarching theoretical paradigm, but a different paradigm to that within the social sciences and one that would probably neither be accepted by those within religious traditions. In a similar vein other phenomenologists of religion – such as Bleeker – have attempted to reduce religion to essences or essential types. That this paradigm contains implicit metaphysical assumptions about the nature of religious 'objects' or the existence of the 'sacred' outside of its cultural instantiations, is merely to point to different underlying assumptions to those in the social sciences (which might contain methodological assumptions about the non-existence of the sacred). That the social sciences are themselves based upon unreflexive assumptions has been made very clear by the 'reflexive turn' in sociology and anthropology, as witnessed, for example, in the work of Bourdieu,[17] Gadamer,[18] as John Milbank has so forcefully argued,[19] and as Habermas has argued in criticizing the presupposition of epistemological neutrality in social research.[20]

That research programmes have underlying presuppositions is not in question, although the existence of a transcendent focus beyond its expression in a tradition or believer is not the object of the religionist's inquiry. As Smart pointed out long ago a distinction can be made between objects which are *real* and objects which *exist*. On this view 'God is real for Christians whether or not he exists'.[21] On a related point, Idinopulos claims that for Segal whether the interpreter is a 'believer' or not is relevant to the acceptance of reductionism; belief is irrelevant as 'a concept about the meaning of religious practice'.[22]

Indeed the highlighting of belief in Segal's argument, if I do not misrepresent him, is itself problematic as being a feature of the 'religious person', for while belief may be central to some traditions (such as Christianity) it is by no means an important feature of others such as 'Hinduism' where ritual is more central and unifying. A Hindu might well believe any number of things, but it is not belief which makes her a Hindu.

These points however do not affect Segal's central proposal that for the explanation of religion, models from the social sciences have to be introduced and the data of religion have to be explained in terms of those models; that questions of origin and function take precedence over questions of meaning and intentionality. The present project is generally sympathetic to this view, while wishing to stress the dialogical nature of research and its hermeneutical character. Segal's is an important point, for the future of the academic study of religion lies in its closer proximity to the social sciences. However, we must deal with a number of problems associated with the naturalist enterprise. First, it might be claimed that naturalist explanations do not take meaning and the self-interpretation of social actors seriously enough, in not recognizing emic accounts as having, at one level, equal validity to etic ones. While emic accounts which make empirical claims about the world are certainly open to scientific critique, non-empirical, metaphysical claims are not (see chapter 7). But the primary claim of naturalist accounts does not directly concern the truth of religious propositions, but rather the origin and function of religious ideas and behaviours. In the end, an emic account which speaks in terms of a transcendent object is resistant to any sociological or psychological reductionism, though such a reductionism might well make claims, with conviction and legitimacy, about the function and origin of emic accounts. While sociology or psychology might be sceptical of such emic accounts, they themselves can only make claims about origin and function and not about the truth content of such claims (though many naturalist accounts have done so). In other words, after any reductionist account of religion there is always a remainder, a residue which is part of the believer's perspective, perhaps a 'sense of God' to use Bowker's phrase, and which is as open to a theological understanding as to a naturalist account of origin and function. In this sense Segal is quite correct when he maintains that a non-believer cannot really penetrate the believer's world for whom a transcendent focus, such as God, is true.[23] There is a very strong sense in which the discourse of theology (in the primary sense explained in chapter 1) in defining itself and its object, is resistant to reductionism, and this position is as equally valid as the reductionist when truth is understood in terms of competing narratives or rhetorics. As Lash has observed, the human grasp of truth cannot be other than tradition-constituted.[24]

Secondly, a problem with the naturalist position is not the principle of reductionism, or even the hostility to emic accounts, but rather that – as Lorne Dawson has also noted[25] – it is based upon an objectivist model of the social sciences and committed to a objectivist account of truth that needs to be problematized. The third criticism is that naturalist accounts of religion do not take seriously enough the inevitability of the hermeneutic circle, that interpretation and 'historical prejudice' are present in any explication; and fourthly the naturalist-reductionist position does not appreciate the need to explicate material in terms of appropriate constraints. It is these last three criticisms to which I now turn, for the first issue of the irreducibility of subjective meaning pervades all three.

The objectivist model of the human sciences: Hempel and post-empiricism

The objectivist model of the human or social sciences, based on the natural sciences, maintains that objective truth can be arrived at through a repeatable, methodological procedure involving logical deduction, or at least inference, and empirical evidence. This model contrasts epistemology with hermeneutics and generally maintains that a set of statements arrived at through a repeatable, rational process reflects what is 'really out there'. This is the model appealed to by those who favour naturalist reductionism in the study of religions; a model which owes much to the work of Carl Hempel, but a model which is problematic in our attempts to explicate human intentionalities and ways of life.

Hempel argued for a model of scientific explanation – that in his early work he called 'deductive-nomological' explanations – in which a set of statements (the *explanans*) explains another set of statements which is to be explained (the *expanandum*). This is also called the covering law model; the idea that an event is explained when deduced from a general law or set of conditions and so the law 'covers' that event or the *explanans* covers the *explanandum*. Although Hempel later developed an inductive-probabilistic model, we shall here focus on deductive-nomological explanations as a clear example of a naturalist account of human action. In this model what is to be explained follows deductively from the explanatory statements: the '*explanandum* sentence' follows deductively from the '*explanans* sentences'. Hempel cites the example of Perier's experiment that the length of a mercury column in a Torricelli barometer decreases with increasing altitude. This is the *explanandum* explained by a series of *explanans* sentences, the first of which is the general rule that at any location, the pressure that the column of mercury in the Torricelli apparatus exerts upon the mercury below equals the pressure on the surface of the mercury in the open vessel by the air above it (therefore the mercury column during an ascent becomes shorter).[26] This kind of explanation is a deductive argument whose conclusion (the shortening of the mercury column) is derived from general laws (such as concerning the pressure of the mercury column) and assertions about particular relevant facts (such as Perier carrying the apparatus to the top of the mountain). General, predictive laws ($L_1, L_2 \ldots L_r$) (hence 'nomological' from 'nomos' or 'rule') along with particular facts ($C_1, C_2 \ldots C_k$) result in a certain phenomenon. The predictive laws and the facts are the specification of operational constraints. The *explanandum* sentence is reduced to or explained by the *explanans* sentences. Hempel diagrammatically represents this formula:[27]

$$L_1, L_2 \ldots, L_r$$

                          Explanans sentences

$$\underline{C_1, C_2 \ldots, C_k}$$

       E   *Explanandum* sentence

While this is effective within natural science, it is not clear that such a model works adequately when applied to human behaviour, for there could be no deduction which could establish a connection between general laws of the *explanans* sentences and the human behaviour of the *explanandum* sentence. For example, 'a girl offers a flower to an icon of Lord Krishna' is an *explanandum* sentence that might be accounted for by the *explanans* sentences including 'facts' such as 'the girl has been raised as a Hindu', 'offerings are regularly made to Lord Krishna at this time or on this occasion', 'the girl is from an observant Vaiṣṇava family', 'the girl is acting rationally within her world-view in order to obtain a blessing', or whatever. These are all *explanans* sentences or the specification of the constraints upon the *explanandum* sentence describing the girl's action. But there is no *necessary* entailment between these *explanans* sentences and the *explanandum* as there is in the mercury example. There could be a number of reasons or constraints to account for the behaviour but no *deductive* entailment between them and the action. Similarly, it would be impossible to establish general laws that would account for the girl's reverential behaviour, and the formulation of any such hypothetical law would itself be based on a theory of religion, economics, history or whatever. A Freudian 'law' might be formulated along the lines that 'neurotic impulses are displaced into ritual action', but not only would such a law itself be highly questionable, in a way in which the law concerning air pressure and mercury is not, but the action of offering a flower would not be entailed by it. Social action is characterized by its indeterminacy and to date there has been no successful formulation of general, predictive laws regarding social action, although Hempel did attempt to account for action in terms of reasons, beliefs and desires in his later work.[28]

While not wishing to dismiss Hempel lightly, particularly in the light of the inductivist position of his later ideas, the point I am trying to make is that there are fundamental problems in the adoption of models derived from the natural sciences (as exemplified by nomological-deductivism) by research programmes within the social sciences. General rules of inference or deduction cannot easily be applied to human behaviour that involves meanings and intentions. The study of human beings entails the recognition of humans as self-interpreting. Hempel did attempt to argue against his critics by showing that the human sciences, such as history, are not methodologically distinct from the natural sciences, in that deductive-nomological inference can be used by taking agents' beliefs and desires into account as causes of behaviour; that reasons are the cause of action. But it is impossible to establish true general laws which would account for all cases.[29] It is hard to see how the reasons behind the Hindu girl's offering a flower could be construed in terms of general laws applicable in all cases, other than as very general, culturally construed rules concerning ritual obligations within that particular context. As Bohman has cogently argued, the 'old logic' of the social sciences – exemplified by Hempel among others – has been superseded by a 'new logic' characterized as 'post-empiricist' in which indeterminacy prevails and 'objectivity now concerns the choice of a research program and of its standards of evaluation'[30] rather than any external measure of objectivity.

The debate is by now well rehearsed concerning the problem of epistemological privilege in the natural sciences and to the understanding that science itself is as value-based as any other cultural enterprise. The work of Kuhn has brought our attention to the history of science as a series of ruptures or paradigm shifts, and Feyerabend has argued against the rationality of science, that its development depends upon rhetoric and wider political circumstances.[31] That knowledge-making is a collective enterprise involving trust in others has been made by philosophers of science such as Polanyi and Steven Shapin.[32] This work presents us with a picture of knowledge acquisition as historically contingent with the implication that the idea of scientific or objective truth is agreement, though this idea is not universally accepted. Indeed, as Rorty observes, the debate between Kuhn and his critics is informed by a moral sense that the undermining of objectivity threatens the preservation of Enlightenment values that are perceived to be 'our best hope'.[33] In this line of thinking, in the critique of objectivism 'matters of taste' or 'aesthetics' become foregrounded over 'matters of fact' or 'truth' and subjectivity replaces objectivity that, for the objectivist, perniciously undermines epistemological certainty. However, there can be some degree of certainty in a post-empiricist world if we take 'objectivity' to refer to an inter-subjectively shared or 'agreed discourse' (rather than a correspondence theory of truth) in which what is at one time 'subjective' can soon become 'objective' once accepted within a discourse as part of a body of knowledge. As Rorty says, subjective considerations are regarded as 'being either "kooky" (if he loses his point) or "revolutionary" (if he gains it)'.[34] In Rorty's model, objective truth becomes 'unforced agreement' and rationality becomes 'civility'.

The general point to which this discussion leads is that 'objectivity' can be glossed as 'agreement' or intersubjective consensus. Both the critical hermeneutics of Ricoeur and Habermas' critique of ideology overlap here in that consensus can be understood as the eradication of distorted communication that has an emancipatory and therefore ethical dimension (see chapter 8). The critique of objectivist social science shows that there are no data independent of theoretical assumptions and the deeper values they articulate. All theories are embedded within wider cultural and historical contexts which constrain theory and its outcomes. What is lacking in the naturalist understanding of social science and in naturalist, reductionist programmes is a reflexivity that allows those engaged in the application of a method to human behaviours and intentionalities to understand the context of its occurrence and the power issues involved in its application.

That social science has shifted from an outmoded objectivism towards various forms of perspectivalism and towards an acknowledgement of the indeterminacy of knowledge, is one of the most important criticisms of the naturalist position.[35] When studying human behaviours and intentions we cannot escape the unavoidably intersubjective nature of the enterprise in which subjects cannot be reduced to 'things' as Bakhtin observes:

> The exact sciences constitute a monologic form of knowledge: the intellect contemplates a *thing* and expounds upon it. There is only one subject here – cognizing (contemplating) and speaking (expounding). In opposition to the subject there is only a *voiceless thing*. Any object of knowledge (including man) can be perceived and cognized as a thing. But a subject as such cannot be perceived and studied as a thing, for as a subject it cannot, while remaining a subject, become voiceless, and, consequently, cognition of it can only be *dialogic*.[36]

Bakhtin contrasts the 'double-voiced' depth of the humanities with the 'single-voiced' precision of the hard sciences. A naturalist, reductionist science of human behaviour and intention is unnuanced in not allowing the subject of inquiry a voice or response. A dialogic model of the human sciences, by contrast, recognizes the dialogic nature of research and seeks to allow voice to the 'object' (i.e. subject) of inquiry. Like some forms of critical theory, dialogism is reflexive in its appreciation of understanding as perspectival, from a viewpoint (*Sehepunkt*) or a view both from 'somewhere' and from 'elsewhere'. Rather than a method explaining an object, we have an interactional model of different perspectives in dialogue. Bakhtin has spoken of an 'excess of seeing' or 'unfinalizability' (*nezavershennost*), meaning that everything in the world is 'open and free'.[37] More specifically I am not able to perceive myself from the outside (from outside my body and my birth and death), whereas an external viewer can perceive me in this 'objective' way. The other's objective perception of me seeks to complete or finalize me, yet I cannot be finalized from my perspective if I am to continue a dialogue with the world and others. In a similar way externalist social science can view social actors and texts from that perspective, but from the social actor's perspective there is an unfinalizability: self-perception is always more than perception by others.

Rather than causal explanation, what becomes important is interpretation. When we look more closely at the work of the researcher into religion, whether a quasi-theological religionist or a hard-nosed sociologist, the primary activity of both is the analysis and explanation of texts or behaviour. It is texts about human actions and thoughts or human actions themselves that are the focus of research and there is a strong sense in which human behaviour can be understood as a text analogue as Ricoeur and Taylor have argued and Bakhtin has implied. The work of the sociologist, psychologist of religion, or religionist, does not involve the explanation of 'religion' or even of sub-categories such as 'religious experience' or 'belief'. Rather, the primary data of investigation are either written and oral texts or behavioural text-analogues. That which is 'beyond the text' is not given within representation and so is beyond explanation. That is, only that which is represented can be explained. If something is not represented as knowledge within human sign-systems, it is beyond explanation at that time; quarks are only given meaning within scientific models. That which cannot be represented is unknowable.

The object of the social sciences is meaningful action, within which general rubric religion falls. In an obvious sense much of the religionist's work is concerned with texts, but even in investigating 'religious experience' the psychologist of religion is primarily investigating *reports* – written or oral – of religious experience. She may also be investigating physiological states or behaviour, but these are only meaningful if related to a narrative context; physiological states of arousal do not mean anything of themselves. Even the anthropologist studying 'religious behaviour', such as possession, is studying a text-analogue in the sense that behaviour to be meaningful must be set within the context of a narrative (the work of Obeyesekere on possession in Sri Lanka is a prime example of this).[38] Nor does the category of 'religious practice' fall outside of narrative, for it is within a narrative context – the context of a life and the context of a tradition – that practice (prayer or yoga for example) are given meaning. Once set within a narrative context, rather than any naturalist, causal explanation, it is primarily understanding and interpretation which become central and hermeneutics must take precedence over epistemology. The interpretation of texts and text-analogues is the primary activity of the religions researcher.

Charles Taylor defines interpretation in the following terms:

> Interpretation ... is an attempt to make clear, to make sense of, an object of study. This object must, therefore, be a text, or a text-analogue, which in some way is confused, incomplete, cloudy, seemingly contradictory – in one way or another, unclear. The interpretation aims to bring to light an underlying coherence or sense.[39]

Interpretation is the primary task of the social scientist on this view because the object of interpretation is ultimately for a human subject. This object – which for Taylor is a text or text analogue – comprises a sense or meaning and its expression which are distinguishable.[40] If an interpretation is to be successful then the interpreter must be able to distinguish the sense of something from its expression and to reconstitute that sense in a different context – for example by attempting to make coherent that which was incoherent. The task of the religionist is initially the making coherent of that which is vague or opaque and 'other' by reconstituting that other in a different mode which makes it coherent for the interpreter or community of interpreters. This might well be to reconstitute the object in terms of paradigms external to the material, such as psychological or sociological models, but while such paradigms claim epistemological authority, they remain nevertheless interpretations of their data. The objectivist mode of explanation is itself an interpretation of data in terms of models distinct from it. Traditionally in the social sciences and humanities we have on the one side naturalist, causal explanations, while on the other we have an emphasis on interpretation and meaning. Rorty sees this as a distinction between epistemology and hermeneutics in which hermeneutics resists the epistemological desire for discourses to be commensurable or able to be subsumed under a set of rules leading to rational agreement.[41] However, explanation and interpretation are not entirely distinct or mutually exclusive and, as Bohman shows, there has been a tradition in the social sciences from Weber to Habermas which recognizes methodological complexity and incorporates elements of explanation and interpretation in research; this tradition has recognized that interpretation is necessary to explanation[42] and both can be reconciled in hermeneutic discourse (as Taylor, Ricoeur and others have argued). As regards the academic study of religion, Segal makes the point that while the distinction between explanation and interpretation corresponds to that between cause and meaning, they are not necessarily opposed and attempts to identify cause with *physical* cause opposed to mentalist meaning are mistaken. Causes are not necessarily physical and a meaning can be taken as a cause, an interaction as an explanation, as in the work of Weber and Geertz.[43]

There is also a relation here between interpretation and critique. If we take critique to be understood as a discourse which lays bear contradictions within narrative, the social and historical conditions of narrative and indeed, of interpretation itself, then critique can be seen as both a form of interpretation and as that which reflexively undermines interpretation. As regards religion, it is difficult to see how an explanation is not also an interpretation, and it is difficult to imagine an explanation which does not bring understanding to the scholarly community. Explanation can also be implicit or explicit critique.

The problem of the hermeneutic circle: Heidegger and Gadamer

If what the religionist or social scientist is doing is primarily interpretation of texts and text analogues, then how, given that understanding is constrained by historical prejudice, can we distinguish between 'correct' and 'distorted' interpretations? What are the epistemological standards or criteria for judging between conflicting interpretations? How do we know *this* interpretation to be correct and *that* to be wrong if there are no objective standards beyond interpretations to which to appeal? Surely naturalist reductionism offers certainty, closure, and clarity in the face of the non-closure of interpretation? These are difficult questions for any research programme that must appeal to criteria of adequacy within the parameters of that programme. But criteria of adequacy can themselves only arise out of a research programme. In trying to convince somebody that *my* interpretation is correct, I can only appeal to the text and to other readings or other texts: the force of conviction must arrive through the force of the 'reading' in the context of other possible readings within a tradition of interpretation. As Vattimo says, hermeneutics cannot appeal to a true reality outside of interpretation, but can only establish a coherent picture.[44] The telos of complete understanding is unobtainable. Even naturalist explanations entail the interpretation of data, which are in turn partially constructed by the method and determined by the questions asked. The social scientist in the end is appealing to texts or behaviours and relating these to traditions of explanation, which is why social science is itself inherently hermeneutical in a general sense.

This is the ineluctable problem of the hermeneutic circle, that a particular element can be understood only in terms of the whole text, yet the whole text can itself only be understood in terms of that particular element. The meaning of the parts depends upon the whole and the meaning of the whole on the parts. The interrelation between the whole and the parts will lead to deeper or richer interpretations. One way of putting this might simply be trial and error: a 'reading' is always modified in relation to the whole and the view of the whole further modified in the light of particular readings. This is even the case with philology, arguably the most objective of the human sciences, in which a pre-understanding is necessary to arrive at the objective text. Knowledge in this sense entails the idea of foreknowledge or the intuition of a meaning yet to be fully disclosed.

This concept owes everything initially to Heidegger, who applied the method of interpretation developed in the context of understanding texts to the understanding of Being itself, and latterly to Gadamer. For Heidegger the forestructure of understanding is a prelinguistic orientation or way in which we are 'thrown' into the world; these forestructures are integral within Being (*Dasein*) and are not a matter of choice, but are the inevitable projections operative in any act of understanding. We cannot choose not to understand in this way. Heidegger attempts to map out the forestructures of forehaving (*Vorhabe*), foresight (*Vorsicht*) and foreconception (*Vorgriff*) which need to be worked out in terms of the objects or the entities and the Being in which they share.[45] The objects of interpretation are already governed by our pre-understanding of being; an interpretation 'is grounded in something we grasp in advance – a foreconception',[46] for all understanding is still within the being we wish to interpret. Even science, for Heidegger, has shared theoretical and technical assumptions – its 'forehaving' – and operates through projection, in the light of which the 'fact' is found.[47] Understanding here is not so much a form of knowledge as a 'knowing one's way around' (*Sichauskennen*) or 'being at home with something' (*sich auf etwas Verstehen*).[48] In order for interpretation to come about, the forestructures of understanding need to be reflexively brought to awareness as far as possible.

Although reliant of Heidegger's understanding, for Gadamer the hermeneutic circle is concerned primarily with texts, that the very enterprise of understanding involves a projection of meaning into the text, corrected with further readings. Although hermeneutics certainly has wider ontological implications beyond texts,[49] it is Gadamer's hermeneutic problematic that is of greatest relevance to the study of religions rather than Heidegger's ontological one, because the religionist deals with texts and text analogues. Gadamer himself recognizes the different natures of the problematics. He writes: 'Our question, by contrast [to Heidegger's], is how hermeneutics, once freed from the ontological obstructions of the scientific concept of objectivity, can do justice to the historicity of understanding.'[50]

In answer to the problem that all interpretation is the projection of historical prejudice, Gadamer, following Schliermacher and Dilthey, sees that meaning is initially projected into the text and these projections are subsequently modified with further reading in the light of the text. He writes:

> A person who is trying to understand a text is always projecting. He projects a meaning for the text as a whole as soon as some initial meaning emerges in the text. Again, the initial meaning emerges only because he is reading the text with particular expectations in regard to a certain meaning. Working out this foreprojection, which is constantly revised in terms of what emerges as he penetrates into the meaning, is understanding what is there.[51]

This process will be readily recognized by those who read texts in other languages such as Sanskrit: the meaning is gradually illumined by repeated readings. All understanding arises due to the process of projection which is modified in the light of further enquiry. This implies that the text is a totality or complete and this completeness functions as a constraint upon interpretation: there is an 'anticipation of completeness' or 'perfection' (*Vollkommenheit*) on behalf of the interpreter. This anticipation of completeness maintains that a text expresses its meaning which is its complete truth and that understanding, which is interpretation for Gadamer, implies a movement from the whole to the part and back to the whole. Understanding develops or progresses because of the assumption of the text's completeness and there is an attempt to make sense of individual parts and relate them to the context of the whole. The pre-understanding of the text is a necessary condition for any understanding at all. There can be no passive receptivity of meaning, but rather meaning only occurs *because* of preconception, *because* of prejudice and it is this feature that constitutes the universal (and in Gadamer's sense the ontological) character of hermeneutics. There can be erroneous preconception in so far as an erroneous meaning is projected onto the text, but without preconception there could be no understanding. Understanding, as it were, is the skill of relating meanings found in a text to one's own situation and to the questions brought to bear upon it. Indeed, Gadamer denies that his conception of hermeneutics is a method, for we cannot choose not to understand in this way; we cannot help but understand through the route of the hermeneutic circle, for the very structure of understanding involves the projection of anticipation or foreunderstanding.[52] As the title of the work *Truth and Method* suggests, Gadamer is concerned with the relation of 'truth' arrived at through the tradition-constrained understanding of the human sciences, to 'method' of the objectivist sciences, arguing that scientific method is inadequate. Indeed, 'culture' (*Bildung*) is more relevant than 'method' in the act of understanding.[53]

This sentiment is echoed by Rorty when he argues that hermeneutics is not a discipline or method to achieve what epistemology sought to achieve, namely the establishing of rational foundations for a theory of knowledge, for it cannot fill the gap left by the demise of epistemology.[54] Hermeneutics cannot provide the sure foundations of knowledge but, at most, intersubjective agreement. While this position might ring alarm bells for an epistemological foundationalism, and for a naturalist reductionism, in replacing certitude with indeterminacy hermeneutics allows for the development of research programmes that are freed from the quest for determinate knowledge, that recognize that experience is linguistically and historically constrained, and that are open to the multi-faceted and multi-vocal cultural world that provides the data for the human sciences. This is especially true of religious studies where the plurality of texts, ideologies, and ritual behaviours provides a very wide range of phenomena, about which any foundational, epistemological explanations would be restrictive in a way a hermeneutical approach is not.

In one sense it is a truism that a textual understanding develops through interaction with the text and modification of the interpreter's views as that understanding deepens. In any reading there is an anticipation of what is to come and a modification of that anticipation – perhaps of disappointment or surprise – as the text unfolds. But the problem arises when the anticipation of perfection is not met by the text and there is a rupture between anticipation or fore-understanding and the text's contents. A text might appear to be incomprehensible and, on Gadamer's account, there is no way of determining whether the problem lies in the anticipation or whether the text itself is discordant and fragmented. Warnke has drawn attention to this problem, noting how deconstructionist critics have highlighted the inconsistencies of the text, that the assumption of the text's unity overlooks the contradictions within it.[55] However, Gadamer's response to these criticisms, Warnke notes, is that while he partially agrees with the deconstructionist critique of textual unity, it does not resolve the problem of misunderstanding. Indeed, for Gadamer the idea of truth revealed in the text, or behind the text, is still important in the sense that understanding involves insight into 'the things' (*die Sache*). To understand the 'thing itself' (*der Sache selbst*) is to understand its meaning, that in turn points to a universal ontological structure, namely that the 'being that can be understood is language'[56] (in stark contrast to Husserl's differentiation between existence and meaning as we shall see). On the other hand, for deconstructionists such as Derrida, rather than a relation between a 'signifier' and a 'signified' all we have is a differential network of meaning; the sign is divorced from its signifieds and all we have are texts and their interconnections.[57] This is to deny the distinction between the subject of research and the object, one configuration of the postmodernist enterprise, but a distinction that needs to be maintained (although in a different way to Husserl) if there is to be theory, criticism and an ethic that reflexively acknowledges the situated nature of research and the centrality of language.

In contrast to the objectifying attitude of science, the hermeneutics of Gadamer aims to refute the 'alienating distanciation' (*Verfremdung*) in that hermeneutics must begin with the bond between interpreter and interpreted. That is, there are enabling prejudices that allow something to be understood and these prejudices and foremeanings are not something that can be chosen, but are given. Because of this, Gadamer claims that hermeneutics is not a procedure or method brought to bear on a text, because there is no choice – hence his dichotomy between 'truth' and 'method'. Yet nevertheless, although the interpreter is intimately bound up with the object of interpretation through prejudice and foreconception over which she has little control, it also entails the notion of an inside and an outside perspective because of the distanciation between what one is and what one is not,

required in interpretation. Indeed, hermeneutic work, claims Gadamer, is based on 'a polarity of familiarity and strangeness', and the
'true locus of hermeneutics is this in-between'.[58] Any sharp distinction
between the theorist and agent, as Kögler claims, is 'a methodological
fiction'.[59] It is here that the friction with critical theory – especially the
Gadamer–Habermas debate – arises, critical theory wishing to create a
critical distance with tradition and claiming that hermeneutics cannot
break free from its constraints. In contrast to hermeneutics, critical
theory requires an overarching theory of justice as the basis of its
critique.[60] These positions are not, however, mutually exclusive and
the idea of belonging within tradition is not incompatible with critique; there can be a critical hermeneutics, as Ricoeur and Kögler have
argued.[61] McCarthy has similarly argued for critical theory supported
by philosophical hermeneutics 'which insists on the context-
boundedness of understanding and sees theories as interpretations, not
as pictures'.[62]

For hermeneutics, because we are embedded within history and
within the narratives of our traditions, there can be no closure of the
process of understanding, and the clarification of misunderstanding
can only occur with further interaction between interpreter and text.
In the romantic hermeneutics of Schliermacher, the hermeneutic circle
was closed once full understanding of the text occurred. Erroneous
pre-understanding would become full or complete understanding in
the movement from the part to the whole. But Gadamer rejects this
individualistic view on the grounds that understanding a text is not an
act of individual subjectivity, but is rather the result of tradition in
which the individual is bound and which in turn is produced by the
individual in participation in a tradition's evolution.[63] Interpretation
on this account becomes transindividual and is set within historical
tradition in which the individual is subject to historical contingencies
and whose prejudices are moulded by historical circumstance. Gadamer writes: 'Every age has to understand a transmitted text in its own
way, for the text belongs to the whole tradition whose content
interests the age and in which it seeks to understand itself.'[64] This can
be seen in conflicting interpretations of texts. To take a Hindu example, a famous verse of the *Bhagavadgītā* about grace (the *carama
śloka*) is interpreted in two distinct ways by different branches of the
Vaiṣṇava tradition: the 'cat' school reading it as advocating a doctrine
of pure grace, the 'monkey' school as advocating a doctrine of effort
combined with grace.[65] Or again, in interpreting the fifth-century

Sanskrit grammar of Pāṇini, nineteenth-century philologists misunderstood certain principles within the text because they did not know about context-sensitive rules in modern linguistics.[66] An interpretation can never be complete.

Our question of how we can distinguish between 'correct' and 'distorted' interpretations or what the epistemological criteria are for judging between conflicting interpretations, is a question concerning the legitimacy of a discourse, such as hermeneutics, and the problem of from whence derives its authority. Once we have abandoned the possibility of a foundational epistemology upon which naturalist reductionism rests – an acknowledgement that we cannot step outside of discourse and narrative – we are faced with a choice of two routes. On the one hand the sceptical view adopted generally within postmodern social science, that there can be no certainty as regards knowledge, for we are embedded within cultural narratives from which we cannot break loose, albeit intertextual narratives of free-floating signifiers. On the other a modification of this position in the fallibilist view that while there can be no certainty about knowledge, scepticism is not a consequence of this and there can be intersubjectively agreed public knowledge which is open to revision. That is, there can be a linguistic discourse or criticism that is a type of cultural narrative, both reflexive in self-criticism and having the power to critique other narratives. Thus a text can indeed assert its truth against our fore-understandings, 'a person trying to understand a text is prepared for it to tell him something'.[67] This is a position within the hermeneutical tradition, but also arguing for a critical distance. While not existing outside of narrative in the sense that all critique is a practice temporally produced within cultures, narrative critique can nevertheless distance itself from the culture and the history which produced it through reflexivity – although of course only because of that history – and provide a rupture with tradition and so eventuate potentially radical change.

We can recapitulate the three positions in the following terms. The naturalist claim to objectivity and access to truth is a claim that critique can exist completely outside of narrative as if in some atemporal zone. This is Gadamer's conceptualization of science as 'alienation'. This contrasts with the sceptical view that there can be no critique outside of narrative and no objective access to truth, and with the fallibilist view that although knowledge is indeterminate and criticism is a practice inevitably within narrative and history, critique can nevertheless reflexively comment upon itself as a narrative tradition and comment upon other narratives. This latter position, I would argue, remains open to its own limitations and open to the complexity of constraints operating within diverse narrative traditions. Unlike objectivist, naturalist reductionism which ironically distorts its object through a non-appreciation of the complexity of constraint, the fallibilist position of narrative criticism attempts to highlight and specify constraints operative within any tradition.

Levels of constraint and explanation

Different disciplines operate at different levels of human being, ranging from the social, to the psychological, to the biological. For naturalist reductionism the constraints specified are functional at the level of the disciplines' operation. A sociological functionalist account of religion – such as the Stark and Bainbridge hypothesis that religion functions to secure rewards and compensators operate to satisfy human desires in the face of their absence[68] – will specify constraints within social processes that function to provide compensators. A cognitivist theory of religion – such as Pascal Boyer or Lawson and McCauley's theory of religion as an idealized model of the world which operates in a way akin to science[69] – specifies the explanatory functions of religion, while a sociobiological theory – such as Wilson's explanation of religion as functioning to protect the process of gene replication[70] – specifies its evolutionary, genetic constraints. It is not my intention to critique or assess these different research programmes that make claims about religion, but rather to underline the important point that different research programmes specify different levels of constraint, and that the more extreme forms of naturalist reductionism, such as sociobiology, are inadequate because of the limited constraints they account for. The example of sociobiology will briefly serve to illustrate this. My understanding of constraint in the context of religion is due to the work of John Bowker and it is his critique of sociobiology that I largely follow here.

Sociobiology is an example of a research programme that attempts to show that the most important constraints upon human cognition and behaviour are genetic, but while it operates as critique upon the narrative of religion, it tends to be blind to the narratives out from which its critique has developed. Sociobiology claims that religions are systems which have evolved to protect gene frequencies and to enhance the likelihood of gene replication. Wilson argues that the genes programme the functioning of the nervous, hormonal and sensory systems of the body and thereby influence the learning process: 'They constrain the maturation of some behaviours and the learning rules of other behaviours.'[71] Religions which determine so much in human behaviour as systems of learning, are therefore constrained indirectly via physiology, by the genes. This would equally be true of other aspects of culture. This is a strong and well corroborated claim. As Bowker says, '(t)he value of religions as protective systems for gene replication and the nurture of children is dramatically obvious in the preoccupation which all long-running religions display, with sex and food.'[72] There is a strong case for the specification of genetic constraint in the explanation of religion. However, the genetic constraints specified by Wilson operate at a level too low to account for both the diversity and specificity of religious traditions. Theological differences between traditions, the variety of ritual behaviours, and ascetic practices cannot be accounted for – even within the spectrum of naturalist explanations – in terms of the genetic level of constraint. The Digambara Jain monk, Acarya Shantisagar, in 1955 withdrew from the world in order to achieve liberation (*mukti*) by ritual fasting to death (*sallekhana*).[73] This is behaviour with no clear genetic or evolutionary advantage and explanation of it in terms of genes rather than in terms of reasons and emic accounts, is simply inadequate. Such behaviour must be understood within the constraints of the tradition, by its internalized ideology and by reference to the intentions and desires of practitioners. This is not to preclude other constraints, but the explanation of religion must arguably occur at a level which can take account of the terminologies, texts, practices and ideologies of the tradition.

Segal has criticized Eliade for claiming that religion has to be understood at its own level on the grounds that this is to go against the spirit of the scientific enquiry into religion and in effect to exclude explanation in favour of implicitly theological assertion.[74] While this is not the place to defend Eliade,[75] it is certainly arguably the case that once we take human meanings, intentions, and behaviours embedded within particular social and cultural structures, as the 'texts' in need of 'explanation', we are immediately in a dialogical relationship with that material and must acknowledge constraints above the genetic. The explanation of genetic inheritance is simply not enough to understand the Jain monk's behaviour, nor is it sufficient to dismiss the worldview of which such extreme asceticism is a part, as irrational or an example of religious error in the light of the modern reason. In the Jain monk's eyes, and in the eyes of his community, his ritual death is the highest achievement of his monastic career and the vindication of his life of non-violence and asceticism. We need to view such behaviour, not primarily in terms of genetic constraints, but in terms of religions, to use Bowker's phrase, as route-finding activities[76] that construct a life from birth to death and, for our Jain monk, beyond. Genetic explanation does not account for the diversity of religious constraints, and to understand a religion research strategies need to specify constraints operating within it. Religions as route-finding activities operate within constraints external to them – such as physiological and environmental – yet also comprise various constraints which directly affect the lives of those who follow them. As Bowker says, 'religions offer various forms of constraint, which, if they are appropriated or internalized delimit the life of an individual or group, and help to control it into its particular outcomes.'[77] The specification of these constraints is the job of different research programmes. Naturalist reductionism in specifying constraints external to religion to account for it, ignores the equally important internal constraints of a tradition; the level of intention, meaning and action at which enquiry must begin and to which it must always return in order to clarify understanding in an ongoing process. The level of constraint specified – the social-functional, personal-psychological, rational-intentional or whatever – will determine the quality of understanding, which allows for the operation of hermeneutics. This in turn depends upon the questions brought to bear on the material and the interaction or dialogue between the interpreter and system, text, or person.

Summary

The general position I have argued privileges hermeneutics over epistemology and sees explanation as a form of interpretation. Although these distinctions are not clear cut I hope that the position I have argued is sufficiently nuanced. The relation of research programmes to religion is complex and I have here focused upon the issue of naturalism and non-naturalism, arguing that a strong naturalistic reductionism is open to criticism on four accounts. First, it does not give sufficient space for emic perspectives. It is far from clear that beliefs, intentions, and behaviours can be explained in the naturalist terms of external constraints such as genes or social processes. Hempel's early model of nomological deductivism is insufficient in explaining human intentionalities. Secondly, the objectivist model of social science under which naturalist reductionism operates is itself highly questionable in the context of critiques of the 'view from nowhere' and the plausibility that there can be a discourse outside of history and place. All accounts of religion are from a location. This leads to the third criticism that prejudice or fore-understanding is inevitable and needs to be acknowledged in the process of interpretation and refinement of the hermeneutic circle. Lastly, naturalist reductionism only specifies constraints external to the narratives and behaviours of religion and in so doing neglects to appreciate that different research programmes will arrive at different results depending upon the level of constraint specified.

The question of constraint has bearing upon the very nature of religion and the deepest experiences in human lives. Controls within religious traditions largely operate through internalized narratives and through action, particularly ritual systems which are informed by narratives although not always dependent upon them. It is these narratives or 'texts' and ritual systems or text analogues which are the primary material wherein 'religion' is encountered by research programmes. The phenomenology of religion has resisted naturalist reductionism and has attempted to take into account emic perspectives, but this enterprise is itself problematic and to this we now turn. The critique of phenomenology will lay the ground for developing a dialogical research programme in the following chapters.

4. The limits of phenomenology

In the preface to the second edition of *the Eternal In Man (Vom Ewigen im Menschen)* Max Scheler makes a distinction between reconstructive and essential phenomenology, the former being 'relativistic' in being concerned with the description of the original empirical contents of a religious or metaphysical system, the latter being concerned with the essential correlations which are true of the essence of an object.[1] This distinction has been at the heart of much phenomenology of religion which has sought to describe the phenomena of religion while suspending truth judgements, and which has sought to find correlations between the phenomena of diverse traditions and to establish types and patterns of religious consciousness. The present chapter does not intend to trace the history of the phenomenology of religion[2] nor to explore the sometimes rancorous distinction between the phenomenology of religion and the history of religions. Rather I wish to discuss the function of phenomenology within the study of religions by examining its foundational concepts, referred to by Scheler, and in offering a critique of these foundational concepts shall thereby offer a critique of the phenomenology of religions; a critique which itself is located in the confluence of phenomenological and narrativist traditions. Anticipating my conclusions, I shall argue that phenomenological method alone is inadequate for understanding religions because it entails a particular philosophy of consciousness, and that description needs to be located within narrative (and so disallows a reduction to essences).

The history of the term 'phenomenology' has been traced by Spiegelberg from its first documented occurrence in 1764 by Johan Heinrich

Lambert, a follower of Christian Wolff,[3] for whom the analysis of appearances leads to ascertaining truth or error, and by Ryba with particular reference to the study of religion.[4] Lambert's thought can be traced through Fichte to Kant and Hegel, though the roots of phenomenology can be traced back to Plato's concept of changing appearances or 'phenomena' being related to the underlying forms or 'logos'. In 1798 John Robinson used the term in the *Encyclopaedia Britannica* to denote philosophy as 'the study of the phenomena of the universe with a view to discover the general laws which indicate the powers of natural substances.'[5] A common theme in the uses of 'phenomenology' has been the emphasis on consciousness and modes of awareness, especially for Hegel for whom consciousness is the immediate being of spirit (*Geist*). But it is Husserl who is the founder of modern phenomenology and who is so pivotal in the history of Western thought in the latter half of the twentieth century. From his phenomenology at least three paths of development can be traced. First, the central tradition of philosophical phenomenology represented in the work of the phenomenological circle (Edith Stein, Adolf Reinach and so on) through to the French phenomenologists Merleau-Ponty and Gabriel Marcel. The theological phenomenology of Max Scheler can be located within this tradition, though there are also strong 'sociological' leanings in his work. Secondly, a path of existential phenomenology in Heidegger which leads into the hermeneutics of Gadamer on the one hand, and the existentialism of Sartre and de Beauvoir on the other; and thirdly a sociological phenomenology in the work of Moritz Geiger and especially Alfred Schutz, which draws on Weberian sociology and develops into ethnomethodology. In relation to these traditions the phenomenology of religion does not develop only from Husserl, but absorbs key concepts developed by him.

Although the phenomenology of religion predates Husserl, he is nevertheless of central importance in its development, for it is to Husserl that it owes its three most fundamental analytical concepts, namely 'bracketing' (*epoché*), the 'eidetic reduction', and 'empathy' (*Einfühlung*).[6] The bracketing of questions of objective truth, which Van der Leeuw calls 'intellectual suspense', can be taken to be a defining characteristic of the phenomenology of religion; in Ninian Smart's words 'the attempt at value-free descriptions in religion'.[7] The eidetic reduction has similarly had a deep impact upon the science of religion in the idea of understanding the 'essence' of a 'religious manifestation' and in the idea of developing typologies of religion and religious phenomena, or the grouping together of diverse phenomena which share the same essence. Similarly 'empathy' has accompanied the idea of bracketing; that bracketing allows empathy or the ability to enter into the life of another, characterized by Ninian Smart, citing a native American proverb, as the ability 'to walk a mile in another's moccasins'.[8] While they have functioned to liberate the study of religions from theological dogmatism, these concepts now unnecessarily limit the range of methodological possibilities within the study of religions; are closed to an open-ended dialogical understanding in which language is central; and disenable an explanatory level that seeks to link 'religious' phenomena to other cultural practices. In order to examine these three vital concepts more closely we will return to their source in that giant, Husserl.

Husserl's phenomenological project

The development of Husserl's thought is complex and his work is open to different readings, from his early work on the philosophy of mathematics, to the idealist emphasis on consciousness and essence, to an emphasis on the intersubjective life-world in his later years. The work that has influenced the study of religions has come from Husserl's development of phenomenology and the analysis of intentionality. For Husserl phenomenology is both a method or practice and a philosophical discourse about the nature of metaphysics and epistemology. Ultimately the purpose of such a practice is universal self-knowledge and Husserl ends the *Cartesian Meditations* with the Delphic motto 'Know Thyself' (*gnothi seauton*) and a quote from Augustine to 'go back to yourself' (*in te redi*) and that 'truth dwells in the inner man' (*in interiore homine habitat veritas*).[9] This truth lies in consciousness and the indubitable experience of the *cogito* ('I think') and its objects. In his famous phrase Husserl characterizes phenomenology as a return 'to the things themselves' (*Zu den Sachen*), a return to the data given in our experience or consciousness. What is presented to consciousness is apodictically given – not the factual existence of the world, but rather appearances to consciousness – and needs no further legitimacy to be an object of understanding or investigation. The central characteristic of consciousness is therefore that it is conscious *of* something or is 'intentional'. The intentionality of consciousness, a term which Husserl inherited from his teacher Brentano, is the foundation of phenomenology in so far as it allows any object of consciousness to be a legitimate field of enquiry. Through turning our 'inquiring gaze' (*des erfahrenden Blickes*) inwards to our own psychic life, every experience (*Erfahrung*) can be subject to phenomenological reflection (*Reflexion*). Through reflection we grasp not the objects themselves, but rather the experience of those objects as subjectively given in which they 'appear' (*erscheinen*). Husserl goes on to explain:

> For this reason, they are called 'phenomena' (*Phanomene*), and their most general essential character (*Wesenscharakter*) is to exist as the 'consciousness-of' or 'appearance-of' the specific things, thoughts (judged states of affairs, grounds, conclusions), plans, decisions, hopes and so forth. This relatedness resides in the meaning of all expressions in the vernacular languages which relate to psychic experience – for instance, perception *of* something, recalling *of* something, thinking *of* something, hoping *for* something, fearing something, striving *for* something, deciding *on* something, and so on ... [10]

Each conscious process or *cogito* means something, and this meaning is its object or *cogitatum*. That each conscious act has an object, that we are always conscious *of* something, is what is meant by intentionality, which Husserl regards as a universal property of consciousness.[11] In *Ideas Pertaining to a Pure Phenomenology and to a Phenomenological Philosophy 1 (Ideen zu einer reinen Phänomenolgie und phänomenologigischen Philosophie 1)* Husserl introduced the terms *noema* and *noesis* to describe intentionality. Although Husserl is ambiguous about the precise meaning of these terms, *noesis* can be taken as referring to the subject's experience and intention towards an object of consciousness, while *noema* refers to the content of experience or object of intentionality. Intentionality is therefore the correlation between the *noema* and *noesis*. This makes clear the distinction between the real objects of experience and the intentional contents of experience; the *noema* referring to the latter and being the realm of phenomenological investigation. It is judgements concerning the relation between the 'real' objects of experience and the *noema* or contents of consciousness which is suspended in bracketing. Phenomenology seeks to explore that which is given to consciousness and in so doing to suspend judgements about objective existence or non-existence of the objects of consciousness, or more specifically, to suspend judgement about the solutions to this problem posed in the history of philosophy.

This suspension of judgement is the phenomenological reduction or 'bracketing out' (*epoché*) of questions of objective truth. Description in this sense is, in Husserl's phrase, a 'universal depriving of acceptance, (an) ... "inhibiting" or "putting out of play" of all positions taken towards an already given objective world and, in the first place, all existential positions ... '[12] This is to put the objective world in parentheses by which firstly I know myself as an ego with a conscious life, a *cogito*, and secondly I am aware of that which allows conscious life to be, namely the flow of consciousness or the objects of consciousness, the *cogitationes*. The ego perceives the constant flux of profiles or perspectives (*Abschattungen*) from which meaning is acquired. This is not to posit a psychological truth about the self for Husserl, but rather to present a transcendental truth; that in stepping back from belief in the objective world and in directing one's gaze to being conscious *of* the world, the self acquires itself as a pure ego with the 'pure stream' of its *cogitationes*. Through the phenomenological reduction the self in the mode of *psychological self-experience* has been reduced to a *transcendental-phenomenological self-experience*.[13] This is a transcendental truth for Husserl and not a psychological truth, for psychology itself is subject to the *epoché*.[14] Through *epoché* there occurs the complete suspension of judgement concerning the objective world which thereby disallows both solipsism and scepticism and allows for the certainty of the ego and its objects of consciousness. The primary enterprise of phenomenology for Husserl is therefore the description of the totality of meanings in the stream of consciousness; a mapping of their structure. There is a deeper level than this, the genetic phenomenology which seeks for the foundations of these mapped structures, for example in terms of teleology and the ego's motives,[15] but it is this first, descriptive level which is important for the phenomenology of religions.

In order to secure the grounds for any knowledge, having performed the phenomenological reduction, the bracketing of the ontological status of the objective world in which I as a transcendental ego become conscious of the *cogito* and its objects, the *cogitationes*, there remains a second reduction to be done, a further step must be taken. This is the *eidetic* reduction, the reduction of an object of consciousness to its essence (*eidos*), in which the 'facts' present to consciousness are understood through intuition. The intuition of essences occurs through considering the diverse aspects of the objects of consciousness, such as those apprehended through acts of perception. To clarify this idea Husserl gives the example of the perception of a table. A table, or any percept, is always seen from a particular angle or view and its totality is not directly perceived. Through varying in the imagination all possible perceptions of the table – by changing its shape or colour for example – we remove perception into 'the realm of non-actualities'. In this way, through this 'method of free variation' we arrive at the intuition of the essence of the table's perception. Removed from actuality, perception has become 'a pure *eidos*' comprising all possible perceptions constructed in the imagination.[16] It is this process of phenomenological bracketing and the reduction to essences which is adopted by the phenomenology of religions.

The phenomenology of religion

The phrase 'phenomenology of religion' is first used by the Dutch theologian P. D. Chantepie de la Saussaye in his *Lehrbuch der Religionsgeschichte (Textbook of the History of Religions)* published in 1887, in which his aim is to understand the essence or rather unity (*Einheit*) of religion's manifold forms (*der Vielheit ihrer Formen*).[17] In this text he gathers together groups of religious phenomena – sacred stones, trees, animals, gods and so on – and presents us with an early comparative religion. As Sharpe remarks, '(e)vidently in its earliest form "the phenomenology" of religion was meant to be no more than a systematic counterpart to the history of religion, an elementary method of cross-cultural comparison of the constituent elements of religious belief and practice, as opposed to their treatment in cultural isolation and chronological sequence.'[18] After Saussaye this method of systematic description has remained central to the phenomenology of religion, especially as developed by scholars in Holland and Scandinavia, of particular note being Van der Leeuw who is largely responsible for the incorporation of the Husserlian *epoché* and empathy into the study of religions. Van der Leeuw defines phenomenology as 'the systematic discussion of what appears'[19] and locates its origins in the eighteenth century, but particularly in Christoph Meiner's *Allgemeine kritische Geschichte der Religionen (General, Critical History of Religions)* published in 1807. There are certainly precursors of the phenomenology of religion in the Enlightenment (the very practice of explaining religion scientifically is an Enlightenment enterprise) and early romantic periods, and Saussaye's use of the term 'phenomenology,' which feeds in to the phenomenology of the Dutch and Scandinavian school, would seem to be taken from Hegel. This is supported by Tim Murphy who argues that the contemporary phenomenology of religion 'is more heir to Hegelian rather than Husserlian phenomenology' with its central concept of an essential and unified human nature.[20] It must be remembered, however, that whereas Hegel's phenomenology is not concerned with present meaning but is rather concerned with teleology and the final closure of his system in absolute being in and for itself, what Lyotard refers to as 'the total recovery of total reality in absolute knowledge', phenomenology of religion is primarily concerned with present meaning, and in this way is closer to Husserl's understanding of phenomenology.

Although the phenomenology of religion in the sense of description and taxonomy developed before Husserl, and religionists are often keen to distance the phenomenology of religion from philosophical phenomenology,[21] Husserl's influence even being described as 'at best a folk tale',[22] it is nevertheless to to Husserl that the phenomenology of religion owes its central methodological concepts of bracketing, the reduction to essences, and empathy. Bracketing is central to the proclaimed neutrality and objectivity of the phenomenology of religion, the reduction to essences has been important in the development of types of religious phenomena, and empathy is a key feature in the enterprise of understanding the 'religious other'. These concepts have played a vital role in the work of phenomenologists of religion such as Van der Leeuw and Ninian Smart. Without them, particularly bracketing and empathy, there would be no phenomenology of religion. But in religious studies this bracketing is sometimes mistakenly taken to be the suspension of *subjectivity*, which is hard to understand in a system which places such great emphasis on intentionality and the *cogito*. For Husserl bracketing is clearly the 'suspension of the natural attitude' or the *objective* existence of phenomena in order to circumvent the problems of solipsism, idealism and realism which Husserl thought had plagued the history of philosophy. Bracketing for Husserl clearly means that the question concerning the objective status of phenomena is suspended and that meaning can be separated from existence. This is quite different from the puzzling religious studies doctrine that *subjectivity* or *subjective* attitudes are suspended in the phenomenological reduction. Max Scheler in 1921 introduced Husserlian ideas of description and essential phenomenology into the study of religion in his *On the Eternal in Man (Vom Ewigen im Menschen)* but it was Van der Leeuw's work *Religion in Essence and Manifestation* in 1938 that became most influential. He introduced a sophisticated understanding of the *epoché*, in broad agreement with Husserl, that it is concerned with bracketing of what lies behind appearances, not with the bracketing of subjectivity, and moreover, that the *epoché* is intimately linked to subjectivity as 'the distinctive characteristic of man's whole attitude to reality'.[23]

While Van der Leeuw is clear that *epoché* is not a denial of subjective faith or belief, other phenomenologists of religion have misunderstood the *epoché*. One of the first indications of this confusion occurs, some years prior to Van der Leeuw's publication of *Religion in Essence and Manifestation*, in Gaston Berger's claim that we can 'put into parentheses' our own beliefs and personal feelings, though Berger does admit, with some contradiction, the difficulty or impossibility of suppressing subjectivity.[24] Translated into terminology of the social sciences, bracketing becomes, in Ninian Smart's phrase, 'methodological agnosticism' or the suspension of truth questions concerning the focus of a religion. Echoing Joachim Wach's plea – and before him Weber's – for the necessity of the distinction between statements of fact and value judgements,[25] in the suspension of the natural attitude 'we neither affirm nor deny the existence of the gods'.[26] On this account the suspension of truth claims allows for pure description without evaluation or explanation, without the affirmation or denial of existence, and phenomenology becomes 'the attempt at value free description in religion'.[27] Such description can allow for the development of typologies or the grouping together of phenomena which share a common essence or common features. Husserl's eidetic reduction becomes, in religious studies, the creation of typologies and the grouping of religions or religious phenomena into patterns of coherence. Joachim Wach, directly influenced by Husserl whose lectures he had attended, provides examples of this strategy,[28] though the creation of typologies is a common feature of even contemporary religious studies.[29] If we take the creation of typologies to be the mapping of intersubjective networks of communication and the relating of diverse networks to each other, then this is an important part of the enterprise of religious studies, but the methodological problem arises when such mapping of intersubjective networks is taken to be 'objective' and value free.

Over three decades ago Ninian Smart made a fundamental distinction between the expression of religion (e.g. 'Jesus died for our sins') and its description ('Christians say "Jesus died for our sins" ').[30] While religious expression entails structures of authority (that might include education in Weber's charismatic, traditional and bureaucratic forms); values; theologies; and structures of practice (ritual, asceticism, meditation), description, on the other hand, is the phenomenological enterprise, and aspiration, of representing the theory and practice of expression in terms of a neutral or 'value free' discourse, distinct from any commitment or engagement with any 'political' agenda (see chapter 1). In Husserl's sense this is to bracket ontological questions and rather to investigate meaning as distinct from being. Through bracketing the scholar lets subjective religious facts speak for themselves, which thereby become objective.[31] Value-free description becomes the goal of the research programme which is the phenomenology of religion, to which the practices of bracketing, eidetic reduction and empathy are foundational. However, the limits of this research programme can be demonstrated through showing the problematic nature of these foundational practices. Through offering a critique of these foundational ideas, I hope to demonstrate the limits of the phenomenological method in the study of religions and to suggest some different approaches to 'religious appearances' in the following chapters. The following critique will identify three problematic areas in phenomenology which function to restrict its scope in the study of religions: the issue of representation and language; the issue of subjectivity and bracketing; and the issue of intersubjectivity. All of these are, of course, interlinked. The central problem of empathy will be examined in the following chapter.

The problem of representation

Perhaps the greatest problem within phenomenology relevant to the study of religions concerns the place of language and the understanding of representation through language. Two issues stand out here, the problem of the separation of meaning from being and the issue of whether meaning is locked up in the language of its expression. These two problems are inseparably related and entail the enormous questions of whether language is representation or imitation of an already given reality or truth, or whether language is purely constructive, articulating representations of representations, rather than referring to something already given in experience or in 'the world'. Let us discuss this complex of issues with reference both to the phenomenology of religion and to Husserl.

For Husserl, when we are within the natural attitude existence is accepted, but the phenomenological reduction demands that the natural attitude be suspended; that positions taken towards the objective world are 'put out of play' (see above). Although the world is experienced in the same way, in philosophical or phenomenological reflection the ego 'abstains' from the world's affirmation or denial. The phenomena within consciousness are sensations in the case of perception or presentation, or memory and imagination in the case of representation (*Vergegenwartigung*), though their ontological status is suspended.[32] Representations remain within the stream of the *cogitationes*, but the ego abstains from taking a position regarding them: the question of existence is removed leaving their meaning as an appearance. Although the ego abstains from 'position takings' as regards judgements, values and theories etc., all of which presuppose the world in the natural attitude ('involve believing in its existence'), having bracketed existence, there still remains the *meaning* of those phenomena. Husserl writes, 'everything *meant* in such accepting or positing processes of consciousness (the meant judgement, theory, value, end, or whatever it is) is still retained completely [after the phenomenological reduction] – but with the acceptance-modification, "mere phenomenon"'.[33] The being or existence of phenomena is suspended, yet appearances still remain within the stream of consciousness and retain their meaning within consciousness, or more specifically within *my* consciousness. Husserl eventually, towards the end of *Ideas 1*, is concerned to distinguish existing things from imagination, through intuition,[34] but these ontological inquiries are long deferred in the phenomenological method. With the suspension of the natural attitude 'the image floats before us without our deciding about its existence or nonexistence'.[35] Understanding language is the apprehension of the relation between the sign and what it represents; a relation in which the signification is not restricted to 'real objects', but rather to any object within consciousness whether 'real' or 'fictional'.[36] Through distinguishing the meaning of representation from its existence, *any* appearance to consciousness becomes a legitimate area of inquiry.

But while this path holds promise for the desired goal of simply mapping appearances to consciousness, its limitations soon become apparent, especially when we translate the separation of meaning from existence into the separation of language from ontology as it is far from clear that questions of existence can be so easily separated from language. Here Derrida's critique of Husserl comes into play. For Derrida, Husserl is a prime example of logocentrism, the privileging of cognition over affect, and of speech over writing. This can be seen in Husserl's emphasis on monologue or the flow of 'speech' in private or inner consciousness. Even though Husserl distinguishes being from meaning, there remains, according to Derrida, a 'metaphysics of presence', the self-authenticating truth haunting the history of Western thought which Derrida wishes to deconstruct. According to this view it is impossible to distinguish language from ontology because of the remaining presence of being within language which cannot be eradicated (though which can be deconstructed).[37] This denial of the distinction between being and meaning is to privilege the status of language and the sign: all meaning is constructed within language and its referents cannot be separated from it. For Husserl the question of the correspondence between a statement within language and the world is not at issue because of the distinction between meaning and existence, though the question – which is also the question of truth – still hangs in the air. Even in Husserl there is the echo of an imitation or *mimesis* pointing towards a truth or reality beyond the inscribed text. For Derrida the question of correspondence between language and the world – and even between language as *mimesis* and some inner revelation – is circumvented through the privileging of the sign. There can be no distinction between meaning and an independent existence, for the being of the world is largely constituted by language. Meaning does not depend upon some pre-given correspondence between words and objects, but rather the understanding and definition of an object depends upon language. Objects within the world are determined through the web of linguistically and culturally constructed meanings, grounded in history, rather than through pre-existing distinctions. On this view meaning is not representation or imitation of a pre-existing reality, but is inextricably bound to the language of its expression. Here repetition becomes repetition of other signs and representations of representations. Language does not mediate in any correspondence sense, so language, as Derrida has argued, cannot *refer*. Rather than an 'original act of imitation' we have 'the trace'; imitation without origin within a series of texts and particular narratives. It is significant that not only Derrida, but Foucault and Deleuze have the critique of Husserlian phenomenology as their point of departure.[38]

The phenomenology of religion inherits the Husserlian view of language that existence can be distinguished from meaning and representation, which results in a tension or even contradiction between this and the idea of phenomenological neutrality. The separation of meaning from being is implicitly a denial of the being expressed in language. Paying attention to the 'facts' of religious statements (such as 'Jesus died for our sins') while at the same time being agnostic as to their truth content or relation to existence, creates an immediate tension if the claim of phenomenology is that an accurate understanding of religious statements can be made by its method. This is because an existence claim is implicit within the religious statement and if this relation is denied, or the existence claim is bracketed out, then there is a limit to the degree to which the religious statement is understood. 'To worship Śiva one must become Śiva' (*śivam bhūtvā śivam yajet*) is a statement which entails an existence claim, and while this can certainly be understood externally within the ritual and theological systems of Śaivaism, its existential force cannot be penetrated by the phenomenological method. Part of the meaning of the statement for the practitioner is that Śiva exists (in some sense, as either other than the self or as self-identical). There is, as it were, a limit to phenomenology, and a barrier beyond which it cannot venture into the realm of insider discourse, because of its separation of meaning from existence. It might be the case that 'religious' statements, such as the Śaiva pronouncement, are a kind of rhetoric made within bounded, ritual circumstances whose existential force is limited or confined to the parameters of the ritual situation. But even so, the separation of meaning from existence, of language from ontology, inevitably entails a quite distinct, external understanding which is implicitly sceptical. The implication here is that a phenomenological bracketing, agnostic to existence, is impossible and that rather we are left with a choice between either an insider discourse, which accepts the link between meaning and being, or an outsider discourse which denies the link. A position which claims to be agnostic regarding the link is, in the end, an implicit denial of it and an implicit hermeneutics of suspicion.

Two objections to this position might be constructed. First, a reductionist understanding of religion could be made which is mostly or wholly accepted by the insider discourse. Indeed, many within religions are happy to agree with such explanations, though these do not effect their confidence in the tradition or religious identity. But this does not threaten my point that the phenomenology of religion is an outsider discourse, though it might mean that an insider perspective can accept a great deal of reductionism; it even might accept a 99 per cent explanation of the tradition in reductionist terms, though one per cent would still remain outside of that explanation. The second objection might be that I can well imagine describing in different language to the emic account, the beliefs and behaviours of a group of people without that description entailing a hermeneutics of suspicion: I simply describe what I perceive or give an account of it in terms which describe those beliefs and behaviours, even if direct translation is impossible. The problem here is that beyond the most basic description, interpretation comes into play by the observer which entails judgements. Beyond unremarkable thin description, presumably the purpose of a phenomenological account is 'thick description', to use Geertz' term following Ryle, in which intentions are taken into account and the 'stratified hierarchy of meaningful structures' are elaborated.[39] Once interpretation and judgement come into play – which they inevitably do fairly quickly in even a most basically descriptive account – then these interpretations and judgements are formed within the context of a wider method which implicitly entails the values of secular reason and explanation.

This is, of course, a perfectly legitimate position, but it becomes another competing narrative alongside other outsider discourses, and alongside the *equally legitimate* insider discourse. Rather than an overarching, universalist, rational understanding of religious phenomena as *data*, reflexively understood the phenomenology of religion becomes another competing discourse about religion, containing within it a particular view of consciousness and subjectivity, and the implicit values of Enlightenment reason which critiques myth as error. From an outsider perspective, or from a rational perspective which seeks to distinguish meaning from being, the history of religions which does not distinguish existence from language – particularly from mythological language – is a history of error.[40] In the end, the discourse of religion is either from within, in which case the entailment of existence by language is implicitly accepted (even if demythologized), or from without, in which case it is denied: there cannot be both an acceptance and a non-acceptance of an existence claim.

Part of the problem here concerns the rationality of discourse and the degree to which rationality stands independently of language and culture (the key issue between modernity and postmodernity). A position – such as phenomenology – which denies the link between existence and meaning is necessarily a critical position as regards religion and must see the history of religion in which ontology is embedded within its language, as critically as an overtly antireligious critique from, say, secularism or Marxism. Even a position such as Eliade's which has been criticized for an implicit universal theology, goes against the historical particularity of specific traditions. From a religious perspective, the representations of a religion contain or refer to a tradition-specific reality, whereas from a phenomenological perspective because of the separation of meaning from existence, this link in broken. This is not to say that religious discourse, such as traditional Christian Theology, is irrational, but rather that the legitimacy of a discourse is governed by the wider historical context in which it is embedded as opposed to some notional, independent rationality. Certainly, rational process is a property of most discourse, though based upon sometimes unreflexive, unquestioned presuppositions. An Islamic discourse about Qur'ānic law clearly operates according to processes which are rational, but within the boundary of the presupposition of the Qur'ān as revelation, while a phenomenological or philological discourse about Qur'ānic law operates according to a secular rationality, itself founded upon the ontological presuppositions of modernity. Rather than the notional value-free discourse which is the claim of phenomenology, we have competing narratives and critiques stemming from those narratives, which indicate that all representations of the world are historically and linguistically mediated. Perhaps a more accurate way of putting this is that from a narrativist perspective, because of the differential nature of the sign, there are truly no 'outsider' views but only competing 'insider' ones.

The problem of subjectivity

The phenomenology of religion absorbs two major currents in the recent history of Western thought. On the one hand there is the transhistorical, cognitive perspective of the Enlightenment with its emphasis on universalizing values, the idea of a common human nature, and claims to epistemological privilege through reason.[41] This is articulated in Husserl's metaphysical assumption of the transcendental subject. On the other we have the romantic, affective perspective in which the individual self apprehends – and longs for – the infinite; i.e. longs for that which is other to itself. This is the tradition from Schliermacher, of the self apprehending an infinite other and also of the self experiencing the exotic other of orientalism, as found in the work of the early Sanskritists and philosopher-critics such as Schlegel and Schelling.[42] This stream of thought emphasizes feeling, intuition and aesthetic appreciation and is inherited by Rudolf Otto who significantly influences the phenomenology of religion. Both streams of influence can be found in Husserl with his rationalism, on the one hand, in which cognition is highlighted and, on the other, his insistence on intuition as the immediate ground of truth in which the self apprehends itself. Husserl's transcendental ego spontaneously apprehended in intuition is reminiscent of Kant's unity of appercep-tion, but more directly reminiscent of Fichte's idea of the transcendental ego as the ultimate ground (*Letzbegrundung*) of expla-nation for all phenomena,[43] and indeed Fichte was the subject of Husserl's lectures in 1917.[44] Husserl's thought, as Ricoeur notes, can be seen to be in the line from Descartes, Kant and Fichte.[45] Although inevitably daughters of both the Enlightenment and Romanticism, postmodern, postcolonial and feminist perspectives have criticized the idea of a unified self and of epistemological privilege giving access to objective truth on the grounds that truth is, with some qualifications, tradition-specific, and reason itself is embedded within traditions; critique is always founded upon a narrative base. It is not so much these general aspects of the phenomenological inheritance I wish to focus upon, but rather the problem of subjectivity. Behind the phe-nomenology of religion's emphasis on 'religious experience' is the assumption of the unified subject – what Husserl called the transcen-dental ego – dwelling behind experience, and it is this assumption which can be brought into question.

For Husserl phenomenological bracketing leads to the eidetic reduc-tion in which the essential structures of appearances to consciousness can be intuited. A further step in the eidetic reduction reveals the essence of the subject and Husserl is concerned with the 'universal laws of genesis' which produce the unity of the subject within a history. That is, he wishes to show how the transcendental ego is particular (a monad) and that the imaginative variation of possible egos is restricted; the ego is unitary, but not all types are compossible within a single history.[46] The particularity of the transcendental ego with its thought-habits or habitualities and experiences is understood through realizing the constraints operative upon it. I can imagine other possi-bilities having occurred for me in my life history, but these could never be actualities given my particular stream of experiences. I can imagine being an Olympic runner but through understanding the historical and cultural constraints operative in my life I can thereby understand, through elimination, the actuality of myself as a transcendental ego who is the ultimate source of the structure of my experience.

From the particularity of the transcendental ego with its habitualities, Husserl wishes to demonstrate its universality through showing the principles which constrain its *eidos* or essence. He wishes to show the genesis of the particularity of the transcendental ego revealed in the eidetic description or reduction. The principles operative here are what Husserl calls the active and passive genesis which, put simply, refer to what is experienced (the passive genesis) and how that experience is understood (the active genesis). Through the active genesis the ego constructs new objects of consciousness from the given data – 'objects already given' – of the passive genesis:[47] for Husserl, as for Kant, the subject constructs and structures experience from what is given in experience. This idea of preconstructed experience allows Husserl to state the famous motto 'to the things' (*Zu den Sachen*), which feeds into the phenomenology of religion in so far as the phenomenology of religion wishes to abdure theory and to apprehend religious appearances in themselves, but also to actively order these phenomena into coherent patterns.

While Husserl is seldom referred to in the literature of the phenomenology of religion, it is pervaded by this understanding of subjectivity. Through adopting the phenomenological method of bracketing, the eidetic reduction and empathy, the phenomenology of religion also inevitably adopts the Husserlian view of the subject. As Hans Penner has observed, phenomenology is not simply a 'neutral method or pure description of phenomena' but a transcendental philosophy.[48] The Husserlian (and ultimately Cartesian) philosophy of consciousness is smuggled in with the method. This subject is a particular but universal, detached but rational ego, who partially receives experiences in the stream of the *cogitationes* and who also partially constructs them. Because of the flux of perspectives (*Abschattungen*) within the given stream of the *cogitationes*, meaning is partially constructed, being constituted by intentionality: the flux of phenomena given in experience are actively made coherent. It is this transcendental ego who can penetrate otherness through empathy, but who yet remains distinct and detached as the witness and partial constructor of experience. In accord with Husserl, the subject of the phenomenology of religion brackets the objectivity of religious phenomena appearing to consciousness and arranges the phenomena – or *data* – into types and themes, thereby partially constructing their meaning. Like Husserl's subject apprehending the *cogitationes*, the phenomenology of religion seeks to apprehend and imaginatively construct religious appearances. The idea of bracketing entails the idea of a universal, rational subject who does the bracketing and who is also the subject of religious experience. This is certainly the case for Max Scheler for whom the psychic experience of the sacrament is based on subjective belief and even that description of the psychic state demands this.[49] This is also the case for Joachim Wach who, quoting Paul Tillich, refers to the demand for ultimacy in 'the structure of our existence' being the basis of religious experience. In this religious experience we are involved as 'integral persons'.[50]

From Husserl – and ultimately from the general backdrop of Western thought from Christianity to the Enlightenment – the phenomenology of religion inherits the idea of the detached self as subjective, intentional consciousness and of detached theory apprehending its object (religion) through a rational method (the *epoché* and eidetic reduction). In this Husserlian understanding of subjectivity, there is a radical distinction between subjective consciousness (albeit intentional) and the world of other subjectivities: there is a gap between subjectivity and the other which needs to be bridged through the mechanisms of *epoché* and empathy. This isolated subjectivity leads to the focusing upon the *experience* of the flow of consciousness or the self's intentional structure, and an emphasis on experience as the focus of phenomenological inquiry. This view can be generally critiqued – and a critique which will be implicit in the following chapters – from a position which maintains that we are intersubjective prior to the *cogito*, a position which moves from consciousness to language and culture and which sees the observer as integrally bound up in the dialogical process of understanding.

Within the phenomenology of religions the emphasis on experience and the philosophy of consciousness is seen over and over again in the work of Eliade, for example, for whom the experience of the sacred is constitutive in any analysis of religious phenomena; in the work of Joachim Wach; and, well before them, in Otto's and Schliermacher's understanding of religion as the subject's affective apprehension – or 'creature feeling' – of the 'wholly Other'.[51] The emphasis on consciousness within phenomenology has led to a highlighting of inner experience and subjective states such as 'faith', 'belief', or 'enlightenment', at the cost of religion as intersubjective performance in which consciousness is not central. Indeed, intersubjective performance is a feature of religions which is more important in the maintenance of their boundaries and temporal continuity than any subjective experience (even the theology of sin and redemption is subordinate to the Eucharist in Christianity). It is ritual structure and performed narratives which are primary in the transmission of traditions through the generations and not any individual experience or state of consciousness. Even in traditions such as the *teyyam* possession dancers of Kerala, it is only consciousness as the 'substance' of the deity in intersubjectively agreed narrative performance which is important; the inner state of the possessed dancer is irrelevant.[52] The proclaimed objectivity of the phenomenology of religion assumes the universality of the rational subject who wishes to adopt its method, who can, through objectification, have access to a truth external to any particular historical and cultural standpoint. The position I would wish to promote, by contrast, will argue that such an objectivism is not possible, first because subjects are always constructed within their particular narratives and within the wider historical narratives of their cultures, and secondly because the knowledge of the subject arises within intersubjective networks of communication within what Husserl was to call the 'life-world' (*Lebenswelt*).

The problem of intersubjectivity

With the *epoché* the phenomenologist apprehends all appearances within the stream of ego's consciousness; as Husserl writes, the 'transcendental reduction restricts me to the stream of my pure conscious processes . . .'[53] Within the stream of consciousness other egos appear. However, other egos are more than merely appearances to my consciousness, they are other selves, and Husserl wishes to provide a foundation for knowledge of other selves within the same world as 'myself'. It is this problem which Husserl addresses in the fifth meditation of the *Cartesian Meditations*, which addresses the issue of intersubjectivity and through the phenomenological method seeks to understand the sense of existence which the other self has. For Husserl, knowledge of other selves is indirect and must be established through a methodical, phenomenological process. This process, akin to the

phenomenological reduction, requires the bracketing of the ontological status of other subjects, what Husserl calls 'a peculiar kind of
epoché'.[54] Whereas the first *epoché* bracketed out the question of the
objective existence of phenomena, this second *epoché* brackets out the
existence of other selves – 'we *disregard all constitutional effects of
intentionality relating immediately or mediately to other subjectivity*'
– *which is a reduction* to '*my transcendental sphere of peculiar
ownness*'.[55] This sense of myself stripped of all that is alien (*Fremde*, a
term that has the connotation of 'other' rather than 'strange'), as
within a sphere of 'ownness' which is non-alien (*Nicht-Fremdes*), can
then phenomenologically understand other selves through an 'analo-
gizing apprehension' that the body of the other, over *there*, is 'another
animate organism',[56] akin to myself over *here*. This is not inference,
but rather the transfer of sense from the one case (myself) to the other
(another person). These other selves expressed spatially in their bodies
can be 'read' as analogues of the self in its ownness which has been
intuited in the second *epoché*, a reading which is facilitated through
empathy (*Einfühlung*). Other selves through their bodies appear to me
within a spatial location as I appear to them. But we are all locked into
our own subjectivites characterized by monologue and any connection
between us is without communication – or dialogue – as part of our
constitution. Steinbock puts Husserl's position well:

> The intersubjective nexus is that which occurs between two absolute
> original spheres who express themselves to themselves, repeating, ideal-
> izing silence, 'over there', imagining that 'over there', there is another
> *monologue*, self-presence, self-expression, just 'as if' I were there. Tran-
> scendental experience of the other – through intropathy [i.e. empathy] – is
> essentially transcendental silence.[57]

Having established other selves in this way Husserl then tries to
show how the self and other selves experience the same world as a
'community of monads'. Within the community of monads the self
perceives other selves in 'presentive' and 'appresentive' modes of
perception. The other is experienced *there* in body (presentive perception), though this self is not directly perceived but is nevertheless
'indeed there too' (appresentive perception).[58] For Husserl we share
the same world, have distinct bodies in separate locations, and perceive the world from different perspectives. Moreover this
intersubjective community is constituted through a shared perception
and apperception. Husserl writes:

just as his animate organism lies in my field of perception, so my animate organism lies in his field of perception and that, in general, he experiences me forthwith as an Other for him, just as I experience him as *my* Other. Likewise I shall find that, in the case of a plurality of Others, they are experienced also by one another as Others ... [59]

Just as I perceive other bodies, so others perceive me, and potentially perceive the others for me, as I can perceive the others for them. This constitutes the 'community of monads' which Husserl designates as 'transcendental intersubjectivity'. This has inevitable ethical implications for Husserl in that all human personal communication is established through social acts and the individual in relation to others is 'fashioned into a *cultural world*' or 'concrete life-world'.[60] These cultural worlds which comprise the 'constitution of humanity' while sharing the transcendental subjectivity of each person, are nevertheless alien to each other. On this model if a person is to understand another culture it must be through the bridging devices of the phenomenological reduction and empathy. Husserl writes:

> To me and to those who share in my culture, an alien culture is accessible only by a kind of 'experience of someone else', a kind of 'empathy', by which we project ourselves into the alien cultural community and its culture.[61]

Husserl developed the idea of the life-world in his later work,[62] and well understood the paradox that knowledge originates in the 'primal I' (*Ur-Ich*) which in its essence is transhistorical, yet the idea of the life-world entails historicity. Gadamer notes that the reconciling of the life-world which is the communal world of being with other people, with an epistemology based on subjectivity is 'the most difficult task of all' for Husserl.[63] While the theme of the life-world is taken up by Merleau-Ponty, for Husserl it must remain secondary to the project of grounding epistemology in the transcendental ego who reaches into the life-world via the phenomenological method, but who in the end remains in a transcendental silence.

Perhaps the main criticism of Husserl in this respect is, put bluntly, that we do not infer the existence of others through a detached method of inference or intuition, having bracketed the world's existence, but rather immediately apprehend ourselves and others as being in a world; 'I' and 'thou' are co-constituted within the world and immediately apprehended as bodies. As Bakhtin says, and as we shall explore much further in later chapters, subjectivity or consciousness is not self-sufficient, for the subject only exists in dialogue with others and is constructed out of contending voices; consciousness cannot exist alone but is multiple. He writes:

> The consciousness of other people cannot be perceived, analysed, defined as objects or as things – one can only relate to them dialogically. To think about them means to talk with them; otherwise they immediately turn to us their objectivized side: they fall silent, close up, and congeal into finished, objectivized images.[64]

Consciousness is not self-revealing or a primary, *sui generis* category that can be derived from nature – or stripped of content – but is rather constituted of signs and language. Rather than a transcendental ego, consciousness becomes within the philosophy of the sign constituted only in the 'semiotic interaction of the social group', stripped of which there is nothing left.[65] For Husserl this socio-linguistic interaction is simply the natural attitude that must be suspended for scientific understanding and the arrival at certainty. Husserl's account of the essentially Cartesian epistemological problem of explaining how appearances to consciousness relate to the world, is simply inadequate because the intersubjective world – as the Russian dialogists understood – is already given.

Criticism of Husserl's subjectivity pervades Heidegger's work, who shows the problem of the relation of the knower to the known is itself founded upon questions concerning the nature of the being we are, or the meaning of our being beyond the *cogito* in the already given intersubjective world.[66] This kind of critique, though not directed primarily at Husserl, is also found within Wittgensteinian philosophy: I simply respond to the suffering of others rather than infer their existence. As Gadamer has observed, for Husserl the data of consciousness do not include a 'thou' in any immediate or primary way[67] and all knowledge is mediated via consciousness within the structure of the *noesis–noema* relationship. Husserl's transcendental ego and rational method for arriving at knowledge of others and the world are implicitly ahistorical and universal, standing outside the life-world yet paradoxically enmeshed within it: the detached subject of the *epoché* is within both a personal and a wider, cultural narrative.[68] Because of the *epoché*, the eidetic reduction and empathy, the phenomenology of religion is constrained within the same Husserlian model. Bracketing the objective status of religious phenomena and penetrating those phenomena through empathy is thought to result in objective description and understanding. For the phenomenology of religion the 'religious world' is the field which is, in Husserl's term, an 'alien world' (*ein fremde Welt*) to be understood and penetrated by the phenomenologist who stands outside of it. This religious world has often been constructed – in the work of Otto, Eliade and Cumpsty – as being characterized by a quality of sacredness which is distinct; a sacredness which is apprehended in experience by the 'religious subject' who is understood by the phenomenologist through empathy, but which understanding must be transformed into 'data' for objective representation to occur. The use of the phenomenological method in the study of religion inevitably brings with it Husserlian assumptions of the transcendental ego who infers the intersubjectivity of the cultural or social world through the process of bracketing and intuition. If, however, intersubjectivity and communication are accepted as given, that the starting point for any inquiry is not the ahistorical, rational self detached from the object of its investigation, but rather the social world in which meaning is primarily constituted within intersubjectivity rather than within consciousness, then surely this distinct starting point needs distinct methods which do not bring the Husserlian baggage with them.

One path in this direction would be the recognition of the narrative nature of all discourse, that critique is always founded upon a narrative bed, and that the primacy of intersubjectivity and communication is already given. This would be to recognize that understanding always arises within a context of sign systems and is inherently interactive or dialogical. Voloshinov arguing against the privileging of consciousness in 'idealism' and 'psychologism', emphasizes the importance of understanding in terms of interaction. He writes:

> Idealism and Psychologism alike overlook the fact that understanding itself can come about only within some kind of semiotic material . . . , that sign bears upon sign, that *consciousness itself can arise and become a viable fact only in the material embodiment of signs*. The understanding of a sign is, after all, an act of reference between the sign apprehended and other, already known signs; in other words, understanding is a response to a sign with signs.[69]

As religions can be seen in terms of sign systems, as systems of signification and communication, then the mode of their study must be primarily in terms of semiosis rather than consciousness. Jensen has observed, '(i)f Religion has any essence it is not the Sacred, but precisely the same essence of other socio-cultural systems, namely communication'.[70] And it is precisely communication which, perhaps with some reticence, Husserl abjured.

Phenomenology and narrative

The phenomenology of religion inherits the epistemological problems of Husserlian phenomenology due to its Cartesian assumptions. The recognition of the narrative nature of all discourse means that the phenomenology of religion reflexively recognizes the historical context of its own method, and thereby its limitations, and simultaneously recognizes the narrative nature of the phenomena it claims to illumine. Description as the primary enterprise of the phenomenology of religion needs to locate the 'facts' it describes within narratives or in what Ricoeur has called 'plots'.[71] If phenomenology is essentially description, description can be understood as the representation or *mimesis* of action which needs to be located within narrative, where narrative is, following Ricoeur, the 'organization of events'.[72] This is also to place language – and particularly narrative language – at the centre of discourse. On this view the history of religions is the history of particular narratives, or binding narratives, which have been highlighted by the method to seek the illumination of particular questions. Phenomenology as a research programme can become the active enterprise of construction within a dialogical encounter with its 'object'. Description then becomes not an attempt to passively observe and map what appears to consciousness, but the active construction of the historical narrative or the relating of the 'facts' to 'plots' with the awareness that such narratives are constructed within the constraints of the questions brought to the material and by the intentionalities of the material itself. That is, the narrative of, say, the Kerala tantric tradition is constructed through the interplay of the questions brought to bear by the scholar on texts and people within the tradition and by the constraints of the tradition itself. The representation of action constructed at the level of phenomenological description is translated into narrative or the organization of events.

Locating description within narrative language moves completely away from any essentialist understanding of religion: through narrative we see that religious meanings are temporal, relative to context, and do not contain a timeless essence such as 'the sacred'. From this narrativist perspective, the sacred becomes a concept contingent upon other circumstances and, as J. Z. Smith has observed, something becomes sacred by having our attention drawn to it in a certain way.[73] This might be regarded as a first level of description which is not so much a passive letting appearances show themselves, as the active construction of material into narrative structures, into 'emplotment'. Here phenomenology both allows the intentionalities of the 'objects' – such as the Eucharist or a Kerala possession dance – to be manifested through the active construction of the narratives of their occurrence. Such constructions are in response to the specific questions brought to the material, which themselves have been constrained by it in, as it were, a circular motion. Engaging with religious phenomena in this sense of locating 'data' within narrative, does not give privileged position to religion and places it within the context of its wider cultural history. It also reflexively locates the enquirer, who is methodologically outside the tradition, within the enterprise of enquiry in a dialogical relationship to the process of emplotment. All subjects – and all knowledges founded upon or assuming such subjects – are within narratives and inevitably within particular perspectives. A second level of explanation in which the material established within a narrative context is related to paradigms external to it might then be brought to bear, along with the reflexive awareness of the historical or narrative situatedness of explanation itself.

This shift away from the epistemological problem of subjectivity and its relation to the world confronted by Husserl, puts language and culture at the centre of a discourse in which narrative therefore becomes dominant. This relocation of the problem of the other into language, culture and narrative – and of the problem of understanding religion – has its origins in the work of Hamman and Jacobi in the late eighteenth century, who demurred the idea that knowledge can be established within a system, and can be traced through hermeneutics into the narratology of Ricoeur, what might be called the 'philosophy of the sign' to use Voloshinov's phrase,[74] and into linguistic anthropology and discourse analysis. It is this tradition emphasizing the primacy of language, narrative, culture and the intersubjectively given, which can move away from the problematic nature and veiled assumptions of epistemological privilege within the phenomenology of religion and, indeed, that are implicit within other naturalist or reductionist understandings.

Phenomenology as description becomes on this view a moment in a process in which description is important, but which is recognized as the representation of action and the setting of action in a narrative context, moreover that the enterprise of setting the representation of action in a narrative context is itself part of a narrative context. Such a recognition would be to acknowledge that all representations are lingustically and historically mediated and that language does not mimic a reality beyond it. While the emplotment of phenomena comes from the perspective of a rational, scientific discourse – such as the academic study of religions – or from the perspective of *logos*, this perspective can become reflexively aware of its own mythic dimensions. Critique, especially of 'myth' in its widest sense, is always from the perspective of *logos*, but through narrativity, through emplotment, rational method becomes aware of itself as *logos* investigating or constructing *mythos* and aware of the mythological dimensions to its own narrative. Cassirer's contention that myth is a cultural form alongside, and equal to, others such as science, is an example of such awareness[75], and Blumenberg has studied the persistence of myth in the modern world in the face of Enlightenment reason.[76] Such an approach that locates rational critique within the narrative of its own grounding, does not set religion apart from other cultural practices and does not give absolute epistemological privilege to the 'rational observer' or 'scientist'. From a narrativist perspective, rational discourse is always founded upon a narrative base and we are in a constant situation of competing – and sometimes complementing – narratives. Narratives can overlap with each other – in which case there is consensus – or, more often than not, simply clash. As postmodernism has argued, there is no leverage on this situation from a place outside of narrative; there is no grand narrative outside of local narratives as the place of critique.

Summary

This chapter has argued that the phenomenology of religion owes its fundamental concepts of bracketing, eidetic reduction and empathy to Husserl, and that it implicitly carries with it Husserlian assumptions about the transcendental ego and an overarching rationality. The phenomenological method smuggles into the phenomenology of religion a Husserlian philosophy of consciousness. Through examining these fundamental tools within phenomenology I have attempted to indicate the problematic nature of the phenomenology of religion, particularly as concerns representation and language, subjectivity, and intersubjectivity. This is certainly not a plea for a return to a situation in which the insider has precedence – Ninian Smart reminds us that he once heard a Baptist minister give a lecture on Christianity which was 'phenomenologically absurd'[77] – but it is a recognition of the limits of phenomenology and the necessity of contextualizing both phenomena and academic practices within the narratives of their occurrence. This investigation shows that implicit assumptions within the phenomenological method are carried over into the phenomenology of religion and that today this is simply inadequate for understanding religions as embedded within culture and history, because of its imported rationalist and universalist assumptions. This is not to abjure rationalism – indeed I hope that the present argument is rational – but it is to argue that rationality is constrained by the narrative bed within which it arises and whose values it articulates. It is to the possibility of a narrativist understanding of religions to which we now turn.

5. Narrative theory

In the last chapter we have seen how phenomenology involves a philosophy of consciousness that developed from Descartes through Kant and Fichte to Husserl. This phenomenological philosophy of consciousness involves the idea of a detached, neutral observer performing the operations of bracketing and so on, in order to arrive at epistemological representation which is certain; to arrive at truth. In adopting phenomenology, the science of religion carries with it the idea of the detached observer or epistemic subject who understands the presentations to consciousness from a privileged distance. However, the shift of emphasis from a philosophy of consciousness to a philosophy of the sign, from consciousness to language, culture and intersubjectivity, entails a different view of the epistemic subject and a critique of the view of the detached observer. As Benhabib says, '*the paradigm of language has replaced the paradigm of consciousness*. This shift has meant that the focus is no longer on the epistemic subject or on the private contents of its consciousness but on the public, signifying activities of a collection of subjects.'[1] This idea reflects Derrida's assumption that the intention of the Cartesian subject does not determine meaning, that the sign does not belong to the author, my words 'no longer belong to me'.[2] Similarly with critical theory, Habermas has developed a theory of intersubjectivity based on language rather than consciousness.[3] The same shift has been discussed at length by Karl-Otto Apel who argues that ontological metaphysics was replaced by a transcendental philosophy of the subject of consciousness (that is phenomenology) that is now replaced by the (transcendental) philosophy of language, communication and intersubjectivity.[4] The phenomenological analysis of understanding, as Kögler observes, has given way to the hermenutic significance of language and conversation.[5]

The aim of this chapter is to follow the implications of this critique of the philosophy of consciousness by the sign, and to present an argument to show that if the subject of knowledge is always situated in a particular, historical and social context, then all understanding is dialogical. The implications of this for the study of religion are far reaching. The shift to the sign deprivileges consciousness, experience and inner states, and places religion squarely within culture and history, that is, within narrative. In emphasizing narrative, the insider/outsider problematic is reconfigured in terms of competing narratives. That is, there is no lived reality external to or unmediated by narrative. To establish this claim I shall first discuss the importance of narrative given the shift to the privileging of the sign, a discussion that must entail some consideration of the 'text'. Secondly, given the importance of narrative, three positions regarding it emerge: narrative realism, that stories are lived; narrative constructivism, that stories are told; and narrativism, that stories are both lived and told. I shall support the third view, based largely on Ricoeur, that while narrative emerges from life (from history and biography) it is also constructed. Thirdly, the implication of this for the study of religion is that insider and outsider discourses must be seen as competing – or perhaps complementing – narratives and that therefore there can be no epistemic privilege or distanciation provided by phenomenology, but only situated and contextual dialogue.

Narrative theory and religion

In examining narrative theory in relation to the phenomenology of religion, I shall approach the question of the epistemic subject through considering the relation between 'story' and 'explanation'. This relation focuses our attention on key issues in the study of religion. Religion has been understood in terms of story – a 'true story' for those standing inside of it, 'a fiction' for those outside, while postmodern views would wish to blur the distinction between narrative as fiction and narrative as history; on this view 'a fiction' can be a 'true story' in some sense of the term and a 'true story' understood in ways akin to the understanding of fiction. Phenomenology has aimed at the accurate representation of religion within the field of consciousness, while social science has aimed at its explanation. In both enterprises the 'story' of religion – as meaningful articulation of human truth or as expression of social or psychological forces – is seen to be distinct from its representation in phenomenological description and categorization, and from its explanation by falsifiable sociological or psychological theories. Both of these accounts, the phenomenological and the social scientific, are based on the assumption of the observer's distance from the object of study, that the observer or social scientist is distinct from the narratives she wishes to represent and explain, and that critique and explanation are themselves distinct from any narrative. The view I would wish to support is that neither the method nor the object are free from narrative and that the theories and descriptions proffered in phenomenology and the social sciences always stem from a narrative context; the narrative of history, the narrative of scientific development or even the narrative of the individual scholar.

Located within this general problem of representation and explanation in the humanities and social sciences, this chapter will begin to argue for the centrality of narrative in the process of understanding religion, particularly as regards three propositions which follow from the non-Cartesian or Husserlian view of the observer, namely that insider and outsider perspectives can be understood in terms of different narrative accounts; that insider and outsider perspectives provide competing, though sometimes overlapping, narratives; and that 'polyglossia' is a feature of religion and its study revealed through narrative theory, particularly dialogism. These propositions are related to each other and show how narrative theory is central to understanding religion. Arguing for the centrality of narrative in the study of religion will take us into debates in other disciplines, particularly history, philosophy, and literary criticism, and will draw primarily on the work of Ricoeur, White, and Bakhtin. In so doing we shall see how their problematics are directly relevant to the study of religions. These issues need to be taken into account if the discipline of religious studies is to develop beyond descriptive mapping into a deeper engagement with human subjectivity and meaning.

The field of narrative

Gerard Genette in his *Narrative Discourse* developed the distinction found in the Russian Formalist Tzvetan Todorov between narrative as story (what happened) and narrative as discourse (about what happened) and on this basis has distinguished three meanings of the term 'narrative'. The first is that of common usage which refers to a written or oral discourse telling about a series of events, the second is the 'analysis of narrative' which refers to series of events which are the subject of that discourse, and the third is the act of narrating in itself, or the event of someone recounting something. Accordingly he uses the terms *story* (*histoire*) for the first meaning of that which is signified or the narrative content, *narrative* for the signifier, discourse, narrative statement, or text which expresses the *story*, and *narrating* for the act of producing the narrative.[6] In his text Genette is primarily concerned with the relationship between *narrative* and *story*, on the one hand, and *narrative* and *narrating* on the other.

Taking my lead from Genette, I am interested in the issues of the relation between religion as narrative or *story* in Genette's first sense, narrative as a discourse about religion, and the production of narratives about religion (both by the narrator of religious discourse and by the scholar of religion). The relation between narrative as story, or the 'stories' of religion, and narrative as a discourse about religion, can be understood in terms of our three problematics outlined above. That is, the nature of the relation between story and narrative in Genette's sense, is articulated first in terms of the connection between insider and outsider discourses, secondly in terms of the degree to which distinct narratives compete or complement each other, and thirdly in the ways in which the many voices within religions, and within its study, are heard or not heard. I shall here examine more closely the theoretical issues behind the relationship between story and narrative in the context of the insider/outsider issue in the study of religion. In the next chapter I shall examine the narrative-narrating relation, paying particular attention to the role of the situated observer, and in chapter seven I will examine the story-narrative relation in the context of problems of truth, language, and text.

Narrative as story I take to be a meaningful chronological sequence expressed through the genres of oral tradition, written text, conversation or personal narrative and music (song and opera), and which is in language embodied in texts, however widely that term is understood. On this view, without text there is no narrative, though this is problematic when understanding a life-process in terms of narrative, as we shall see, and goes against some thinking on narrative that would include all genres as narrative expressions, such as sculpture or pictorial representation.[7] This understanding of narrative is in accord with Ricoeur's characterization of story as describing 'a sequence of actions and experiences done or undergone by a certain number of people, whether real or imaginary'.[8] These people, Ricoeur explains, are in changing situations that reveal 'hidden aspects of the situation' and the responses they make to the new situation leads the story to its conclusion.

Long ago, Lessing made the fundamental point that a painting exists in space and all of its parts are perceived simultaneously, whereas narrative exists in time and its parts are perceived sequentially. A painting, even if depicting a mythological scene, is not in itself narrative, but narrative can be brought to it to give it sense.[9] Similarly the representations on the 'gateways' at the Sanchi *stupa* depicting scenes in the Buddhist scriptures need narrative to be brought to them in order to understand them. Such plastic representations echo narrative and although they may be 'intertextual' they feed off narrative in a way that narrative does not feed off plastic representation. In contrast to the plastic arts, narrative as text involves temporal sequence and the sequential unfolding of a situation or idea. This can, of course, be disrupted – as has been done in many modern narratives from Joyce to Burroughs – but temporal sequence is nevertheless the frame within which narratives are constructed, even in the temporal disruption of that construction such as is characteristic of Burroughs' work.[10] Narrative as text pervading culture need not be coherent but can be fragmentary, and the fragmentary nature of texts can serve in turn to create new narratives.

Text, a complex of signs given coherence through narrative, is therefore the primary object of investigation for the study of narrative. Text, as Piatigorsky has observed, is one of our most basic cultural categories 'which on the one hand presupposes an *idea* of text in general, and on the other, an idea of a *text* as a concrete thing'.[11] Any culture comprises a range of texts that constantly affect each other; as Bakhtin and Kristeva have shown, any text echoes and transforms others. The concept of 'text' is itself difficult to pin down precisely because as an abstraction it operates on a number of levels: a single text can itself be broken down into a multiplicity of texts and two or more texts can be regarded as a single text, as Piatigorsky shows with reference to Vedic material.[12] Indeed in a very real sense the text only comes into being because it is perceived, read or heard, and understood,[13] and so embedded, in Bakhtin's terms, in a second, framing text of comment, analysis and critique. Within the spectrum of cultural texts we have 'religions', generally with boundaries clearly defined by their narratives – stories of beginnings and endings, stories of lives which should be emulated, theological discourses, ethical codes – that constrain the lives of those within them from birth to death. People live within religious narratives articulated as texts, which are subjectively appropriated in the context of a particular life. In this sense, the narrative of a personal biography might become fused with that of the metanarrative of the religious tradition. Indeed, this is a common pattern. The Buddha's journey to *nirvāṇa* becomes the internalized narrative of the Buddhist nun (*bhikuni*) diligently seeking the same goal through adherence to the *vinaya* code and meditation; or Christ's journey to the cross becomes a narrative to be internalized by the Christian and performed liturgically. But narrative not only provides the context and legitimacy of a life, it also expresses power by legitimizing particular social groups, through representing a local interest or story as universal (as Paul with Christianity), through making its ideals appear to be objective (as in utopian hope), and through being internalized by individuals (as in a monastery or inner asceticism).[14] In other words, narrative functions as ideology and is subjectively appropriated and taken to be true by those who live within them.

Within the general category of narrative, the kinds of texts that have been most important in the phenomenology of religion are placed within the category 'myth'. Derived from the Greek distinction between *mythos* and *logos* with its deeper contemporary echoes of 'error' and 'truth,' *mythos* has been regarded as narrative in contrast to *logos*, as reason outside of *mythos* which can critically reflect upon it. While both *mythos* and *logos* meant 'word' and 'story', *mythos* referred in Homer to aesthetic ornamentation and the term came to refer particularly to stories of origins and of past greatness. Aristotle used *mythos* in a more restricted sense to refer to plot (*fabula*) in contrast to *logos* as rational debate. Indeed, rational discourse which becomes the defining feature of the academy, has its roots here, as expressed by the historian Heroditus who sees himself as a writer of *logos* rather than of *mythos*.[15] The early Christian fathers saw that the reason for the continuance of a mythical narrative through time is that it contains a truth subject to analysis in terms of allegory.[16] Truth, embedded in narrative, is illumined through processes of reason and analysis. With the Enlightenment, truth comes to be regarded as being accessed via reason alone and by the time we reach Hegel, the truth of philosophical reason, or reflexive thought, has superseded even the Christian narrative.

122

Yet in spite of its claims to transnarrative privilege, *logos* is never completely free from *mythos* and there are strong mythical dimensions in the discourse of reason. One is reminded here of Hegel's mythological understanding of Napoleon entering Jena as representing the end of history, yet an interpretation which for Hegel is under the sign of reason,[17] or Lévi-Strauss' interpretation of Freud's 'rational' reading of the Oedipus myth as being itself part of the myth.[18] More recent, structural studies of myth have therefore tended not to sharply distinguish it from other genres such as advertising.[19] Examples of such proximity of reason to mythic narrative abound in the Indian material, though the terms *logos* and *mythos* do not map on to any directly equivalent Sanskrit terminology (perhaps *tarka* or *nyāya* and *itihāsa* would serve). The Hindu and Buddhist philosophical tradition can be understood in terms of a protracted conversation articulated in commentaries on texts – narratives such as the *Bhagavadgītā* – in which rival reasons for particular readings are given. The 'science of the self' (*ātmavidyā*) is established through readings of texts that are themselves narratives or that are understood within the wider narrative context of revelation.

The shift from a discussion about 'myth' to a discussion about 'narrative' in contemporary academic discourse, or even a discussion in which myth is simply a metonym for narrative, is an important one for it allows us to understand the proximity, on the one hand, of contemporary narratives such as the films *Santoshi Ma* or *Star Wars*, to the category 'myth,' and on the other, the proximity of reason to narrative. The distinction between *logos* and *mythos*, reason and narrative, is variable and the distance from narrative, often claimed of reason, is not as obvious as it at first might appear.

Explanation, culture and narrative

Narrative is central to the understanding of human meanings and institutions, a centrality which is partially recognized by the phenomenology of religion in emphasizing myth, but whose particularity and temporal dimension is diminished in the phenomenology of religion's emphasis on ahistorical universals and patterns. Influenced by Jung, the work of Eliade has argued for the archetypal nature of myth at the cost of its historical particularity. Phenomenology foregrounds consciousness as the starting point of inquiry, that, as we have seen, leads

123

to intractable epistemological problems of understanding the social – and thereby religious – world. My connection with others and with the world becomes apparent only through the phenomenological reduction in which subjectivity is revealed in intuition and meaning mediates between me as subject and the world. In this view the world becomes simply a correlate of intentionality and so excludes any real communication or dialogue.

The model of consciousness excludes the linguistic and/or cultural model as the basis of understanding because there is no real communication; the object of consciousness is the flow of the *cogitationes*, some of which are the intentional correlates of other people, and so communication is always between transcendental egos mediated through consciousness. Even in the *Crisis of European Sciences and Transcendental Phenomenology* Husserl maintains that the subject, through the phenomenological reduction, stands above the life-world which itself becomes a phenomenon.[20] Alternatively, rather than consciousness as the starting point of inquiry, an equally legitimate beginning could be the givenness of language, intersubjectivity and culture, that would also give primacy to ethics. Indeed ethics as first philosophy replaces the first philosophy of consciousness for thinkers such as Levinas in reaction to Husserl. Rather than the *cogito* with its stream of *cogitationes* being the methodological basis of inquiry, the centre of gravity becomes the intersubjectivity of the social world mediated through language. Indeed, Husserl himself begins to move away from the primacy of consciousness (though not very far) with the introduction of the life-world in the fifth *Meditation* and the development of this idea in the *Crisis*, where a 'new way' to the phenomenological reduction that begins from 'natural world-life' is introduced.[21] He claims, for example, that the life-world is already given, being for us in advance as the 'ground' for everyone.[22] But even so, for Husserl consciousness and subjectivity are still the inevitable foundation upon which knowledge of the life-world depends.

If the intersubjectivity of the social world in its historical specificity is our starting point, then language rather than consciousness becomes the focus of investigation, open to linguistic analysis and semiology. In a general shift away from the totalizing perspective of the phenomenology of consciousness, placing language and culture as the focii of understanding allows us to begin with human lives bounded by time. It allows us to prioritize communication and to begin with narratives lived out in history. The shift to language and culture opens up the field to understanding in terms of narrative and intersubjectivity which the ahistorical aspirations of transcendental phenomenology could not do. Once language and culture are the central objects of epistemological investigation, then narrative becomes a dominant theme along with the historical and intersubjective nature of the human subject.

Viewing the study of religions through the lens of narrative provides a fresh understanding of the relationship between insider and outsider discourses. Discourses from within a religious tradition give accounts of themselves in terms of the tradition's narratives, and individuals within a tradition imbue their lives with meaning through the internalization of these accounts and by relating the narratives of their own lives to the larger narratives of the tradition. John Bowker has presented ways in which this occurs from the perspective of ordinary believers in his *Worlds of Faith*.[23] Furthermore, external accounts, such as a psychoanalytic explanation, might relate a person's actions to a narrative of which they themselves are unaware. This can be seen, for example, in Obeyesekere's psychoanalytic interpretations of Sri Lankan priestesses at the Kataragama shrine.[24] Outsider discourses – such as the sociology or psychology of religion – necessarily offer different explanations as to why a particular tradition is as it is, or why a particular individual behaves or thinks in this way. But the outsider discourse itself will be critique or explanation from the perspective of its own, perhaps implicit, narratives. In this way narrative as story (the insider perspective) is explained or critiqued by narrative as discourse (the outsider perspective). These insider and outsider narratives can and do clash, though not necessarily and there can be continuity between them. A Catholic devotee's account of why she is attending mass at a particular time can be related both to the narrative of the tradition – the origin of the mass and the historical development of the Church – and to her personal narrative of feeling the need for spiritual sustenance or having strayed from the Christian path, or whatever. An etic account might place her personal narrative in a broader context of explaining patterns of Church attendance in a particular area or among a particular social group, or might even, for example, construct a different narrative for a particular individual's attendance at mass based on a psychoanalytic construction of her biography. The insider – outsider distinction can therefore be related to different kinds of narrative account.

Equally, scientific or causal explanations of human thought and behaviour do not stand outside narrative in a position of privileged critique. Rather they are themselves embedded within traditions of intellectual history, though often questioning of these traditions. Alistair MacIntyre has observed that intellectual traditions on occasion lapse into incoherence, and at such time 'can only be recovered by a revolutionary reconstitution'.[25] Such a reconstitution would be found, for example, in the work of Galileo or in Newton, each of whose physics proved to be rationally superior to its predecessor. But this rational superiority can only, claims MacIntyre, be understood within the history of the tradition; we can only say wherein this rational superiority consists by reference to Newton's predecessors.[26] On Mac-Intyre's account, a long view of history will show continuities between the old and new models and will be able to locate the new within a narrative of tradition. 'Scientific reason', writes MacIntyre, 'turns out to be subordinate to, and intelligible only in terms of, historical reason: And if this is true of the natural sciences, *a fortiori* it will be also true of the social sciences.'[27] This is clearly true of the study of religion. Freud's explanation of the narrative of religion in terms of projection, repression, the Oedipus complex and so on, must itself be understood in the cultural narrative of late nineteenth- and early twentieth-century Viennese society, and within the history of psychology and other social sciences. Similarly Marxist theory and phenomenology are within their own historical narratives. The criticism which MacIntyre makes of Descartes, that it is impossible for him to stand outside of history through the method of radical doubt, for he still must know something, especially language, in order to perform the task in the first place,[28] can equally be levelled at the ahistorical claims of Husserl's method.

Theories of narrative

On the one hand, a narrative account develops from within the tradition or within the individual who reads her life in this way, and so is *story* in Gennette's first sense. On the other hand, the explanation of the emic narrative in terms of paradigms external to it – though such external paradigms are themselves a part of a larger scientific narrative – is narrative in Genette's second sense. To argue that insider and outsider perspectives are different kinds of narratives is to place them on a much more equal basis and to refigure the debate about insider and outsider accounts in terms of competing, though sometimes complementing, narrative traditions. The emic account on this view is not simply relegated to the realm of superstition or error, but in so far as both share forms of rational discourse and questioning, rests alongside etic accounts. Those emic narratives that do not participate at all in the process of rational exposition or inquiry – and that may aggressively reject this process – become competing narratives which share nothing with the outsider narratives that try to explain them. But let us defer this discussion of competing narratives for a later chapter and focus instead upon the relation between narrative as story and narrative as discourse in narrative theory.

The extent to which narratives are objectively given in history and culture or are imposed on history and culture is an issue central to our concerns. On the one view narrative structures are inherent in history, culture and human life, on the other narrative structures are imposed upon history, culture and human life from the outside. On the one hand human life and biography comprises narratives that are not distinct from it, on the other narratives are created from the raw material of the passage of time, somewhat similar to the narrative or manifest content of a dream being imposed upon the non-narrative, latent content in the dream work (the translation of the latent content into the manifest content), to use a psychoanalytic metaphor. The former position maintains that narrative is lived, the latter that narrative is told.

Three positions therefore emerge based on this distinction: narrative realism that maintains that culture and history enact a lived narrative pattern; narrative constructivism, that narrative is told or imposed upon culture and history; and narrativism, that both lived and told narrative are true.[29] These terms indicate general orientations, though it must be remembered that thinkers who broadly maintain these positions do not defend crude forms of these theses. I take as examples the philosopher Alistair MacIntyre to articulate an essentially narrative realist position; the historian Hayden White to express narrative constructivism; and Paul Ricoeur to express a narrativist position.

Stories lived and stories told: MacIntyre and White

An example of narrative realism can be found in MacIntyre's *After Virtue* whose overall project is to develop a philosophical and historical argument showing how the substance of morality has been fragmented and partly destroyed in the modern world even though the language of morality persists, and showing how narrative is integral to any sense of unified identity and understanding.[30] MacIntyre essentially champions an Aristotelian view – although one which flows through Thomas Aquinas – of the teleological nature of the good to which the virtues aspire. This contrasts with the modern, non-teleological view of disengaged reason that is autonomous, and free to make choices outside of the context of any transcendent good. Within this general view, highlighting the virtues, teleological goods and tradition, narrative is central to the understanding of human life. Indeed, narrative embodies a moral order. Arguing against narrative constructivism, MacIntyre maintains that 'stories are lived before they are told';[31] we live out narratives and understand others in terms of narrative or because of narrative. On this view there is no standpoint of epistemological privilege from outside of narrative; the epistemic subject must be located within it. For the narrative realist, all subjectivity is understood within a sequence of actions, stemming from intentionality that forms a narrative. MacIntyre says that we are both the authors and the actors of our own narratives, or rather the co-authors for '(o)nly in fantasy do we live what story we please'.[32] The present is formed by the image of a future and represented in the present by aims and goals, as well as being constrained by the past. All human beings on this view are born into a set of pregiven narratives but can act to create intelligibility within those constraints as one narrative in a complex of interlocking narratives. For MacIntyre the pursuit of the virtues as goods given within a narrative – or equally the pursuit of vice – can be understood within this model of intentionality producing action, that both comprises a narrative and is embedded within larger or wider narratives.

Against the liberal conception, inherited from the Enlightenment, of the self as a free agent, MacIntyre presents a view in which the self is embedded within narratives which precede it and any choices to be made. He writes:

> man is in his actions and practice, as well as in his fictions, essentially a story-telling animal. He is not essentially, but becomes through his history, a teller of stories that aspire to truth. But the key question for men is not about their own authorship; I can only answer the question 'What am I to do?' if I can answer the prior question 'Of what story or stories do I find myself a part?'[33]

A life as the consequence of intentions and actions can itself be seen to embody a tradition which, as it were, speaks through the body (for MacIntyre, albeit a male body judging from his exclusive language). An example here would be Levin's point that religion as a tradition of ritual binds and fastens the body, 'it binds us to the performance of special tasks, special postures, gestures and movements'.[34] The body expresses tradition whose narratives are inscribed upon it, although in gender-specific ways.

In modernity, life has been partitioned into discreet segments and actions are not perceived to be within the context of larger wholes or parts of wider narratives. The modern self as a consequence does not have such a unified sense of identity because it does not have the unity of a narrative linking 'birth to life to death'. But even the modern self cannot be wholly stripped of narrative identity, for in the temporal nature of life, narrative is generated inevitably from the process of birth and death. Even at a mundane level statements can only be understood through a narrative; MacIntyre gives the amusing example that a young man at a bus stop who randomly says 'the name of the common wild duck is *Histrionicus histrionicus histrionicus*' can only be made meaningful by a narrative context and the reasons for its utterance.[35]

Narrative is essential in the establishing of a moral identity for the self within communities, such as the family, city, neighbourhood, or tribe, who is bound by their restrictions.[36] Narrative is central to the development of both a sense of personal identity as well as historical or traditional identity and it is through narrative that ethics are linked to the unity or coherence of a particular life. MacIntyre does not, however, relate these insights to gender and the differing narrative experiences of men and women within the constraints of the communities which bind them. But even given the hierarchical nature of gendered narratives within tradition, or conflicting narratives, MacIntyre's general point that narrative provides continuity and the context for individual actions that make life intelligible, albeit intelligible in gender-specific ways, remains intact. An individual is born into a particular cultural narrative and does not have the option to say 'I don't want to start from here.'[37] The loss of intelligibility can be seen as the loss of narrative that MacIntyre sees as a characteristic of modernity, articulated, for example, in Sartre's Roquentin, for whom to present life in the form of narrative is to falsify it and for whom '(h)uman life is composed of discreet actions which lead nowhere, which have no order'.[38] On this view a narrative order in modernity is imposed on an almost random sequence of human events and actions after their occurrence, but human action is not itself the expression of a lived narrative.

Whether MacIntyre's representation of Sartre's position here is accurate I do not wish to pursue, but MacIntyre draws our attention to the issue of whether narrative is imposed upon human events or whether human actions express narratives inherent in human life. Actions are only intelligible in the light of intentions, beliefs and meanings. History, on this view, is a discourse that reflects the past, though which, as MacIntyre acknowledges, will reflect the past according to the understanding derived from its contemporary situation and value. The alienation and indifference of Meursault to the consequences of whether he fires the gun or not,[39] must be seen within the wider cultural narrative of modernity and the break with the tradition of the virtues.

The issue of whether narrative develops from a life lived or is imposed retrospectively is important in all the humanities and social sciences, for it relates to the ways in which we conceptualize the past; whether past events 'occurred' or whether they are constructed only in narrative. If events and areas of academic discourse are pure constructs, then there are 'no true stories'.[40] That events are constantly being reconstituted in the light of present circumstance, then, quite apart from the individual re-evaluating and making sense of her life in a continuous process, history is constructed through historiography, an 'ethnos' is constructed through an ethnography,[41] and 'religion' is constructed through the methods of its study. On this view there are no facts outside of theories; the given is created by the 'delicate and fascinating labour' of hypotheses and conjectures.[42] Decisions about this issue have ethical and political implications. For example, holocaust revisionism would deny the reality of the holocaust; that the narrative was rather constructed by historians out of political motives. The epistemological difficulty of knowing the past expressed in this debate is in fact conceded by Lyotard and Hayden White.[43]

While not at all wishing to be associated with revisionism, White's point is that historical representation is essentially fictitious and that the kind of writing called 'history' is locked into a nineteenth-century model of representation in which historical writing transparently reflects a pre-existent reality, as is evidenced, claims White, in the work of historians such as Tocqueville and Ranke.[44] Narratives are created out of sequences of events which have no *inherent* narrative features of beginnings, middles and ends.[45] The resulting discourse is one of ironic representation in which the past is constructed through the metaphors which 'construe fields or sets of phenomena in order to "work them up" into *possible objects of narrative representation* and *discursive analysis*'.[46] While undoubtedly wishing to draw together the fictional event and the historical event, White is careful to distinguish between them in so far as historical events are assigned to specific time–space locations which could have been observed. But there is overlap between the imaginative writer and the historian who writes 'fictions of factual representation'.[47] The historical text here becomes a 'literary artefact' and history as narrative is imposed upon the events in the past. Earlier forms of historical representation, the annals and the chronicle, recorded sequences of events but did not turn them into narrative. Rather the annals is simply a list of years with apparently random events listed by them that have no conclusion but simply end, and the chronicle, while being closer to narrative, is still nevertheless without conclusion. They present sequences of events without beginnings or ends or sequences that never conclude but 'simply terminate'.[48] On White's model, authoritative narrative is imposed on these sequences of events in the interests of power for the narrating voice.

Extrapolating from this into the field of religion, it could be argued that the study of religion, like history, constructs the narratives it presents as 'fact' from an array of cultural expressions, texts and events and that the authorial voice is a voice of power that seeks, perhaps unconsciously, to control a domain. Religion on this view, like White's view of the past, is constructed or created through the writing of it. 'Hinduism' can in this way be seen as a construction of Western scholarship, founded upon Western political motivations and projections,[49] or the story of the 'Aryan invasion' in the second millennium BCE can be read as a construction of nineteenth-century scholars projecting Aryan supremacist views upon the subcontinent.[50]

Paralleling White's understanding of history, Russell McCutcheon and Timothy Fitzgerald have argued that the category 'world religions' and the equivalents of 'wisdom traditions' and 'world faiths', are constructions that express 'unarticulated theological agendas'.[51] In *Manufacturing Religion*, McCutcheon, arguing against the *sui generis* conception of religion, claims that 'religion' as the object of scholarship within departments of religious studies is constructed, and that

131

this construction has fostered the idea that religion as an essence can be studied as something outside of sociopolitical institutions. McCutcheon persuasively argues that scholarship about religion, mainly from the phenomenology of religion, has been blind to its own implicit assumptions privileging such concepts as 'the archaic', 'experience', and 'tradition', at the cost of an awareness of the historical contingency of 'religious data'. Through blindness to its own implicit assumptions, the field of religion has been 'manufactured' without regard to its material, sociopolitical, and geopolitical implications 'concerning such issues as individual expertise, social power, and politico-economic privilege'.[52] On this view scholarship has constructed an essence of religion – as we have seen in the second chapter – divorced from its historical context and is reflexively unaware of the process of construction. While the field of religion is no doubt partially or largely constructed – as the work of McCutcheon, Harrison and others have shown – this is not the complete story and there are, I have argued, patterns of behaviour and narratives to which the term 'religion' points, the constraints of which need to be specified in developing theoretical models for religious thought and behaviour. Religions provide narratives within which people construct their lives over and above the constructions of scholarship. Acknowledging, after MacIntyre, that narrative is generated from simply being born and dying within human communities, as well as acknowledging the force of the narrative constructivist position of White and Mink in history, and McCutcheon in the study of religion, it is possible to articulate a position that acknowledges both the role of categorization in the construction of knowledge, as well as the constraints of narratives independent of scholarship. Such narratives have often been occluded because of the dominance of unreflexive models or scholarly constructs that have highlighted an ideologically dominant position or that correspond to the implicit assumptions of the method. A discourse of religion which simply finds its own reflection in its object, is open to an accusation of the occlusion of other voices and the implicit non-acknowledgement of the polyglossia of cultures and those cultural discourses we have called religions.

Narrative as the mimesis of action: Paul Ricoeur

In *Time and Narrative*, Ricoeur defends a version of narrative theory which does not deny the narrative nature of existence, yet which is also strongly constructivist. Here Ricoeur seeks to show the structural identity of historiography and fiction and to show how the temporal character of human experience is presupposed in these two forms of narrative, with particular reference to Augustine and Aristotle.[53] In contrast to Hayden White, and in agreement with MacIntyre, Ricoeur maintains the general position that historical sequence possesses the characteristic of narrative and that narrative is not simply imposed upon a temporal sequence. Narrative, claims Ricoeur, can deal with the problem of time in a way that philosophy cannot. The central problem of the text is the irresolvable relation – or *aporias* – between 'cosmic time' and 'individual time' or the 'time of the soul'. Cosmic time is irreconcilable with the phenomenology of subjective temporality except in a poetic, narrative resolution. Ricoeur's general proposal is that in narrative we can see a connection between the metaphysics of time and its human, phenomenological aspect. But it is not so much time, but Ricoeur's understanding of narrative that I wish to pursue here.

While Ricoeur is happy to admit of a great difference between life and fiction and that in one sense life is lived whereas stories are told,[54] the situation is more complex than this. Human actions are always within the bounds of personal biography and the narratives we apply to ourselves given by our cultures. Time is the central feature of human experience, but time only 'becomes human' when it is articulated through narrative 'and narrative attains its full meaning when it becomes a condition of temporal existence'.[55] Narrative has the power to refigure both the past and future in human imagination and to construct a coherent sense of identity. Because of the narrative identity of human experience – lives are understood and lived through the stories we tell of ourselves – the gap between 'lived life' and 'told narrative' is not as great as might at first appear. Ricoeur tries to establish this through an argument that leads from the understanding of narrative, taken directly from Aristotle and building on structuralism and the Russian formalists, as the imitation of an action (*mimesis praxeos*) and as emplotment (*mythos*), to narrative as constructing personal identity.

Narrative for Aristotle is imitation of action which is not, observes Ricoeur, a copy or identical replica but rather the production or organization of events through plot or emplotment (*mythos*).[56] Plot is the synthesis of multiple events that serves to transform these events into a single story which thereby becomes a totality and forms a coherent narrative.[57] Such a narrative is regarded with varying degrees of suspicion concerning its 'reality', thus fiction is imaginary whereas historiography is less clearly so, though both share the quality of emplotment which creates coherence or homogeneity from the discordance of human action and suffering.[58] Mimesis is thus translated as 'imitation' or 'representation', though not, Ricoeur insists, in the sense of a copy of some pre-existing reality, but rather as a creative imitation or representation seen as 'the break which opens the space for fiction'.[59]

Using Aristotle's *Poetics* as his starting point, Ricoeur distinguishes between a 'real domain' covered by ethics – which can be taken to be 'world of action' or 'lived experience' – and an imaginary domain covered by poetics. He then delineates three senses of mimesis. The first of these, called mimesis 1, if I understand him correctly, is the connection between the real and the imaginary domains through a transposition of emplotment on to the practical field of human action. This initial mimesis is grounded within the world of action which entails the meaningful, temporal structures of that world and its symbolic nature. That is, the world of action which entails culture and symbolism, is subject to emplotment: action is symbolically mediated through this first level of mimesis. There are three features or anchors for mimesis 1. The first is that it is a conceptual network that enables the distinguishing of a domain of action: emplotment is always grounded in 'a pre-understanding of the world of action, its meaningful structures, its symbolic resources and its temporal character'.[60] The second feature which controls representation is that action can be narrated, or in other words the 'practical field' already contains symbolic resources such as signs, rules and norms. Ricoeur says that this feature is accessed through the work of anthropologists such as Geertz and is the realm to which *Verstehen* sociology gives access.[61] The third feature is the recognition of the 'temporal structures which call for narration'.[62] That is, action itself which is represented in mimesis contains temporal structures and that time is integral to action. It is here that we can see how Ricoeur differs from any pure narrative constructivism, for here action is characterized by a temporal structure which needs to be narrated. This temporal structure is none other than Augustine's characterization of the threefold present as the present of future things, the present of past things and the present of present things.[63] In other words all action contains implicitly within it this temporal dimension as present action in the past, present and future. Action thus contains potentially a narrative structure and the representation of action will reflect this. The difference here between Ricoeur's position and MacIntyre's is that whereas for Mac-Intyre narrative is inherent in the process of action, for Ricoeur narrative is potential in action because of its ineluctable temporality. Summarizing mimesis 1 Ricoeur writes:

> To imitate or represent action is first to preunderstand what human acting is, in its semantics, its symbolic system, its temporality. Upon this pre-understanding, common to both poets and their readers, emplotment is constructed and, with it, textual and literary mimetics.[64]

Ricoeur's second sense of mimesis, mimesis 2, is that of creation or the organization of events. This is the mediation between what precedes fiction and what follows it, or 'the postunderstanding of the order of action and its temporal features'.[65] This second mimesis refers to the representation of action in text and, to use Ricoeur's phrase, 'opens the kingdom of the *as if* ... the kingdom of fiction'.[66] This kingdom of 'as if' embraces both fiction and historiography, and while fictional and historical narratives differ in so far as they relate to the 'imaginary' and the 'real', nevertheless both share the paradigm of 'emplotment' or both share a narrative structure. Both historical and fictional narrative are engaged in the refiguring of time which affects the reader's imagination. This aspect of representation mediates through the text in which it is articulated, between the pre-understanding of action in mimesis 1 and its postunderstanding in the text. Finally Ricoeur's third sense of mimesis 3 is the intersection of the world of the text with that of the reader or hearer.[67] This refers to the response of the reader/hearer to the text, or what the reading subject brings to narrative as mimesis 1 and 2. In a succinct summary of his position 'Life in Quest of Narrative' Ricoeur argues that plot, as Aristotle shows, is not static but is an operation which is only completed by the receiver of the narration. There is a sense in which narrative only comes into being when it is read or heard and is refigured by the reader. Thus the meaning of narrative and its transforming effects on a person occur, in Ricoeur's words, from 'the intersection of the world of the text and the world of the hearer or reader',[68] an idea that has echoes in Wolfgang Iser's theory of reading and Robert Jauss' reception theory and, as Ricoeur acknowledges, in Gadamer's 'fusion of horizons' in which the world horizon of the text becomes fused with that of the reader's own, real action.

Both Ricoeur and MacIntyre highlight narrative as the focus of discourse and problems concerning the nature of the self, the relation of subjectivity to objectivity and the relation of fiction to action. While Ricoeur has a sustained and philosophically more important treatment of narrative than MacIntyre, MacIntyre's work is a clear statement of a narrative realist position; to write the truth and to write an intelligible history are not exclusive of each other. Two ideas are particularly important to this position, first that narrative is inherent to the structure of life's process – in one sense history writes itself – and secondly that action arises from human intentionality. Regarding the first point, to the critiquer of narrative realism (in this particular passage, Louis Mink) MacIntyre responds: 'And to someone who says that in life there are no endings, or that final partings take place only in stories, one is tempted to reply, "But have you never heard of death?"'[69] The rhetorical force of this does indeed question any purely constructivist position. For MacIntyre beginnings, endings and the life between comprise the very structure of narrative. Narrative is inherent in the process of life itself and not imposed externally or after the event. However, as Brian Fay points out, for many in different religious traditions for example, death is not the end, nor birth the beginning but episodes in a much longer story.[70] In such cases a narrative is brought to bear upon birth and death that goes beyond the constraints of physical occurrences, and those occurrences are understood in terms of identity-giving and nourishing narratives that proclaim these events not to be the beginning nor the end. In such cases the narrative does not come from the realm of action itself but is projected onto the world of action to endow it with meaning and sense.

Ricoeur is quite close to MacIntyre, echoing many of the same themes, particularly over the issue of narrative identity. But in the end Ricoeur retains the Aristotelian distinction between the real domain of ethics, the life that is lived, and the imaginary domain of poetics, the story that is told, with narrative as the imposition of one plot we inherit from our cultures onto the 'real' domain. The internalized narratives – the 'narrative voices' – which comprise our life provide a sense of identity that constitutes us and that is constantly reinterpreted within the contexts of culture. Unlike MacIntyre, Ricoeur does not think human beings can be the authors of their lives, though we can become 'the narrator and the hero of our own story'.[71] On a larger scale, historiography characterized as emplotment is the creation or refiguring of the past at a level of productive imagination. Here narrative is constructed in historiography – and thus is parallel to fiction – and not generated through action within history. Narrative creates order and concordance out of the discordance of temporal acts or lived experience.

Both positions, it seems to me, have a lot to be said for them. On the one hand time does constrain life from birth to death and intention does impact upon the world as non-random action within the context of a *telos*. This *telos* can range from personal objectives and agendas to the long-term goals of entire nations or the collective *telos* of a religious group. But this life narrative and sense of identity need not be unitive to be meaningful, as MacIntyre might claim, for it might be argued that there can be many narrative voices within a single life. There is also, therefore, merit in the narrative constructivist position that any understanding of the world is generated by the narratives we bring to it – whether it be a pre- or post-Copernican narrative, whether it be a narrative of endless beginnings, or a materialist narrative of collective, political emancipation. Of course our narratives are always constructed by and within the cultures we inhabit and our identities given by those cultures, but this does not mean that narratives are not constrained by the temporal limits of birth, life and death, and of genetics and physics.

Narrative theory and the study of religion

What, then, has this discussion to do with the study of religions? We can now return, by way of MacIntyre and Ricoeur, to our contention that in the move away from the philosophy of consciousness, narrative is central to any understanding of, or attempt to explain, religion. The phenomenology of religion, I have argued, is limited by its ahistorical pretensions and by the Husserlian baggage concerning the epistemic subject and the philosophy of consciousness which it inevitably assumes. Given that phenomenology entails the detached observer and that such a view can be criticized from a perspective in which language, communication and intersubjectivity take centre stage, then this reemphasis entails a different model of the observer. Rather than the transcendental ego performing the acts of bracketing, eidetic reduction and empathy, in order to objectively understand the data presented to it, we have the observer within her own narratives engaging in a dialogical process with another narrative. In this dialogical process, the work of scholarship is produced and knowledge generated.

Rather than consciousness we can take the philosophy of the sign or language, culture and intersubjectivity, as given. In this case, 'description' becomes a moment in a process or the relating of action to narrative in Ricoeur's sense of mimesis. Rather than appearances to consciousness in the flow of the *cogitationes*, some of which are identified as 'religious' because of their 'sacred' quality, we are engaged in a more dynamic or active process in which actions – forms of behaviour and also texts appearing in the field of practice – are made sense of in their narrative context. The atemporal and ahistorical essences or structures of phenomenology are replaced with the recognition of the historically contingent nature of the cultural practices and textual resources we identify as religions. This involves the understanding that the narratives identified through emplotment are both created by the method and by the questions we bring to the intersubjective nexus of culture, and by the narrative structure inherent within the temporal dimension of action itself.

The study of religions, like history, is inherently narrative in nature. This is not to say that papers and monographs of religious studies are hidden narratives, but rather that they achieve intelligibility through being embedded within narrative, within the context of ongoing research within the history of an institution or institutions. As Chidester has urged, the academic study of religion needs to be a narrative of historically situated practices.[72] Writing on natural science Rouse claims that 'both the practices of scientific research and the knowledges that result from them acquire their intelligibility and significance from being situated within narratives'.[73] Kerala tantric tradition, formed through the actions and writings of generations of Nambudri Brahmans, has a narrative dimension inherent within it – the emic perspective of the tradition – yet this has to be related to the etic questions brought to bear upon it, which serve to create a scholarly or external narrative. This narrative – the monograph or paper – is the product of a dialogical process or interaction between the historically situated observer or scholar and the people, texts and practices of the 'object' tradition. The emplotment of texts and behaviours in certain configurations is then determined by the observer and the scholarly apparatus brought to bear. The monograph or paper is itself then 'entextualized' or placed within the context of a temporal, academic culture. There is, of course, no reason to relate the emic narrative of the Kerala tantric tradition to the external questions brought to it, other than the imperatives of scholarship itself. These in turn might be – and have been – severely criticized for the assumption of epistemological superiority and, in the South-Asian context, an implicit dominance and colonization of the emic perspective.[74]

Moving the centre of discourse away from consciousness towards language, culture and narrative is to see religion as historically contingent in terms of narratives and practices highlighted by scholarship but also by traditions themselves. Narrative theory can recognize both that stories are lived and stories are told. It can highlight the narrative nature of religion as both readings and transmission of texts, and as actions repeated through the generations. It also reflexively understands hermeneutical pre-understanding (mimesis 1), the representation of action in texts in the realms of fiction and historiography (mimesis 2) and the interaction between text and reader (mimesis 3).

These two kinds of narrative – the narrative of the tradition and the narrative construction of scholarship – are equivalent to insider and outsider accounts within the field of religion. Insider accounts are from within the narrative of the tradition and articulate that tradition as normative. Outsider accounts are from within the narrative traditions of their own discourses, notably the naturalist tradition, though specific traditions in the study of religion could also be specified. Sketched in broad brushstrokes these modern narrative traditions of the critique and interpretation of religion can be identified as the consciousness tradition from Kant and Fichte through to Husserl; the hermeneutical tradition from Schliermacher through Dilthey which develops into the narrative theory of Gadamer, Ricoeur and Bakhtin; the psychoanalytic tradition from Freud, which in one reading can be seen as part of the narrativist tradition; and the sociological traditions from Durkheim and Weber, on the one hand, and from Marx, on the other, which develops into critical theory. There are significant cross-fertilizations between these traditions, all of which offer significant critiques and explanations of religion, and postmodernism inherits elements of, and responds to, them all.

But the point I would wish to underline is that these Western intellectual narrative traditions – perhaps with the exception of phenomenology, and the work of Jung in psychoanalysis – take a critical look at the narratives of religion and attempt to explain those narratives in naturalist terms external to them. As I have suggested, this is a perfectly legitimate goal which gives epistemological privilege to reason and empiricism and is inevitably sceptical of the claims made by the narrative traditions which are its object. However, if knowledge, as MacIntyre has argued, is tradition specific, and the grand narrative of Enlightenment reason can be shown to be historically contingent, then this means that we are in a situation of competing narratives. There are, in the end, no criteria other than those derived from tradition, whereby one tradition can claim rational superiority to another. Of course, some paradigms are more successful than others in specific areas – allopathic medicine can claim more success than homeopathy – but the scientific paradigm cannot, for example, refute metaphysical claims of narrative traditions. Insider and outsider discourses on this view, must be seen in terms of competing narratives and so the issue becomes one of power. This is, however, not the full story, as narratives are not wholly constructed by the practices which seek to explain them and the battle for the truth of different narratives must also be understood in terms of different levels of constraint. The narrative of objectivist science accommodates more levels of constraint in the empirical world than earlier narratives, thus Copernican science accommodates more levels of constraint than pre-Copernican cosmologies, and relativity theory specifies different constraints to those of Newtonian mechanics. But in all these cases, the narrative of the scientific tradition cannot falsify or prove religious traditions: quantum mechanics does not 'prove' Hindu metaphysics nor Newtonian science disprove a creator God.

An objection to this scenario might be that the idea of competing narratives leads to an unwelcome relativism in which critical reflection is made impossible. There are no objective grounds, on this view, for accounting for different narratives: a Western rational inquiry cannot claim superiority to an orthodox Christian or Islamic narrative. The arguments for different forms of relativism are well developed – perhaps the most influential in social sciences by Winch[75] and in philosophy by Margolis[76] – as are the counterarguments – by Gellner for example.[77] Science – a rational discourse *par excellence* – has abandoned narrative, particularly religious narrative, in favour of explanation that discerns laws and discovers causes. But even science is within a tradition, although a particularly successful one in terms of practical application.[78] Indeed, rational discourse crosses many narrative divisions, but it always operates from a particular narrative base or from within a particular history. There is no rationality independent of tradition. Even formal rules of logic, such as the law of the excluded middle and the law of non-contradiction, although they might be applied across cultures, are embedded within a discourse and a history, as Margolis has consistently argued.[79]

On this account there can be no grounds outside of tradition for establishing overlapping narratives. We can simply operate Davidson's principle of charity, that to avoid total scepticism we must maximize faith that the other's rationality or truth is akin to our own. That narratives can overlap does not entail any universal, non-contingent truths, but does entail, on the contrary, that narratives are always historically located. Narratives within traditions are necessarily temporal and constrained by the historical circumstances of their occurrence. Indeed, as Greenblatt has shown in the context of literature, texts need to be read as interrelated to wider historical narratives and other, parallel fields.[80] Similarly with religion the placing of religious texts alongside non-religious ones of the same period, allows them to 'interrogate' each other. Insider and outsider accounts in religion might be competing narratives, and any epistemological privilege claimed by the outsider discourse, needs to be reflexively, and critically, aware of its epistemological grounds. What scholars of religion are doing, is examining and critiquing other narratives from the perspective of their own, whose presuppositions can be reflexively revealed, but which cannot claim epistemological privilege.

Summary

Reading the past, and social science discourse through the lens of narrative, shows us that contemporary academic disciplines are confronted with differing and sometimes competing accounts. The present chapter has attempted to examine ideas of narrative as story and as discourse about religion, in relation to insider and outsider accounts. I have argued that with the move away from the philosophy of consciousness and the privileging of the epistemic subject entailed by the phenomenological method, narrative becomes central to the enterprise of understanding religion. Insider and outsider discourses can therefore be understood in terms of different kinds of narrative, and we have here examined how constructivist views of narrative, as exemplified particularly in the work of MacIntyre and Ricoeur, map onto insider and outsider accounts.

The implications of this position is that there can be no privileged view outside of narrative, or outside of history, and that critique assumes a narrative base. The relation between narrative as discourse about religion and narrative as story, reveals the often competing nature of insider and outsider accounts. To develop this idea further, in the following chapter we will see how these different kinds of narrative reveal the polyglossic nature of religion and explanations of it. This will serve to counter the objection that the reduction of accounts of religion to mere narrative serves to repress naturalist explanations of religion, though I would accept that on this view naturalist explanations become competing narratives without privilege, for there can be no place outside of narrative from which to adjudicate. We will then be able to enquire more fully into the relation between narrative as discourse about religion and the act of narrating a discourse about religion; in other words an inquiry into reflexivity and the production of scholarship.

6. Dialogue and the situated observer

The shift from consciousness, to language and the sign, questions both the disengaged observer of phenomenology and modernist social science. Rather than the detached, epistemic subject penetrating the alien world of the other through the phenomenological process, the shift to language and the sign as the focus of inquiry means rather that the subject must be defined in relation to other subjects. The inquiry into the nature of religion or quasi-religious propensities within culture, becomes a dialogical enterprise in which the inquirer is situated within a particular context or narrative tradition, and whose research into narrative traditions, that become the objects of investigation, must be apprehended in a much richer and multi-faceted way. The observer is a situated observer or, to use Rosaldo's term, a 'positioned subject',[1] with all the implications of human complexity and relationality entailed by that phrase. The relationship between the situated observer and situation of observation, becomes dialogical in the sense that the observer is thrown into conversation with people and texts of the object tradition. Rather than the disengaged reason of the social scientist observing, recording and theorizing data, we have a situation in which research is imaged as 'conversation', or more accurately 'critical conversation', in which the interactive nature of research is recognized. Research, says Bakhtin, 'becomes inquiry and conversation, that is, dialogue'.[2] This is not to abjure theory, but on the contrary to recognize the pervasive nature of theory and the situational nature of all inquiry; that knowledge is generated through the interaction of inquirer and object of inquiry which produces 'data' or 'phenomena'. The present chapter will develop the critique of the detached phenomenological observer or epistemic subject, begun in chapter four, through examining the perspectival and dialogical nature of the process of religious and cultural research. This is to place social scientific discourse within the contexts of its narrative traditions and also to reveal the narrative nature of religions at both micro and macro levels.

The claims to detached objectivity in phenomenology and positivistic social science can be questioned because of the problematic natures of positing a disinterested observer and of the idea that there can be pure description without evaluative judgements. The mind as the mirror of nature[3] is widely considered to be untenable in a world in which facts can be shown to be constructed by the method or theory, and objectivity is thought to be the result of the process of inquiry, rather than a pregiven reality prior to inquiry. The shift from consciousness to language and the sign means that the epistemic subject must be defined in relation to other subjects and that the subject or observer is not outside of historical and cultural situations. All academic inquiry is from a place. De Certeau articulates this point well by describing 'place' as the sum of determining factors that delimit an inquiry: 'However scientific it may be, an analysis always amounts to a localized practice that produces only a regional discourse'.[4] This is, of course, nothing remarkable and has been understood for a long time in some areas of social science, particularly anthropology. But within the field of the study of religions this idea has not been given the serious attention it demands, first because, as we have seen, the phenomenology of religion entails the Husserlian philosophy of consciousness, which, while being open to the diversity of 'phenomena' (by which we can read 'cultural practices'), is resistant to the contextualization of the observer. Secondly, because the situated nature of the observer means that knowledge cannot be objectively certain; it leads to a fallibilism.

But fallibilism, the view that there can be no certainty as regards knowledge, does not lead to scepticism. Indeed, fallibilism, whose origins are in Peirce, is akin to Popper's idea that theories can never be verified, only falsified, and that science is contingent upon the social communities in which it is embedded. In the context of the study of religions this simply means that all knowledge and explanations concerning beliefs and practices are historically contingent and dependent upon the hermeneutic circle. Bohman presents a convincing fallibilist argument in the following terms. Interpretation occurs within the hermeneutic circle and so is circular, indeterminate and perspectival. This circularity is defined by the necessity of a background, which is a set of shared and accessible conditions as its possibility. These shared background constraints are, rather than limiting conditions, enabling conditions which allow for the production of revisable, public knowledge through interpretation. These interpretations can be revised in the light of better interpretations and the close comparison of competing interpretations.[5] We see here that, for Bohman, fallibilism allows for interpretation and the understanding of constraints upon it, as enabling conditions, or conditions which allow an understanding to develop. This is to recognize the contingent nature of interpretation and that knowledge is always from a perspective.

If this is true of all knowledge, it is certainly the case in the study of religions where explanation and understanding are always contingent upon the wider interpretative community of the epistemic subject. Understanding and explaining religion occur within a conceptual scheme and are always from a particular situation, perspective and gendered place. The positioned subject is an embodied subject. All understanding is therefore dialogical, by which I mean the situation of subject and 'object' or 'other subject' is one of dialogue. This dialogue can be understood as 'critical conversation' for not only does the situated observer investigate, comment upon or offer explanations in terms of external paradigms, but is in turn interrogated by those who would be the objects of explanation. In dealing with living persons in the particularity of their lives, the scholar of religion or other social scientist is thrown into a situation in which she not only interrogates but is interrogated, even implicitly, by that tradition and those people who are the object of research. In any particular research situation there is a sense in which we all have an equal stake in understanding. Within religious studies the application of this kind of research model occurs principally in two ways, in the study of living traditions through the interaction of situated observer and people (ethnography for all intents and purposes), and in the study of texts which itself is a form of interaction. While the study of people and texts demand different methods and skills, neither can assume the privilege of the epistemic subject and both must recognize the embodied, situational nature of research. In the critique of the phenomenological philosophy of consciousness, dialogical theory becomes particularly important in demonstrating the linguistic and interactive nature of research in both ethnography and in the reading of texts.

Dialogue and critical conversation

That all research is interactional has brought into question modernist assumptions of social scientific truth arrived at through objective method. The observer in interaction with the object of inquiry, say a religious tradition or community, is always situated and research becomes dialogue. Indeed dialogue is more than simply a 'method' – as Gadamer understands hermeneutics to be – but is fundamental to human being which is dialogical. Understanding occurs in conversation and in this sense – in contrast to a scientific method – '(u)nderstanding or its failure is like an event that happens to us'.[6] This is also to say that all research is situational, from a dialogical perspective. Rather than any proclaimed value-free, monologic investigation, we have a dialogical situation in which preconceptions, as well as the epistemic subject of research, are inevitably changed and challenged in the process of dialogue.[7]

The situated nature of research has long been accepted within anthropology because it is defined by fieldwork. Renato Rosaldo observes how the ethnographer is a positioned subject who observes the object community from a certain angle, and that 'age, gender, being an outsider, and association with a neo-colonial regime influence what the ethnographer learns'.[8] The traditional model of sociology and ethnography, as found in Weber and Radcliffe-Brown for example, has been that detached, value-free observation at a critical distance from the material creates an objective account of the society or aspect of culture. Rosaldo claims that, while it is certainly possible to do research at a distance in this way, its results are only partial and can just as equally conceal aspects of culture as reveal them. Objectifying descriptions can appear as ludicrous when applied to 'our own' culture (Rosaldo cites the example of Miner's famous 'Nacirema' paper which describes mundane activities of Americans in a detached, ethnographical language)[9] and this should alert us to the possibility that there are other descriptions and accounts equally as valid. The ethnography which is the result of anthropological investigation, while displaying what Tyler has called the 'rhetoric of distance' and claim to objective description, is embedded within other texts which it alludes to or, indeed, ignores.[10] The totality of events which comprises classical ethnography tends to suppress other voices and other narratives, whose claim to give an account is as equally valid as the ethnographer's. If the situational nature of research into culture and society is taken seriously, then analysis becomes relational and the embodied subject of research, who is not morally indifferent or emotionally empty in the interests of objectivity, is in a discursive relationship with her informants. The dialogical nature of enquiry then highlights the diversity of narratives and the different ways of understanding a cultural formation, including emic accounts. Any distanced, analytical account of an ethnographer must become one among other, competing insider accounts (or alternative outsider ones).

This kind of approach moves away from overarching theories to microsocial description in which the ethnographer reflexively understands the process of analysis she is engaged with. Karen Brown's *Mama Lola*, for example, shows the ethnographer in a dialogical situation in which she is deeply affected by the 'object' of inquiry and the participants in the voodoo community are in turn affected by her presence.[11] There are many other ethnographic studies of this type.[12] Knowledge is contextual and the embodied nature of the positioned subject means that she will inevitably bring to the analysis not only questions stemming from the research programme, but also questions stemming from personal biography. This emphasis on the situational in anthropology is not a move into relativism, but rather a highlighting of the particular. James Clifford, citing the example of Marjorie Shostak who describes the birth of a child for a !Kung woman, suggests that such ethnographies speak to readers in very direct ways and the ethnography becomes an allegory, in this case of female humanity.[13]

The situated observer inevitably brings to the ethnographic situation, not only the methods of her analysis but also a personal biography which influences research. This is not so much an obstacle to objectivity but can be a resource which facilitates understanding. A poignant example of this is from Rosaldo who claims that the personal loss of his wife allowed him a deeper understanding of bereavement among the Ilongots.[14] In the field of religion the question of personal involvement raises again the issue of whether the objective researcher can understand or explain 'religion' without some personal religious emotion or experience. We are reminded here of Otto's claim in *The Idea of the Holy* that only those who have had a numinous experience can understand it. This is a deeply problematic issue. On the one hand a piece of research about religion – in my own work, phenomenological accounts of Hindu traditions – needs to be from an outsider perspective if it is to command the interest of the scholarly community and be made accessible to a contemporary, secular, Western audience, yet on the other there should be some ability for identification with the 'object' of research if it is to be insightful or explanatory.

This is not to say that we have simply a choice between a dichotomy of reductive explanation, say along the lines of the Stark–Bainbridge thesis of religion as promising compensation for the deficiencies and pain of the world,[15] and an empathetic, phenomenology or history of religions, along the lines of Eliade's religion as hierophany. A third position, the one which I am attempting to unfold here, is possible. This position is both critical and dialogical. It desires both to understand and to offer explanations of religion or religious practices as completely embedded within other cultural practices, but reflexively recognizes the embodied/embedded, narrative nature of the enterprise. In this way it draws upon postmodern critiques of modernist, overarching rationality, but recognizes that any embodied narrative draws upon cultural values which it inevitably articulates, and, at least in the late modern world, is sensitive to the human reasons as to why people elect certain cultural practices. The idea of 'empathy' is relevant here, though the term is problematic, as we shall see, for it has unnecessary implications of a philosophy of consciousness which a dialogical model would wish to avoid. The researcher is herself within a culture and community and we need to recognize that, in Taylor's phrase, 'we are embodied agents, living in dialogical conditions, inhabiting time in a specifically human way, that is, making sense of our lives as a story ... '[16]

Inevitably, in any rich account of a religious tradition, the situated observer will be affected as will be the informants of the research. If the critique of the privileged, epistemic subject is accepted, then inquiry into religion becomes a dialogical process in which the observer is located within her own narrative tradition engaging with a tradition which is the object of inquiry. In this situation emic, narrative accounts must be taken seriously, not only as 'data', but as accounts which have an equal claim on validity. These narratives will inevitably compete with those of the outsider discourse as they cannot be unified into a grand synthesis. A dialogical model recognizes the temporal dimension of all cultural analysis; emic and etic accounts exist through time and are subject to constant revision and reassessment in new situations. There will be always something incomplete about research which accepts its situational and temporal nature. Objectivity can therefore be understood in terms of interaction or dialogue among participants within a social field, where one of those participants is a situated observer or social scientist. This kind of dialogue is critical in so far as different narratives and accounts are placed under critical scrutiny; indeed each is subjected to the critical scrutiny of the other and social analysis becomes 'a relational form of understanding in which both parties actively engage in the interpretation of cultures'.[17] Following the logic of this, it means that those aspects of culture we label 'religions' can be analysed both from within by the questioning insider, as well as from without by the social scientist. Both would have different perceptions and reach different, perhaps radically different, understandings, though both could constructively converse.

Rather than the disengaged reason of the social scientist observing, recording and theorizing data, we have a process in which research is modelled on critical conversation. This is not to espouse a situation in which any explanation is as good as another or in which 'anything goes', for the standards of assessment concerning evidence, rigour, and coherence still apply. But it is to argue that all explanation is situated; there is no 'view from nowhere' and there are competing narrative accounts which might be totally incompatible, being based on wholly different presuppositions. Critical conversation also means that there can be no ethical or value neutrality and divergent accounts of any cultural practice will contain divergent value systems. On this view, rather than simply an attempted value-free account of the revival of the illegal practice of *sati* in some Hindu locations (the generally coerced, immolation of widows on their husband's pyre), it is perfectly coherent to critique such a practice from a consciously other perspective – such as a feminist perspective – without compromising explanation or understanding. The issue as to whether such a critique would be an example of a covert exercise of reminiscence in colonial power, is a complex problem to which we will return. But this kind of dialogical approach is resistant to the idea that the etic discourse or ethnography is objective because based on empirical evidence and reason, and the emic discourse is purely subjective and based on myth (and therefore error). There are strong mythical dimensions in scientific processes as there is rationality in the emic accounts from 'traditional societies' or from within religions. The dialogical model has been operating for some years within anthropology – a discipline which is radically self-critical – and has produced ethnographies which significantly contribute to social scientific understandings of cultures and the people who comprise them. It has also operated successfully as regards texts within literary studies and social scientific studies of texts, a development whose source is the Russian thinker Mikhail Bakhtin. His work has great significance for the social sciences and is particularly relevant to the study of religion in involving a critical inquiry into utterance and in showing the centrality of narrative in culture.

Dialogical theory: Bakhtin

If a characteristic feature of modernity is the disengaged subject of scientific discourse, then a characteristic feature of postmodern scientific discourse is the situated observer working within a context and responding to the problems of a particular environment. Within a world in which paradoxically there is an increasing tendency, on the one hand, towards a universalization and simultaneity through the development of information technologies and, on the other, towards localization of knowledge and exchange, dialogue becomes central.[18] Dialogue gives the situated observer access to universalization through cyberspace as well as being the basis of intersubjective engagement with people and texts. While the idea of dialogue is, of course, an ancient one at the heart of the reasoning process in Plato, with Bakhtin it becomes the central focus of investigation. Bakhtin's ideas have come to the attention of Western scholars relatively late, due largely to the historical contingencies in which he lived, and his work is important in anticipating many developments within postmodernism and within Habermas' critical theory, with the centering of dialogue in the processes of social science and the recognition of the plurality of voices, or 'heteroglossia', within cultures.[19] His thought also has strong parallels with Ricoeur's and Kögler's critical hermeneutics.[20] Although Bakhtin did not actually use the term, dialogism is a discourse which focuses upon dialogue, utterance and heteroglossia. Bakhtin formulated this as the science of ideologies whose objective is the study of utterance in its specific historicity as well as utterance functioning as an element within the larger signifying system of language.[21] At the heart of dialogism is the concept of 'dialogue', the idea that every utterance or thought enters into relationship with other utterances and thoughts not only in the present but stretching into the past and future. While Bakhtin is the figure most associated with dialogical understanding, other figures also stand out, particularly Martin Buber, who influenced Bakhtin, his younger contemporary,

Emmanuel Levinas, Gadamer, Ricoeur and, more recently, Kögler. With their emphasis on alterity and dialogue, these figures stand against the philosophy of consciousness tradition in recognizing the primacy of communication and relationship; in dialogism consciousness is identified with otherness and is entirely relative to the dialogical situation.

Although Bakhtin was influenced by neo-Kantian German philosophy – though radically moving away from the Kantian position – the theme of dialogue has precursors in the *Verstehen* tradition which saw that the natural and human worlds require different modes of understanding, and which placed lived experience (*Erlebnis*) over cognition as the centre of cultural inquiry.[22] The distinction between natural science whose methods entail objectification and the identification of causes, and the social or human sciences whose methods entail understanding subjectivities, is one of the bases from which dialogism develops. But dialogism is not subjectivism, rather a focusing on intersubjectivity and communication, articulated by Bakhtin as the understanding of the 'I' 'in interrelation with other persons, that is *I* and the *other, I* and *Thou*'.[23] Indeed, with the demise of the subject of the philosophy of consciousness, the other becomes the catalyst of self-understanding. As Kögler remarks, '(i)n critical interpretation, the reconstruction of the other and of her symbolic background serves as a critical foil from which to become, as it were, one's own other'.[24] Understanding the other in critical conversation is also to develop self-understanding, though not the understanding of the transcendental ego, but the understanding of the historically contingent subject through the distanciation.

The dialogical critique of the philosophy of consciousness can be summarized by focusing on three themes, the relationship between 'I' and 'other', the idea of utterance in dialogue, and in the idea of 'live-entering'. I shall examine each of these in turn in order to further contribute to the critique of the disengaged, epistemic subject of phenomenology begun in chapter four, and in order to point to ways in which dialogism can contribute to the discourse of method in the study of religions.

The I and the other

In the relationship between 'I' and 'other', the 'I' is invisible as an abstraction or transcendental subject, but, by contrast, is visible in performance and in the body: the 'I' is constructed in relationship. There are therefore three co-ordinates within the dialogical encounter, the 'I', the 'other' and their relationship. This relationship between two subjectivities is simultaneous and cogenerated, yet occurs in distinct locations; two bodies exist in different spaces and cannot share the same time/space co-ordinates. On this view the human subject cannot be studied, as the natural world, as if it were a 'thing' without voice, and while this may be to ignore macro-problems of social and cultural formation, the dialogical approach emphasizes the crucially important intersubjective aspect of immediate encounter. Bodies occupy difference in respect to space, but are temporally spontaneous, in which partners in dialogue actively participate. The recognition of the body as the locus of inquiry and the place on which are inscribed the patterns, life and power-relations within a culture has long been recognized in anthropology and sociology.[25] Given that the human subject who gives voice to her concerns (or indeed, is silenced) is the 'object' of the human sciences, all knowledge of the human realm, on this account, is therefore dialogical, entailing the subject of dialogue hearing and responding to the voice of the 'other' of dialogue, from a particular, embodied location. Indeed, in a reflexive mode, Bakhtin says that the object of the human sciences is not one 'spirit' but two, the studying and the studied,[26] though the term 'body' in place of 'spirit' would perhaps reflect more accurately the nature of contemporary theorizing about culture.

Outsideness (*vnendkhodimost*) is necessary for understanding and all dialogue entails a distinction between 'subject' and 'object', 'author' and 'hero'.[27] In 'Art and Answerability', an early essay by Bakhtin, he begins to express the relationship of 'I' to 'other', through discussion of the problem of the relation between an 'author' of a text and its 'heroes'. Set within the general problem of what Bakhtin, following Kant, calls 'architectonics' or how beings relate to one another, this essay examines the way in which the author and hero are correlative moments in a work ('the artistic whole'), from which he generalizes to the relationship between subjects. The author is the bearer of the 'consummated whole' of a work – knowing its completion – who stands outside of its constituent features and temporal moments.[28] This standing outside or transgredience (*transgradientsvo*) of the author to the work is in contrast with the hero who is incapable of being guided by the consummated whole accessible to the author, though as readers we only have access to that whole through the hero.

The author in maintaining a position outside the hero completes him 'by supplying all those moments which are inaccessible to the hero himself' and to justify and consummate the hero outside of his own 'forward directed life'.[29] The structures of the author – hero relationship are recapitulated in life where 'I' and 'other' are always transgredient to each other, though never wholly so for both share time and (different) spaces. But unlike the narrative to the author, unlike art, we can never be consummated or completed, for human life has no neat closures, except perhaps for death, though even then our life outcomes have consequences for others. Bakhtin writes:

> If I am consummated and my life is consummated, I am no longer capable of living and acting. For in order to live and act, I need to be unconsummated, I need to be open for myself – at least in all the essential moments constituting my life; I have to be, for myself, someone who is axiologically yet to be, somebody who does not coincide with his already existing makeup.[30]

This idea of incompletion and self-construction, emphasizes the temporal and narrative dimension of the unique event (*sobytie*) of human life in a way, as we have seen, not dissimilar to Ricoeur. For Bakhtin, in life the self is always unfinished or unconsummated, in contrast to art which is finished off by the 'author'. In the realm of life we create ourselves, for the self is not something given (*dan*) but is rather conceived (*zadan*) or constructed in dialogue: 'we have no alibi in existence'.[31] This non-closure of any biography inevitably has consequences for understanding others and, indeed, for the construction of any human science. Any apparent consummation of a self – in art or indeed in social science – must always be from the outside and must always, therefore, remain ultimately as an incomplete account. There can never be the total appropriation of another – and so never a complete understanding or transgredient explanation of them – because each, being in a distinct location, has what Bakhtin refers to as an 'excess of seeing.' This excess of seeing is what I perceive and the other does not being in a different location, and conversely what the other perceives and I cannot: our horizons do not coincide, for 'regardless of the position and the proximity to me of this other human being whom I am contemplating, I shall always see and know something that he, from his place outside and over against me, cannot see himself . . . '[32]

That knowledge of others must of necessity be incomplete has important consequences for the human sciences. The human sciences which aspire to explain thought and behaviour are necessarily limited by the 'excess of seeing'. Yet the excess of seeing also allows for a critical distance between observer, or research programme, and observed; the external perception can see what self-perception cannot, yet without objectivism. Any explanation will inevitably be incomplete because of the temporal nature of human life and the inaccessible dimension of self-experience within a specific embodied context. This does not entail a total scepticism towards the human sciences, but does entail fallibilism and the reflexive understanding of the limits of explanation, because selves stand outside of each other in particular, embodied locations. This standing outside is not a return to a philosophy of consciousness, far from it, for 'standing outside' is standing in another place and not in 'no place'. The self is only constituted within a dialogical relationship to another, within a linguistic environment, whose cognition is determined by that relationship.

Unlike Husserl's transcendental ego, Bakhtin's 'I' is constructed purely in relationship. The relationship between I and other determines the constraints of understanding and sets the boundary for explanation. For Bakhtin all understanding arises from the dialogical encounter between two bodies and the communication between them. Once we accept communication and language as the starting point of all inquiry, within which the self–other relationship is constructed, then this allows approaches in the social sciences to develop which focus on the analysis of communication and language, such as discourse analysis, sociolinguistics, linguistic anthropology, narrative analysis and dialogics. On this view, having abandoned the privilege of the epistemic subject, religion must be understood in terms of communication, and the modes of its study as not different from other approaches to culture.

Dialogue and utterance

All understanding is embedded – and embodied – within the dialogical encounter, and the focus of this analysis is the 'utterance' (*vyskazyvanie*). The utterance is the basis of the analysis of communication that is active or performed, and is always a response to some previous utterance. That utterance is performed is an important aspect of dialogism which links the approach with the speech-act theory of

154

Austin and Searle and pragmatics in linguistics, that emphasizes the deixic nature of language.[33] In its particularity utterance is from a specific spatial and temporal location, a specific 'chronotype', yet it also participates or draws from the general inheritance of a language and grammatical structure.

Rather than the sentence being the focus of interest, which is an abstraction defined by a theory of grammar, utterance takes centre stage, which can itself be a sentence or fragment of a sentence, though issued in a particular context. Every speech act assumes the existence of other utterances. Bakhtin writes:

> [The speaker] presupposes not only the existence of the language system he is using, but also the existence of preceding utterances – his own and others – with which his given utterance enters into one kind of relation or another (builds on them, polemicizes with them, or simply presumes that they are already known to the listener). Any utterance is a link in a very complexly organized chain of other utterances.[34]

Every utterance is 'filled with echoes and reverberations of other utterances' and each utterance is 'a response to preceding utterances of a given sphere'.[35] Not only is the utterance responsive to previous utterances, but it anticipates response and is directed to somebody; it has the quality of *addressivity*. This means that not only the content of the utterance is important but also its social context and intonation. Understanding and explanation focus on the utterance in the particularity of its context, rather than on the sentence and the implicit system of language (*langue*), which had been the focus of Saussurian linguistics. In one sense understanding, claims Bakhtin, is distinct or stands opposed to utterance, which is its immediate object, but only in the sense that one reply is opposed to another within a dialogue. Because understanding is within a dialogical context, and is inevitably ideologically suffused, it already contains within it the embryo of an answer, or the anticipation of an answer born within the pre-understanding of an utterance. Voloshinov writes: 'Any true understanding is dialogic in nature. Understanding is to utterance as one line of dialogue is to the next. Understanding seeks to match the speaker's word with a counter-word.'[36] While this brings to mind the hermeneutic circle, that understanding of the whole entails an understanding of the part which in turn entails an understanding of the whole, for Bakhtin it is a hermeneutic spiral: understanding is gradually deepened and discourse illumined in the activity of dialogue.

Understanding is not a passive reflecting of the other's utterance, or a redoubling of the other's experience within the self, but is rather a translation of that experience into new categories and evaluations. It can only arise within meaning or a system of signs, and is inevitably ideologically informed.[37] The redoubling of the other's experience within me is impossible because of the distinct locations of bodies in dialogical encounter. Because of this, the phenomenological enterprise of mapping other's experience within my consciousness is not possible without reinterpretation and recategorization: the utterance of the dialogic partner must be interpreted from my perspective, it must be a response from a location.

The concept of utterance is central to Bakhtin's project. In perhaps his most famous essay outlining his theory of language 'Discourse in the Novel', published in Russia in 1975, he writes:

> The living utterance, having taken meaning and shape at a particular historical moment in a socially specific environment, cannot fail to brush up against thousands of living dialogic threads, woven by socio-ideological consciousness around the given object of an utterance; it cannot fail to become an active participant in social dialogue. After all, the utterance arises out of this dialogue as a continuation of it and as rejoinder to it – it does not approach the object from the sidelines.[38]

At the heart of all dialogue is 'utterance'; a speech act occurring in a language within a specific social, cultural and historical situation. Utterance occurs within a context and reaches out towards an answer. In its simplest form, utterance comes from a person and is directed at another and, indeed, directed towards, in anticipation of, the other's answer. But utterance also 'brushes up' against the 'thousands of living dialogic threads'; it assumes preceding dialogues, echoes other dialogues and reaches into the future. Dialogism is the discipline of understanding the interconnection of utterances or their intertextuality. The meaning of an utterance is dependent upon the meaning of other utterances and indeed, there can be no utterance without a relation to others.[39] Rather like the web of Brahma in which the drops of water at each of the intersection points of the threads reflect all the others, so utterance *in order to be utterance*, reflects other utterances. Kristeva understands this to mean that any text is a mosaic of quotations and a transformation of previous texts:[40] all texts reflect a diversity of discourse or heterology (*raznorecie*), which is also termed the diversity of language or 'heteroglossia' (*raznojayzycie*). At one

156

level, dialogism is understanding intertextuality or the interrelation of utterances, at another it is simply dialogue, a conversation between two people.

This tendency in the intertextuality of discourse towards unending diversity and fragmentation or heteroglossia, Bakhtin calls the 'centrifugal force' (*centrobeznyi*), contrasted with the opposing tendency towards the centralization of meaning, the 'centripetal force' (*centrostremitel'nyi*). In every concrete utterance both forces occur:

> The processes of centralization and decentralization, of unification and disunification, intersect in the utterance ... Every utterance participates in the 'unitary language' (in its centripetal forces and tendencies) and at the same time partakes in social and historical heteroglossia (the centrifugal, stratifying forces).[41]

Discourse is therefore riven with tension and contradiction inherent within it, the centripetal force tending towards unified, clear meaning, giving voice to a dominant, powerful ideology and social group, the centrifugal force tending towards difference, ambiguity and allowing other voices to speak, and other, subversive ideas and subaltern social groups to be expressed. In his study of the history of the novel, Bakhtin demonstrates these tendencies, arguing that the genre of the novel (as realized supremely in Dostoyevsky) and its antecedents expresses heteroglossia, and is genuinely dialogic (expressed in themes such as the carnival), in contrast to poetry and the epic which tend towards monologue and the articulation of a dominant ideology. Ultimately all discourse is dialogic to some degree, though some discourse, such as Dostoyevsky's work, is explicitly 'double-voiced'; utterances expressing double and hidden meanings, expressing diverse world-views, and moving against the centripetal tendencies of the dominant discourse in late nineteenth-century Russia. These forces are in all language. Indeed, the disciplines of linguistics, stylistics and the philosophy of language have been, according to Bakhtin, shaped by the centralizing tendencies in language which ignore heteroglossia, and which therefore cannot understand the dialogic nature of language, emphasizing instead an ahistorical, static structure abstracted from the life of divergent discourse.[42] Disciplines such as linguistics, particularly as articulated by Saussure, have 'served the great centralizing tendencies of European verbal-ideological life' in seeking unity in diversity. Such tendencies in concentrating on elements of language such as the phonetic, have moved far from the semantic aspects of discourse which are always embedded in a social matrix and are always hetero-gossic. Bakhtin sees his task as counterbalancing these unifying, static tendencies which cut themselves off from the plural voices of actual discourse and the social reality which makes up language and occurs in concrete, historical circumstances.

Dialogism is therefore more than merely a description of human interactions or interactions with the diverse voices of texts. It is a theory of knowledge and a theory of language as understood in its historical specificity: knowledge arises within language through the dialogical encounter. In his influential distinction between language as an abstract system (*langue*) understood synchronically, and speech (*parole*), utterances apprehended diachronically, Saussure had empha-sized the synchronic, abstract system in developing the science of linguistics.[43] But in emphasizing language as an abstract system sus-ceptible to scientific analysis as its object, Saussure rejects speech or particularized utterance, which for Bakhtin is to miss the most impor-tant point about language, that it lives as communication in the diachronic mode of utterance.[44] This initial critique of Saussurean linguistics occurs in the early text, *Marxism and the Philosophy of Language* (1929), written by Voloshinov, one of Bakhtin's associates, which offers a materialist interpretation of signification (or language as a system).[45] This text attempts to move between the 'abstract objectivism' of Saussure on the one hand, and the romantic 'individu-alistic subjectivism' from Humboldt to the Russian representative of this tradition, Karl Vossler, on the other. The system of language emphasized by Saussure and studied by the objectifying science of linguistics, stands in contrast to utterance emphasized by Bakhtin, understood through the dialogic process. Whereas Saussure's linguistics sees language as a system of structural relations, Bakhtin hears voices in everything 'and dialogic relations among them'.[46]

Hearing voices everywhere is to hear the unique, non-reiterative utterance of speech acts in context. Whereas Saussure is not interested in the contexts in which speech occurs, indeed, he is only concerned with abstract language as a system of signification (and in this respect he differs from Peirce), Bakhtin is acutely aware of the dialogical nature of language and the historical and linguistic construction of subjects. Similarly for Voloshinov, every linguistic sign (a term not used by Bakhtin) is 'constructed between socially organized persons' and only exists in the context of dialogue.[47] Utterance assumes the wider community in which it takes place and it is because of the wider context of dialogue that non-repeatable utterances can be the object of scientific investigation. In analysing the abstract system of language, Saussurian linguistics ignores the particularity of utterances and the contexts in which they occur, yet in investigating utterance, which is to say investigating 'texts' in a broad sense, dialogics is not merely investigating particular, individual meaning, but rather the transindividual realm of the social order. Utterance within texts occurs, always, within the social realm, and can be called 'discourse'. And it is types of discourse, particularly within the history of literature, that Bakhtin primarily investigates.

The model which Bakhtin presents of understanding discourse through dialogical encounter has implications and applications beyond those of literary history to which Bakhtin largely devoted himself. Dialogism can become a model for understanding wider cultural processes and for the social sciences.[48] Indeed, dialogism as expressed by Bakhtin is a way of avoiding the objectivism of natural science which seeks causal explanations of behaviour and reduction to 'nature', and subjectivism which only accepts the interior perspective of the text or discourse. In dialogism we therefore have a fruitful way to develop an understanding of the range of cultural utterances we call 'religion' which avoids the Scylla of an objectivist reductionism and the Charybdis of subjective, insider accounts. The range of cultural texts and practices we call 'religions', open to social scientific inquiry, are open as dialogical encounter. Understanding and explanation of religion from a social scientific perspective inevitably entail an ideological context in which interpretation takes place, though a perspective which is changed in dialogue with its 'object', the 'data' under consideration, or person being spoken to.

Live-entering and empathy

Dialogism provides a very different model of understanding from Husserl's philosophy of consciousness. Rather than the world and people within it being phenomena or appearances which are then penetrated through bracketing, the eidetic reduction and empathy, the world and communication are the starting points with the recognition of my embodied nature in a historical context. For Husserl empathy (*Einfühlung*) is a way for the transcendental ego to go beyond itself and access others behind appearances. For Bakhtin, by contrast, we do

159

not begin with transcendental subjectivity, but rather with communication in which the 'I' is the product of a process of self-creation in interaction or dialogue with the 'other' in a historically located world. There is no need of empathy, in Husserl's sense, for understanding. But Bakhtin does develop the parallel concept of 'live-entering' (*vzhivanie*) which occurs within the dialogical process and which has antecedents in the history of social thought, particularly in Dilthey and Lipps, who also influenced Husserl.

For Dilthey the human sciences (*Geisteswissenschaften*) are to be distinguished from the natural sciences (*Naturswissenschaften*) through the understanding (*Verstehen*) of expression and action. This understanding, at least initially for Dilthey, is by reliving (*nacherleben*) the mental states of others which are inferred on the basis of our own experience, though Dilthey later refined this model by locating human expressions within a framework of linguistic meaning, which is itself embedded within wider cultural forces.[49] In the idea of reliving the experience of others, Dilthey is echoing the founding father of the science of society, Vico, who thought we could penetrate historical traditions through an imaginative entering into the modes of consciousness which produced them.[50] Empathy (*Einfühlung*) is a term which became important in a theoretical context in the nineteenth century with the German philosopher Theodor Lipps,[51] and Husserl developed his own interpretation which he related to intuition and intersubjectivity. For Husserl, empathy is the penetration of the 'object' by consciousness; an intuition in which the object is actually reached and immediately apprehended or possessed by an intentional consciousness.[52] Intuition which penetrates or reaches its object is therefore distinguished by Husserl from a 'signifying act' which refers to representation within consciousness. Both intuition and signifying acts might aim at the same object, but they differ in the degree to which they penetrate the object. In intuition there is contact with reality, an experience, whereas there is no experience with the pure thought, or representation, of signifying acts. As Levinas observes, a signifying act only thinks about an object, whereas an intuition 'gives us something of the object itself'; intuition is thus not necessarily opposed to thought or intellection, but rather, as Levinas comments, 'is an act which possesses its object'.[53] In possessing its object, intuition possesses a 'fullness' (*Fülle*) in contrast to the 'emptiness' of merely signifying acts.[54]

This understanding of empathy must be seen in the context of

160

Husserl's whole philosophy of consciousness. The penetration of an object through intuition as part of the structure of intentionality is, for Husserl, an actual touching or experiencing of the object and not merely an occurrence in thought. Through empathy there is a real contact with others and with the given world, arrived at indirectly through bracketing and intuition. In this way intuition is identified by Husserl with intersubjectivity. Empathy is the intuition of the other understood as intersubjectivity. In the context of repudiating the accusation of solipsism in the fifth *Cartesian Meditation*, Husserl, as we have seen, tackles the problem of intersubjectivity and the idea of the *alter ego* in relation to 'me'. The problem is, given the reduction to the transcendental ego, how can the accusation of solipsism be avoided?[55]

Husserl circumvents the problem in two ways, firstly by describing how the ego experiences others: as humans in the world, as subjects who experience the same world as oneself, and as subjects who experience oneself, as oneself experiences them. (This of course begs many questions such as how is it possible, given Husserl's egology, to *know* that others experience the world as oneself?) Secondly, in a more promising direction he circumvents the problem through the idea of another self intuited in intersubjectivity, beyond transcendental subjectivity. The temporal community of other selves, so intuited, forms a *cultural* community. All selves exist for themselves as monads while yet existing in communion, with intentionality towards each other: '(s)omething that exists is in intentional communion with something else that exists'.[56] At this level of communion there is a mutual recognition of 'being for one another' which Husserl calls an 'objectivating equalization', that is, my own understanding of the other's perception of myself as another. This perception is an intercommunion and a knowing that the other is constituted by a self which perceives others (perceiving oneself), also designated by Husserl as 'transcendental intersubjectivity'.[57] This mutual comprehension of egos in transcendental intersubjectivity is empathy; a cognitive, intuitive penetration of another's being.

From a dialogical perspective, Husserl's ideas of empathy, intuition, and the life-world are deeply problematic. Although Steinbock in a far-reaching study claims that dialogical philosophies do not challenge Husserl's basic structure articulated in the Fifth Meditation,[58] it seems to me rather, that they fundamentally challenge the Husserlian scheme on account of a quite distinct view of intersubjectivity. From the

161

perspective of dialogism, Husserl's empathy or intuition of the *alter ego* can be critiqued, first because it does not take account of communication and active understanding, secondly because it does not take into account the historicity of the understanding encounter, and thirdly it cannot deal with conflict, or the other's being closed to empathic penetration. Let us look at these three problems of communication, historicity and conflict.

THE PROBLEM OF COMMUNICATION

Rather than a process of my penetrating in empathy a distant other, and from that, inferring a shared world through appreciation of the subjectivity behind the seen body, from a dialogical perspective such a process is unnecessary, for the other is already given in the dialogic encounter. For Husserl the process of empathy is one in which the solitary ego understands the intersubjectivity of 'transcendental egos' or 'monads', but it is an empathy which occurs in intuition and not in real communication. As Gadamer says, Husserl's empathy is 'still oriented to the interiority of self-consciousness and fails to orient itself toward the full circle of life . . . '[59] This line of criticism has indeed been developed within phenomenology itself in going beyond Husserl's understanding of the relationship between the 'homeworld' (*Heimat*) and 'alienworld' (*Fremdewelt*). Recent scholars have explored this relationship and offered fresh readings of Husserl's later works. David Carr has stressed the idea of 'community' rather than the 'ego' in understanding Husserl's problematic,[60] and Anthony Steinbock has developed a 'generative phenomenology', also using the work of Klaus Held, in which the homeworld is 'our world' rather than that of the solitary ego.[61] We have already seen how for Steinbock Husserl's account is a 'transcendental silence' (p. 109). These recent phenomenological accounts are more compatible with dialogism, but still find it difficult to move away from the Husserlian problematic.

The silence of Husserl's intersubjectivity contrasts sharply with the many voices of Bakhtin's dialogism. For Bakhtin dialogical encounter makes empathy possible as the projection of myself into another. Such a projection and experiencing what the other experiences must always be constrained by limits, for I can never completely lose myself or become the other. This projection – especially important in aesthetic appreciation[62] – or 'live-entering' (*vzhivanie*), Bakhtin contrasts with empathy (*Einfühlung*) in which there is a total merging and experiencing of the other from the other's place. For Bakhtin this would be the momentary eradication of the self, whereas in live-entering I enter the other's place while maintaining my own place, without losing for a moment my place outside of the other individual.[63] We cannot experience another's suffering as our own – this would be anesthetizing and pathological for Bakhtin, merely a doubling of suffering – but we can creatively respond from the outside: 'When I project myself into another's suffering, I experience it precisely as *his* suffering ...'[64] In his contrast between empathy and live-entering, Bakhtin regards empathy as a passive understanding which attempts to reproduce in consciousness what is already there outside of it. Live-entering, by contrast, is a creative understanding in which something new is produced through the dialogic interaction of self and other and so is a form of communication. For Husserl empathy is a solitary, cognitive, imaginative act (*Einfühlung* does not have the affective connotation of the English 'empathy'), whereas for Bakhtin live-entering is a communicative, immediate experience involving simultaneity but also spatial distinction and the distinction of persons within the dialogical triad of 'I', 'other' and their relationship.

THE PROBLEM OF HISTORICITY

In contrast to Husserl's intuition, Bakhtin's dialogical encounter is always embedded within history. Bakhtin is acutely aware of historical processes which affect consciousness and indeed, his live-entering into a past historical event entails an aesthetic visualization of that person situated in her historical context. For Bakhtin the understanding between self (*svoi*) and other (*drugoi*) is through the historicized, communicative encounter which above all else means through language. Language as communication in a social and historical context is the given, rather than a transcendental, prelinguistic ego. This criticism of ahistoricism can be levelled against Husserl, whom Bakhtin and Voloshinov mention but do not systematically critique. Furthermore, all historically situated speech has an evaluative accent, and all utterance entails a value judgement (and so is ideological) from within a social perspective. Indeed the attempted separation of word meaning from evaluation, such as occurs in phenomenology, is an attempt to create a philosophy divorced from temporality, 'divorced from the historical process of becoming'.[65] It is various, conflicting, evaluative contexts which create semantic shifts within dialogue and language and which generate the energy of the dialogic encounter. The conflict of evaluative modes given in particular historical circumstances (related to wider issues of economics and social change) leads to transformations in linguistic meaning and the development of dialogue which, of course, can have no end or final resolution.

THE PROBLEM OF CONFLICT

For Husserl, the intuition of the *alter ego* is the understanding of the identity of the structure of intentional consciousness within two subjectivities who perceive one another as distinct locations. Communication is here of little importance and, because of this the conflict of meanings, or indeed, interpersonal conflict in the social world, is not relevant to the phenomenological project of empathic intuition, even though Husserl does admit that life-worlds are essentially shared. For Husserl, self and other, although ontologically distinct, share an identity in their respective spheres of 'ownness'. The intentional structure of consciousness revealed in the phenomenological reductions is universally the same; a universality which thereby circumvents the problem of interpersonal – or intertextual – conflict. Such levelling or universalizing tendencies in Husserl's phenomenology are absent in Bakhtin's dialogism. Indeed, conflict is entailed in the dialogic encounter of different voices at both interpersonal and intertextual levels. 'Deep conversation' involves a process in which conflict is confronted and resolved. There is, of course, the possibility and actuality of the non-resolution of conflict, but whereas phenomenology cannot adequately address this, for its enterprise is primarily descriptive, dialogism entails an ethical commitment to conversation. Whereas phenomenology sees first philosophy as grounded within consciousness, within the *cogito*, dialogism sees first philosophy as grounded in the communicative encounter; it is the communicative encounter, which may entail conflict, and recognition of alterity that marks dialogism off from the egology of phenomenology.

Levinas, in a paper that marks an important shift away from Husserlian phenomenology and that criticizes the monopoly of a metaphysics of presence in Western thought, comments that first philosophy as self-consciousness attempts to assert its 'place in the sun' as the 'usurpation of spaces belonging to the other man, whom I have already oppressed or starved or driven out into a third world ...'.[66] Empathy for Husserl is integrated into his philosophy of consciousness and brings with it the model of transcendental subjectivity locked into its world of appearances and only through empathy breaking into intersubjectivity. Bakhtin's dialogism, on the other hand, sees live-entering as the mechanism within the dialogical encounter in which I can project into another, while yet inevitably maintaining my distinction and embodied location. How then, is this related to the study of religions?

Empathy is a key term in the phenomenology of religion, derived from Husserl via Scheler and Van der Leeuw, and reinforced through the Schliermachian emphasis on locating religion in feeling rather than will or cognition. In contrast to the physicist who places himself at a distance from the object of study, the historian and psychologist should, says Van der Leeuw, make every effort to penetrate into the object through empathy which is the 'transposing of oneself into the object or re-experiencing it'.[67] Such as transposing of the self into the object is not to perceive it in its spatio-temporal actuality but to understand its inner truth. It is to 'contemplate the essence of the phenomena, and not to comprehend their factual existence ... [The phenomenologist] analyses in an intuitive, or in a rational manner; he is concerned not with empirically comprehensible events, but with events that are directly intelligible in their general being.'[68] Such empathy or the transposing of the self into its object occurs through phenomenological analysis and the discerning of the essence from what is not the essence. Van der Leeuw is here directly adopting the classical phenomenological understanding of *Einfühlung* from Husserl and has wholly adopted, as we have seen, the method developed in philosophical phenomenology. This idea of empathy, walking a mile in another's moccasins, has had wide influence in the non-confessional study of religion. Ninian Smart characterizes the practice of contemporary religionists as 'the use of *epoché* or suspension of belief, together with the use of empathy in entering into the experiences and intentions of religious participants'. This is an attitude of 'informed empathy' which 'tries to bring out what religious acts mean to the actors'.[69]

While this understanding of empathy contains many Husserlian assumptions (about transcendental subjectivity, about disengaged reason, and about freedom from values), the image of moccasin walking is potentially a dialogical image. The Husserlian legacy implies that the religionist is the detached observer who crosses the boundary between self and other through the conscious act of empathy: re-enacts in imagination the other who is the object of inquiry, without imposing judgements, and retreats back into transcendental silence. This is the reconstitution of the other's experience within the self. Such a reconstitution is, in Bakhtinian terms, a 'passive understanding' which ignores the social and historical contingencies which shape and control experience. While there can be a partial entering into the other through imagination, there is still the inescapable 'standing without' which is standing within one's own historical circumstances, but meeting the other in the dialogical situation. While empathy remains static, trying to relive the experience of the other and placing both subject and object outside of a spatio-temporal world, dialogism and live-entering move on to actively establish new meanings in new social and historical contexts which constantly arise. Empathy in the Husserlian and phenomenological sense implies closure of analysis, a passive reconstruction of knowledge (which is anyway impossible), whereas dialogism implies openness and ongoing exploration in the context of particular locations and views which cannot be decontextualized. In one sense this is to take moccasin walking very seriously, though perhaps the more accurate image is walking alongside in open dialogue in which a discourse is produced in the interaction of self and other. In the social scientific study of religion this discourse or conversation, might be the critical construction or emplotment of the narrative in which the other is embedded.

Religion, dialogue and narrative

Dialogism seeks to reconcile the gap, explored in the previous chapter, between 'life' and 'narrative' or rather to allow both realism and constructivism. A number of texts attempt to bring together these positions,[70] but it is Bakhtin's dialogism which effectively demonstrates the ways in which told narratives are produced from the lived narratives of human, historically situated experience. Apart from the implicit critique of the phenomenology of consciousness, Bakhtin's ideas are important in the understanding of religion primarily for three reasons. First, because Bakhtin provides a methodology in the social sciences and humanities which does not rely on the deeply problematic

166

model of the natural sciences. In developing a method which promotes the 'dialogical' understanding of utterance, Bakhtin promotes the idea of stepping into the 'object' while simultaneously maintaining a remaining outside the object; an idea not dissimilar to 'empathy' in religious studies discourse, though which rejects the idea of epistemic privilege implied by its use in that context. Secondly, Bakhtin is important because he stresses the contextualized nature of all utterance, including the utterances of scholarship, and developed what has become known as a pragmatic understanding of language; an understanding which is directly relevant to the study of texts and behaviour. Thirdly, the dialogic enterprise in forging a way between objectivism and subjectivism, reveals an ethic which develops out of the dialogic encounter and which can be used in resolving the tension between semantic relativism and the ethics of the intellectual practice of understanding.

The inquiry into utterance shows the centrality of narrative in so far as chains of utterance form narratives. Critical inquiry from a dialogical perspective occurs between rival inquirers, which, in the case of religion refers to the emic inquiry of the tradition itself and the etic inquiries of competing social scientific claims to explanation. Dialogism shows that we do not live outside of narrative: the narratives of religion function within the constraints of revelation, cosmology and soteriology, whereas the narratives of social science function within the constraints of rationality and empiricism. For dialogism, knowledge is generated through the interaction of inquirer and object of inquiry, a process in which the epistemic subject is not a detached but a situated observer, reflexively aware of reasons for a particular research programme. Dialogical research is accountable research. To regard the sciences and academic discourses as narratives is to place them in their own historical and social context as well as to undermine the privileged position which they claim. Eugene d'Aquili, following Rappaport,[71] has made a distinction between a cognized environment and an operational environment.[72] The cognized environment is a worldview, the belief system of a people who act within it, in contrast to the objective, operational environment which directly affects a person's survival and which is accessible through, for example, anthropological or biological analysis. The operational environment is the 'real' environment which constrains the cognized environment. However narrative analysis and dialogism show that even the objectivist operational environment which is constructed through observation and measurement of empirical entities, is itself a cognized environment; the emic narrative of an objectivist science.

Summary

The question of objectivity in the social sciences has been put into question in recent years. The present chapter has continued the critique of the phenomenological philosophy of consciousness and epistemic privilege, from the perspective of dialogism. Rather than the detached observer viewing and mapping data, free from value judgements, I have argued that the observer is always situated and embodied, within a specific, historical context, in a relationship of dialogue with the 'object' – in fact fellow 'subjects' – of inquiry. The relationship between inquirer and people enquired about, or, indeed, tradition, is one of dialogue in which communication and inter-subjectivity, rather than the certainty of consciousness, are given. If the epistemic subject is situated in a particular, historical location, in a particular body, then understanding is dialogical and critically evaluative. The problems of rationality which arises out of this position – how can we formulate criteria of judgement for the assessment of public knowledge claims? – and the problem of the compatibility of dialogism with the need to explain macro-problems of social and cultural formation, will be the subject of the next chapter. The correlative problem of the ethics of inquiry in a postmodern world will follow in chapter eight, in which we shall examine more closely the question running through the present text, of 'how can we understand another?' and its implied Levinasian answer, 'by not effacing them'.

7. Text, language and truth

While the central project of Husserl, as we have seen, was the descriptive enterprise of mapping appearances that has been so important in the phenomenology of religion, Husserl was also concerned with ontology. The existence of the world beyond appearances, however, could not be accessed from the phenomenological attitude because of the suspension of questions of objective truth, although ontological questions could, of course, be posed in the natural sciences which take their stance in the natural attitude.[1] Husserl seems content to relegate an investigation of an ontology of the natural world to natural science, though only as a consequence of the phenomenological process; reality, as it were, being given back to the world after its suspension in the *epoché*. But in spite of Husserl's quoting Augustine at the end of the *Cartesian Meditations* that truth dwells in the inner man, a statement in complete concordance with his transcendental subjectivity, Husserl does not develop the possibility of giving back reality to religious appearances. John Bowker observes that while the existence of 'God' as an appearance to consciousness is bracketed out in the phenomenological process, Husserl does not face the question as to whether such appearances simply give rise to the sense of God, or 'whether they are the sense of God', though Husserl did begin to ponder this question at the end of his life,[2] thereby taking a route towards a ground of being – as in so much else – directly parallel to Fichte.

The problem of religious truth (I am assuming that truth and ontology are coterminous) has been deferred, not only in the present text but in the phenomenological method, and will be so again here but via a different route. The question of truth in religions is relevant to a metatheoretical inquiry only in so far as, on one line of thinking, the truth of a religious statement or claim within a religious tradition will affect the theory of religion. This chapter will argue that the question of truth needs to be reformulated in tradition-specific terms and, from the perspective of religious studies, becomes a question of coherence and the representation or transmission of systems of signification and communication through the generations. That is, any crude formulation of the problem of truth as a question of accessing some unmediated, pristine reality is rejected. I wish to propose that the question of religious truth for the inquiry into religions, become a question of language and interpretation within tradition-specific or narrative boundaries.

To support this claim I do not intend to rehearse old arguments about rationality, but rather first to suggest that any understanding of truth as representation sheared of context is simply a recontextualization of claims in a different system. Secondly, this implies that the inquiry into religious truth is an inquiry into language, specifically narratives of traditions and the processes of their replication, a theme which takes up again the critique of the philosophy of consciousness by the philosophy of the sign. The implication of this is that one of the primary tasks of the study of religions is therefore an inquiry into the ways in which truth-embodying narratives (texts) are transmitted through the generations and even across cultures. I wish to argue that a dialogical approach to language, particularly as developed in linguistic anthropology, offers crucial insights into cultural and religious replication. Thirdly, in contrast to the transcendental subjectivity entailed by phenomenology, the dialogical analysis of cultural replication entails a dynamic, interactive view of subjectivity constructed in utterance. This kind of analysis therefore has relevance beyond methodology, for a view of self and other that is semiologically grounded. A dialogical religious studies does not contain an implicit philosophy of consciousness, as does the phenomenology of religion, but an implicit ontology of self-in-relation.

The question of truth

The question concerning the ontological status of religious appearances to consciousness is, naturally, a compelling and important one, but an impossible question in the study of religions when approached from a perspective that claims neutrality and assumes the detached

170

privilege of the epistemic subject. From both the phenomenological and the hermeneutical perspectives the question of the ontological status of religious appearances, which can be taken to be the question of the truth of religious propositions in so far as existence entails truth, cannot be asked outside of specific contexts and traditions. The path through this thorny problem is, for me, stated in bald terms, to argue for the total contextualization of religious truth within language and tradition and to disclaim any privileged access to the question, for example on empirical grounds. The truth value of religious language that is metaphysical (and does not make empirical claims subjected to contradiction by strong counter-evidence) cannot be recognized by criteria of truth brought in from another discourse, particularly a scientific one.[3] Metaphysical truths proclaimed by a religious tradition are internal to the tradition and can be understood in terms of coherence within given frameworks and their significance within those frameworks. The question of significance rather than truth, as Rouse has argued in the context of science, is the more fundamental issue,[4] and the question of origin and function more germane to a social scientific method. We cannot assert or deny the central truth claims of any tradition from a position of neutral, rational privilege, in the same way that we cannot ask whether a poem is true. This is, of course, based on the contention that the central doctrinal claims of religions are not empirical claims, at least in the late twentieth century. It could, of course, be argued that poetry does not make claims about reality, as religions do, but the general point is that the major, metaphysical claims of religions are not open to scientific inquiry. It is far from clear, for example, what the grounds could be whereby the invisible, super-natural objects of a religious discourse could be ascertained to be 'true' or 'real' or, on the contrary, 'disproved'. A naturalist research pro-gramme would, of course, assume their falsity, an assumption which is coherent within certain research frames of reference, but no more. Let me give some examples of religious truth as tradition-specific.

It is simply incoherent to ask about the truth of *nibbāna* outside of a Theravāda Buddhist context: whether *nibbāna* is true could have no meaning outside the tradition because it is a term, and indeed a Buddhist experience textually instantiated over generations, that makes sense only within the Buddhist tradition. The term has no meaning outside of that tradition and conceptual framework. In speaking of *nibbāna* we are speaking of a term within Buddhist discourse found in the narratives of the Pali canon and a goal which –

at some level – constrains the individual life-ways of millions of Buddhists. The ideology of *nibbāna* articulates with Buddhist ritual practices, ethical behaviour and meditation. The verification, or falsification, of the truth of *nibbāna* could *only* occur within the framework of a Buddhist soteriology. This is not to claim that there can be no translation between cultures or traditions, indeed the term 'nirvana' is now within popular English where it is recontextualized and embedded within a wholly new context to be roughly equivalent to 'happiness'. Similarly the Christian Orthodox concept of *theosis*, the divinization of the human being, can only be understood within the narratives of Orthodoxy in which the human can become divine, as the divine became human in Christ, and within the binding practices of liturgy and prayer. To ask whether *theosis* could be true outside of that context is meaningless. Let me give one last example. In certain Kerala rituals in which deities are invoked in songs, though are not physically present, it is pointless inquiring as to whether the objects of the nouns and pronouns used are 'really there'. What is far more interesting and important from the perspective of an externalist social science is the *function* of such language within the ritual context and the ways in which such language constructs the participants' identities. Indeed, external perspectives can only examine the function of truth claims – the function of *nibbāna* in the Theravāda context, of *theosis* in Orthodoxy, and of the deity in Hindu Kerala – within a tradition-specific framework. It becomes meaningless to inquire into the truth of these concepts outside of their cultural function, though that function can be critiqued from an external perspective (such as Marxism).

This kind of historicism is broadly to remove religious truth-claims from the field of scientific inquiry and to recognize the contextual nature of that inquiry. It is, indeed, an argument that the translation of concepts between cultures is really very difficult if not impossible, but not an argument for a strong form of incommensurability, for it is certainly possible to learn another religious language and furthermore this language can be recontextualized and reformulated in new contexts.[5] But to ask about the truth of *nibbāna* or of *theosis* from an external, supposedly epistemically neutral standpoint, is in fact to recontextualize the concepts within another framework with its own rules of coherence. Such recontextualizing, while it might be interesting from the within the recontextualizing episteme, tells us nothing about those terms within the traditions of their occurrence, nor about the human experiences to which they are said to refer. Undoubtedly the truth claim of *nibbāna* is a motivating factor in many (though by no means all) Theravāda Buddhists' lives and we need to ask, not whether *nibbāna* is true, but rather how does *nibbāna* feed in to Buddhist practice, how are the texts which speak of *nibbāna* pragmatically effective and how does *nibbāna* function in Buddhist discourse? The truth value of the claim about *nibbāna* – or any religious goal – is not ratiocinative outside the tradition. The question of the truth of religious claims is impossible to answer from an objectivist viewpoint. Existence claims cannot be divorced from the contexts of their occurrence, a point made by Smart long ago,[6] or rather any abstraction of existence claims is a recontextualization or reformulation of those claims in different terms. The question of whether *nibbāna* 'really exists' or whether the gods are 'really there' is a question of whether they are 'really there for us'.

One objection to the model I am proposing could be that religious traditions make empirical claims that conflict with the empirical claims of science. Indeed, in the history of the West before the rise of science, the claims of religion were taken to be empirical claims. Christian accounts of creation, with the exception of some thinkers such as Eckhart,[7] were regarded as being true in a literal rather than an empirical sense. With the rise of science and its staggering explanatory power, religious claims became generally restricted to metaphysical claims. In such cases where religions continue to make empirical claims, it might be argued that it would be quite legitimate to make a judgement about their truth or error if they conflict with empirically established, scientific claims. Indeed, there has been a long and painful history in the West of such conflicts, and frequent instances of conflicting truth claims are found in the contemporary world. The empirical claim of the Hare Krishna movement that meat-eating Americans could not have landed on the moon in 1969, is evidently false in the realm of historical action, but can be understood and seen to be coherent from within the history of the movement's theology in which the moon is regarded as a pure, sacred place. Or the claims of Sai Baba or his followers that he can magically produce material objects and perform other miracles, is open to empirical investigation (such as whether he belongs to a caste of magicians) but not the claim that his more important work is the disciple's inner or spiritual transformation. Regarding cases in which empirically testable claims are made, a judgement is required inevitably based upon rational criteria for acceding to or denying the claim. A religious, empirical claim faces the

173

problem of contradiction in the face of counter-evidence. There are more problematic cases than this in which metaphysical claims begin to intrude upon the publicly testable. Associated with *theosis*, for example, is a phenomenon of light, such as light emanating from the face of a saint, which could arguably be susceptible to a truth or falsity claim on empirical grounds, though the broader claims of Orthodoxy regarding *theosis* are unaffected either way. While this is a deeply problematic area, the main point is that the major metaphysical truths of religious traditions – truths which became metaphysical with the development of science – are outside of scientific inquiry.

In spite of the rise of science and the deep questioning of the status of religious truth claims, religions have not died out. This suggests that truth claims in religions are performing a function unrelated to scientific investigation. Religious truth claims are, I would argue, most importantly about religious, personal or community identity, perhaps perceived to be under threat, and form part of a framework, part of the rhetoric of a tradition, within which an individual or group formulates their life-objectives and organizes their time. Religious truths are part of the narratives which inform and constrain the lives of religious people. This is an important point for the majority of religious claims are beyond the pale of verification or falsification from an external, empirical perspective. As we have seen, the entire rationalist tradition from the Enlightenment might be read as the critique of religion as the history of error. But as the 'sea of faith' subsides from the realms of scientific empiricism, most religious truth claims are removed outside of the scientific, empirical realm and the question of truth in religion becomes a question of how truth-claims function within tradition. To view religious language and religious propositions as making verifiably empirical claims is, in my view, methodologically mistaken if the aim of inquiry is understanding or explaining religion.

To separate the question of truth from its contexts as a question of empiricism, is to embed the question within a different context; in the very act of reformulating the question of being, of abstracting it, we are simultaneously re-embedding it or reframing it in other terms. Rather than the question of truth outside of context, the question of the process of the translation of truth-claims from one context to another demands our attention and takes us in a different, more fruitful direction. The question of truth becomes a question of representation within traditions. Given that it is impossible to assess the truth or falsity of religious truth-claims except in those cases where an empirical claim is contradicted by counter-evidence, there are never-theless questions about transmission which can legitimately and fruitfully be asked (and answered). In other words truth becomes a cultural trope, and the question of truth becomes subordinated to the question of representation, to questions of cultural transmission, and to questions about the formation and re-formation of tradition.

The transmission of tradition

The truths of religious traditions, or more specifically the communities who hold those truths, are their self-representations. These representa-tions are both transmitted through the generations and constantly reformulated in the temporal instances of their occurrence. While cognition is no doubt important in this process, it is primarily in the representation or imitation of sign-systems (the systems of commu-nication and signification) in the history of communities that is paramount. The success or survival of tradition in late modernity would seem to be the degree to which tradition adapts its representa-tions to the modern world and processes of globalization. The response to modernity could mean the demise of tradition, on the one hand through the erosion of its boundaries in total accommodation to modernity, on the other through a shoring up of its boundaries in an attempt to keep back the tides of the present. Alternatively, traditions can ensure continuity through the necessary appropriation of moder-nity, in terms of technology for example, while at the same time rejecting late modern ideologies (as can be seen in fundamentalist Islam). The degree to which a tradition is either formed through 'retention', the immediate inheritance of primary remembrance, the 'retained past' in Ricoeur's terms, or due to 'recollection', the con-struction of the past or 'reproduced past',[8] is disputed (see the discussion of the nature of narrative as lived or told in chapter 5). From an emic perspective, traditions will regard their recollections as retentions, even though it might be shown from a critically distant or historical perspective, that traditions are engaged in a constant recon-struction of their pasts, their self-representations, and in their re-evaluation in contemporary contexts.

The truths and values of any tradition are reformulated and repack-aged to meet the needs of fresh generations. Paul Morris has convincingly argued with particular reference to Judaism, how the detraditionalization accompanying the rise of modernity and the foregrounding of the individual, is paralleled by retraditionalization in which the past is 'invented (re-membered) to suit current purposes'.[9] For example, the past of modern Jewish communities was constructed in response to the granting of citizenship rights after the French Revolution, and the creation of a Judaism compatible with modern citizenship, education and a professional life. This reconstruction, Morris notes, was either prejudicial in constructing the past negatively as a time of isolation, or romantically as a model of community providing security. Contemporary calls for a return to tradition are in fact a call for a return to the tradition as it was in the nineteenth century. Morris observes that '(a)s a tradition undergoes detraditionalization, its 'past' becomes frozen, as it were, in its retraditionalized ('premodern') form'.[10] The recollection of tradition means that truths are constructed in tradition-specific ways, in response to the competing truths of the ideological marketplace and, since the rise of modernity, to liberal individualism.

Tradition is intimately linked to the idea of community as a group of people that inherits tradition, or is constrained by a set of binding narratives and behaviours. In another sense a community as a local, face-to-face or geographically restricted entity might inherit different traditions and so be bound by different values and texts. As has been so evident in recent history, this situation can lead to extremes of violence and ethnic conflict. It is therefore important to remember that recollection of the past or of narratives of identity for the reconstituted tradition or imagined community, is not imaginary. The term 'represent' corresponds within traditions to a truth-claim and, as Ricoeur observes, recollection is distinguished here from imagination 'by the positional value (*Setzung*) attached to recollection but absent from imagination'.[11] These forms of representation, reconstituted in each generation, are regenerated by tradition-bound social actors who replicate forms of action through mimesis. Tradition is inscribed on the body through ritual behaviour, cultural gestures, and, indeed, by all systems of signification (even cooking) and passed on through imitation. As we shall see in more detail presently, imitation is the identification of the self with another within a frame of discourse. These routinized forms of behaviour subordinate individual action to tradition (which for Weber and others is not meaningful, in contrast with the meaningful, intentional actions of the modern subject).[12]

Although the imitation or mimesis of action is central in the transmission of tradition, or in some cases its reconstruction and invention, it is above all the transmission of texts, the narratives of origin and identity, that is of particular importance in traditions' boundary maintenance. Texts are often performed and it is in performance that cultural transmission occurs through the identification of the everyday self – or the referential 'I' – with the self of the narrative in varying degrees (see below). Rather than any truth-claims contained within texts, it is the process of their transmission and their reinterpretation in each generation that become the more important focus of the inquiry into religion. It is precisely this process of the reformulation of tradition and the redefining of identity that is open to critical, though dialogical, academic inquiry, through examining the processes of self-representation and cultural replication.

Cultural replication and the text

Two sources are important in understanding the processes of cultural transmission, especially the transmission of texts. On the one hand, Bakhtinian dialogism provides us with a general orientation towards language and the significance of utterance, and on the other the semiotic mediation of linguistic anthropology furnishes us with a terminology and empirical studies for locating the processes of textual transmission.

Although undoubtedly action, particularly ritual action, is important, it is through language that the narratives of a tradition are conveyed and the reasons or reinterpretations of action in each generation are given. It is often the case that cultural texts cannot be separated from their performance and the transmission of cultural action and the transmission of texts can be coterminous. This can especially be seen in the recitation of mythic narratives and the identification made between social actor and the subject or 'hero' of a narrative. Explaining this process within a general dialogical framework shows how language is used in cultural transmission, especially the first person pronoun as demonstrated by Greg Urban. But the theoretical advances made by dialogism need to be seen against the background of the structuralist, linguistic model it rejects. To understand the processes of cultural, and therefore religious, transmission, we need first to look in general terms at the linguistic analysis of cultural replication through the analysis of the transference of contextualized meaning, and secondly to see how this occurs through the transmission of texts and the use of linguistic indexicality within texts.

THE LINGUISTIC ANALYSIS OF CULTURAL REPLICATION

The founder of modern thinking about language, Saussure, focused on the structure of language or language as an abstract system (*langue*) rather than on living language or the individual speech-act or utterance (*parole*) and its transmission; on synchrony rather than diachrony. According to Saussure, linguistics should have *langue* rather than *parole* as its object, as synchronic linguistics is 'pure' linguistics, concerned with the logical and psychological relations within language, as opposed to diachronic linguistics concerned with 'relations binding successive terms together'.[13] The normatively identical linguistic form, on this view, is the standard controlling utterance against which it is measured. This 'abstract objectivism' is criticized by Voloshinov precisely for focusing on language as an abstract system at the neglect of utterance. It is utterance rather than the abstract, synchronic system that is historically located and for Voloshinov therefore, more real. Language is constantly changing and adapting to concrete, historical situations and is not 'a stable and always self-equivalent signal'. Language for the speaker is always related to concrete situations. Voloshinov writes:

> For him (the speaker), the center of gravity lies not in the identity of the form but in that new and concrete meaning it acquires in the particular context. What the speaker values is not that aspect of the form which is invariably identical in all instances of its usage, despite the nature of those instances, but that aspect of the linguistic form because of which it can figure in the given, concrete context, because of which it becomes a sign adequate to the conditions of the given, concrete situation.[14]

On this view the meaning of words is governed by the contexts of their occurrence, so utterance cannot be accounted for in terms of what Voloshinov calls 'individual subjectivism', but only as a social phenomenon. Language is a process generated in the interaction of speakers within social contexts.

The implication of this is that cultural replication occurs primarily (though not exclusively) in the linguistic interaction of social actors, an interaction which is time and location specific. Apart from the critique of the abstract objectivism of Saussure, there is the concomitant criticism of formalism. The Russian formalists were concerned with the structure of literature and its methods rather than its content or message and its historical and social location. The aim of poetry, for formalists such as Shlovsky, is to defamiliarize the familiar through the 'making strange' (*ostranenie*) of language in literary devices such as rhyme and metre.[15] Indeed, for Shlovsky art can be understood wholly in terms of the formal device contrasted with meaning, artistic truth and social comment.[16] Similarly with regard to ordinary, transactional speech or practical language, the formalists were concerned with the formal properties of language. Speech is a transmission from one person to another, of an addresser to an addressee, within set boundaries controlled by the formal properties of language. This model for linguistic replication and the structure of communication was developed by Jakobson and expressed in terms of the addresser sending a message to an addressee, a message that requires 'contact' between the two, a 'code' in which the message is formulated, and a 'context' which gives sense to the message.[17]

From a dialogical perspective, the limitations of this model become evident. Although privileging the sign, the problem is that the message must first be encoded by the addresser and then sent out to the addressee who decodes it. There is an ideal sender and receiver or hearer of the message without acknowledgement of the processes' historical particularity. But understanding is more than a matter of decoding and the utterance is not only shaped by the addresser but also by the receiver: the utterance belongs to at least two people[18] and so is dialogical, as we have seen (pp. 154–9). Rather than the formal properties of language controlling meaning, it is the historical and social particularities of its *use* that are most important in replicated communication.

The dialogical nature of the communicative act is at the heart of cultural transmission. Through communication the social agent can take on different roles and identify with distinct social forms at different times. Rather than the formal properties of language and the sender encoding a message which is then decoded by a receiver, meaning is generated in social and historical transaction. The transmission of language, and by extension of culture, always occurs in the social field.[19] This is in one sense obvious, but what is significant is that the process of cultural transmission continues beyond childhood through the dialogical encounter of the agent with others within a historical context. Put simply, a dialogical understanding of cultural transmission is that we are changed by the contexts we inhabit and linguistically identify with different roles and social forms within which we find ourselves. The discourse which is prior to the agent forms her in significant ways, such that the discourse is perpetuated, though inevitably intersubjectively modified, through the generations: a point not dissimilar to MacIntyre's argument that we are born to a set of pregiven narratives which constrain our possibilities of freedom (see p. 128).

A theory of cultural replication is not explicitly developed by Bakhtin and his school, though such a theory is implicit in his work and is developed in linguistic anthropology drawing on pragmatics. Within these disciplines, a general dialogical understanding of cultural transmission is related to specific grammatical structures and an analysis of the ways texts are transmitted; language becomes a resource for reproducing social reality. This extension of dialogic theory is important because it shows, by referring to the particularity of language use, how cultural forms are replicated, which has important implications and applications in the study of religions.

TEXT AND INDEXICALITY

As dialogism privileges speech or articulated language over the abstract language system, so pragmatics privileges utterance over sentence, where utterance refers to the articulation of a sentence, or part of a sentence, in a context. Pragmatics is particularly concerned with deixis, the ways in which language encodes or reflects the contexts of its occurrence.[20] Deixis or indexicals, such as first and second person pronouns and locative and temporal adverbs such as 'here' and 'there', are contrasted with anaphoric terms which refer to a previous item in a discourse (such as 'he', 'she', 'it' and 'they'). Thus, indexicality always refers outside of itself to a context (as would be indicated by 'you' or 'there') whereas anaphora does not refer outside of the utterance; the term 'he', for example would refer to a previously named person. The qualities of indexicality are both generalized and referential, inexorably linked to the context of utterance. When we shift to anaphoric terms, to the third person for example, discourse ceases to have the indexical qualities of deixic language. Anaphora is always discourse-internal in that terms such as 'he' or 'her' are substitutes for some previously named person or entity. A complication arises when apparently indexical terms are used anaphorically in direct discourse. 'I' becomes anaphoric, for example, when placed in a sentence such as 'She said "I'm going to the river," ' where the 'I' does not refer to anything outside of the narrative itself. Based on this distinction and drawing on the work of Ricoeur, Milton Singer and especially Benveniste, Greg Urban in an important paper has proposed that cultural replication occurs through the use of this kind of anaphora and its extensions.[21] His argument runs approximately as follows.

Urban makes the assumptions based on work in pragmatics, first that personal pronouns are 'empty' signs, empty in sense that they are not referential with respect to a specific reality. This empty character of pronouns, such as the first person 'I', arises because it is indexical: it can be filled out or point to a particular person but as an abstraction it does not refer to any class of objects (in the way that 'table' does). In this way, to use Ricoeur's terms, oneself can be seen as another and another as oneself (see p. 213). But the use of 'I' in quotation marks – as in narratives – allows anyone, or anything, to be construed as a speaker. Secondly, there is a split in language between indexical, referential pronouns – 'I' and 'you' which indicate a particular reference – and semantically referential pronouns and nouns – such as 'he'. Centred around the indexical versus anaphoric, and pragmatic versus semantic distinctions, Urban shows that there is an amplified use of the 'I' pronoun in texts, that is central to our understanding of cultural replication. That is, the 'I' provides the key to understanding cultural replication in supplying the hinge between the indexical-referential 'I' (that points to a subject) and the reported 'I' of quoted discourse (that can point to any being, real or imaginary, within a discourse). In expressing his position in these terms, Urban is transforming Benveniste's understanding of the 'I' as a hinge between language as an abstract, Saussurean structure and discourse as specific instances of language use.

The use of quotation marks within a text – such as in the example 'he said "I am going" ' – indicates that personal pronouns are freed from their usual indexical value and can be used to refer to persons and objects internal to the discourse: they become, in Urban's words, 'available for coreferential use in a situation where it is necessary to manage cohesion relations between a number of discourse subjects'.[22] That is, reported speech clarifies ambiguities of reference which can occur within a text in which there are several subjects or several uses of the anaphoric 'I'. But while the anaphoric 'I' must be distinguished from the indexical-referential 'I', there is nevertheless a metaphorical relation between them. In a statement 'he said "I am going"', Urban notes, the 'I' refers anaphorically to 'he', who is not indexed, but the words within the quote are like 'the words in some original but now non-present utterance'.[23] The anaphoric 'I' is therefore a metaphorical 'he' in so far as 'he' can be understood to be like an 'I'. This is important because it allows for the identification of the indexical 'I' with the anaphoric 'I' and so opens up the field to role-play and to the imagination. Once we have the anaphoric 'I', the 'I of discourse', we have the innumerable possibilities of identification with narrative heroes and innumerable roles told and acted out within texts. Such imaginative role-play allowed by the anaphoric 'I' is central to culture and cultural replication through imitation, for it brings to imitation the control of others, it creates 'the weight of tradition'.[24] This metaphorical 'I' can indeed become an ideal to which the self aspires.

It is here where Urban's most important point lies. The anaphoric 'I' within the text allows for the metaphorical identification with it of the indexical 'I' and so allows for role-play and the imagination. The anaphoric 'I' becomes, as it were, an extension of the indexical 'I'. Having made this fundamental distinction and suggested the metaphorical relation between the two 'I's, Urban then goes on to develop further the anaphoric 'I' into degrees of removal from the everyday situation or from the indexical-referential 'I'. These degrees of removal are marked by being embedded within frames which at first clearly indicate the anaphoric nature of the utterance (as in the case of the anaphoric 'I'), but which gradually drop the linguistic matrices in which anaphora occurs. What he calls the dequotative 'I' is distinct from the anaphoric 'I' in that the matrix clause within which the 'I' of quotation occurs, has disappeared, though there are preceding frames which allow for the interpretation of the dequotation. That is, the first person appears independently of any surrounding clause which makes it clearly anaphoric, but the function of the 'quotation' is provided by the preceding sentences, as in a story in which direct, first person speech might be used. Further down this path we have the theatrical 'I' in which there is no trace of quote framing. Here speakers refer to themselves in the first person, as actors on a stage, but this first person reference does not indicate their everyday self outside of the performative context. Speakers use the first person pronoun to point to themselves, but not as themselves. Further along this route we have

what Urban calls the projective 'I', the 'I' of trance states and possession in which the indexical 'I' is completely submerged and a
non-ordinary self is assumed. Indeed Urban's continuum represents
degrees of the loss of the indexical 'I' or everyday self. In theatrical
role-playing the self is hidden, but in possession the everyday self is
completely submerged. In the case of the projective 'I' Urban notes that
'the context of language use must be highly marked and salient with
respect to everyday contexts, if the 'I' is to be interpretable as referring
to a non-ordinary self.'[25] If there are no linguistic markers between the
everyday self (the indexical 'I') and the trance or possession self (the
projective 'I'), then the two 'I's cannot be differentiated (and Urban
observes that such cases are susceptible to being labelled as mentally
unstable).

There are often no clearly defined boundaries between the different
kinds of 'I'. Some forms are prototypical, such as the actor on a stage
of the theatrical 'I' or a trance/possession state of the projective 'I', but
some forms fall between these states. Urban cites the examples of the
Shokleng, among whom he has worked, where the group's origin myth
is narrated by two speakers facing each other. The syllables of the
myth are shouted by one and echoed by the second performer who
begin to take on the qualities of the projective 'I'. That is, the
performance is midway between the theatrical and the trance state.[26]
Another example might be the Hindu dance-possession rituals of
Kerala, the dancing of the *teyyam*s described by Rich Freeman. Here
the dancer in an elaborate costume and mask/face-paint becomes
possessed by the deity of a shrine, parades around the shrine area and
the rite culminates in the sacrifice of a chicken or chickens. There is a
point at the beginning of the possession dance where the performer,
gazing into a mirror, initially addresses the deity in the third person,
then in the second person and finally in the first person and the
possession is complete.[27] In this case there is a gradual shift from
anaphoric statements in the third person to statements of the projective 'I' in which, although an extension of the anaphoric 'I', all
linguistic framing around the first person pronoun is gone. There is a
surface or linguistic identity between the indexical and projective 'I's,
but the context of the performance clearly distinguishes the projective
'I' of the *teyyam* from the indexical 'I' of the dancer. It is the socially
sanctioned degree of removal from the everyday situation towards the
projective 'I' that distinguishes different types of ritual performance.
Hence, an Anglican liturgy in which the priest utters the words of Jesus

is clearly an example of the anaphoric 'I', the 'I' of discourse, whereas the *teyyam* speaking *as* the deity is the 'anaphoric I' completely devoid of linguistic framing (and so not strictly or technically anaphoric) and wholly identified with that non-ordinary self.

Linguistically, the various degrees of the dequotative 'I' are indistinguishable from the indexical-referential 'I', for they are devoid of quote-framing clauses and so promote a more complete identification or submersion of the indexical 'I'. That is, the dequotative 'I' looks just like the indexical 'I', but its roots are in the anaphoric 'I'. There are then, two levels operating here. Anaphora, the 'I' of discourse in its various stages of removal from the everyday, provides the subject with a range of culture-specific identifications encoded in texts and, conversely, this textual self – the anaphoric 'I' – functions as an ideal or 'blueprint' for the everyday self. The identification, in varying degrees, of the self or indexical 'I' with the anaphoric 'I' of narrative, creates an awareness of the 'I' as a social being and ensures cultural replication or transmission through the identification of the two 'I's.

Urban's argument is powerful in that it develops a model that shows how cultural replication occurs through the linguistic appropriation by the self of different 'I's. Placed within a specific narrative context, the first person becomes anaphoric and so becomes metaphorical, allowing for a diversity of identifications on the part of the social agent. Perhaps a criticism of Urban's argument is that he assumes too wide a gap between the everyday social world in which indexicality functions, and the world of fiction and mythology in which the anaphora functions. It must be remembered that both the realms of the indexical and anaphoric 'I' are realms of narrative and due to the identification of the indexical with the anaphoric I, can become merged. Indeed, to hang on the distinction between a 'real' cultural narrative and a fictional cultural narrative is problematic, except in so far as there are material constraints upon the social world that do not operate in the realm of fiction.

Nevertheless, the use of the first-person pronoun in an anaphoric context provides for the possibility of multiple identifications and becomes, to use Bakhtin's term, polyphonic in giving space to a plurality of distinct voices, unsubordinated to an overarching narrative voice. The use of indexicality within anaphora is thus the linguistic mechanism for cultural replication, providing the means whereby the 'I' can function within a range of different frames and identifications. The 'I of discourse' is the form by which cultural replication occurs, by allowing the social actor to be projected into a number of contexts or to take on different roles and personae. The personal pronoun of the text can point to many different things and we are faced with 'an infinitely variable ventriloquation of the "I" '.[28] This linguistic phenomenon is therefore central to the understanding of narratives, both as mythology and as theatre.

Dialogical religious studies

This work on cultural replication in the field of linguistic anthropology is highly relevant for the study of religions: first, because it provides a language-based model for the replication of religious traditions; secondly it is dialogical in recognizing the contextual nature of research, the linguistic constraints upon it, and is sensitive to issues of power; and thirdly it does not entail a problematic subjectivity, as does phenomenology, but rather assumes a 'dialogic self' constructed in interaction, it privileges a philosophy of the sign over a philosophy of consciousness. Dialogism understood in these terms, as drawing on Bakhtinian dialogism and linguistic anthropology, provides a coherent and forward-looking research programme in religious studies. While there are questions arising from such a research programme over the issue of power, because of its inherent reflexivity it does not bring with it the problem of epistemic privilege to the same degree as phenomenology.

The implications of the linguistic research of Urban and Silverstein grounded in the Boasian tradition of linguistic relativity as well as in the Bakhtin school, for the study of religions is immediately obvious. If religion is to be understood in terms of 'value-laden narratives and behaviours that bind people to their objectives, to each other, and to non-empirical claims and beings' (p. 47), then investigating the processes of transmission and subjective appropriation of traditions are central in order to understand the ways in which religion is so binding. The internalization of religious traditions by individuals and their consequent modification in contemporary life situations, how and why this occurs, are central questions in religious studies which the linguistic approach can constructively contribute to. Understanding the relation between the indexical-referential 'I' and the anaphoric 'I' of religious texts allows us to see the ways in which religious ideologies and identities are internalized and allows us to see how the indexicality of everyday life relates to language references in ritual.

The transmission of religion through the generations or religious replication, occurs partially through the transmission of texts and partially through the replication of behaviours. The mechanism whereby texts and behaviours are replicated can be seen in the ways the social agent identifies the indexical-referential 'I' with the anaphoric 'I'. The religious social agent internalizes religious ideologies and images through this kind of identification. For example, the New Testament is filled with instances of anaphora and the dequotative 'I'. Taking a passage almost at random from the King James version of the Gospel of John we read at 6.35: 'And Jesus said unto them, "I am the bread of life: he that cometh to me shall never hunger; and he that believeth on me shall never thirst".' Here we see the first person pronoun used anaphorically, embedded within a framing clause that makes clear whom the anaphoric 'I' refers to and to whom the speech is addressed – a 'them' which we know to be the disciples by the previous verses. This use of the first-person singular allows for a relation to be set up between the indexical 'I', or self-referent of the text's reader, and the 'I' of the discourse. It is almost as if an identification at some level is invited between the two 'I's: the empty sign of the 'I' being filled out by both the indexical referent and the anaphoric referent functioning as though indexical.

This kind of usage, so common in religious and literary texts of the West, allows for the possibility of the identification of the indexical 'I' with the 'I' of discourse which not only has aesthetic implications (as in a literary work), but moral implications as well. It is, moreover, the mechanism whereby texts are transmitted and their content internalized in the life-way of the religious social agent. Indeed, the tension or gap between the indexical 'I' and the 'I' of discourse of a religious text, is the area in which personal transformation occurs and in which the individual life-way is moulded to a religious ideal. The 'I' of discourse becomes a moral exemplum to be emulated by the indexical 'I'.

The identification of varying degrees of the indexical 'I' with the 'I' of discourse, will depend upon the anaphoric context of the discourse within a text, also on the ideological parameters of the wider text and the religious social agent who is its receiver. In the example cited above from the New Testament, Jesus is indeed a moral exemplum within the Christian tradition, but there is a limit to the identification of the indexical and anaphoric 'I's, in that Jesus is understood to be not only human but divine. Indeed it might be possible to formulate a general principle that the further from the human the anaphoric 'I' moves – the further it is removed, in Urban's terms, from everyday situations or the everyday self – the less becomes the possibility of the indexical 'I's identification with it at the same time as maintaining a distinct identity. The further a narrative moves from a narrative of the social world constrained by material conditions, the greater the disjunction between the indexical and the anaphoric 'I', and the more extreme must be the identification in which the indexical 'I' is wholly sub-merged and momentarily lost.

If the 'I' of discourse is human, either in anaphoric discourse or in dequotative, theatrical discourse, then identification between the two 'I's is more possible than if it is not, and rupture with everyday indexicality becomes less. Indeed, it is this kind of human identifica-tion about which Aristotle speaks in the catharsis of aesthetic experience and, indeed, of which Abhinvagupta speaks in the identi-fication of human emotions with aesthetic ones. But if the 'I' of discourse is not human, but is rather divine, animal or theriomorphic, then the social agent's identification is either extremely restricted or is total, in the sense that the indexical 'I' is submerged by a possession or trance state. If the 'I' of discourse is bereft of human features, then either identification does not happen, because the gap between the indexical 'I' and 'I' of discourse is too great, or the identification is total with the momentary eradication of the everyday self; there is a rupture with the indexical 'I' and a total identification with the projective 'I' in which a mythological narrative takes over an everyday, social narrative. In a *teyyam* ritual possession the deity Viṣṇumūrti, half human and half lion, wholly possesses the dancer so that the everyday, indexical 'I' of the dancer is submerged. This variability in the identification of the indexical 'I' with the 'I' of discourse is probably related to the wider social matrix and concept of the individ-ual, in that where the indexical 'I' retains a strong reference, there the projective 'I' is minimized, but where it is weaker the identification between the indexical and the projective is greater.

It is arguable that a developed concept of the individual, as in the Western tradition, will encourage an identification between the two 'I's in a text, but will discourage the total absorption of the indexical 'I' into the 'I' of discourse. Rather there will be an appropriation of the 'I' of discourse into the indexical 'I'. But the possibilities of reader identification and the possibilities of anaphora within the text will depend upon the kind of text it is. Bakthin has identified three kinds of discourse: direct discourse which is 'directed towards its referential object' and is under clear authorial, semantic control; objectified or represented discourse, the discourse of a represented person usually by the direct speech of characters indicated by quotation; and double-voiced discourse, a discourse oriented towards another or a discourse in which two intentions or two consciousnesses coexist. In contrast to the third, the first and second types are 'single-voiced' discourses.[29] In direct discourse the possibilities of other voices are limited and the text is kept under strict authorial control, whereas in objectified discourse we have the possibility of multiple anaphoric 'I's. This possibility is developed in the Western novel and finds its most extreme extension, according to Bakhtin, in the nineteenth century with the work of Dostoevsky in which we find dialogic relationships within a single utterance.

Because of the degree of authorial control, religious texts seldom elicit the feature of the double-voiced discourse of the late nineteenth- and twentieth-century novel, yet while some religious texts would seem to be direct discourse, many are objectified discourses, such as is the New Testament which uses the anaphoric 'I' to great effect for contemporary readers. The converse effect of the anaphoric 'I' in the New Testament passage cited above can be found in texts which, while being objectified discourses, try to consciously downplay the role of the individual. This can be seen in the medieval, Sanskrit tantras and ritual manuals in which the objective performance is paramount (though there *are* rites for the fulfilment of individual desires). For example, in the *Jayākhya Saṃhitā*, a text of the Vaiṣṇava Pāñcarātra, the following is typical of the style of ritual prescription:

hastaśuddhiṃ tataḥ kuryād yathā tacchṛṇu nārada /
dve tale hastapṛṣṭhe dve sarvaścāṅgulayastathā //

Hear this, O Nārada, one should then perform the purification of the hands, on both palms, on the backs of the hands and on all the fingers.[30]

This text is a dialogue between the Lord (Bhagavān) and the sage Nārada whom the Lord here addresses in the second person. The second person singular imperative is anaphoric in that the implied *tvam* ('you') refers to the sage named in the vocative. But the ritual prescription is in the third person singular optative, 'he should per-form' (*kuryād*). Here the third person in effect takes the place of the second person directed to Nārada and indirectly to the reader of the text, but serves to formalize and distance the discourse from any direct indexical reference. The 'you of discourse' that would be an indexical used in an anaphoric way, is replaced within the text by the clearly anaphoric third person. Within the discourse the instruction by Bhagavān are to what the ritualist 'reader' should do who is being spoken to indirectly through Nārada. Nārada stands in for the practitioner. Indeed the school of philosophy called the Mīmāṃsā explicitly states that the use of the third person optative in Vedic injunction actually refers to 'me', the reader of the text, performing the ritual injunction.[31] In this way the text tries to control and objectify the dialogic relations between the characters and the reader. In the passage from the *Jayākhya* the anaphoric third person is indirectly understood by the text's receiver or reader to be referring to the indexical 'I'. Unlike the New Testament passage, there is no direct relation or identification between the indexical 'I' and the subject of the third person verb, but rather the reader has to understand that the third person refers to the indexical 'I', through Nārada, the object of the second person discourse.

The response of the indexical 'I' to the anaphoric 'I' of religious texts is therefore variable. On the one hand there might be a highly regulated response which controls the degree of identification of the two 'I's, on the other an unregulated response that highlights the particular individual's appropriation of the text. In the former case we have the highly controlled transmission of texts in particular, formalized circumstances – such as the formal reading of a text, be it the Bible or the *Adi Granth*, in a religious service – on the other we have the private reading of a text and personal identification of the indexical 'I' with the text's anaphoric 'I'. An example here would be a Protestant use of the Bible as the word of God to which the individual human conscience responds. Further down this route we simply have 'literature' in which the indexical 'I' identifies, positively or negatively, with the various anaphoric 'I's of the novel or even of the poem. We here venture into the area of the aesthetic response of the reader and reader-response criticism where the dialogical nature of the text as a construction of both reader and text-artefact is recognized.[32]

The significance of the 'I' of discourse within religious texts is first that it allows the identification, in some sense, of the indexical 'I' which thereby allows for the possibility of moral change or even a transformation of consciousness, and secondly it has the function of perpetuating the tradition. The identification of the two 'I's is a mechanism whereby tradition is replicated. Let us take each of these in turn. The stated intention of most religious traditions is a transformation of the individual and/or community in some sense. The hope of Christianity, for example, has been the moral transformation of both individual and society, and the practices of yoga or Buddhist meditation have aimed at transforming individual consciousness, suffering due to its limiting constraints, to some higher level of awareness (such as *samādhi* in the former case or *jhāna/ dhyāna* in the latter).

In these cases the social agent wishes, as it were, to close the gap between the indexical 'I' and the anaphoric 'I' of the texts through imagination. Imagination provides awareness of the possibility of transformation and the possibility of behaving in a way that allows the goals of the tradition, internalized through the identification of the two 'I's, to be realized. These possible transformative ways of behaving are often ritual performance in which the indexical 'I' becomes identified with the anaphoric 'I', or deferred anaphoric 'I', of a ritual text or injunction. Indeed, transformation can be so complete in cases of ritual possession and trance, that the indexical 'I' is completely submerged and overridden by the projective 'I' of the ritual prescription (which is an anaphoric 'I' stripped on framing clauses and sentences). The kinds of shift implied by these different identifications can be seen, for example, in ritual performances of the Hindu epic, the *Mahābhārata* which are midway between 'theatre' and 'ritual festival' and midway between the dequotative 'I' and the projective 'I'. Hiltebeitel describes some of these performances in Tamilnadu, one of which is during the day, the other at night, and it is only during the night performance where possession occurs.[33] The shift into the first person and the consequent submersion of the indexical into the projective 'I' can be particularly seen in the *teyyam* rites described by Freeman. Again, these rites, midway between theatre and ritual, illustrate the process whereby the social agent as performer becomes identified with the beings postulated by the tradition.[34] Further examples, analysed in terms of his 'I' of discourse, are found in Urban's work.[35]

This process of the multiple dequotative contexts of the 'I' is a key mechanism in cultural replication. Through the identification of the indexical 'I' of the performer with the anaphoric or even projective 'I' of the text, the text – or the figure portrayed, be it a character in a play or a deity – is replicated in the performer, and also in the audience whose own indexical 'I's are further identified with the performer in

190

varying degrees. Hence in some Hindu festivals there is secondary possession by members of the audience. The replication of the text and the truth-value it contains for a community, suggests furthermore that the text, as Urban and Silverstein have argued, is a trope of culture which is constantly decontextualized, or liberated from a specific historical context, and recontextualized in a new context. These processes they call 'entextualization' and 'co(n)textualization.'[36] Texts are the result of continuous cultural processes which create and recreate them over again as meaningful objects or tropes that are constructed as having detemporalized and despacialized meanings. This process can particularly be seen with religious texts, which transcend the boundaries of their production and are reconstituted through the generations, especially through the contextualization process of the identification of the indexical 'I' with the 'I' of discourse. Religious truths embedded within texts function as tropes within tradition that inform the individual practitioner through the process of the indexical identification with the 'I' of discourse. One of the primary tasks of religious studies therefore becomes the inquiry into the ways in which texts are transmitted, their internalization by the individual practitioner, and the function of texts and truth claims within the practices of the tradition.

But the implications of this kind of analysis, this kind of dialogical research programme, do not end simply with an enhanced understanding of cultural replication. Not only does this account contribute to an understanding of religious traditions, but also reflexively reveals a view of the self as constituted in relation to others and not as a disengaged subject. In contrast to the phenomenology of religion which entails, as we have seen, a problematic philosophy of consciousness, a dialogical research programme that focuses on the centrality of language in cultural replication entails a view of the self as culturally and historically situated. As Ricoeur has outlined, history of the *cogito* from Socrates, to Augustine, to Descartes, to Kant, Fichte and Husserl, has been challenged by semiology and by the 'consideration of *signs* which questions any intention or any claim that the subject's reflecting *on* himself or the positing of the subject *by* himself is an original, fundamental, and founding act'.[37] The rejection of the Husserlian transcendental subjectivity is replaced by a view of the self constructed in social interaction and through language – as is shown by Urban's work on indexicality – and so to an epistemic subject who is in a dialogical relation with the objects of inquiry.

Summary

The question of truth in the study of religions has been problematic. On the one hand there has been a deep questioning of religious truth-claims from the perspective of scientific, epistemological neutrality (a hermeneutics of suspicion), while on the other there has been the phenomenological distancing from questions of religious truth and the claim to an epistemological agnosticism. I have argued here that metaphysical claims are not subject to empirical investigation, and that a more fruitful way of proceeding for the academic study of religions is to ask questions of how religious truth-claims function within the traditions of their occurrence. Indeed, it is often meaningless to ask about the truth of a religious claim outside of the context which frames it. I have suggested that an abstracting of metaphysical truth-claims is a recontextualization of those claims within the system of inquiry. This translation of questions of truth into questions about the transmission of tradition places greater emphasis on language and the narratives of tradition, which has important implications for the study of religions. Rather than an emphasis on 'religious experience', on 'belief', or on 'phenomena' understood as material expressions of tradition, there is an emphasis on the way in which language functions in the transmission of tradition and the replication of culture, and a more dynamic understanding of the processes of both transmission and understanding.

This replication can be shown to occur through linguistic mechanisms of identification of the subject – the indexical 'I' – with the subject of texts (understood in a wide sense). The 'I' as an extensible linguistic sign, as the point of intersection of subjectivity and culture or tradition, becomes the central point of cultural replication. This general approach is dialogical, but sharpened through the application of linguistic anthropology that shows how cultural replication occurs. The relevance of this for religious studies can be spelled out in that the dialogical model provides a rigour in cultural analysis absent from the phenomenology of religion, it accepts epistemological uncertainty, and does not entail the view of the detached, epistemic subject. Rather, the dialogical understanding of a research programme entails an interactive view of the self as grounded within language; a view distinct from that entailed by phenomenology and the philosophy of consciousness. The implications of this, to be explored in the next chapter, are that dialogism not only means that cultural knowledge arises from the interaction of self and other, of research programme and data, but it also entails an ethics of practice that recognizes the historical and situated nature of research.

8. The ethics of practice

So far, I have traced an argument for a dialogical inquiry into religions that begins from a philosophy of the sign rather than from the philosophy of consciousness of traditional phenomenology. Having argued for a dialogical discourse and practice within the study of religions, we must now come to the ethical implications of the shift from consciousness to the sign, from the self to language and culture, and see how these impact upon the inquiry into religions. The issues involved here are extremely important and touch upon the deepest values in contemporary culture. The study of religions and academic disciplines in general do not stand outside of these debates and are often the ground for their articulation. Indeed, the issue of academic practice and its ethical implications is important across the board of academic inquiry in the human sciences, perhaps especially in anthropology where the encounter with others in fieldwork can be particularly sensitive, but ethical issues are also present in the examination of historical documents and religious texts. The inquiry into religions is not ethically neutral. The difficult question of ethics and the deeper values contained within any inquiry has so far only been implicit in the present work and the question now needs to be brought into the open. In investigating religious traditions and individual intentions and aspirations, the outside inquirer inevitably draws from and relates to the resources of her own cultural inheritance. The trained anthropologist would be pressed to be ethically neutral in some field situations – such as an execution in a southern American state or aboriginal claims to land rites – even if she does not act. Similarly the textual scholar cannot be ethically neutral when confronted with a narrative describing the genocide of one group by another under the sign of religion, such as Basava's description of pogroms against the Jains, even though this might not effect actual philological practice.

We are not only faced with the problem of ethical judgement in particular situations or when dealing with specific examples, but must face the deeper questions of whether any understanding or explanation of a human cultural practice or ideology is possible without some common basis of shared values, of the relation of ethics to politics, and of the relation of ethics to jurisprudence. The question of method therefore merges into the broader philosophical questions of the values inherent within Western culture, of ethical relativism and universalism, and into political questions of dominance and occlusion, especially as articulated in feminist and postcolonial critiques.

In the limited space available here, after some necessary remarks on the relation between ethics and aesthetics, I shall argue first, that religious studies conceived in terms of dialogism has the 'ethics of authenticity' as its foundational value; secondly that a dialogical ethic in the study of religions can draw on postmodern ethics as articulated in postmodern ethnography; thirdly that religious studies, reflexively understanding its assumptions, can both promote difference and offer cultural critique; and lastly that a dialogical ethics implies a view of the self in relation, in contrast to the philosophy of consciousness.

Ethics and aesthetics in late modernity

Before discussing the problem of the ethics of practice, I need to make some remarks about the relation between ethics and aesthetics in order to situate the place of ethics in contemporary culture. The shift from the philosophy of consciousness to the philosophy of the sign places emphasis on aesthetics rather than teleology. This dichotomy goes back to Kant who distinguishes teleology from aesthetic judgement which he characterizes as the free-play of the imagination and the cause of delight.[1] Goal-orientated, purposive action can be contrasted with spontaneity, action for its own sake, play and *jouissance*, which have become features of the postmodern landscape. The move from teleology to aesthetics privileges the imagination and the idea of self-cultivation; an idea that developed with Romanticism and which can be seen in the concept of 'cultivation' or *Bildung* and the development of the *Bildungsroman*.[2] The idealization of the aesthetic further links in to the idea of self-cultivation within the institutional, educational

195

context of the humanities, especially developed in the twentieth century. Aesthetics becomes a defining feature of late modernity in which metaphysics disappears with the collapse of being into appearance, of depth into surface, of territory into map.[3] This foregrounding of the aesthetic, whose immediate source is Nietzsche, that can be seen in Foucault's notion that 'we have to create ourselves as a work of art', and, citing Baudelaire, that man produces himself as self-creation.[4] Bakhtin himself has a similar idea in that through our actions we become the authors of our lives in future oriented self-determination.[5] In this sense, there is a close assimilation of ethics to aesthetics. Even in modern theology we have the idea of the transcendent manifesting in aesthetic appreciation,[6] and at the level of popular culture in the predominance of the 'pleasure principle' as an ideal and in cultural commodification that links aesthetics to capitalism.[7]

It is within this aestheticized culture and ideology that religious studies, and all academic disciplines, must locate themselves. At a pedagogical level religious studies attracts large numbers of students drawn to self-cultivation, the desire to legitimate some form of religiosity, and the desire for self-transcendence; students who are looking for significance and meaning and looking around in the supermarket of religions. Although this is admittedly anecdotal, to assume that a student is reading for a degree in religious studies primarily motivated by a desire for market success, or that the curiosity driving the religious studies student is of the same kind as that driving the geographer, is surely mistaken. Very often the student is drawn by personal attraction and what gives pleasure (i.e. the aesthetic response of the modern world). There is an identification between the true and the pleasurable. The question I am encircling is, therefore, within the context of a pedagogy in which aesthetics is a primary consideration and in which ideas of self-cultivation are of utmost importance: what is the place of ethics, especially in the light of its Kantian teleological preclusion?

One response to this question would be to argue, not for ethics in favour of aesthetics, but for a level of values that allows the aesthetic response to the world so characteristic of our age. This level of value or ethical basis is the repersonalization of morality outside of justification by rational systems, as Bauman argues,[8] and has been called the ethics of authenticity. Aesthetic response and self-creation as features of late modernity can be said to rest upon this ideal. It is to this ideal, one might even call it a 'base line', within the aestheticized, Western world that any ethics of practice must be related. A dialogical religious studies implies such an ethics of authenticity. I shall take my lead from Taylor's account and analysis of the contemporary ethical situation.

The ethics of authenticity and dialogue

According to Charles Taylor the modern, Western world is characterized by the culture of authenticity in which highest value is given to the right to be true to oneself, to seek one's own fulfilment and values in a world without absolutes. He writes:

> There is a certain way of being human that is *my* way. I am called upon to live my life in this way, and not in imitation of anyone else's. But this gives a new importance to being true to myself. If I am not, I miss the point of my life, I miss what being human is for *me*.[9]

This ideal, which Taylor generally wishes to defend against both the 'knockers' and the 'boosters', has in many ways degraded into a culture of narcissism. Indeed, this is a theme particularly associated with contemporary culture[10] and contemporary spiritualities in which the self is seen to be divine and the fundamental resource from which the individual's life flows.[11] The origins of the ideal can be seen in nineteenth-century liberalism with its emphasis on the individual as possessing value,[12] in the idea of the self as having inwardness,[13] with the link between inwardness and ontology,[14] and beyond this to the ideal of disengaged reason and Kant's understanding of the nature of the Enlightenment as autonomy.[15] A consequence of this ideal is the 'liberalism of neutrality', that the good life is simply 'what each individual seeks in his or her own way, and government would be lacking in impartiality, and thus in equal respect for all citizens, if it took sides on this question'.[16] The moral subjectivism to which this leads means that morality is not grounded in reason which cannot, therefore, 'adjudicate moral disputes'. This position has affinities with Bauman's postmodern ethics where morality is 'repersonalized'.[17]

But while promoting the ideal of authenticity, that everyone has the right to be true to themselves and seek their own fulfilment and their own values, individualism becomes a problem because in focusing on the self, other important concerns – the religious, the political, the historical – are excluded. Yet it is not necessary, argues Taylor, that the ethics of authenticity should exclude these areas that make demands upon us. Indeed, he argues that the ethics of authenticity should be taken seriously as a moral ideal that can be retrieved from its degraded expressions in modern culture, through agreeing that the ideal is valid and in maintaining that there is agency not imprisoned in a capitalist, industrial or bureaucratic system.[18] Taylor's argument articulates an ethical position that sits well with dialogism in having affinities both with liberal, humanitarianism and communitarianism. On the one hand liberal ethics is universalist, concerned with the primacy of justice and individual rights, the rejection of teleology, with an emphasis on the good life as that sought by each individual within the legislative task of reason.[19] On the other hand, communitarian ethics, as articulated in Sandel's critique of Rawls, disparages liberal notions of impassive justice and cannot support the view of neutrality regarding the good life. Indeed, the regulative principles of a society should determine what the good life is, though such principles are always historically contingent as are divergent views of the self linked to ethical views.[20] The self-knowledge entailed by responsibility and agency within social constraints becomes more complicated when 'encumbered by a history' shared with others.[21]

The ethics of authenticity advocated by Taylor attempts to circumvent the impasse between these two positions. It draws both on liberal and communitarian ethics in highlighting the particularity of each individual, along with emphasizing the individual self-in-relation with others and the community as the mediator of morality. This particularity and emphasis on the self is not the narcissistic ethics that Taylor critiques, but is rather the foundation of morality grounded on the self-in-dialogue with others. Ethics are certainly subject to reason, but reason means the dialogical relationship between self and others. Our identities and our values are developed through our acquisition of language and defined in dialogue with others, with our 'significant others', and within communities. Reason is therefore linked to the ethics of authenticity through dialogue. There are no absolutes in this picture, but humans in particular communities – what Alphonso Lingis has called a 'rational community'[22] – growing and developing, whose identities remain dialogical, and whose authenticity therefore remains within a horizon of significance. The 'rational community' provides the horizon of significance beyond individualism and so prevents the slide into narcissism.

Dialogical ethics must be based upon the ethics of authenticity in so far as open dialogue assumes the self in relation, assumes the self as an end rather than a means, and assumes a community of speakers interacting through sign systems. Indeed, a dialogical ethics based upon the ethics of authenticity that does not assume the universality of any ethical content, but does assume the universality of people in communication, is an argument against total incommensurability. The Nazi must make a judgement that the Jew is a non-person. An incommensurable ethical theory would have to claim that this is a judgement fundamentally about power, whereas some form of universalism would need to claim that this is a fundamental ethical judgement, the reaction against which is equally a fundamental response. A dialogical ethic would wish to maintain, along with communitarianism, that values are relative to their social and historical contexts, but also, along with liberalism, that there is a universalist obligation to treat people as ends. Dialogism implies an ethics based not on an egoistic self-interest, nor on an absolutist moral code, but rather, in the words of Michael Gardiner, 'implies an ethics rooted in a "neo-humanism" ... [which] refuses to entirely abandon such notions as "communication", "responsibility", or "intersubjective understanding".'[23] It is the ethics of dialogism that is important for a dialogical religious studies that I wish to develop.

Gardiner characterizes dialogical ethics as represented by three thinkers in the dialogical tradition, namely Bakhtin, Buber and Levinas, as comprising a suspicion of reductionist and totalizing theories, the valorization of alterity between self and other, and a stress on the everyday life-world.[24] For Bakhtin, as indeed for Levinas, ethics can only develop out of the relationship between self and other; or rather the ethical is a structure of that relationship. Indeed, Levinas would wish to replace 'dialogue' with 'responsibility',[25] though Ricoeur has criticized him for not allowing the ethical project to arise out of reciprocity, but rather out of the injunction to morality by the 'epiphany of the face' of the other.[26] For Bakhtin, in contrast, the ethical arises out of the encounter, out of negotiation and conversation, not out of injunction.[27]

Dialogical ethics and the study of religions

As we have seen in chapter one, an academic discipline or symbolic culture is given legitimacy by the wider rational community that surrounds it. Such a community establishes a commonality of values and, above all, establishes truth. An academic discourse does, of course, question this truth but is always constrained by the same forces that gave rise to it; a discipline is always on the leash of the culture that gave it birth. As regards the human sciences, the central ethical question is not so much the relation of the discipline to the rational community (though this is important), but the relation between the discipline and the 'other community', the community outside of the 'home' rational community that is the discipline's object of inquiry. The encounter of a symbolic culture – such as religious studies or anthropology – with the 'other community' is one aspect of the wider issue of the encounter of the rational community with the other. Indeed Lingis sees this encounter as fundamental in human interaction and in some sense prior to the rational community. He writes:

> Before the rational community there was the encounter with the other, the intruder. The encounter begins with the one who exposes himself to the demands and contestation of the other. Beneath the rational community, its common discourse of which each lucid mind is but the representative and its enterprises in which the efforts and passions of each are absorbed and depersonalized, is another community, the community that demands that the one who has his own communal identity, who produces his own nature, exposes himself to the other with whom he has nothing in common, the stranger.
>
> This *other community* is not simply absorbed into the rational community; it recurs, it troubles the rational community, as its double or its shadow.[28]

Within the wider rational community, religious studies has traditionally wished to maintain a liberal, ethical neutrality, while at the same time paradoxically has advocated pluralist values and empathy. Religious studies departments offer courses on many religions, and religionists writings are often driven by a strong liberal, ethical vision of pluralism (this is true of Smart's work, for example, as well as Eliade and liberal theologians such as Hick). Indeed the promotion of pluralist values is inevitable in a subject area that functions within educational institutions whose doors are open to anyone who abides by the rules of the academy or participates in the process of rational analysis, and which rigorously polices its borders (through status hierarchies, peer reviews and examinations).[29]

The question of shared values is of utmost importance in the inquiry into religions. Religious studies in the phenomenological mode is arguably more straightforward in situations where both the method and object-tradition share some common ground (as theology's inquiry into Christianity), but religious studies is most challenged in situations of radical otherness, where there is no apparent common ground and in which a liberal, pluralist ethic is implicitly or explicitly challenged. The test of religious studies, so to speak, is how, in Lingis' terms, it exposes itself to the stranger and how, in consonance with its ethic of authenticity that recognizes the importance of difference and of being true to oneself, it maintains a genuine recognition of the radically other. We are then left with the questions of whether and how understanding and explanation can be achieved while respecting radical otherness?

One response to this question – that argues against the proclaimed 'value-free' religious studies – is the postmodern response that genuinely recognizes difference, accepts the situated nature of inquiry, and that claims that a conflict of values is a conflict of power. This postmodern approach to religions rejects liberal notions of tolerance and empathy in favour of an analysis that highlights conflicting power in a world with no basis of common values. It is this orientation that has recently been critical of a pluralist religious studies based on phenomenology,[30] and indeed would wish to replace dialogue with 'mutual suspicion'.[31]

But dialogism offers another response that draws on both liberal notions of the ethic of authenticity (and the implicit recognition of others as ends in themselves) and on the recognition of contextuality. It maintains the genuine recognition of difference and the situated nature of inquiry within communities, but also recognizes the power of dialogue and the non-reduction of understanding to power relations. Dialogism can be both sensitive to power relations in the dialogical encounter highlighted by postmodernism, but can also draws on liberal conceptions of universal agency in treating people as ends in themselves. In dialogism subjects are not, to quote Kögler, 'reduced to "power dopes" but become interpretive partners in the dialogical effort to reconstruct the underlying truth about power in the social field'.[32] This is to see the inquiry into religions not simply as an encounter in the contested field of power, nor to simply accept a detached objectivism neutral to ethical questions, but to foster a reflexive dialogue that allows critique and allows the other the power of critique and self-determination. To explore this further we need to look more closely at Lingis' stranger.

The religious stranger

The need to understand and to recognize the interests and the values of
the radically other is perhaps the greatest imperative in religious
studies that, by its own definition, seeks an external examination of
religion. In the study of religions the religious other or stranger
impinges herself upon me and confirms or, more likely, disrupts my
pre-understanding of the religion she expresses. The other can come,
as Lingis observes, as an intruder into my preconceived understanding.[33] Following Lingis, the religious stranger presents to me a surface
which I perceive but which I can also see through into the constraints
that affect that surface presentation. Speaking with a low-caste
Malayali in Kerala I am confronted initially with a surface – a facial
expression, a posture, a judgement of me, and an expectation – that is
penetrated only gradually, through the strange becoming familiar. He,
similarly, is presented with the strangeness of me and my expectations
of him. Again, taking a group of students to the Saddam Hussain
mosque in Birmingham which happened to coincide with the Gulf
War, we are presented with surfaces that display suspicion, indeed
mutual suspicion, perhaps hostility, and a desire for those wishing to
talk to find common ground. But seeing through the surface we can
perceive in the other the constraints that result in the eventuality of
that particular surface – the particular narrative of the low-caste
Malyali's life, his intentions within his horizon of expectation, his
psychology, the caste into which he was born, the economic constraints upon him and his family, the language that constrains his
perception, and the ideologies that constrain his behaviour. Beyond
this are further levels of constraint located in regional and national
history or in genetics, of which any one person may or may not be
aware. A surface perception can become a depth perception that can
include even the specifying of biological constraints. I shall quote a
passage by Lingis on this:

> When the other speaks, it is with the tongue of the nation, the intonation of
> a class, the rhetoric of a social position, the idiom of a subculture, the
> vocabulary of an age group. When one perceives the other, one sees behind
> her posture and movements the demands of a job, the codes of etiquette,
> the history of a nation. One sees behind his feelings the structure of
> hierarchies, the rites of passage of a culture, the polarities of ideologies.
> One envisions behind her speech the semantic, syntactic, grammatical, and
> phonetic patterns of a cultural arena and a history. The depth perception of

the other requires the thought that represents the concepts and laws of disciplining, education, job training, professional etiquette, kinesics, linguistics, and ultimately ethnobiology and animal psychology.[34]

Lying behind or beneath the surface are the layers of constraint that result in the presentation of the other to us. It is the penetration of these layers in dialogical exchange that is one of the primary functions of a religious studies that acknowledges the situated nature of research and begins from the face-to-face encounter with the religious other in a fieldwork context. Beneath the phenomenological surface we can specify layers of constraint that might be the object of different disciplines (such as cognitive psychology or sociobiology), but which cannot exhaustively explain the surface (see chapter 2). To understand the religious other is not only to explain him in terms of lower level factors such as biology, though this is arguably important, but nor is it simply to perceive and describe the surface as one understanding of phenomenology would have it. A dialogical research programme is an ongoing endeavour to reveal the religious other and the constraints at work within that life and more broadly within the wider body of a community, and also thereby to illumine the constraints operative within the rational community of the discipline and the inquirer.

There are certainly major problems here. How do we maintain otherness and difference without the other's appropriation into the models and explanations stemming from the rational community of the discipline? Or how do we maintain, in Deleuze's terms, both difference and repetition? Whose religion is to be told and for what purpose? What do we do in cases where the religious stranger is so other that there is mutual incomprehension or in cases where there is a refusal to enter into a dialogical encounter? What do we do in cases of religious violence? Are the values of the religious stranger incommensurable with those of my own community and if they are what moral obligation do I have towards her?

The response to these questions rests upon basic assumptions concerning the nature of the self and the relation of communities to each other. I have already sketched the broad parameters of the problem in terms of liberal and communitarian ethics. On the one hand behind the liberal view we have a Kantian universalism and the principle of treating people as ends in themselves rather than as means, on the other, behind the communitarian view we have an ethical relativism and an implicit idea that ethical systems are incommensurable. Lingis, while maintaining a strong recognition of otherness, nevertheless argues that the rational community as a 'republic of autonomous agents' is formed through the Kantian imperative which each subject individually discovers: while the subject is situated he recognizes the universalist principle that people are ends in themselves and agents, at least potentially, of their own lives.[35] While dialogism can accept the Kantian idea of treating people as ends, and so must accept some form of the universalist claim that human being is fundamentally ethical being, it nevertheless wishes to absorb the postmodern insights about power. It is to this postmodern ethics and its impact upon anthropological practice that we must now turn.

Postmodern ethics

Bauman has argued that the hope of modernity has been the dissolving of ethical conflict; modernity 'is about conflict-*resolution* and about admitting of no contradictions except conflicts amenable to, and awaiting resolution'[36] but there is little prospect of arriving at any non-ambivalent, non-aporetic ethical code. What is *post*modern, argues Bauman, is the disbelief in such a possibility, for most moral choices are inherently ambiguous, 'made between contradictory impulses'.[37] Having said this, there are some general conceptions of ethics, prior to particular ethical choices, that are made by postmodern thinkers, including a strong tendency to reduce ethics to either aesthetics or politics. These conceptions of ethics are deeply rooted in differing conceptions of the self, some thinkers, such as Foucault, wishing to view the self as constructed,[38] even as an aesthetic creation, while others, such as Touraine, wishing to maintain the integrity of the self as a social actor.[39] This antihumanist tradition that is opposed to Enlightenment objectivism, whose emphasis is on desire, power and the unconscious, can be traced from Nietzsche through Freud to a number of thinkers representative of postmodernism, notably Foucault, Lyotard, Deleuze and Guattari.[40] It is arguably Foucault who has had most effect upon the humanities and social sciences and whose work has been a strong influence upon postcolonial and feminist critiques, though Deleuze might, in the long run, prove to be the more significant thinker. This tradition has also impacted upon theology, especially in the work of Milbank and others,[41] work that challenges religious studies as traditionally conceived. I shall take Deleuze as an example of this tradition.

Two ideas in particular are important for ethics in the work of Deleuze: difference and immanence. In *Difference and Repetition* Deleuze deconstructs the opposition between essence and appearance, as found in Plato and Kant, and wishes to articulate pure, unmediated difference or difference in itself that cannot be represented, outside of any relation to the same or the identical.[42] Deleuze is faced with, as far as I can see, the insurmountable problem of freeing difference from representation, because, as Deleuze says, 'difference becomes an object of representation always in relation to a conceived identity, a judged analogy, an imagined opposition or a perceived similitude.'[43] Deleuze also highlights what he calls 'immanence' over subjectivity and objectivity, which contains an ethic that transcends the ethics of a subject and object. He cites an example from Dickens. A rogue and good-for-nothing is dying and those around him display great devotion and respect in their care for him, but as he comes out of his coma he returns to his malevolent attitude and his carers grow cold. But during this period of unconsciousness between life and death, pure immanence is shown, an impersonality that is yet singular: 'The life of the individual has given way to a life that is impersonal but singular nevertheless, and which releases a pure event freed from the accidents of inner and outer life; freed, in other words, from the subjectivity and objectivity of what happens.'[44] The ethical implications lie in the nature of this immanence, a singularizing haecceity that yet contains pure power.

It is bodies that are important here as affects on this plane of immanence, yet which are in a sense beyond the subject and so potentially beyond normalizing and limiting forces. Developing the themes of power and desire as forces outside of consciousness, Deleuze and Guattari in the two volumes of *Capitalism and Schizophrenia* (*Anti-Oedipus* and *The Thousand Plateaus*) attempt a programme of the emancipation of desire from the constrictions of the processes of normalization and capitalism. Schizophrenia, for example, becomes an image for liberation from the oppressive regimes of modernity.[45] Deleuze's ethics is therefore not so much concerned with the subject of consciousness but, as Goodchild has shown, with the unconscious determinants of thought and action.[46] Deleuze presents a non-egotistical ethics that stems from the forces that he believes to be the deepest constraints on subjectivity and objectivity.

Deleuze with other postmodern thinkers have in common the rejection of the subject and the view that the subject is a construct of history and sociopsychological forces. These forces have generally functioned in the interests of oppression either of one group by another or as self-repression. Indeed, both Foucault and Deleuze/Guattari seek to liberate desire, the former from limiting sociohistorical conditions, the latter from the ego and superego that restrict its reign. Readings of history for Foucault are not the illumination of an impassive truth, but rather readings that illustrate something that has immediate relevance for the present. In this way, Foucault's genealogy has parallels with cultural materialism that similarly seeks to illumine the present and to contribute to political debate through the analysis of history and past literature.[47] Readings in the history of philosophy for Deleuze are similarly not the unveiling of a hidden truth but the promotion of a ethical view that devalues consciousness in favour of an ethics of the unconscious.[48] There are therefore political implications in their work and a link between ethics and politics in the broadest sense or a seeing of politics as ethics.[49] Postmodern thought claims not simply to be a hermeneutic but a re-visioning of society and rereading of history that has emancipatory implications for late modernity and which criticizes academic, liberal neutrality. The ethical implications of scholarship are also political implications.

Yet at the heart of a postmodern, power-orientated ethics, there is a tension if not a contradiction. On the one hand it claims to recognize the limitations of any ethical system, particularly one based on the universalizing force of reason and on subjectivity, and so ethical systems are in the end only local. On the other it wishes to claim that genealogical and deconstructive analyses produce an emancipatory discourse. On the one hand there is a recognition of the local nature of ethical systems and an emphasis on the recognition and non-occlusion of difference, on the other there is the implicitly universalizing claim to critique and liberation. The work of Foucault, Deleuze and Guattari are not simply analyses of discourse and practice but are prescriptive with deep ethical implications which have been adopted by emancipatory discourses, especially feminism.[50] Is it possible to hold both a communitarian-oriented ethic that claims values to be relative to a particular community, and the Kantian claim that there are ethical universals? Of course, the answer to this question will depend upon presuppositions and views of the self, but arguably both can be held together by dialogism which recognizes that social actors are ends in themselves, but also that we live in an ethically pluralist world without absolutes and that all positions towards the encounter between self

and other must be worked out in practice, dialogically. There can be
no end to the question of ethics.

Dialogical ethnography

What is most important for the human sciences in the work of the
postmodern theorists are, following Goodchild's characterization of
Deleuze, first, that all practice has ethical and political implications,
secondly that there can be no primary encounter of self and other prior
to systems of power that precede the encounter, and thirdly there can
be no free, rational agent independent of a body and fields of signification.[51] These points emphasize the embedded and embodied (and by
implication the gendered) nature of research and have been internalized by some emergent discourses, particularly postmodern
ethnography, feminist discourse, historical materialism, the new historicism, and post-colonial studies. An important volume edited by
James Clifford and George Marcus, *Writing Culture: The Poetics and
Politics of Ethnography* emphasizes that ethnography is above all
writing and that the writing of culture does not occur in a neutral space
but entails a relationship, with power implications between the ethnographer and the informant. Rather than the objective representation
of culture in the interests of scientific neutrality and the impersonal
quest for knowledge, the ethnographer, it is argued, constructs a
culture through the writing of it; a culture is invented[52] and ethnography is evocation rather than representation.[53]

While the invention claim might be an exaggeration and has been
the subject of much debate,[54] it is nevertheless the case that ethnography is situated between systems of meaning, between cultures, and
there is a moral demand in the fieldwork situation in the responsibility
of the ethnographer to the represented. A postmodern ethnography,
Tyler claims, is not a monologue, but a dialogue, made in conjunction
with the represented; it 'emphasizes the co-operative and collaborative
nature of the ethnographic situation in contrast to the ideology of the
transcendental observer'.[55] We have already had an example of ethnography that recognizes the situated nature of research in the work of
Rosaldo (p. 146). A further example can be found in the work of
Karen Brown whose *Mama Lola* is an evocative biography of
Alourdes, a voodoo priestess in New York.

In her work Brown found herself becoming deeply involved with voodoo and the priestess who became her friend. This personal involvement meant that she could gain a far deeper understanding of the healing tradition of voodoo through Alourdes and from her personal experience of the tradition than from any objective study. This shift towards a subjective and internalized meaning of voodoo necessitated a change in method from recording interviews, to simply informally conversing and writing up the results embellished with contextual descriptions and observations. Another dimension of this creative partiality is Brown's feminist reading of voodoo. In taking gender as a primary category and through focusing on the matrilineage of Alourdes' family and on an implicit feminist reading of religious symbolism, Brown is able to reveal meanings that would otherwise not be highlighted. These meanings are developed through the narratives of her informants and in her own narrative style interspersed with analytical comments as she moves from surface to depth.

This emphasis on narrative has the effect of an evocation, in accord with Tyler's characterization, of the world of voodoo: 'In *Mama Lola*, I am most interested in telling rich, textured stories that bring Alourdes and her religion alive.'[56] This emphasis on narrative stands in stark contrast to Alfred Métraux's study, in the Durkheimian tradition, that seeks a strictly etic explanation in terms of objective sociology.[57] Brown is implicitly sceptical of this idea of anthropological, scientific neutrality, for ethnography is inevitably based on some form of human relationship between ethnographer and informant. Indeed friendship might be seen as an important factor in the method that enabled Brown to proceed so successfully. Rather than the informant being a means to an end (the ethnography) the informant is treated as an end in herself. Rather than an objective anthropologist making sense of an alien culture from a distance, we have a situation in which two cultures meet, that of the anthropologist and voodoo priestess, in a dialogic encounter. Brown writes:

> What the ethnographer studies is how people create meaning or significance in their lives, how they interpret objects and events. An ethnographic study such as *Mama Lola* is thus an exercise in bridge building. It is an interpretation within one web-spinning tradition (in my case, my own) of the interpretations of people who follow a largely different aesthetic in their spinning (in this case, Haitians).[58]

The dialogical method followed by Brown has produced a compelling and fascinating study that makes voodoo shine for the Western

reader. While the purely narrative account has limitations in preclud-
ing a detailed, external analysis of the language used (perhaps along
the lines of linguistic anthropology), the approach undoubtedly brings
out the qualities of the tradition. The ethical nature of this fieldwork
encounter is implicit in the relationships between Brown, Alourdes
and other informants, which are above all encounters between persons
in which the usual moral imperatives would apply. The other makes
demands upon me not overtly but simply through her presence. Lingis
writes:

> To respond to the other, even to answer her greeting, is already to
> recognize her rights over me. Each time I meet his glance or answer her
> words, I recognize that the imperative that orders his or her approach
> commands me also. I cannot return her glance, extend my hand, or respond
> to his worlds without exposing myself to his or her judgement and
> contestation.[59]

The encounter between Brown and Alourdes creates a new ethos and
opens out a new world of experience that might be seen in Deleuzean
terms as an 'aesthetic of existence'. In this postmodern ethnographic
encounter there is no epistemological privilege but an ethnography
that is deeply informed by emic accounts, including the emic account
of the ethnographer. In her engagement with voodoo it is almost as if
Brown and Alourdes meet on a plane of immanence, to use Deleuze's
phrase, and the particularity of their personalities becomes displaced
by the power within their meeting, by the force of voodoo. There is a
movement from surface to depth on the part of the ethnographer that
could not have happened outside of the human, and therefore ethical
encounter with Alourdes.

But this kind of ethnography is not without problems and a number
of questions arise. In the movement from surface to depth in any
ethnographic analysis, does it mean that any external account has to
conform to an internal one? What happens if the ethnographer's
account is rejected by the informants? In cases where there are competing epistemological claims, what are the ethical responsibilities to the
other? And what if the informants refuse to dialogue?

I would argue that a dialogical model demands the integrity of the
ethnographer in that in the movement from surface to depth, the
ethnographer inevitably, and desirably, brings paradigms to bear on
the material that are external to it. While Karen Brown is deeply

209

affected by her fieldwork encounter, she still brings to it the anthropological terminology of kinship and also feminist theory through which the other culture is read. Inevitably in applying paradigms external to the material there is a rupture of emic narrative, but dialogical ethnography entails difference and the distinction between subject and object. But although she does bring external paradigms to bear, one problem with Brown's approach is that there is a tendency for the subject to merge into the object of inquiry; for the integrity of the academic and the religious realms to be blurred. A consequence of this is, while the ethnography is fascinating and compelling and there is evidently a strong bond between ethnographer and informants, inquiry into the constraints affecting, say, a particular ritual, of moving further from the surface into a depth, is limited.

While a narrative is constructed through a chorus of voices,[60] distance from those voices is also important and inevitable in the dialogical encounter. The ethnographer's account does not, cannot, be conterminous with the emic account. Indeed if it were conterminous this would disallow not only analysis but also critique and would fall to the illusion that the emic account can be made transparent through some detached method. Although understood only in dialogical encounter, the history of the Kerala brahmanical tradition can be analysed in terms of caste relationships and royal patronage, even though such an account might be rejected by a Nambudri brahman in favour of a model of the Nambudris being the recipients of divine grace. We must simply accept an epistemological clash which inevitably limits my moral obligation to how the other is represented by me. These are difficult questions for which there are no clear answers. Taking some of the qualities expressed in Brown's work and using some of the concepts developed by Bakhtin, we might say that a dialogical method involves the following elements: (1) a focus of language as the location of evaluation and values; (2) an emphasis on an ethos of friendship; (3) the necessity of distance and outsideness; and (4) the recognition of boundaries and unfinalizability or non-closure.

LANGUAGE AS THE LOCATION OF VALUES

To return to the point made in the last chapter, language must be the central focus of inquiry into religions in so far as it establishes contact between inquirer and informant, creates evaluative schemes, and allows us to reflect on values. In some ways the point is obvious, but it needs to underlined, that there can be no neutral language of description shorn of intentions, and the ethics of practice must be rooted in the reflexive use of language. Language is always dialogical existing within situations of encounter, a 'concrete heteroglot conception of the world'. Bakhtin writes:

> As a living, socio-ideological concrete thing, as heterglot opinion, language, for the individual consciousness, lies on the borderline between oneself and the other. The word in language is half someone else's. It become 'one's own' only when the speaker populates it with his own intention, his own accent, when he appropriates the word, adapting it to his own semantic and expressive intention. Prior to this moment of appropriation, the word does not exist in a neutral and impersonal language ... but rather it exists in other people's mouths in other people's contexts, serving other people's intentions: it is from there that one must take the word, and make it one's own.[61]

Understanding involves the attempt to make the other's language one's own, which has inevitable ethical consequences. In the context of fieldwork research this is to reconfigure the language of the other in terms of the language of the interpreter brought to the situation. This language itself will comprise paradigms or models exterior to the language of the informant and it is in the interaction of the two languages that explanation, for the researcher and her community, occurs. The language of the researcher will inevitably evaluate the language of the other in terms of structures and imperatives within it and the language of the other will always be changed in the encounter: there can be no transparency of representation (as phenomenology would have it) but only, as Taylor has argued, an ongoing conversation which expresses the inherently social nature of language and academic inquiry, and the inherently ethical relationship between inquirer and informant. The emphasis on language in the encounter of self and other is important in terms of the social sciences and in the explanation of religion, an emphasis that moves away from Husserl's transcendental silence.

211

Friendship

This ethical relationship can best be characterized as friendship. Friendship and its corollary trust[62] are of central importance in a fieldwork encounter as can be seen from Brown's monograph, and indicate not only an interpersonal relationship but a general ethos of inquiry. This ethos should be understood as the creation of bonds between the ethnographer and her informants, the creation of an atmosphere or context in which occurs the reciprocal exchange of knowledge and a kind of immersion of the ethnographer in the fieldwork experience. The importance of friendship as a theme in the history of philosophy since Aristotle cannot be underemphasized and has been highlighted by Ricoeur in *Oneself as Another* where he develops the idea not as a psychology of attachment, but in terms of ethics, as a virtue. Friendship is based on mutuality (in Kantian terms as treating people as ends in themselves) and not on utility (people as means). But this mutuality is not based, argues Ricoeur, on the Husserlian idea of the same, the sameness of the *cogito*, for this is to abdure otherness, but nor can it be established on Levinas' idea of the other, for Levinas' other is so other as to elude vision. For Levinas, the other demands responsibility and commands justice, but in the end the initiative of the other towards the self is actually no relation at all: injunction precludes the intersubjectivity that Ricoeur must maintain in developing his thought between the total exteriority of Levinas' other and the total sameness of Husserl's transcendental *cogito*. Ricoeur writes:

> this initiative [of the other in the intersubjective relation] establishes no relation at all, to the extent that the other represents absolute exteriority with respect to an ego defined by the condition of separation. The other, in this sense, absolves himself of any relation. This irrelation defines exteriority as such.[63]

As Ricoeur so astutely observes, for Levinas with the injunction that comes from the other, 'it is in the *accusative* mode alone the self is enjoined'.[64]

Ricoeur analyses friendship into three structures or elements: reversibility, non-substitutability and similitude. Reversibility is the reversibility of the pronouns 'I' and 'you', for from the perspective of the receiver, the 'you' refers to an 'I', and '(w)hen another addresses

212

me in the second person, I feel I am implicated in the first person'.[65] This is to recognize the social and contextual nature of 'I' and 'you', as well as to recognize the importance of language and its pragmatic analysis in the interachangeability of pronouns (which we have discussed in chapter 7). By contrast, and paradoxically but necessarily, non-substitutability says that 'I' yet remain distinct and cannot lose my place; the I/you distinction cannot be eliminated. Lastly, similitude means that in the relation between myself and another, I recognize you as an agent, as being like myself, which is to see 'oneself as another'. Ricoeur expresses this in a passage which is arguably the heart of the volume and from where the book's title comes:

> All ... ethical feelings belong to this phenemenology of 'you too' and of 'as myself'. For they well express the paradox contained in this equivalence, the paradox of the exchange at the very place of the irreplaceable. Becoming in this way fundamentally equivalent are the esteem of the *other as oneself* and the esteem of *oneself as another*.[66]

In the fieldwork encounter these structures of friendship are inevitably brought into place in the process of understanding. There must be mutuality in the fieldwork encounter that entails not only the recognition of the non-substitutability of self and other, perhaps divided by wholly contrasting narratives, but also entails reversibility and the recognition that 'you' are an 'I'. Such a relationship or encounter in effect precludes an objectivist understanding. Rather it facilitates a more complete ability to represent the other, first in terms of exterior paradigms in the recognition of non-substitutability, and secondly in terms of mutuality in a shared social context.

Friendship, of course, cannot be forced but can and does emerge through the dialogic encounter, though this is often written out of ethnographies in the interests of a notional objectivity. Fieldwork is encounter of different narratives – the narratives of individuals but also of cultures in history – and friendship will partially depend upon the overlap of these narratives. Yet it is friendship that so often facilitates understanding in the fieldwork encounter and is a positive force rather than an impediment to objectivity.

Outsideness

Having said this, immersion can never be complete in the inquiry into religions if scholarship and tradition are to maintain a distinct integrity, which they must for they pursue different goals and have different intentions. Not only friendship but distance, or to use Bakhtin's term, 'outsideness' (*vnenkhodimost*), is crucial for understanding culture[67] and for the ethics of encounter. Outsideness does not contradict the idea of the dialogue, that we are embedded in 'webs of meaning', but is an important part in the dialogical process that entails a surplus (*izbytok*) of seeing or transgredience (*transgradientsvo*); the idea that we are always outside of each other (through being different bodies). The excess of seeing allows me to have a perception of the other that she cannot have, similarly it recognizes the other's perception of me that I cannot have. Only with outsideness can there be understanding and the ability of entering into the other (as the live-entering of aesthetic appreciation) and friendship that leads to understanding and explanation.

Unfinalizability and boundary

This brings us on to our final considerations, the notion of boundary and unfinalizability. For Bakhtin a boundary or borderline is essential in the dialogic encounter; it not only marks the difference between self and other, between one culture and another, but also connects them. I am connected to the other only through the boundary where we interact, which is the field of language. It is the boundary where self and other meet, where a method engages with its object, and in religion is the contested ground between insider and outsider discourses and between conflicting explanations. It is on this ground that we understand the unfinalizability (*nezavershennost*) or non-closure of tradition: that everything temporal changes and so there can never be a complete closure of understanding.[68] Exactly as my perception of the other cannot exhaust her possibilities, because of the excess of seeing, so any method applied in the field of language to a tradition cannot exhaust the possibilities of explanation. All that a dialogical programme can do is to seek to articulate a problem or set of problems within this field and to offer answers which are inevitably provisional, constrained not only by the history of the tradition but by the interests of the researcher or theoretical programme. The boundary is therefore potentially the ground of ethical contestation and conflict even in cases where friendship and openness inhere within the dialogue.

Dialogical ethics is based upon the face-to-face encounter within a linguistic field, rather than in a transcendent realm of the solitary *cogito* inferring others through the processes of the phenomenological reductions and intuition. A Bakhtinian ethics of encounter arises not out of the self, as it ultimately does for Husserl, nor out of injunction, as it does for Levinas, but rather out of reciprocal communication. The study of religions conceived in terms of a dialogical programme contains within it a dialogical ethics that recognizes language as the contested ground of meaning and the other as a conversation partner, a partner in dialogue with whom there can be no closure of understanding, though with whom there are distinct assumptions and values. This is in complete accord with the ethics of authenticity, the right for persons to be true to themselves, as the foundational values of dialogic religious studies.

This ethic would be wholly rejected by many. Indeed, most religious traditions would probably reject it as foundationless. Yet in the secularized, Western world in which the academic discipline of religious studies has its institutional base, it is really the only ethical basis on which to proceed. The study of Islam is different depending on whether it is based on a consciously outsider position that assumes both a hermeneutics of suspicion and the ethics of authenticity, or whether it is based on Islamic principles that assume a hermeneutics of faith and an Islamic ethic. The insider position might be critical in a certain way, but could not be critical of its foundations. The outsider position allows for critique that the insider position does not and the nature of scholarship and language become contested areas in competing claims to explanation. Similarly the ethics of authenticity could hardly be contested from within a dialogical ethic in favour of a more deferential or authoritarian system. These positions are irreconcilable and a dialogical programme would not wish to reconcile them, but rather to continue to talk in the field of language.

But what happens when the field of language becomes a field of weapons? What happens when religious violence disrupts dialogue or when traditions or sub-traditions seek to enforce a different ethical vision through violence, as we have witnessed with fundamentalist Christian groups in the USA or Islamic groups in Algeria? Although a dialogical perspective can operate at a deeper level than the rational community, at Lingis' fundamental level where the 'lucid mind' exposes itself to the other 'with whom he has nothing in common', there is a problem of how a dialogical ethics can respond. Dialogism must assume rational communities, howsoever diverse, must assume rational agency, and must assume the potential for speech and communication and the potential for agreement or 'co-voicing' (*soglasie*). In this sense dialogism is not dissimilar to Habermas' discourse ethics and ideology critique, though unlike discourse ethics is less concerned with consensus and is not concerned with the creation of the ideal speech community.[69] There can be no closure to the dialogical situation. Dialogism (nor any other rational method within the human sciences) cannot make the other talk or lay down arms and in such situations we are simply left with a conflict of power and must resort to wider political institutions. In the West there is recourse beyond ethics and outside the academy, to jurisprudence within the democratic nation state, and at this point law mediates between individual ethics and the politics of the rational community. This finally brings us to the explicit consideration of what kind of self is implied by the dialogical model that accepts historical contingency and the dialogical nature of inquiry.

The dialogical self

This rejection of the philosophy of consciousness from a post-empiricist perspective, as we have seen, has taken two forms: a semiotic understanding of the self contextualized within 'webs of meaning' as articulated in the work of Bakhtin, and a deconstructive understanding in which any notion of the self or the self/other distinction is rejected, as in the work of Derrida and Lyotard. Benhabib articulates these positions in the following terms:

> the bearer of the sign cannot be an isolated self – there is no private language as Wittgenstein has observed; the epistemic subject is either the community of selves whose identity extends as far as their horizon of interpretations (Gadamer) or it is a social community of actual language users (Wittgenstein). This enlargement of the relevant epistemic subject is one option. A second option, followed by French structuralism and post-structuralism, is to deny that in order to make sense of the epistemic object one need appeal to an epistemic subject at all. The subject is replaced by a

216

system of structures, oppositions and différances which, to be intelligible, need not be viewed as products of a living subjectivity at all.[70]

Throughout the present study, I have argued from the former position; that meaning and explanation occur within a community of selves. This recognition of the linguistic community, the community of selves, as the arbiter of meaning allows for a language-orientated, dialogical understanding of tradition, that maintains a distinction between self and other, insider and outsider, and that therefore can be both explanatory and critical. Within such a dialogical research programme the self is recognized to be a part of a linguistic community – say an academic community – and scientific inquiry into the nature of another community (or another person) to be an exchange within a circumscribed context. This circumscribed context is the historical constraints inherent within the research programme as well as the constraints operating within the object tradition. On this view the self is intimately related to utterance and defined by interaction within language communities: the self is reflexively given meaning through the encounter with the other. This recognition of the self as interactive and the research programme as dialogical encounter, not only has epistemalogical implications (that knowledge is indeterminate and culturally constrained) but has the ethical implication that a dialogical encounter is an encounter of values. There are three important features to the dialogical view of the self. First, that the ethics of authenticity, foundational to a dialogical research programme assumes the concept of a self in relation to others, as a social agent or potential social agent, an idea that owes much to Ricoeur and Bakhtin. Secondly, the social agent entails the body, and thirdly the moral nature of social agents and their cultural particularity allows for cultural critique.

THE SELF-IN-RELATION

A dialogical ethics founded on the ethics of authenticity is grounded in the notion of the self-in-relation as (or potentially as) a social agent engaging with others. While this most definitely does not entail liberal notions of legislative reason or detached subjectivity, it does entail the concept of a person as embedded (and embodied) within a social and cultural context with the ability to act upon that context; an ability constrained by extrinsic factors such as economics, status and gender.

217

But before all social constraint there is the axiological demand of the self in response to the other. Although we have already discussed Bakhtin's concept of the self, it is worth reiterating it here in order to emphasize the ethical obligation entailed by it. In his essay 'Author and Hero in Aesthetic Activity' that sets out his stance on ethics, Bakhtin writes:

> No one can assume a position towards the *I* and *other* that is neutral. The abstract cognitive standpoint lacks any axiological approach, since the axiological attitude requires that one should occupy a unique place in the unitary event of being – that one should be embodied ... Being is ... irrevocably between myself as the unique one and everyone else as others for me; once a position has been assumed in being, any act and any valuation can proceed only from that position – they presuppose that position. I am the only one in all of being who is an *I for myself* and for whom all others are *others for me* – this is the situation beyond which there is and there can be nothing axiological for me: no approach to the event of being is possible for me outside that situation; it is from here that any event began and forever begins for me.[71]

In contrast to a postmodern view that eradicates the self, replacing it with free-floating simulacra as in the work of Baudrillard, dialogism entails a self, but a self that only exists in relation to the other within the linguistic community. Self and other are actively co-productive and demand an ethical response from the other. Moreover it entails the self's ability to act and to affect the other and the other's ability to affect the self. In this sense dialogism is not relativism and polyphony entails, on the contary, communication and contact across human divides.[72] Emerson observes Bakhtin's ethical system does not tolerate relativism if by that we mean a principle 'invoked to release us from the obligation to evaluate and commit'.[73]

When I meet the religious stranger, that meeting demands my taking her as a social agent, capable of language and interaction. It demands interaction, and assumes that the realm of our meeting is language and the sign. I cannot approach her as a pure *cogito*, but must approach her as a socially embodied one who simply evokes in me a non-rational, ethical response. It is only in the meeting of distinct narrative identities that we encounter religions or religious strangers as our necessary outsiders.[74] The study of religion must position itself outside of its object, yet remain in dialogical relationship with it; the religionist or anthropologist must position herself outside of the religious stranger yet remain in dialogue, reflexively recognizing the context of the encounter and embarking on 'power sensitive conversation'.[75] Such power sensitive conversation takes time, is aware of different agendas in interaction, aware of different assumptions, and aware of the potential for a conflict of interests, perhaps due to a clash between secular and religious narratives, or due to a colonial past.

AGENCY AND COMMUNICATION ASSUME THE BODY

Without the body and the cultural construction of gender, there is no dialogue and no understanding. While this is an obvious point, it is not a trivial point. So often the episteme of objective knowledge has ignored the embodied nature of human life and gender difference. As Benhabib has observed, the 'deepest categories of Western philosophy obliterate differences of gender as these shape and structure the experience and subjectivity of the self'.[76] Because of the assumption of the philosophy of consciousness and the adoption of Husserlian phenomenology, religious studies has predominantly been blind to the body and gender, though there are significant publications that seek to readdress these issues.[77] The body is both for-oneself and for-others. It is the body for others that is first encountered and which expresses the self and impresses the other.[78]

AGENCY AND CRITIQUE

The recognition by the study of religions that the self is embodied and embedded within personal narratives that articulate with the wider narratives of culture, is to reconfigure research in terms of dialogue as well as to recognize cultural critique. The move away from phenomenological distance to a dialogical distance-in-communication, is the recognition that all inquiry occurs within a wider framing culture and is from a gendered place. This is to recognize the problematic notion of ethical neutrality and to allow for cultural critique. If we acknowledge that all research is culture-bound, then we free ourselves from the impossibility, and undesirability of ethical neutrality, which thereby allows for cultural critique from specific perspectives that would otherwise not occur. For example, reading culture and religion through the lens of feminism, which does not proclaim ethical neutrality, produces provocative and important research. Similarly, postcolonial theory has highlighted politically consequential assumptions in 'objective' scholarship and has drawn attention to groups

219

whose voice has been ignored or misrepresented. It is to the possibility of a critical religious studies that we now turn.

Summary

The inquiry into religion is not ethically neutral, but the question of the ethics of practice is deeply problematic. Ethical positions arise within traditions, though scientific objectivism, in disclaiming that its truth is tradition-specific, has wished to be ethically neutral. With the turn to the sign and the recognition that all systems of knowledge are tradition-specific and embodied within particular cultural narratives, ethical neutrality can be recognized as impossible and undesirable. In the context of liberal, communitarian and postmodern ethics, I have argued that ethics entailed by dialogical practice develops out of the ethics of authenticity and that the encounter with the 'religious stranger' in a fieldwork context is inevitably, and richly, an ethical encounter. Drawing on Bakhtin and Ricoeur, I have argued that a dialogical research programme in religions cannot be reduced to a will to power – as postmodernism would have it – but most focus on language as the field of ethics, the cultivation of friendship, outsideness, and unfinalizability. A reflexive, dialogical inquiry will acknowledge the context of research, and the distanciation created through reflexivity will allow for cultural critique and the perspectival theories that not only question what is outside the rational community of their inquiry, but also reflexively critique that rational community.

Epilogue: Towards a critical religious studies

In 1882 Nietzsche published *The Gay Science* and there told his famous story of the madman who runs into the marketplace on a bright morning, holding a lantern and shouting 'God is dead! God remains dead! And we have killed him.' It is as though, the madman declares, we have wiped away the horizon with a sponge or loosened the earth from the sun.[1] Today, as those of us who use the Roman calendar move towards a new century and new millennium, we can appreciate the power of Nietzsche's prediction which perhaps echoes in a more extreme form Hölderlin's idea from an earlier generation that the gods have absented themselves from human affairs. The present century has seen the rise (and in one case the demise) of the great atheisms (Chinese and Russian Communism), the rise of secularism, and the demise of traditional values in detraditionalized Western societies. It has also been witness to human suffering on an immense scale and historical developments of momentous importance that have directly affected the lives of millions of people. Movements of populations and the spread of mass communication have rendered the world into a globe and we live amidst both the forces of globalization and the fragmentation of more narrowly conceived nationalisms and ethnicities. The history of modernity has indeed been seen, since Nietzsche, as the history of nihilism.[2] But amidst this turmoil and conflict of ideologies, religions have not died out. Indeed, religious and moral concerns are at the centre of wider social debate. God may be dead for some, but for millions of people of the book and for millions of Hindus, God, however the concept is constructed, is far from dead, but is a living presence active in the world and dwelling in the hearts of women and men. There are, moreover, structures in the spectrum of human aspirations, non-empirical claims and practices we refer to as 'religions' which do not invest *ultimate* importance in the concept of God, most notably Buddhism and Jainism, and there are also secular ideologies – such as Marxism or the many nationalisms that pervade the world – which have nevertheless functioned in analogous ways to religions. Although I have problematized the term 'religion', I would nevertheless maintain that religions – certain kinds of culturally or locally constructed practices, ideologies and values – continue to have enduring presence in the late modern world and will conceivably continue to do so into coming centuries. Arguably, religious studies is a potentially excellent subject area in which to pursue the inquiry into these cultural expressions.

In an article critiquing contemporary religious studies as taught in Western, particularly British, universities, Gavin d'Costa has argued that religious studies is based on the deeply problematic assumption of the neutral study of religion, that its success is sociologically explicable, and that similarly its downfall is inevitable.[3] Whilst I share many of d'Costa's concerns and his general argument is compatible with the argument against the objectivism of phenomenology presented here, I do not share his overall scepticism regarding the enterprise of religious studies. Undoubtedly d'Costa is right in locating the origins of religious studies (one might add along with most other disciplines) 'in the Enlightenment marriage to objectivity and scientific neutrality'.[4] The factors he highlights in its development in the 1960s and 1970s are the multi-religious nature of modern society, the demise of Christianity in many (if not most) households that leads to an increased interest in Buddhism and Hinduism (an interest aligned with romanticism), and the introduction of phenomenology as an objective, scientific method. With postmodernism and the critique of the objectivist episteme, this kind of proclaimed neutrality has been questioned, as we have seen, a questioning that also allows theology, or rather theologies as critical, 'insider' discourses, a legitimate place in the study of religions.

But while I share d'Costa's concerns, I do not share his pessimism about the institutional future of the subject area on two accounts. First, in spite of Nietzsche's declaration, religion is still an important force in contemporary cultures throughout the modern world, especially when aligned with nationalism and ethnicity, and religion is undoubtedly one of the factors that contributes to war.[5] Cultural factors which can be construed as 'religious' cannot be left out of attempts to understand contemporary societies or indeed civilizations.

'Religion' continues to impact upon millions of people and simply because of this should be one of the central focuses in the human reflexivities that are academic disciplines. Secondly, religious studies could not be done adequately in other subject areas alone (such as anthropology or oriental studies) because religion has two ingredients, text and ritual, that are often integrated and cannot be adequately understood if philology and anthropology are quite distinct. Religious studies can combine philological and anthropological interests and methods: anthropology can illumine texts as textual studies can inform anthropology.[6] Such work can ideally be done under the umbrella of religious studies.

The critique of phenomenology on the grounds articulated here suggests that the inquiry into religions can be reflexively aware of its assumptions and limitations, and rather than a proclaimed value-free description, can consciously bring to its object paradigms external to it. These paradigms might include theory developed in other disciplines, such as reader-response criticism, dialogism (as argued here), linguistic anthropology, critical theory, feminist theory and so on. While many of these approaches are at variance with each other, some – particularly postcolonial critique, feminist critique, and critical theory – have consciously emancipatory agendas. They wish to criticize religions as legitimizing certain kinds of social institutions and practices that they perceive as causing suffering and preventing human freedom. Such an agenda might be from a relativist perspective, that critique is from a certain position within a society but has no absolute foundation, as Adorno thought, or it might be from an absolutist perspective, that agents will desire emancipation or the freedom from distorted communication once the coercive conditions of their world-views or ideologies are illumined, as Habermas thinks.[7] Dialogism does not have such a consciously emancipatory agenda in that the only epistemological superiority it can claim is outsideness or transgredience – a view from elsewhere rather than the view from nowhere of the ideal speech situation. But the important point is that religious studies' future lies in its developing into a critical endeavour that is in dialogical relationship with its object, the most important boundary here being language, or rather utterance in the social world, the contested area of dispute and the place where insider and outsider discourses converge. Different intellectual traditions, especially critical hermeneutics and dialogism discussed here, can meet in language as the common realm of analysis. McCutcheon has developed some of these ideas, arguing for the scholar of religion as critic and as 'public intellectual' who can 'see religion as a powerful means whereby human communities construct and authorize their practices and institutions (i.e. their "regimes of truth")'.[8]

Although predictions usually turn out to be wrong, it might be suggested that the future of religious studies as it moves into the twenty-first century, lies in its closer alignment with other disciplines and subject areas, particularly critical, cultural theory. Postmodernity as social movement or characteristic of a late capitalist culture of consumerism, and postmodernism as theory or intellectual movement, has loosened up academic discourses in a way that breaks free from restrictions of objectivism and scientism, and while it might produce eccentricities, has also produced new and innovative ways of reading the past and present to great effect throughout the academy.

Nietzsche presaged the 'rupture with modernity' that can been seen not only in the wider context of social diversity, the fragmentation of centralized values, and the rise of religious fundamentalisms, but also at the level of theory with the development of postmodern critical perspectives and the development of feminist, gay and postcolonial critiques of Western rationalism. There is no way around these developments, the force of the postmodern critique of Enlightenment processes and values cannot be ignored, and religious studies as a whole needs to engage with these issues to a far higher degree. This needs to be done both at a metatheoretical level, to which the present volume is a contribution, and in engaging with the contemporary religiosity of late modern culture. There is much interesting work taking place in the latter field, but little at the metatheoretical level. If it abandons its objectivist episteme, recognizes its late modern basis and agenda, religious studies can have an important role in influencing wider, crucial debates about religion and culture. The closer alignment of religious studies with other disciplines, particularly the social sciences, is facilitated by the reconfiguration of disciplines into new forms, especially with the development of new technologies and virtual educational institutions. In Nietzsche's 'rupture with modernity', religious studies has an important place in becoming a forum for the development of many kinds of critical awareness, critical not only of object traditions, but also of itself. These alignments across the traditional boundaries of academic discourses are desirable from a dialogical viewpoint, for a dialogical religious studies is a critical religious studies. It remains here to identify some ways in which religious studies can interface with contemporary theology and with the important developments of gender studies and postcolonial theory.

Theology and religious studies again

David Ford has presented a view that overlaps to some degree with D'Costa's, that specific faith positions should have a legitimacy within the academic study of religion,[9] a position strongly opposed by Ninian Smart for whom faith as such cannot be allowed in the academic study of religions, though for whom empathy is important.[10] Ford argues that there are no convincing intellectual arguments for the divisions between theology and religious studies, simply on the grounds of the exclusion of faith by religious studies in the interests of a proclaimed objectivity. He characterizes extreme positions of the two disciplines in the following terms:

> Religious studies at its crudest uses an ideology of academic neutrality which presumes a cool, objective approach to the phenomena of religions. The arbitrariness or at least seriously problematic nature of this emerges when the ethical and even quasi-religious claims of that ideology are questioned, when its presumption of a superior overview is suspected of being a bid for power, and when it is asked to give any intellectual justification for cutting off the pursuit of certain questions of truth and of practice which it labels 'theological'. Theology at its crudest presumes sole privileged access of believers to theological truth. Is reluctant to engage fully with the whole range of intellectual disciplines concerned with religious traditions and the questions they raise, and draws its boundaries with reference to one community's confessional position.[11]

Ford is right to criticize any extreme objectivism in religious studies in this way. This criticism of the boundary within religious studies that does not permit the pursuance of certain questions, is determined by the practice of *epoché* and the Husserlian assumptions it entails concerning objectivity and detachment that have been the object of critique by the present study. But Ford's desire for the eradication of the boundary between religious studies and theology is problematic simply because of the underlying presuppositions of the two disciplines. Certainly, at a pedagogical level both theology and religious studies are engaged in a common enterprise within the secular university (see chapter 1), and at this level it makes little difference

225

whether a particular lecturer (is he is adequately skilled) belongs to any particular faith community or none; simply because one is a Buddhist does not mean that one has the ability to teach about Buddhism, similarly a Catholic theologian should not be *de facto* barred from teaching Karl Barth simply on confessional grounds. The student body reading for degrees in these subject areas will reflect the wider society and belong to a whole range of religious traditions and none; in any class in a Western university there will be Moslems, Christians, Neo-Pagans and agnostics. To uncritically propagate a particular faith position is therefore unprofessional and against the spirit of critique that should characterize academic institutions.

But to admit that theology and religious studies meet at a ped-agogical level is not to endorse a proclaimed value neutrality. Both theology and religious studies have distinct histories with distinct presuppositions, and while both practice critique, say of presuppositions within religious texts, these critiques are themselves based on different narrative foundations. Neutral critique is, as I have argued, impossible and undesirable, but reflexive critique in dialogical relation with its object, what might be called 'dialogical reflexivity', is potentially the method shared by both theology and religious studies. In the light of this, what becomes important in the study of religions is not so much the distinction between insider and outsider but between the critical and non-critical, along with the recognition that theological and religious studies critiques are themselves founded upon distinct narratives. On reflection it might be argued that Ford's position that wishes to give legitimacy to faith positions within the academy is less hegemonic because reflexive, than the proclaimed objectivity of the phenomenology of religions.[12] Whether specific faith positions should be represented at secular universities is a matter for debate, but at a pedagogical level (including a research level) it is critique rather than faith that is all important. Indeed it is in the practice of critique that religious studies overlaps not only with theology, but with gender studies and post-colonial theory.

Gender and religious studies

Although this study is not a feminist critique of religious studies – a genuine feminist engagement can surely arise only from one's own life – and it might seem as though I have banished a short section on feminist readings of religion to a mere epilogue, this does not reflect the importance of these developments for the study of religions. Feminist theory is a consciously perspectival position that abnegates objectivism and argues that an objectivist position is an androcentric one. From a feminist perspective, as Bowie has argued following Ruether, both theology and religious studies begin with the critical principle of the promotion of the 'full humanity of women'.[13] Feminist critique in religion therefore wishes both to reread religious history from the perspective of women – or rather from a gender-sensitive hermeneutic – and to critique the androcentric ways in which religions have been studies. O'Connor lists five points in the feminist programme: suspicion of sources, the recovery of women's lives and history, criticism of received concepts, particularly universals, rethinking the methods of scholarship, and self-criticism.[14] This is clearly a reflexive and dialogical programme (indeed Bakhtin has been influential on feminist discourse).[15] There has been much work done from a feminist perspective on many areas of cultural life and on religion, especially the important developments in feminist theology. But rather than review this large body of literature,[16] let me take one argument that, while not directly relevant to the study of religion, is very significant as an indication of future cultural developments that have impact upon the forms of communication we call religions.

Donna Haraway argues for what she calls 'cyborg feminism' by which she means that the cyborg is a contemporary model or image for the construction and transformation of gender roles. The cyborg image is a fiction that represents the late-twentieth-century breach in the distinction between animal and human in evolutionary theory and organ transplants, a breach in the distinction between animal, human and machine in the technological reconceptualizations of machines, and a breach in the boundary between the physical and the non-physical in, for example, micro-electronic devices. These transgressions point to a 'cyborg world' that has the potential either to be the imposition of a totalizing power (bad news), or a world of fragmented identities in which animals, persons and machines are interconnected (good news).[17] The cyborg feminism that Haraway promotes is non-totalizing in taking pleasure in the confusion of boundaries and in the criticism of old dichotomies such as base/superstructure, public/private, and material/ideal. In her vision the self is dismantled, not only conceptually but through biotechnology, and can be recreated and new (presumably egalitarian) social relationships established: a cyborg identity is a fractured identity, conducive to freedom and pleasure. Because of this fragmentation and the open possibilities created by the permeable boundaries in both personal and political bodies, the cyborg is a good image for a postmodern, female identity. Hence Haraway's famous statement 'I'd rather be a cyborg than a goddess.'[18]

Haraway's work is important for the study of religions on a number of accounts. It alerts us to the fluid conceptualizations of body and community with the development of cyberspace, and the importance of inquiry into forms without clear boundaries. Many religions or religious aspects of culture express themselves through the worldwide web, and cyberspace can become a form of religious gnosis and transcendence of matter, as Roberts has shown.[19] It alerts us to the ways in which gender is constructed and the potential for reconfiguring gender distinctions and our reconstitution to 'include the utopian dream and the hope for a monstrous world without gender'.[20] It also alerts us to the theoretical potential of religious studies as a discipline that deconstructs and reconfigures itself beyond the phenomenological paradigm, that recognizes the local origin of theory and inquiry (even inquiry into global processes) and whose fluid, theoretical boundaries accord with the fluid boundaries of contemporary religiosity.

It might be objected that while Haraway's work is important and its implications for the study of religion significant, the vast majority of people, who practice religions and adhere to ideologies, are still embodied (most without access to the technological transformations Haraway writes about). Communities comprise embodied, gendered persons who interact with each other and whose culture is inscribed on the body. In this sense the gendered body is the base line that cannot, yet, be significantly circumvented and must be the beginning of inquiry. It is with embodied persons in communication with each other that religious studies is in dialogical relationship. Yet while there is truth in this, as Sarah Coakley observes, the body is not 'a "natural" datum of uncontentious physicality', that can serve as an anchor now that there are no grand narratives.[21] The body is inscribed by culture, in Bhabha's words in 'both the economy of pleasure and desire and in the economy of discourse, domination and power',[22] and while a body's sex might be given, gender is a cultural construction. Gender, as Haraway's cyborg reminds us, has potentially fluid boundaries and the study of religions needs to be sensitive to these constructions.

The deconstruction of gender by thinkers such as Haraway, relates

228

to the broad area of debate in gay and lesbian cultural theory, broadly termed 'queer theory', a discourse that, as far as I am aware, is absent from the field of religious studies. In the way in which feminism problematized gender and developed a gender-sensitive hermeneutic, so queer theory develops a sexual-orientation-sensitive hermeneutic, making sexual orientation a fundamental category of analysis in reading texts and history.[23] This kind of criticism deconstructs the idea of an essential male or female identity and generally argues that sexuality is a construction subject to change. It calls into question traditional dichotomies and identity categories, particularly 'gay' and 'straight'. Judith Butler, along the lines of Foucault, argues that these categories are instruments of regulatory regimes and the very term 'homosexual' is itself a consequence of homophobic discourse, in reaction to which the category of 'heterosexuality' developed. Sexual identity, on this account, is a construction or a kind of 'imitation for which there is no original',[24] a concept not dissimilar to the fluid boundaries of Haraway's cyborg. As is feminism, queer theory is potentially important for the study of religions in identifying lesbian/gay dimensions in the history of religions, in analysing homophobic attitudes and repressive (for gays) religious ideologies, and in highlighting the influence of religions in the construction of sexualities and the concepts of deviance and normality. Read through the lens of these critiques, dimensions and attitudes are revealed in religions that would otherwise have been taken as unproblematic. But this kind of work has hardly begun.

What both feminist theory and queer theory have in common, is the idea that gender roles and sexualities, along with class, are internalized by us through processes of socialization. These processes are patriarchal and oppressive in so far as women and gays have been regarded as other to the male norm and been in positions of weakness in contrast to male power. This situation is changing in the West and feminist and gay discourses regard themselves as liberating critiques. But while these critiques might be driven by what they regard as strong ethical and political motives, some might argue that feminist or gay analyses of religions do not have the moral right to critique other traditions whose assumptions are very different from those of the West, such as Hindu or Moslem assumptions. This is deeply problematic. To what extent can cultural relativism be accepted by these discourses and to what extent can cultures be open to critique by outsiders? At what point does scholarship become political? Many would argue that scholarship is inherently political and cannot be otherwise once the notion of a pure objectivity is vanquished. Indeed the notion of scholarly detachment has played, argues McCutcheon, a supportive role in international systems of privilege.[25]

In highlighting certain practices and ideologies, say the treatment of women by religions over the centuries, feminist theory must of course be critical and claim that its analysis and prescription are better than the religious prescriptions it critiques, yet also wishes to acknowledge and give space to the other. This issue is dealt with in different ways. Noddings wishes to meet the other morally and to promote an ethic of caring that is based on reception rather than projection.[26] But this must appeal to some overarching ethical position that perceives itself to be superior to a tradition that might be the object of critique, while at the same time wishing to maintain no such ethical superiority. If a moral privilege is disclaimed, then we are simply left with a conflict of power, of one (feminist) ethical system over another (patriarchal) one. There is no neutral ground from which to adjudicate the positions. For example, traditional Islamic understandings of women are regarded as oppressive by some feminists, but this outside interpretation is rejected by many Moslem women. The strong, Western feminist response might be that the Moslem woman's capitulation to the conditions of Islam is simply hegemony in Gramsci's sense of internalized ideology, that the oppressed become their own oppressors. But if there is no objective standard by which to gauge these problems, what are the grounds for making this claim? Are we simply left with a Nietzschean clash of power and acceptance that, in the end, the world is ruled by political and actual violence? I think the feminist would have to accept a perceived superiority to her liberationist, moral position that arises not from a given rule, but from the dialogical encounter and the feminist perspective. Similar problematics are found in post-colonial theory, though here the ethical is strongly politicized as the discourse attempts to unravel the political implications of scholarship; a scholarship that has been generally by Western males about third-world others.

Post-colonial theory and religious studies

Post-colonial criticism or theory began in the area of English literary studies,[27] responding against liberal, universalist criticism, and as 'colonial discourse analysis' has penetrated other disciplines and contributed to the erosion of their boundaries. Indeed, post-colonial theory, in common with the new historicism, seeks to function over a wide range in its reading of texts in their social and historical contexts. Moore-Gilbert has defined it in the following terms:

> [a set of reading practices] preoccupied principally with analysis of cultural forms which mediate, challenge or reflect upon the relations of domination and subordination – economic, cultural and political – between (and often within) nations, races or cultures, which characteristically have their roots in the history of modern European colonialism and imperialism and which ... continue to be apparent in the present era of neo-colonialism.[28]

And Bhabha writes:

> Post-colonial criticism bears witness to the unequal and uneven forces of cultural representation involved in the contest for political and social authority within the modern world order. Post-colonial perspectives emerge from the colonial testimony of Third World countries and the discourse of 'minorities' within the geopolitical divisions of East and West, North and South.[29]

Colonial discourse analysis partially develops out of a Marxist analysis of culture (particularly Gramsci) but also draws on the work of Foucault and other cultural theorists in maintaining that representation and knowledge are expressions of material and political power; the imperial power that oppressed the 'Orient' and projected it as the West's other. Fanon in his *The Wretched of the Earth* first voiced an African cultural resistance against France, claiming that a colonized people must first claim back their history,[30] and indeed, revisionist historiography has been high on the agenda of post-colonial criticism. After Fanon the critique developed with Said's *Orientalism*, a most influential, if controversial, book.[31] Orientalist discourse, as shown by Said, contrasts the East as feminine, irrational, exotic, sensual, female, despotic and backward, with the West as masculine, rational, sober, moral, male, democratic and progressive. In terms of psychoanalysis, the Orient becomes a projection of what the West does not wish to acknowledge about itself, and Said backs up his claims with reference to a wide range of cultural phenomena.

Within the academy, orientalism became largely associated with philology, whose roots are in German Romanticism, and became

231

subdivided into a number of distinct disciplines based on language, namely Indology (focusing on Sanskrit, Prakit and Pali), sinology (Chinese but also Japanese language and literature), and Islamic studies (Arabic and Persian). African studies became the concern of anthropology. In contrast to anthropology that dealt with non-literate 'primitive' cultures, orientalism dealt with literate, 'high' cultures, which – in spite of their qualities – were perceived as being inferior to the West. These disciplines were the 'imperial knowledges' to complement the 'imperial formation' of British colonial power and were part of the colonial ruling machine, as Inden has shown in detail with regard to India,[32] and as Spivak and Guha and the 'subaltern studies' groups have shown with regard to specific historical instances.[33] By the time of the rise of religious studies in the 1960s and early 1970s, the colonial legacy was a trace in wider British culture, felt as nostalgia for the past and as the romantic longing for the exotic other that resulted in the burgeoning of Eastern religions in the Western popular imagination. Although the cultural situation is now more complex with Eastern religions becoming integrated into Western culture in subtle ways, in New Age self-improvement techniques and Western gurus,[34] there are still echoes of this orientalist legacy in popular culture (pop songs that recite Sanskrit mantras, the 1990s revival of 'hippy' styles).

But the serious problem is, given that there are links between forms of knowledge and colonial power formations, does this mean that disciplines such as Indology are somehow invalidated or that the knowledge they produce can be reduced to colonial power and its remainder? This is a complex question. On the one hand we have the argument that all forms of knowledge are – at least partial – constructions due to desire and that data is generated by theory (see chapter 3). This position leans towards the idea of truth as coherence within specified levels of constraint (as argued for here) and that there can be no objective knowledge independent of theory and motivation. We can see that the forms of knowledge generated by colonialism (particularly philology), subordinate local knowledge as inferior.[35]

On the other hand we have the idea that philology is the most objective of disciplines, that its correct procedure involves the eradication of subjectivity because subjectivity is subordinated to the objective system of language. In creating a critical edition of a Sanskrit text from a number of palm leaf manuscript editions in the granthi script, the edition is primarily constrained by the limits of the manuscripts themselves, by the interpreter's competence in the language, and by the system of grammar. In one sense, as Schlegel thought, grammar is the foundation upon which textual criticism and herme- neutics are based. But the objectivity of the text spoken of here is not so much an argument for the objectivity of knowledge, but is rather an argument about perception and seeing whether a particular manu- script accords with another, whether the grammatically correct form of the verb is used, and so on. One small step beyond this into the meaning of the text and we are in the realms of interpretation and the construction (or attempted reconstruction) of meaning. These (re)con- structed meanings must be determined to a large extent by the intentions of the interpreter, the wider culture from which she comes, the wider knowledge of related texts, and the reasons for choosing that particular text or research project. With all of these we are imme- diately thrown back into wider cultural questions and into questions about the motivation behind particular research programmes that post-colonial theory has criticized.

Not only philology, but the very enterprise of religious studies as a discourse about the world religions can be critiqued from a post- colonial perspective. First, the development of religious studies needs to be seen against the context of other historical developments and needs to have a sharper sense of that development. As the post-colonial critics have shown, and as David Chidester has shown with specific reference to the development of religious studies in South Africa, there is an intimate relation between forms of knowledge and category formation, and colonial domination. Chidester shows in great detail how the discourse of religion developed in a specific region – South Africa – initially through missionaries, European travellers, and oth- ers, then in a imperial phase and lastly as apartheid, comparative religion. The discourse about otherness generated by those early 'frontier' interactions is still present.[36]

Secondly, the development of the category 'world religion' can be seen as a historically contingent discourse. 'World religions' have been the object of a discourse independent of Christianity that has only comparatively recently attained this status in departments of religious studies where it is taught as one of the 'world religions'. Traditionally we have 'Christianity' contrasted with 'world religions' and this is a pattern that is perpetuated in many institutions where religious studies is taught. It is still possible to find departments of theology and/or religious studies that have one first-year course on 'world religions' and a plurality of courses on Christianity. The problem with the category 'world religion' is that it must be abstracted from its regional and cultural bed in order to be displayed in the supermarket of religions, almost as a consumer product. This inevitably means the narratives of the tradition must be abstracted and distorted in the transference from a predominantly diachronic dimension (the notion of tradition) to a synchronic one (the notion of a religion spread out across the globe, almost outside of time). The world religion is taken out of its cultural and linguistic emplotment and repackaged by the discourse of religious studies. Whether this is an argument for abandoning the category of 'world religion' is not, however, clear. As a student once said to me, we have to start from somewhere. But there is a more serious point to do with traditions themselves, and that is that in the context of globalization religions are constructing themselves as having worldwide significance. Traditions from the Swami Narayan movement to the Unification Church have a global profile and use electronic technology to reproduce themselves and reconstruct their past narratives. Traditions that were traditions of 'descent' have often become traditions of 'assent'[37]. This process of modernization has an effect upon traditions, and the marketing of religions as global movements by the religions themselves is a significant development that needs to be seen in the context of the converse movements towards localization and the grounding or appropriation of global religions at a local level. (This can be seen, for example, in the identification of Orthodox Christianity with local, earlier Celtic Christianity where it has been established in the West, or in the identification of local deities, such as *teyyams*, with pan-Hindu deities such as Viṣṇu or Śiva.)

Conclusion

All of the discourses we have discussed – feminist theory, queer theory, and post-colonial theory – draw attention to issues of cultural difference and are important for the academic study of religions and for the development of a metatheoretical discourse about the nature of religious studies. The implications of these discourses for religious studies are important on a number of accounts. They reject universalism. Universal symbols in religions, for example, are found only due to a particular theory or research programme, perhaps informed by a theological desire for the oneness of all religions. This is a legitimate enterprise, of course, in the sense that any theological enterprise is legitimate, but needs to be reflexively aware of its agenda and motivation, and needs to question the proclaimed objectivity of its research findings. As Smart reminds us in a sentiment I would heartily endorse, 'be clear about what you are doing, and then do what you like'.[38] Religions are abstracted from the wider cultural narratives in which they are embedded and a discourse about religions cannot be wholly separated from a discourse about culture, society and politics. Post-colonial theory celebrates difference, hybridity and polyvalence. The study of religions should be sensitive to difference and the many layers of cultural meaning as we move into a global world of many faceted self-constructions, including its own place in a dialogical relationship as an outsider discourse with its object, 'religion'. Religions take place within narratives that are constructed and reconstructed from particular perspectives, from particular positions of power, which a critical religious studies can decode. Lastly, post-colonial theory emphasizes marginality and plurality which are seen as forces to change. Bhabha speaks of living on the borderline of history and language, on the limits of race and gender.[39] In the encounter with the religious stranger, the religionist needs to inhabit the borderline between the discourse of religious studies and the discourse of tradition, in the contested borderland of language and dialogical relations.

It is now time to draw these considerations to a close. I believe religious studies to be a subject area of great cultural and personal significance that needs to be located centrally in contemporary debates about meaning, ethics, globalization, capital and power, and needs to develop a more rigorous self-reflection or metatheory. My understanding of what religious studies is and does, or should do, has been coloured by the force of contemporary theoretical developments, particularly dialogism, by cultural developments that have not eradicated religion but have shown its significance in privatized, postmodern life, and by the impact of religions in non-Western, particularly South-Asian, cultures. It remains now to simply summarize the main points that I would consider to be of importance for future research in the continuing development of a critical religions studies.

1. The inquiry into religions should be historicist and examine religions in the context of discrete narratives and practices related to

precise locations and cultural and linguistic areas. This is a very demanding enterprise, for it requires the development of the linguistic skills necessary to interact with the range of textual sources needs to place religious texts in the context of wider social, cultural and political texts. It also needs the skills of historical, textual research and anthropological method and perhaps points to a shift from individual to team research programmes. This kind of work has begun in other disciplines, particularly literary studies with the development of the new historicism and cultural materialism, and is beginning to happen with religions in South Asia (I am thinking especially of the work of Sheldon Pollock).[40]

2. Religious studies should develop a metatheoretical discourse that is more visible or central to the concerns of the discipline. This kind of discourse needs to align itself with similar discourses in the social sciences and humanities and to contribute to those discussions. It also needs to be 'dialogically reflexive' in recognizing research programmes to be themselves historically contingent, driven by desire for certain results, and to achieve results in dialogical interaction with its 'object', 'religion'.

3. Research programmes in religions need to be dialogical and to begin with communication and interaction, rather than with the phenomenological privileging of consciousness, as I have argued here.

4. Developing from the first point, religious research needs to develop the anthropological reading of texts, rather than the simply philological, and to recognize the importance of texts in fieldwork. Indeed, this is why religious studies is so important as a distinct subject area, for it can promote the interpenetration of philology and anthropology, while at the same time as reflexively recognizing their historical contingency. To philology it can bring awareness of social and historical processes, and to anthropology or the encounter with the 'ethnos' it can bring history and text.

Although this list is meant to be suggestive rather than prescriptive, I think there is a need for religious studies to have a higher profile in public debate and within the academy which might be facilitated by further research within the parameters outlined here. There is a famous Sanskrit saying about the science of language:

Anantaraṃ kila śabdaśāstraṃ svalpaṃ tathāyurbahavaśca vighnāḥ/
Sāram tato grahyamapasya phalgu hamsairyathā kṣiramivāmbumadhyāt//

Truly endless is the science of language, but life is short and many are the obstacles. So grasp the essence and leave the worthless, as do geese the milk from the midst of water.

If we were to replace *śabdaśāstra* with, perhaps, *mataśāstra*, the 'science of religion', we are left with an apposite assessment of the situation, though with the added complication that, unlike the geese, we can no longer distinguish the essence from the peripheral.

Notes

Introduction

1. Auerbach, *Mimesis: The Representation of Reality in Western Literature* (Princeton University Press, 1953), pp. 3–23.
2. Blumenberg, *The Legitimacy of the Modern Age* (London and Cambridge, MA: MIT Press, 1983), part 1.
3. Ritzer, 'Metatheorizing in Sociology, Explaining the Coming of Age', in Ritzer (ed.) *Metatheorizing* (London: Sage, 1992), p. 7.
4. Eliade, *The Myth of the Eternal Return* (Princeton: Bollingen, 1971), p. 21.
5. See McCutcheon 'The Myth of the Apolitical Scholar: The Life and Works of Mircea Eliade', *Queens Quarterly*, 100(3) (1993), 642–63; *Manufacturing Religion: The Discourse on Sui Generis Religion and the Politics of Nostalgia* (New York: Oxford University Press, 1997).
6. McCutcheon, *Manufacturing Religion*, pp. 101–26.
7. Quoted in McCutcheon, *Manufacturing Religion*, p. 105.
8. Hannerz, *Transnational Connections: Culture, People, Places* (London and New York: Routledge, 1996), pp. 44–55.
9. See Fichte, *The Vocation of Man* (Indianapolis: Hackett, 1987), p. 45. Also Bowie, *From Romanticism to Critical Theory: The Philosophy of German Literary Theory* (London and New York: Routledge, 1997), p. 42.
10. Husserl, *Husserliana* VI 339 and 271, quoted in Gadamer, *Truth and Method* (London: Sheed & Ward, 1989), p. 243.
11. Gadamer, *Truth and Method*, p. 224.
12. See Bowie, *From Romanticism to Critical Theory*, pp. 35–52.
13. The philosophical landscape of the twentieth century has been characterized by Apel as Marxism, analytical philosophy and phenomenological-existential-hermeneutical thought, though Haber-

mas adds structuralism as a fourth current. See Grondin *Introduction to Philosophical Hermeneutics* (Yale University Press, 1994), p. 8. But there are problems in categorizing hermeneutics so closely with phenomenology because of the tension between epistemology and interpretation and between subjectivity and utterance.

14. e.g. Habermas, 'An Alternative Way out of the Philosophy of the Subject: Communicative versus Subject-Centred Reason' in *The Philosophical Discourse of Modernity* (Cambridge: Polity Press, 1985), pp. 294–335. For a critique of the transcendental subject from the perspective of a shared, communicative reason see Castoriadis, *The Imaginary Institution of Society* (Cambridge: Polity Press, 1987), pp. 104–7. For a critique of the Freudian self pp. 294–300.

Chapter 1

1. Bourdieu, *Homo Academicus* (Cambridge: Polity Press, 1988).
2. Particularly the contributions of the Centre for Cultural Values (director Paul Heelas) which transformed in 1996 into the Centre for Cultural Research and the journal *Method and Theory in the Study of Religion*.
3. Roberts, 'Interpretations of Resurgent Religion', *Theory, Culture and Society* 13(1), 1996, p. 137. I would also thoroughly endorse Lorne Dawson's claim: 'I am simply issuing a call for greater methodological sophistication in the study of religion, based on a finer appreciation of the metatheoretical and theoretical debates that have shaped and disturbed the social sciences for over a century. It is time to end our disciplinary insularity.' ('On Reducing Reductionism in the Academic Study of Religion: Dippman's Spurious Distinction,' *Method and Theory in the Study of Religion*, 5(1), (1993), 27–45, 43.)
4. Capps, 'On Religious Studies, In Lieu of an Overview' *Journal of the American Academy of Religion*, 42 (1974), 727–33. Although in *Religious Studies: the Making of a Discipline* (Minneapolis: Fortress Press, 1995) pp. 338–9 Capps implies that even figures such as the feminist psychoanalyst Luce Irigaray and the anthropologist Renato Rosaldo could be regarded as being within the tradition of religious studies. But the point remains that these are coming from discourses distinct from religious studies which has yet to establish a metatheoretical discourse of its own.
5. Preus, *Explaining Religion: Criticism and Theory from Bodin to Freud* (New Haven and London: Yale University Press, 1987). See also Harrison, *'Religion' and the Religions in the English Enlightenment*

(Cambridge University Press, 1990); Sharpe, *Comparative Religion* (London: Duckworth, 1975), pp. 1–26.

6. Müller, 'Chips from a German Workshop', vol. 1, *Essays on the Science of Religion* (London: Longman, Green & Co., 1867), pp. 18 ff.

7. Ryba, *The Essence of Phenomenology and its Meaning for the Scientific Study of Religion* (New York: Peter Lang, 1991).

8. There have been some exceptions such as John Bowker's *The Sense of God: Sociological, Anthropological and Psychological Approaches to the Origin of the Sense of God* (Oxford University Press, 1973), chapter 6.

9. For an account of these institutional developments see King, (ed.) *Turning Points in Religious Studies. Essays in Honour of Geoffrey Parrinder* (Edinburgh: T. & T. Clark, 1990).

10. There is an abundance of literature on this. For a succinct articulation of the position which sees a clear distinction between theology and religious studies see Smart, 'Religious Studies and Theology' in *The Council of Societies for the Study of Religion Bulletin*, 26(3) (1997), 66–8 (see also other papers in this edition). Isichei, 'Some Ambiguities in the Academic Study of Religion' *Religion*, 23 (1993), 379–90 argues for the continued separation of religious studies from theology. For a position which denies the distinction or sees strong continuities between the disciplines in a university and research context, see Davies, 'Theology and Religious Studies in the University: Some Ambiguities Revisited', *Religion* 26, 1996, pp. 49–68 and Ford, 'Theology and Religious Studies at the Turn of the Millennium: Reconceiving the Field', *Teaching Theology and Religion*, 1(1) (1998), 4–12. See also Edsman, 'Theology or Religious Studies?', *Religion*, 4 (1974), 59–74. Hebblethwaite, *The Problems of Theology* (Cambridge University Press, 1980) pp. 23–43.

11. De Certeau *The Writing of History* (New York: Columbia University Press, 1988), p. 23.

12. This is a commonplace distinction in religious studies and is fundamental to much of Ninian Smart's work. See his *Reasons and Faiths* (London: SPCK, 1958), pp. 2–10.

13. La Barre, *The Ghost Dance* (New York: Dell Publishing, 1970), pp. 2, 25.

14. Drummond, 'Christian Theology and the History of Religions', *Journal of Ecumenical Studies*, 12, 1975, 389–405.

15. Lash, *The Beginning and the End of 'Religion'* (Cambridge University Press, 1996), p. 57.

16. Rorty, *Philosophy and the Mirror of Nature* (Oxford and Cambridge, MA: Blackwell, 1980), p. 378. 'To see keeping a conversation going as a sufficient aim of philosophy, to see wisdom as consisting in the ability

to sustain a conversation, is to see human beings as generators of new descriptions rather than beings one hopes to be able to describe accurately.' Also *New Literary History*, 1978, vol. 10, pp. 146–60.

17. Lash, *The Beginning and End of Religion*, p. 54. Others have made similar claims. Kristeva, for example, says theology is a 'discourse of love directed to an impossible other' (Kristeva, *In the Beginning Was Love* (New York: Columbia University Press, 1988), p. 7) quoted by Ward in 'Kenosis and Naming: Beyond Analogy and Towards Allegoria Amoris' in Heelas (ed.) *Religion, Modernity and Postmodernity* (Oxford: Blackwell, 1998), p. 251.

18. Critchley, *Very Little . . . Almost Nothing: Death, Philosophy, Literature* (London and New York: Routledge, 1997), p. 86.

19. Ferré, *Language, Logic and God* (London: Eyre & Spottiswoode, 1962), p. 69. For an interesting discussion of these issues see Ebeling, *Introduction to a Theological Theory of Language* (London: Collins, 1973), pp. 43–53.

20. Black, 'Metaphor' in Margolis (ed.) *Philosophy Looks at the Arts* (New York: Temple University Press, 1962), pp. 218–35; See also a critique of Black in Soskice, *Metaphor and Religious Language* (Oxford: Clarendon Press, 1989), pp. 38–51.

21. Tracy, *The Analogical Imagination: Christian Theology and the Culture of Pluralism* (London: SCM Press, 1981), p. 447.

22. See Lakoff, *Women, Fire and Dangerous Things: What Categories Reveal About the Mind* (Chicago University Press, 1987); Whorf, 'The Relation of Habitual Thought to Behaviour and Language,' pp. 148–49 in *Language, Thought and Reality* (Cambridge, MA: MIT Press, 1956), pp. 134–59.

23. Milbank, *The Word Made Strange: Theology, Language, Culture* (Oxford: Blackwell, 1997), p. 84.

24. My understanding of theology as comprising a primary and secondary discourse has been influenced by conversations with Dr Oliver Davies.

25. This has been argued by Oliver Davies and myself elsewhere. Davies and Flood 'The Other Tiger: Reflections on Method in Theology and Religious Studies' (unpublished).

26. I take the term 'rational community' from Lingis, *The Community of Those Who Have Nothing in Common* (Bloomington and Indianapolis: Indiana University Press, 1994), p. 10.

27. Code, *Rhetorical Spaces: Essays on Gendered Locations* (London: Routledge, 1995), pp. 44–57.

28. Roberts, 'The Construals of "Europe": Religion, Theology and the Problematics of Modernity' in Heelas (ed.) *Religion, Modernity and Postmodernity* (Oxford: Blackwell, 1998), p. 187.

29. Peukert, 'Enlightenment and Theology as Unfinished Projects', in

Browning and Francis Schussler Fiorenza (eds) *Habermas, Modernity and Public Theology* (New York: Crossroad, 1992).

30. For example, Hauerwas, *Dispatches from the Front: Theological Engagements with the Secular* (Durham, NC: Duke University Press, 1994); and Hauerwas and Willimon, *Resident Aliens: A Provocative Christian Assessment of Culture and Ministry for People Who Know That Something's Wrong* (Nashville: Abingdon, 1989).

31. For key works see particularly Taylor, *Erring: A Postmodern A/theology* (University of Chicago Press, 1984); Griffin, *God and Religion in the Postmodern World: Essays in Postmodern Theology* (Albany: Suny Press, 1989); Milbank *Theology and Social Theory: Beyond Secular Reason* (Oxford: Blackwell, 1990); and Marion, *God Without Being* (University of Chicago Press, 1991). For a good overview of the field see Tilley, *Postmodern Theologies: The Challenge of Religious Diversity* (New York: Orbis Books, 1996) and for useful readers see Ward (ed.) *The Postmodern God: A Theological Reader* (Oxford: Blackwell, 1997) and Bond (ed.), *Post-Secular Philosophy* (Oxford: Blackwell, 1998).

32. Lindbeck, *The Nature of Doctrine: Religion and Theology in a Post-liberal Age* (London: SPCK, 1984), p. 41.

33. Lindbeck, *The Nature of Doctrine*, p. 114.

34. Milbank, *Theology and Social Theory*, p. 386.

35. Pickstock, *After Writing: On the Liturgical Consummation of Philosophy* (Oxford: Blackwell, 1998).

36. Green, 'Challenging the Religious Studies Canon: Karl Barth's Theory of Religion', *Journal of Religion*, 75, 1995, 473–86.

37. Marsden, *The Outrageous Idea of Christian Scholarship* (Oxford University Press, 1997), pp. 5–6.

38. Turner, *Orientalism, Postmodernism and Globalism* (London: Routledge, 1994), p. 8.

39. Preus, *Explaining Religion: Criticism and Theory from Bodin to Freud* (New Haven and London: Yale University Press, 1987), p. xi.

40. Weber, *The Methodology of the Social Sciences* (New York: The Free Press, 1949), p. 72.

41. Rickert, *The Limits of Concept Formation in Natural Science: A Logical Introduction to the Historical Sciences* (Cambridge University Press, 1986), pp. 91–2.

42. Weber, *The Methodology of the Social Sciences*, p. 112. In many ways Weber preempts the critique that hard science is beyond cultural and social processes, articulated by Feyerabend, Lakatos and Kuhn, and that the social sciences are similarly constrained. Feyerabend, *Against Method: Outline of an Anarchistic Theory of Knowledge* (London: NLB, 1975); Kuhn, *The Structure of Scientific Revolutions* (University

of Chicago Press, 2nd ed. 1975); *The Essential Tension: Selected Studies in Scientific Tradition and Change* (University of Chicago Press, 1977); Lakatos, 'Falsification and the Methodology of Scientific Research Programmes' in Lakatos and Musgrave, (eds.) *Criticism and the Growth of Knowledge* (Cambridge University Press, 1970). Winch, *The Idea of a Social Science* (London: RKP, 1977 (1958); Woolgar, (ed.) *Knowledge and Reflexivity: New Frontiers in the Sociology of Knowledge* (London: SAGE, 1991). See Bernstein, *Beyond Objectivism and Relativism* (Oxford: Blackwell, 1983), pp. 20–44.

43.   Kolakowski, *Positivist Philosophy* (Penguin, 1972).

44.   Husserl, *Ideas Pertaining to a Pure Phenomenology and to a Phenomenological Philosophy* (Boston, The Hague, Lancaster: Nijhoff, 1983), p. 16.

45.   Schutz, *The Phenomenology of the Social World* (London: Heinemann, 1972).

46.   Müller, *Introduction to the Science of Religion: Four Lectures Delivered at the Royal Institution with two Essays on False Analogies and the Philosophy of Mythology* (London: Longmans, Green & Co., 1873) p. 35, cited in Waardenburg, *Classical Approaches to the Study of Religion*, vol. 1 (The Hague, Paris: Mouton, 1973), p. 94.

47.   Chantepie de la Saussaye, *Lehrbuch der Religionsgeschichte* (Freiburg, 1887), p. 168. Reference from Sharpe, *Comparative Religion: A History* (London: Duckworth, 1975), p. 224.

48.   Smart, *The Science of Religion and the Sociology of Knowledge* (Princeton University Press, 1973), pp. 8, 22.

49.   Lawson and McCauley, *Rethinking Religion: Connecting Cognition and Culture* (Cambridge University Press, 1990), pp. 1–2.

50.   Lawson and McCauley, *Rethinking Religion*, p. 1.

51.   Lawson and McCauley, *Rethinking Religion*, pp. 32–44. These metatheoretical positions Lawson and McCauley categorize as intellectualist which understands religious systems to be 'rational' explanatory systems, symbolist which sees religious systems as symbolic-cultural systems akin to natural languages, structuralist which seeks underlying categories of thought which give rise to symbolic systems, and cognitivist which develops symbolic and structuralist explanations by adding to these developments from cognitive science (linguistics, cognitive psychology and cognitive anthropology).

52.   Samuel, *Mind, Body and Culture: Anthropology and the Biological Interface* (Cambridge University Press, 1990), pp. 18, 36.

53.   Bourdieu, *Outline of a Theory of Practice* (Cambridge University Press, 1991), p. 106. Cf. Bakhtin: 'What is represented by the diagram is only an abstract aspect of the real total act of actively responsive understanding, the sort of understanding that evokes a response, and one that

the speaker anticipates.' 'The Problem of Speech Genres', p. 69, in *Speech Genres and Other Late Essays* (Austin: University of Texas Press, 1986).

54. De Certeau, *The Writing of History* (Columbia University Press, 1988), p. 57.

55. Haraway, *Simians, Cyborgs and Women: the Reinvention of Nature* (London: Free Association Books, 1991), p. 196.

56. Code, *Rhetorical Spaces: Essays on Gendered Locations* (London: Routledge, 1995).

57. Hufford, 'The Scholarly Voice and the Personal Voice: Reflexivity in Belief Studies', *Western Folklore*, 54, 1995, pp. 57–76. On reflexivity in the Western tradition generally see Barry Sandywell's monumental three-volume work *Logological Investigations* (London: Routledge, 1995), p. 138.

58. Bourdieu, *Outline of a Theory of Practice* (Cambridge University Press, 1977), p. 3.

59. Bourdieu, *The Logic of Practice* (Cambridge: Polity Press, 1992), p. 27.

60. Bourdieu, *The Logic of Practice* (Cambridge: Polity Press, 1992), p. 27.

61. Bourdieu, *The Logic of Practice* (Cambridge: Polity Press, 1992), p. 27.

62. O'Connor, 'Feminist Research in Religion' in Ursula King (ed.), *Religion and Gender*, (Oxford: Blackwell, 1995), p. 48.

63. Bowie writes: 'The degree to which the academic discipline studied and the particular paradigms adopted are determined by an individual's life story is insufficiently acknowledged by most scholars, trained as we are in the use of intellectual reasoning to justify and defend positions arrived at largely as a result of unconscious or semiconscious psychological motivations.' 'Trespassing on Sacred Domains: A Feminist Anthropological Approach to Theology and Religious Studies', *Journal of Feminist Studies in Religion*, 13, 1998, 40–62.

64. This is the general position of structuration theory as developed by Giddens but also, although not by that name, by Bourdieu. See Giddens, Anthony, *New Rules of Sociological Method*, (Oxford: Polity Press, 1993 (1976)); Held, David and J.B. Thompson (eds) *Social Theory of Modern Societies: Anthony Giddens and his Critics* (Cambridge University Press, 1989); Jenkins, 'Pierre Bourdieu and the Reproduction of Determinism', *Sociology*, 16, 1982, 270–81.

65. Bourdieu, *Sociology in Question* (London: Sage, 1993), pp. 56–9.

66. For an excellent discussion of these issues see Milner, *Status and Sacredness: A General Theory of Status Relations and an Analysis of Indian Culture* (New York, Oxford: Oxford University Press, 1994).

67. Smart, *The Science of Religion and the Sociology of Knowledge* (Princeton University Press, 1973), p. 22.

68. Nagel, *The View from Nowhere* (Oxford University Press, 1986), pp. 5–7.

69. Borges, 'The Other Tiger'. Translation by Norman Thomas di Giovanni, *Jorge Luis Borges, Selected Poems 1923–1967* (London: Allen Lane Penguin, 1992), p. 145.

Chapter 2

1. Blumenberg, *Work on Myth* (Cambridge, MA: MIT Press, 1990), p. 67.

2. Blumenberg notes Heidegger's association of the term with the 'worldhood of the world'. Blumenberg, *Work on Myth*, p. 68.

3. Dawson, Lorne '*Sui Generis* Phenomena and Disciplinary Axioms: Rethinking Pals Proposal' *Religion* (1990) vol. 20, pp. 38–51; 'On Reference to the Transcendent in the Scientific Study of Religion: A Qualified Idealist Proposal' *Religion* (1987), vol. 17, pp. 227–50; *Reason, Freedom and Religion: Closing the Gap Between the Humanities and Scientific Study of Religion*, Toronto Studies in Religion (New York: Peter Lang, 1988); Pals, Daniel 'Reductionism and Belief: An Appraisal of Recent Attacks on the Doctrine of Irreducible Religions' *Journal of Religion* (1986), vol. 66, pp. 18–36; 'Is Religion a *Sui Generis* Phenomenon?' *Journal of the American Academy of Religion* (1987), vol. 55, pp. 259–82; 'Autonomy, Legitimacy and the Study of Religion' *Religion* (1990), vol. 20, pp. 1–16; 'Autonomy Revisited: A Rejoinder to Its Critics' *Religion* (1990), vol. 20, pp. 30–37; Penner, Hans, *Impasse and Resolution: A Critique of the Study of Religion*, Toronto Studies in Religion, vol. 8 (New York: Peter Lang, 1989); Segal, Robert 'In Defence of Reductionism' *Journal of the American Academy of Religion* (1983), vol. 51, pp. 97–124; Wiebe, Donald 'Theory in the Study of Religion' *Religion* 13 (1983), pp. 283–309; 'Beyond the Sceptic and the Devotee: Reductionism in the Scientific Study of Religion' *Journal of the American Academy of Religion* (1984), vol. 52, pp. 156–65; 'Why the Academic Study of Religion? Motive and Method in the Study of Religion' *Religious Studies* (1988), vol. 24, pp. 403–13; 'Disciplinary Axioms, Boundary Conditions and the Academic Study of Religion: Comments on Pals and Dawson' *Religion* (1990), vol. 20, pp. 17–29.

4. The term 'culture' itself is problematic and almost as hard to define as 'religion'. Broadly I take culture to be 'habit', 'what we do', and 'the way we represent ourselves to ourselves'. On 'culture' see Jenks, *Culture*

(London and New York: Routledge, 1993). Some thinkers take the cultural to be distinct from the social or have argued that processes since the war have increasingly separated the cultural from the social (Featherstone, *Undoing Culture: Globalization, Postmodernism and Identity* (London, Thousand Oaks, New Delhi: Sage, 1995). This would accord with the general postmodern processes of privatization and fragmentation.

5. See Harrison, *'Religion' and the Religions in the English Enlightenment* (Cambridge University Press 1990).

6. Kitagawa, *Encyclopedia of Religion* vol. 1, p. xv. 'We have assumed that there is no such thing as a purely religious phenomenon. A religious phenomenon is a human phenomenon and thus is not only religious but also social, cultural, psychological, biological, and so on.' Tim Fitzgerald has argued that 'religion' cannot be distinguished from 'culture'. Fitzgerald, 'Hinduism and the World Religion Fallacy', *Religion* (1990), vol. 20, pp. 101–18; 'Religious Studies as Cultural Studies: A Philosophical and Anthropological Critique of the Category of Religion,' *Diskus* 3, 1, 1995, 35–47.

7. An important paper in this direction is Roberts, 'Time, Virtuality and the Goddess', *Cultural Values* (1998), vol. 2 nos. 2 and 3, pp. 270–87.

8. Spiro, 'Religion: Some Problems of Definition and Explanation' in Banton (ed.) *Anthropological Approaches to the Study of Religion* (London: Tavistock, 1978 (1966)), p. 90.

9. Evans-Prichard, *The Institutions of Primitive Society* (Oxford: Blackwell, 1954), p. 9, cited in Spiro p. 90. Staal, Frits, *Rules Without Meaning: Ritual, Mantras and the Human Sciences* (New York: Peter Lang, 1989), pp. 61–4.

10. Clarke and Byrne, *Religion Defined and Explained* (London: Macmillan, 1993), p. 4.

11. McCutcheon, 'The Category 'Religion' in Recent Publications' *Numen* (1995), vol. 42, pp. 284–309. McCutcheon summarizes the positions well. He writes: 'the critical camps in this debate on the status or use of "religion" seem to be divided between, on the one hand, those who maintain that "religion" is, for good or bad, a taxonomic tool that labels, divides, abstracts, and describes portions of human behaviour and belief in relation to other equally constructed aspects of behaviour and belief (one thinks of Jonathan Z. Smith as one of the primary representatives of this position) and, on the other, those essentialist scholars who, along with Cantwell Smith, maintain that the focus of research on religion somehow ought to transcend (or, in the least, not be confused with) human, historical categories of thought and commu-

nication,' (p. 287). This review article has strongly influenced the present chapter.

12. For a history of the term see the survey by Rudolf, 'Inwieweit ist der Begriff "Religion" Eurozentrisch?' in Bianchi (ed.), *The Notion of 'Religion' in Comparative Research: Selected Proceedings of the XVI IAHR Congress* (Roma: 'L'Erma' di Bretschneider, 1994, pp. 131–9). Also in the same volume Hans Dieter Betz 'Christianity as Religion: Paul's Attempt at Definition in Romans' pp. 3–9; Johannes Irmscher 'Der Terminus *Religio* und seine antiken entsprechnungen im Philologischen und Religionsgeschichtlichen Vergleich' pp. 63–73. Also see Feil 'From the Classical *Religio* to the Modern Religion: Elements of a Transformation between 1550 and 1650' in Despland and Vallée (eds), *Religion in History: the Word, the Idea, the Reality* (Waterloo, Ontario: Wilfred Laurier University Press, 1992), pp. 31–43; Harrison, *'Religion' and the Religions in the English Enlightenment* (Cambridge University Press, 1990); Also Sharpe, *Comparative Religion* pp. 1–26.

13. Betz, 'Christianity as Religion: Paul's Attempt at Definition in Romans', Bianchi, *The Notion of 'Religion' in Comparative Research*, pp. 3–9.

14. Feil, 'From the Classical *Religio* to Modern Religion', p. 32.

15. Harrison, *'Religion' and the Religions in the English Enlightenment* (Cambridge University Press, 1990). See also Lash, *The Beginning and End of Religion* (Cambridge University Press, 1996), pp. 1–25.

16. Feil, 'From the Classical *Religio* to Modern Religion', pp. 32, 41.

17. Harrison, *Religion and the 'Religions'*, p. 14. On the category 'religion' see Saler, *Conceptualising Religion: Immanent Anthropologists, Transcendent Natives and Unbounded Categories* (Leiden: Brill, 1993), p.1. For religion as a post-Enlightenment development see Cohen, 'What is Religion? An analysis for cross-cultural comparisons' *Journal of Christian Education* 7 (2/3) 116–38 1964; Cohen, ' "Religion" in non-western Cultures?' *American Anthropologist* 69 (1) 73–76, 1967; Despland, *La religion en occident: evolution des idées et du vecu* (Montreal: Editions Fidee, 1979); Preus, *Explaining Religion*; Smith, *The Meaning and End of Religion* New York: Macmillan (1962); Wax, 'Religion as Universal: Tribulations of an Anthropological Enterprise' *Zygon* (1984), vol. 19 (1), pp. 5–20.

18. On the development of these concepts in the Enlightenment see Davies, 'Culture and Spirituality' (Oxford: Westminster College, 1996); on the origins of 'culture' see Jenks, *Culture*, pp. 6–24; on 'mysticism' see McGinn, *The Presence of God: A History of Western Christian Mysticism*, 1 *The Foundations of Mysticism* (London: SCM Press, 1992), p. xvii, 252; De Certeau, *The Mystic Fable* 1 *The Sixteenth and Seventeenth Centuries* (Chicago University Press, 1992), pp. 16–17; Lash, *The Beginning and the End of 'Religion'* (Cambridge University Press

1996), pp. 166–71. On 'sentiment' in the seventeenth and eighteenth centuries see Taylor, *Sources of the Self* (Cambridge University Press, 1989), pp. 291–302.

19. Sharpe, *Understanding Religion* (London: Duckworth, 1983), p. 39. 'It is all too easily forgotten by Western students that many languages simply do not have an equivalent of the word "religion" in their vocabulary. "Law", "duty", "custom", "worship", "spiritual discipline", "the way" they know: "religion" they do not.' However one might question whether they do in fact know even these other terms, being as they are in English and each carrying with it its own particular baggage. For a semantic history of *religio* see Saler *Conceptualising Religion: Immanent Anthropologists, Transcendent Natives and Unbounded Categories* (Leiden: Brill, 1993) pp. 64–8. For a discussion of the term *religio* see Irmscher 'Der Terminus *Religio* und Seine Antiken Entsprechnungen Im Philologischen und Religionsgeschechtlichen Vergleich' in Bianchi, *The Notion of 'Religion' in Comparative Research*, pp. 63–73.

20. See Lash, *The Beginning and the End of Religion*, pp. 3–25.

21. Pye, 'The Notion of Religion in Comparative Research' *Selected Proceedings of the XVI IAHR Congress* 1994, pp. 115–22.

22. Staal, *Rules Without Meaning: Ritual, Mantras and the Human Sciences* (New York: Peter Lang, 1989), p. 401. For a discussion of Hinduism as a religion which brings out these issues see Sontheimer and Kulke, (eds) *Hinduism Reconsidered* (Delhi: Manonhar, 1991).

23. Brunner, 'Le Sādhaka, personnage oubliée dans l'Inde du Sud', *Journal Asiatique* (1975), pp. 411–43.

24. Kolakowski, *Religion* (Glasgow: Fontana, 1982), p. 10.

25. I am indebted here to Rich Freeman for pointing out the importance of non-empirical beings as well.

26. As Armin Geertz says of his definition. Geertz, *The Invention of Prophecy: Continuity and Meaning in Hopi Religion* (Berkeley: University of California Press, 1994), p. 10.

27. Levi-Strauss, Claude, *The Raw and the Cooked* (Penguin, 1992 (1964)), pp. 48–51.

28. Lakoff, *Women, Fire and Dangerous Things: What Categories Reveal About the Mind* (The University of Chicago Press, 1987), pp. 5–57.

29. Rosch, 'Human Categorization,' in Warren (ed.), *Studies in Cross-Cultural Psychology* (London: Academic Press, 1978), vol. 1, pp. 1–49.

30. See my *An Introduction to Hinduism* (Cambridge University Press, 1996), p. 7.

31. Saler, *Conceptualising Religion*, p. 68.

32. Bowker, *Is God a Virus? Genes, Culture and Religion* (London: SPCK, 1995), p. 147.

33. Bowker, *The Sense of God: Sociological, Anthropological and Psychological Approaches to the Origin of the Sense of God* (Oxford: Clarendon Press, 1973), p. 64.

34. Bakhtin, 'Author and Hero in Aesthetic Activity,' p. 104, in *Art and Answerability* (Austin: University of Texas Press, 1990).

35. For an excellent discussion of these senses of ideology see Geuss, *The Idea of a Critical Theory* (Cambridge University Press, 1981), pp. 4–44.

36. Rumsey, 'Wording, Meaning and Linguistic Ideology,' *American Anthropologist* 92 (1990), pp. 346–61.

37. Bakhtin, 'The Problem of the Text,' p. 104, in *Speech Genres and Other Late Essays* (Austin: University of Texas Press, 1986), pp. 103–31.

38. Baudrillard, *Simulations*, (New York: Semiotext(e), 1983), pp. 1–6.

39. Eco, *A Theory of Semiotics* (Bloomington: Indiana University Press, 1976), p. 8.

40. On religions as systems of information flow see Bowker, *Licensed Insanities* (London: Darton, Longman & Todd, 1987), pp. 112–43.

41. Heelas, Lash, and Morris (eds), *Detraditionalization* (Oxford: Blackwell, 1996). See particularly the paper by Morris 'Community beyond Tradition', pp. 223–49.

42. See Roberts, 'Time, Virtuality and the Goddess,' (Time & Value); Heelas, *The New Age* (Routledge, 1997).

43. 'The culture of the consumer society is therefore held to be a vast floating complex of fragmentary signs and images, which produces an endless sign-play which destabilize long-held symbolic meanings and cultural order.' Featherstone, *Undoing Culture: Globalization, Postmodernism and Identity* (London, Thousand Oaks, New Delhi: Sage, 1995), p. 75.

44. Robertson, *Globalization* (London: Sage, 1992), pp. 177–81.

45. Freidman, *Cultural Identity and Global Process* (London: Sage, 1994), pp. 239–40.

46. Robertson, *Globalization*, p. 100.

47. Beyer, *Religion and Globalization* (London, Thousand Oaks, Delhi: Sage, 1994), pp. 99–109.

48. See Roberts, 'Time, Virtuality and the Goddess,' *Cultural Values*, vol. 2.

49. Heelas, 'Introduction: On Differentiation and Dedifferentiation' in Heelas (ed.) *Religion, Modernity and Postmodernity* (Oxford: Blackwell, 1998), p. 8.

50. There is a vast literature on the privatization of religion. See, for

example, Beyer, *Religion and Globalization*, pp. 70–75; on 'individualization' and 'preference' see Berger, *The Sacred Canopy: Elements for a Sociological Theory of Religion*, pp. 133–34; Luckman, *The Invisible Religion: the Problem of Religion in Modern Society* (New York: Macmillan, 1967); Parsons, 'Religion in a Modern Pluralist Society', *Review of Religious Research*, vol. 7 (1966), pp. 125–46; Wilson, 'Aspects of Secularization in the West', *Japanese Journal of Religious Studies*, vol. 3, 1976, pp. 259–76.

51. See Jaffrelot, Christophe, *The Hindu Nationalist Movement and Indian Politics, 1925 to the 1990s*, (London: Hurst & Co., 1996). On the general point see Featherstone, *Undoing Culture*, pp. 119–20.

52. See Heelas, Lash, and Morris (eds), *Detraditionalization*, pp. 40–46 and *passim*.

53. Hick, *An Interpretation of Religion: Human Responses to the Transcendent* (London: Macmillan, 1989).

54. Hick, *An Interpretation of Religion*, pp. 252–96. For a clear account of Hick's theology see Badham 'John Hick's Global Understanding of Religion' (Tokyo: International Buddhist Study Center, 1992).

55. Hick, *An Interpretation of Religion*, p. 12.

56. Hick, *An Interpretation of Religion*, p. 228.

57. Hick, *An Interpretation of Religion*, p. 15.

58. Segal, *Explaining and Interpreting Religion: Essays on the Issue* (New York: Peter Lang, 1992), pp. 63–75.

59. Hick, *An Interpretation of Religion*, pp. 362–76.

60. Clayton, John 'Thomas Jefferson and the Study of Religion' (inaugural lecture, Lancaster University, 1992), p. 23.

61. Clayton, 'Thomas Jefferson', pp. 26–32.

62. Clayton, 'Thomas Jefferson', p. 32.

63. See Casson, 'Cognitive Anthropology' in Philip K. Bock (ed.) *Handbook of Psychological Anthropology* (Westport: Greenwood Press, 1994); Casson, *Language, Culture and Cognition* (New York: Macmillan, 1981); Janet, (ed.) *Directions in Cognitive Anthropology* (Urbana, IL: University of Illinois Press, 1985); Tyler (ed.), *Cognitive Anthropology* (New York: Holt, Rinehart and Winston, 1969); Colby, 'Ethnographic Semantics: a preliminary survey,' *American Anthropology* (1966), vol. 7, 3–32.

64. Sperber, *Rethinking Symbolism* (Cambridge University Press, 1975).

65. Boyer, *The Naturalness of Religious Ideas: A Cognitive Theory of Religion* (Berkeley, Los Angeles, London: University of California Press, 1994).

66. Lawson and McCauley, *Rethinking Religion: Connecting Culture and Religion* (Cambridge University Press, 1990).

67. Atran, 'Origin of the Species and Genus Concepts: An Anthropological

Perspective', *Journal of the History of Biology*, 1987, vol. 20, pp. 195–279. *Cognitive Foundations of Natural History: Towards an Anthropology of Science* (Cambridge University Press, 1990). See also Atran and Sperber 'Learning without teaching: its place in culture' in Landsman (ed.) *Culture, Schooling and Psychological Development* (Norwood: Ablex, 1990).

68. Atran, *Cognitive Foundations of Natural History*, p. 217.
69. Boyer, 'Cognitive Aspects of Religious Symbolism' in Boyer (ed.) *Cognitive Aspects of Religious Symbolism* (Cambridge University Press, 1993), p. 20.
70. Boyer, *The Naturalness of Religious Ideas*, p. 69.
71. Boyer, *The Naturalness of Religious Ideas*, p. 71.
72. Boyer, *The Naturalness of Religious Ideas*, pp. 77–8.
73. Boyer, *The Naturalness of Religious Ideas*, pp. 110–11.
74. Boyer, *The Naturalness of Religious Ideas*, p. 113.
75. Boyer, 'Cognitive aspects of religious symbolism', p. 6.
76. Boyer, 'Cognitive aspects of religious symbolism', pp. 6–7.
77. Geertz, 'The Impact of the Concept Culture on the Concept of Man' in *The Interpretation of Cultures* (London: Fontana Press, 1993), p. 35.
78. Boyer, *The Naturalness of Religious Ideas*, p. 270–84. See also Dawkins, *The Selfish Gene* (New York: OUP, 1976).
79. Bowker, *Is God a Virus? Genes, Culture and Religion* (London: SPCK, 1995), pp. 40–6 and *passim*. For an interesting discussion on cultural and biological replication in relation to a 'multi-modal framework' approach to anthropological theory, see Samuel, *Mind, Body and Culture: Anthropology and the Biological Interface* (Cambridge University Press, 1990), pp. 158–61.
80. With regard to culture generally, this point is well expressed by Voloshinov in the following terms: 'The objective social regulatedness of ideological creativity, once misconstrued as a conformity with laws of the individual consciousness, must inevitably forfeit its real place in existence and depart either up into the superexistential empyrean of transcendentalism or down into the presocial recesses of the psychophysical, biological organism.' (*Marxism and the Philosophy of Language* (Cambridge, MA. and London: Harvard University Press, 1986), p. 12.
81. Personal communication.

Chapter 3

1. Lakatos, 'Falsification and the Methodology of Scientific Research Programmes', p. 164 in Lakatos and Musgrave (eds), *Criticism and the*

Growth of Knowledge (Cambridge University Press, 1970), pp. 91–196.

2. On the idea of a 'community' in relation to scientific rationality see Bernstein, *Beyond Objectivism and Relativism* (University of Pennsylvania Press, 1983), pp. 77–9.

3. On different kinds of reductionism in the study of religion see Strenski, *Religion in Relation: Method, Application, and Moral Location* (Columbia: University of South Carolina Press, 1993), section 2.

4. On the reductionism issue in the social sciences generally see, for example, Dallmayr and McCarthy (eds) *Understanding and Social Inquiry* (Notre Dame University Press, 1977); Dixon, *The Sociology of Belief: Fallacy and Foundation* (London: RKP, 1980); Peacocke (ed.), *Reductionism in Academic Disciplines* (Worcester: Billing & Son, 1985); Stinchcombe, 'The Origins of Sociology as a Discipline' *Acta Sociologica* 1984, vol. 27, pp. 51–61. For causal realism see Harré and Secord, *The Explanation of Social Behaviour* (Oxford: Blackwell, 1972); Keat and Urry, *Social Theory as Science* (London: RKP, 1975). For a critique of causal realism see Fay, *Changing Social Science* (Albany: Suny Press, 1983). On reductionism in the study of religion see Penner, *Impasse and Resolution: A Critique of the Study of Religion* Toronto Studies in Religion, vol. 8 (New York: Peter Lang, 1989); Yonan 'Is a Science of Religion Possible?' *Journal of Religion* vol. 52, 1972, pp. 107–33; Dawson, *Reason, Freedom and Religion; Closing the Gap Between the Humanistic and the Scientific Study of Religion* (New York: Peter Lang, 1988). On an account of these problems in the academic study of religion after the postmodern turn see Paden, *Interpreting the Sacred: Ways of Viewing Religion* (Boston: Beacon, 1992). Also Taylor (ed.), *Critical Terms for Religious Studies* (University of Chicago Press, 1998); Stone (ed.), *The Craft of Religious Studies* (New York: St Martin's Press, 1997).

5. See Outhwaite, *Understanding Social Life: The Method called Verstehen* (London: George Allen and Unwin, 1975), pp. 13–17.

6. For the irreducibility of religion see, for example, Eliade, *The Quest* (University of Chicago Press, 1969) pp. 3–6; Otto, *The Idea of the Holy* (OUP 1982 (1923)) pp. 5–7; Cumpsty, *Religion as Belonging: A General Theory of Religion* (London: University of America Press, 1991) pp. xxxvi, 8. For a critical review of Cumpsty see Lawson, *Journal of the American Academy of Religion* vol. 62 (1994), pp. 184–86. For reductionist arguments see Segal, *Religion and the Social Sciences: Essays on the Confrontation* (Atlanta: Scholars Press, 1989); *Explaining and Interpreting Religion, Essays on the Issue* (New York: Peter Lang, 1992); Wiebe, *Religion and Truth: Towards an Alternative Paradigm for the Study of Religion* (The Hague: Mouton, 1981).

7. See for example the debate in *Zygon: Journal of Religion and Science* 1995, vol. 25 and the responses by Pals and Segal in *Zygon* vol. 27 (1992) and *Method and Theory in the Study of Religion* vol. 5/1 (1993), 89–111.

8. Wiebe, 'A Positive Episteme for the Study of Religion,' *The Scottish Journal of Religious Studies* vol. 6 (1985), pp. 78–95.

9. Wiebe, 'The Failure of Nerve in the Academic Study of Religion', *Studies in Religion/Sciences Religieuses* 13/4 (1984), pp. 401–22. For a response to the reductionist claim see Pals, 'Explanation, Social Science, and the Study of Religion: A Response to Segal with Comment on the Zygon exchange,' Zygon, *Journal of Religion and Science*, 1992, vol. 27, no. 1, pp. 89–105.

10. Although it should be remembered, as Strenski has pointed out, that reductionism is not a monolithic category and there several kinds of reduction. See Strenski, *Religion in Relation: Method, Application, and Moral Location* (Columbia: University of South Carolina Press, 1993) section 2.

11. Segal writes: 'Whoever projects God onto the world does not discover God in the world but rather imposes God on it. Should God turn out to exist after all, the projection would represent no insight on the believer's part. It would represent mere coincidence. The extraordinariness that such a coincidence would represent is what challenges the truth of religion. A belief originating in projection is statistically unlikely to be true.' Segal, *Explaining and Interpreting Religion*, pp. 72–3.

12. Berger, *The Sacred Canopy, Elements of a Sociological Theory of Religion* (New York: Doubleday, 1990 (1967)), p. 100.

13. Wiebe 'The Failure of Nerve', p. 402.

14. Segal 'In Defense of Reductionism', p. 106.

15. Eliade, *Patterns in Comparative Religion* (Cleveland: Meridian Books, 1963 (1958)), p. xiii.

16. See Rennie, *Reconstructing Eliade: Making Sense of Religion* (Albany: Suny Press, 1996), pp. 191–4; Allen, 'Recent Defenders of Eliade: A Critical Evaluation', *Religion*, vol. 24 (1995), pp. 333–51.

17. Bourdieu, *In Other Words: Essays Towards a Reflexive Sociology* (Cambridge: Polity Press, 1994), pp. 35–6.

18. Gadamer, *Truth and Method* (London: Sheed & Ward, 1989), pp. 265–71.

19. Milbank, *Theology and Social Theory: Beyond Secular Reason* (Oxford: Blackwell, 1990). '(T)heology encounters in sociology only a theology, and indeed a church in disguise, but a theology and a church dedicated to promoting a certain secular consensus,' (p. 4).

20. Habermas, 'On the Logic of the Social Sciences* (Cambridge: Polity Press, 1988), pp. 153–5.

21. Smart, *The Science of Religion and the Sociology of Knowledge: Some Methodological Questions* (Princeton University Press, 1973), p. 54.

22. Idinopulos, 'Must Professors of Religion be Religious? Comments on Eliade's Method of Inquiry and Segal's Defense of Reductionism', in Indinopulos and Yonan (eds) *Religion and Reductionism: Essays on Eliade, Segal, and the Challenge of the Social Sciences for the Study of Religion* (Leiden, New York, Cologne: Brill, 1994), p. 79.

23. Segal, 'In Defense of Reductionism', *Journal of the American Academy of Religion* 51/1 (1983), p. 112–14. Revised in *Religion and the Social Sciences*, ch. 1.

24. Lash, *The Beginning and the End of 'Religion'* (Cambridge University Press, 1996), p. 19.

25. Dawson, 'Human Reflexivity and the Nonreductive Explanation of Religious Action', in Idinopulos and Yonan (eds) *Religion and Reductionism* p. 144. See also his *Reason, Freedom and Religion; Closing the Gap Between the Humanistic and the Scientific Study of Religion* (New York: Peter Lang, 1988), pp. 1–6.

26. Hempel, *Philosophy of Natural Science* (Englewood Cliffs: Prentice Hall, 1966), pp. 49–51. See also *Aspects of Scientific Explanation and Other Essays in the Philosophy of Science* (New York: Free Press, 1965). On the covering law model see Sosa (ed.), *Causation and Conditionals* (Oxford University Press, 1975). For Hempel's application of his model to the humanities see 'Reasons and Covering Laws in Historical Explanation,' in Sidney Hook (ed.) *Philosophy and History* (New York University Press, 1963), pp. 143–63.

27. Hempel, *Philosophy of Natural Science*, p. 51.

28. For an excellent discussion of Hempel and these problems see Bohman, *New Philosophy of Natural Science* (Cambridge: Polity Press, 1991), pp. 18–30.

29. Bohman, *New Philosophy of Natural Science*, p. 19.

30. Bohman, *New Philosophy of Social Science*, p. 4.

31. Kuhn, *The Structure of Scientific Revolutions* (University of Chicago Press, 2nd edn. 1975). Feyerabend, *Against Method: Outline of an Anarchistic Theory of Knowledge* (London: NLB, 1975).

32. Shapin, *A Social History of Truth: Civility and Science in Seventeenth Century England* (University of Chicago Press, 1994), pp. 22–7.

33. Rorty, *Philosophy and the Mirror of Nature* (Oxford: Blackwell, 1980), p. 336.

34. Rorty, *Philosophy and the Mirror of Nature*, p. 339.

35. Not that perspectivalism is without problem. For a critique of the logical instabilities of perspectivalism see Dews, *Logics of Disintegration: Post-Structuralist Thought and the Claims of Critical Theory* (London: Verso, 1987). For a defense of perspectivalism without rela-

tivism see Laudan, *Science and Relativism* (Chicago University Press, 1990).

36. Bakhtin, 'Methodology for the Human Sciences' p. 161, in *Speech Genres and Other Late Essays* (Austin: University of Texas Press, 1996), pp. 159–72. Also 'The Problem of the Text' in *Speech Genres*, p. 111. He writes: 'With *explanation* there is only one consciousness, one subject; with *comprehension* there are two consciousnesses and two subjects.'

37. Bakhtin, *Problems of Dostoevsky's Poetics* (Minneapolis, London: Minnesota University Press, 1984), p. 166.

38. Obeyesekere, *Medusa's Hair: Essays on Personal Symbols and Religious Experience* (Chicago and London: Chicago University Press, 1981).

39. Taylor, 'Interpretation and the Sciences of Man' in *Philosophy and the Human Sciences: Philosophical Papers 2* (Cambridge University Press, 1985), p. 15.

40. Taylor 'Interpretation and the Sciences of Man' pp. 15–17. Taylor claims that any interpretive science involves three conditions: an object or field of objects (i.e. texts or text analogues); the distinction between meaning and expression; and a subject 'for whom these meanings are'.

41. Rorty, *Philosophy and the Mirror of Nature*, p. 316.

42. Bohman, *New Philosophy of Social Science*, p. vii.

43. Segal, *Explaining and Interpreting Religion*, pp. 53–6.

44. Vattimo, *Beyond Interpretation: The Meaning of Hermeneutics for Philosophy* (Cambridge: Polity Press, 1997), p. 11.

45. Heidegger, *Being and Time* (Oxford: Blackwell, 1962), p. 195.

46. Heidegger, *Being and Time*, p. 191.

47. Heidegger, p. 414. Heidegger writes: 'Only "in the light" of a nature that has been projected ... can anything like a "fact" be found and set up for an experiment regulated and delimited in terms of this projection. The "grounding" of "factual science" was possible only because the researchers understood that in principle there are no "bare facts".'

48. Heidegger, quoted in Grondin, *Introduction to Philosophical Hermeneutics* (Yale University Press, 1994), pp. 93–4.

49. Vattimo, for example, argues that hermeneutics in maintaining interpretation over an objective truth is inherently nihilistic. Nihilism is inherent to the history of hermeneutics. He writes: 'If hermeneutics, as the philosophical theory of the interpretative character of every experience of truth, is lucid about itself as no more than an interpretation, will it not find itself inevitably caught up in the nihilistic logic of Nietzsche's hermeneutics? This "logic" may be encapsulated in the statement that there can be no recognition of the essentially interpretive character of

255

the experience of the true without the death of God and without the fabling of the world or, which amounts to the same thing, of Being.' Vattimo, *Beyond Interpretation*, p. 9. See also *The End of Modernity* (Cambridge: Polity Press, 1988), pp. 113–29.

50. Gadamer, *Truth and Method* (London: Sheed & Ward, 1989), p. 265.

51. Gadamer, *Truth and Method*, p. 267.

52. Gadamer, *Truth and Method*, p. 293.

53. 'The modern concept of science and the associated concept of method are insufficient. What makes the human sciences into sciences can be understood more easily from the tradition of the concept of Bildung than from the modern idea of scientific method.' Gadamer, *Truth and Method*, p. 18.

54. Rorty, *Philosophy and the Mirror of Nature*, p. 315.

55. Warnke, *Gadamer: Hermeneutics, Tradition and Reason* (Oxford: Polity Press, 1987), pp. 83–4.

56. Gadamer, *Truth and Method* (London: Sheed & Ward, 1989), p. 474. On the brief encounter between Gadamer and Derrida see Grondin, *Introduction to Philosophical Hermeneutics*, pp. 135–9.

57. Derrida, *Of Grammatology* (Baltimore and London: Johns Hopkins University Press, 1976), pp. 10–18.

58. Gadamer, *Truth and Method*, p. 295. Italics in text.

59. Kögler, *The Power of Dialogue: Critical Hermeneutics After Gadamer and Foucault* (Cambridge, MA: MIT Press, 1996), p. 256.

60. McCarthy writes: '[Critical Theory] simply refuses to equate it [pluralism] with 'anything goes' and insists that an acceptable pluralism requires an overarching framework of justice, so that one group's well-being does not come at the expense of another's.' Hoy and McCarthy, *Critical Theory* (Oxford and Cambridge, MA: Blackwell, 1994), p. 238. On the origins of the critique-interpretation issue see Grondin, *Introduction to Philosophical Hermeneutics* (Yale University Press, 1994), p. 51. See also Thompson, *Critical Hermeneutics: A Study in the Thought of Paul Ricoeur and Jürgen Habermas* (Cambridge University Press, 1981), pp. 66–8.

61. Ricoeur, 'Hermeneutics and the Critique of Ideology', *Hermeneutics and the Human Sciences* (Cambridge University Press, 1981), pp. 63–100; Kögler, *The Power of Dialogue*, pp. 251–78.

62. Hoy and McCarthy, *Critical Theory* (Oxford and Cambridge, MA: Blackwell, 1994), p. 172.

63. Gadamer, *Truth and Method*, p. 293.

64. Gadamer, *Truth and Method*, p. 296.

65. See Mumme, 'Haunted by Sankara's Ghost: The Srivaisnava Interpretation of Bhagavad Gita 18.66' in Timm (ed.), *Texts in Context:*

Traditional Hermeneutics in South Asia (Albany: Suny Press, 1992), pp. 69–84.

66. Staal, *Rules Without Meaning: Ritual, Mantras and the Human Sciences* (New York: Peter Lang, 1989), pp. 53–5.
67. Gadamer, *Truth and Method*, p. 269.
68. Stark and Bainbridge, *A Theory of Religion* (New York: Peter Lang, 1987).
69. Lawson and McCauley, *Rethinking Religion: Connecting Cognition and Culture* (Cambridge University Press, 1990), pp. 172–7.
70. Wilson, *On Human Nature* (Harvard University Press, 1978), pp. 175–92.
71. Wilson, *On Human Nature*, p. 177.
72. Bowker, *Is God a Virus? Genes, Culture and Religion* (SPCK: London, 1995), p. 39.
73. Dundas, *The Jains* (London and New York: Routledge, 1992), p. 156.
74. Segal, 'In Defense of Reductionism'. For a discussion of Eliade's hidden theological agenda see Rennie, *Reconstructing Eliade: Making Sense of Religion* (Albany: Suny Press, 1996), pp. 191–4.
75. For a rigorous defence see Rennie, *Reconstructing Eliade*, pp. 4–6; 133–41.
76. Bowker, *The Sense of God: Sociological, Anthropological and Psychological Approaches to the Origin of the Sense of God* (Oxford: Clarendon Press, 1973), pp. 86–9.
77. Bowker, *Licensed Insanities: Religions and belief in God in the Contemporary World* (London: Darton, Longman & Todd, 1987), p. 152.

Chapter 4

1. Scheler, *On the Eternal in Man* (London: SCM Press, 1960 (1922)), pp. 18–19.
2. For such a history see Ryba, *The Essence of Phenomenology and its Meaning for the Scientific Study of Religion* (New York: Peter Lang, 1991); Hans Penner, *Impasse and Resolution: A Critique of the Study of Religion* (New York: Peter Lang, 1988); Ursula King, 'Historical and Phenomenological Approaches to the Study of Religion' in Frank Whaling (ed.) *Contemporary Approaches to the Study of Religion* (Berlin, New York, Amsterdam: Mouton, 1984), vol. 1, pp. 29–164. See also Capps *Religious Studies*. For the history of the phenomenological movement as a whole see Spiegelberg, *The Phenomenological Movement: An Historical Introduction* (The Hague, Boston, Lancaster: Martinus Nijhoff, 1984 (1960)) and Embree, et al. (eds) *Encyclopedia*

of Phenomenology (Dordrecht, Boston, London: Kluwer Academic Publishers, 1997).

3. Spiegelberg, *The Phenomenological Movement*, pp. 7–19.
4. Ryba, *The Essence of Phenomenology*, pp. 25–41.
5. Robinson, *Encyclopedia*, quoted in Ryba, *The Essence of Phenomenology*, p. 46.
6. James has argued, on the contrary, that the phenomenology of religion is dependent on extra-Husserlian phenomenology (James 'Phenomenology and the Study of Religion' *Journal of Religion* 65, no. 3 (1985)) and Ryba agrees (Ryba, *The Essence of Phenomenology*, p. 4). Hans Penner also argues that Husserl is not of primary importance in the phenomenology of religion, though argues that it should in fact turn to a Husserlian programme for more rigorous results. See Penner, *Impasse and Resolution, A Critique of the Study of Religion*, Toronto Studies in Religion vol. 8 (New York: Peter Lang, 1989). Although extra-Husserlian phenomenology is important in the phenomenology of religion, I wish to argue that it is to Husserl that it owes its central methodology.
7. Smart, *The Science of Religion and the Sociology of Knowledge* (Princeton University Press, 1973), p. 21.
8. Smart, *The Religious Experience of Mankind* (New York: Fontana, 1969), p. 11–18.
9. Husserl, *Cartesian Meditations. An Introduction to Phenomenology* (Dordrecht, Boston and London: Kluwer Academic Publishers, 1993 (1950)), p. 157.
10. Husserl, 'Phenomenology,' Husserl's article for the *Encyclopedia Britannica* (1927) in Kockelmans, *Edmund Husserl's Phenomenology* (West Lafayette: Purdue University Press, 1994), pp. 75–7. This explication and analysis of the article includes the German text.
11. Husserl, *Cartesian Meditations*, p. 33.
12. Husserl, *Cartesian Meditations*, p. 20.
13. Husserl, *Cartesian Meditations*, p. 26.
14. Levinas, *The Theory of Intuition in Husserl's Phenomenology* (Evanston: Northwest University Press, 1995), p. 148.
15. Husserl, *Cartesian Meditations*, p. 75.
16. Husserl, *Cartesian Meditations*, p. 70.
17. Quoted in Sharpe, *Comparative Religion, a History* (London: Duckworth, 1975), p. 222.
18. Sharpe, *Comparative Religion*, p. 223.
19. Van der Leeuw, *Religion in Essence and Manifestation* (New York: Harper Tourchbooks, 1973), p. 683.
20. Murphy, '*Wesen und Erscheinung* in the history of the study of religion: A post-structuralist perspective' *Method and Theory in the Study of*

Religion vol. 6 (1994), pp. 119–46. See also James, 'Phenomenology and the Study of Religion: The archaeology of an approach' *The Journal of Religion* 65 (3), 1985, pp. 311–35. Also the remarks by Jeppe Sinding Jensen 'Is a phenomenology of religion possible?' *Method and Theory in the Study of Religion* 5/2 (1993), p. 113, n. 5.

21. Penner, *Impasse and Resolution*.

22. Penner, *Impasse and Resolution*, p. 42.

23. Van der Leeuw, *Religion in Essence and Manifestation* (Harper Tourchbooks, 1973), p. 674.

24. Berger, 'On Phenomenological Research in the Field of Religion' *Encyclopedie Francaise*, vol. 1957, p. 1932, translated in J. Waardenburg, (ed.) *Classical Approaches to the Study of Religion* (Mouton, The Hague, Paris: Mouton, 1973), p. 665. Even Douglas Allen in the *Encyclopedia of Religion* speaks of *epoché* as 'suspending our beliefs and values' (M. Eliade (ed.) *Encyclopedia of Religion* vol. 11 (New York: Macmillan, 1987) p. 281). John Shepherd sums up this attitude in his own critique of phenomenology when he characterizes bracketing in the following terms: 'The academic student of religion's own beliefs, attitudes, values etc. should be temporarily suspended in order to avoid contaminating one's description with personal prejudice, bias, or one's own personal religious or philosophical commitments.' 'Debating Point (4): Phenomenological Perspectivalism' *British Association for the Study of Religions Bulletin*, no. 71, March 1994, p. 12.

25. Wach, *Types of Religious Experience, Christian and Non-Christian* (Chicago: University of Chicago Press, 1951), p. 7.

26. Smart, *Science of Religion and Sociology of Knowledge*, p. 54.

27. Smart, *Science of Religion and Sociology of Knowledge*, p. 21.

28. See for example Wach, *Types of Religious Experience*.

29. For example, Rawlinson, *The Book of Enlightened Masters* (Chicago: Open Court, 1997).

30. See for example, Smart, *Reasons and Faiths* (RKP 1958) pp. 2–10.

31. Dhavamony, *The Phenomenology of Religion* (Rome Gregorian University Press, 1973), p. 16.

32. Embree, 'The Phenomenology of Representational Awareness' *Human Studies* vol. 15 (1992), pp. 301–14.

33. Husserl, *Cartesian Meditations* p. 20. On Husserl's theory of meaning see Mohanty, *Edmund Husserl's Theory of Meaning* (The Hague: Martinus Nijhoff, 1976).

34. Husserl, *Ideas Pertaining to a Pure Phenomenology and to a Phenomenological Philosophy* 1, (The Hague, Boston, Lancaster: Martinus Nijhoff, 1993), pp. 322–5; 326–48. See Levinas, *The Theory of Intuition*, pp. 65–95.

35. Levinas, *The Theory of Intuition*, p. 58.

36. For a succinct account of language in Husserl see Kelkel 'Language in Husserl' Embree et al. (eds) *Encyclopedia of Phenomenology* (Dordrecht, Boston, London: Kluwer Academic Publishers, 1997), pp. 401–07.

37. For Derrida's critique of Husserl see Derrida, *Speech and Phenomena* (Evanson: Northwestern University Press, 1973). See also Evans and Lawlor 'Jaques Derrida' in Embree, *Encyclopedia of Phenomenology*, pp. 141–3. Also Evans 'Phenomenological Deconstruction: Husserl's Method of Abbau' *Journal of the British Society for Phenomenology* 21 (1990), pp. 14–25; *Strategies of Deconstruction: Derrida and the Myth of the Voice* (Minneapolis: University of Minnesota Press, 1991); Lawlor 'Navigating a Passage: Deconstruction as Phenomenology' *Diacritics* 23 (1993), pp. 3–15. For an interesting critique of Derrida's reading of Husserl see Mohanty, *Phenomenology: Between Essentialism and Transcendental Philosophy* (Evanston: Northwestern University Press, 1997), pp. 62–76. For a critique of the distinction between 'facts' and ontology from the perspective of critical praxis see Castoriadis, *The Imaginary Institution of Society* (Cambridge: Polity Press, 1987). He writes 'the idea of a science of facts which would not imply an ontology has never amounted to more than an incoherent phantasy of certain scientists', p. 335.

38. See Alliez, 'Questionnaire on Deleuze,' *Theory, Culture and Society*, vol. 14, 2, 1997, p. 84.

39. Geertz, 'Thick Description: Toward an Interpretive Theory of Culture' in *The Interpretation of Cultures* (London: Fontana Press, 1973), p. 7.

40. See De Certeau, *The Writing of History* (Columbia University Press, 1988), pp. 22–9.

41. As Jonathan Z. Smith has observed, 'the academic study of religion is a child of the Enlightenment'. Smith, *Imagining Religion, from Babylon to Jonestown* (University of Chicago Press, 1982), p. 104.

42. For a history of some of these developments see Beiser, *The Fate of Reason: German Philosophy from Kant to Fichte* (Cambridge, MA: and London: Harvard University Press, 1987); Bowie, *From Romanticism to Critical Theory: The Philosophy of German Literary Theory* (London and New York: Routledge, 1997). For the impact of India on Romanticism see Halbfass, *India and Europe* (Albany: Suny Press, 1988).

43. See Seebohm, 'Johann Gottlieb Fichte' in Embree, *The Encyclopedia of Phenomenology*, pp. 223–6. See also Rockmore 'Fichte, Husserl and Philosophical Science' *International Philosophical Quarterly* 19 (1979), pp. 15–27.

44. Buckley, 'Edmund Husserl' in Embree et al. (eds), *Encyclopedia of Phenomenology*, p. 328.

45. Ricoeur, *The Conflict of Interpretations: Essays in Hermeneutics* (Evanston: Northwestern University Press, 1974), p. 236.

46. Husserl, *Cartesian Meditations*, pp. 75–7.

47. Husserl, *Cartesian Meditations*, pp. 77–8.

48. Penner, *Impasse and Resolution*, p. 44.

49. Scheler, *On the Eternal in Man*, pp. 157.

50. Wach, *Types of Religious Experience*, p. 32.

51. Opening Wach's *Types of Religious Experience* at random the emphasis on religious experience occurs again and again. For example, Wach writes: 'the study of the historical development of Mahayana Buddhism has to be supplemented by inquiry aiming at an understanding of the *religious experience* which manifests in the theology, devotional practice and world-view of the Great Vehicle. The fruitfulness of Rudolf Otto's categories can be proved by analysing the expression of the experiences of the *numinous* to be found in the Mahayana Sutras.' (p. 108).

52. Freeman, 'Performing Possession: Ritual and Consciousness in the Teyyam Complex', in Bruckner, Lutze and Malik (eds) *Flags of Flame: Studies in South Asian Folk Culture* (New Delhi: Manohar Publishers, 1993).

53. Husserl, *Cartesian Meditations*, p. 89.

54. Husserl, *Cartesian Meditations*, p. 93.

55. Husserl, *Cartesian Meditations*, p. 93.

56. Husserl, *Cartesian Meditations*, p. 111.

57. Steinbock, *Home and Beyond, Generative Phenomenology After Husserl* (Evanston: Northwestern University Press, 1995), p. 74.

58. Husserl, *Cartesian Meditations*, p. 122.

59. Husserl, *Cartesian Meditations*, p. 130.

60. Husserl, *Cartesian Meditations*, p. 133.

61. Husserl, *Cartesian Meditations*, p. 135.

62. Husserl, *The Crisis of European Sciences and Transcendental Phenomenology* (Evanston: Northwestern University Press, 1970).

63. Gadamer, *Truth and Method* (London: Sheed & Ward, 1989), p. 247.

64. Bakhtin, *Problems of Dostoyevsky's Poetics* (Minneapolis and London: University of Minnesota Press, 1984), p. 68. For a good discussion of the Bakhtin circle's attitude to subjectivity see Gardiner, *The Dialogics of Critique* (London and New York: Routledge, 1992), pp. 71–6. Sandywell argues that Bakhtin does not completely follow through the implications of his hermeneutics because he is still hampered by the philosophy of consciousness (Sandywell, 'The Shock of the Old:

Mikhail Bakhtin's Contributions to the Theory of Time and Alterity' in Bell and Gardiner, *Bakhtin and the Social Sciences* (London, Thousand Oaks, New Delhi: Sage, 1998), pp. 196–213). But Bakhtin has good reasons for maintaining some notion of subjectivity, as is entailed by the idea of 'outsideness' crucial to dialogism and arguably to hermeneutics generally.

65. Voloshinov, *Marxism and the Philosophy of Language* (Harvard University Press, 1973), p. 13.

66. Heidegger, *Being and Time* (Oxford: Blackwell, 1987), p. 46.

67. Gadamer, *Truth and Method*, p. 250.

68. On the tension between the ahistorical subject and the historical lifeworld in which the subject exists see Lyotard, *Phenomenology*, p. 32.

69. Voloshinov, *Marxism and the Philosophy of Language* p. 11.

70. Jensen, 'Is a Phenomenology of Religion Possible?', p. 128.

71. Ricoeur, *Time and Narrative*, vol. 1 (Chicago University Press, 1984), *passim*.

72. Ricoeur, *Time and Narrative*, vol. 1, p. 36.

73. Smith, *Imagining Religion*, p. 55.

74. Voloshinov, *Marxism and the Philosophy of Language*, p. 33.

75. Cassirer, *The Philosophy of Symbolic Forms*, vol. 2, (Yale University Press, 1955).

76. Blumenberg, *Work on Myth* (Cambridge, MA: and London: MIT Press, 1985), p. 12. Blumenberg writes: 'The boundary line between myth and logos is imaginary and does not obviate the need to inquire about the logos of myth in the process of working free of the absolution of reality. Myth itself is a piece of high-carat "work of logos".'

77. Smart, *Dimensions of the Sacred*, p. 4.

Chapter 5

1. Benhabib, *Situating the Self: Gender, Community and Postmodernism in Contemporary Ethics* (Cambridge: Polity Press, 1992), p. 208. On the critique of the philosophy of consciousness or subjectivity from the perspective of the sign, namely in psychoanalysis and structuralism, see Ricoeur, 'The Question of the Subject: The Challenge of Semiology' in *The Conflict of Interpretations: Essays in Hermeneutics* (Evanston: Northwestern University Press, 1974), pp. 236–66.

2. Derrida, 'La parole soufflée' in *Writing and Difference* (London: Routledge, 1978), p. 177.

3. Habermas, *Knowledge and Human Interests* (Cambridge: Polity Press, 1987), pp. 15–16, 29–30 etc. See Hoy and McCarthy, *Critical Theory* (Oxford and Cambridge, MA: Blackwell, 1994), pp. 179–80.

4.	Apel, *Understanding and Explanation: A Transcendental-Pragmatic Perspective* (Cambridge, MA: MIT Press, 1984), pp. 232–42.

5.	Kögler, *The Power of Dialogue: Critical Hermeneutics after Gadamer and Foucault* (Cambridge, MA: MIT Press, 1996), p. 37.

6.	Gennette, *Narrative Discourse* (Oxford: Blackwell, 1980), pp. 25–7.

7.	For example, Ochs, 'Narrative' in van Dijk, Teun (ed.) *Discourse Studies: A Multidisciplinary Introduction*, vol. 1. *Discourse as Structure and Process* (London: SAGE, 1997), p. 185.

8.	Ricoeur, *Time and Narrative*, vol. 1 (University of Chicago Press, 1984), p. 150.

9.	Lessing, *Laokoon, an essay on the Limits of Painting and Poetry* (Baltimore and London: Johns Hopkins University Press, 1984), p. 72: 'The principal superiority [of the poem over the painting] is that the poet leads us to the scene through a whole gallery of paintings, of which the material picture shows only one.'

10.	The disruption of the narrative frame is evidenced in the 'cut-up' technique of Burrough's *Naked Lunch* (London: Paladin, 1992 (1959)) and also in the *Cities of the Red Night* trilogy (1981, 1983, 1987).

11.	Piatigorsky, *Mythological Deliberations: Lectures on the Phenomenology of Myth* (London: SOAS, 1993), p. 30.

12.	Piatigorsky, *Mythological Deliberations*, pp. 29–67.

13.	Piatigorsky, *Mythological Deliberations*, p. 34.

14.	For the function of narrative in organizations see Mumby, *Communication and Power in Organizations: Discourse, Ideology and Domination* (Norwood, NJ: Ablex, 1988).

15.	See Doty, *Mythography: The Study of Myths and Rituals* (Tuscaloosa: University of Alabama Press, 1986), pp. 3–4.

16.	Blumenberg, *Work on Myth* (Cambridge, MA: and London: MIT Press, 1985), p. 149.

17.	On this see Piatigorsky, *Mythological Deliberations*, pp. 5–6.

18.	Levi-Strauss, 'The structural Study of Myth' in *Structural Anthroplogy*, vol. 1 (New York: Basic Books, 1963) pp. 206–31, p. 217.

19.	Barthes, *Mythologies* (New York: Hill & Wang, 1972).

20.	Husserl, *Crisis of European Sciences and Transcendental Phenomenology* (Evanston: Northwestern University Press, 1970), p. 150.

21.	Husserl, *Crisis*, p. 154.

22.	Husserl, *Crisis*, pp. 143–4.

23.	Bowker, *Worlds of Faith: Religious Belief and Practice in Britain Today* (London: Ariel, 1983).

24.	Obeyesekere, *Medusa's Hair: An Essay on Personal Symbols and Religious Experience* (Chicago University Press, 1981).

25.	MacIntyre, 'Epistemological Crises, Dramatic Narrative, and the Philosophy of Science,' *The Monist* 60 (1977), pp. 453–71. Reprinted

Appleby et al. (eds), *Knowledge and Postmodernism in Historical Perspective* (New York and London: Routledge, 1996), p. 362.

26.   MacIntyre, *After Virtue: A Study in Moral Theory* (London: Duckworth, 1985), p. 268.

27.   MacIntyre, 'Epistemological Crisis,' pp. 364–5.

28.   MacIntyre, 'Epistemological Crisis,' p. 360.

29.   For an excellent review of these positions see Fay, *Contemporary Philosophy of Social Science* (Oxford: Blackwell, 1996), pp. 178–98. See also Carr, *Time, Narrative and History* (New York: Columbia University Press, 1986).

30.   MacIntyre, *After Virtue*, pp. 1–5.

31.   MacIntyre, *After Virtue*, p. 212. To which Mink has responded that stories 'are not lived but told'. Mink, *Historical Understanding*, (Ithaca: Cornell University Press, 1987), p. 60.

32.   MacIntyre, *After Virtue*, p. 213.

33.   MacIntyre, *After Virtue*, p. 216.

34.   Levin, *The Body's Recollection of Being: Phenomenological Psychology and the Deconstruction of Nihilism* (London and Boston: RKP, 1985), p. 180.

35.   MacIntyre, *After Virtue*, p. 210.

36.   MacIntyre, *After Virtue*, p. 205.

37.   Inglis, *Cultural Studies* (Oxford and Cambridge, MA: Blackwell, 1993), p. 214.

38.   MacIntyre, *After Virtue*, p. 214.

39.   Camus, *The Outsider* (Penguin, 1961), p. 62. See also the discussion by White 'The Burden of History' *Tropics of Discourse* (Baltimore and London: Johns Hopkins University Press, 1978), pp. 37–8.

40.   MacIntyre, *After Virtue*, p. 214.

41.   See Clifford and Marcus (eds), *Writing Culture: The Poetics and Politics of Ethnography* (Berkeley and Los Angeles: University of California Press, 1986).

42.   Lucien Febvre, quoted in Callinicos, *Theories and Narratives: Reflections on the Philosophy of History* (Cambridge: Polity Press, 1995), p. 75.

43.   For a good discussion of the literature and issues with regard to historical narrative and the holocaust, see Callinicos, *Theories and Narratives*, pp. 67–75.

44.   See White, *Metahistory* (Baltimore and London: Johns Hopkins University Press, 1973), pp. 163–229.

45.   On this also see Mink, *Historical Understanding* (Ithaca: Cornell University Press, 1987), pp. 182–203.

46.   White, 'Fictions of Factual Representation', *Tropics*, p. 128.

47.   White, 'Fictions', p. 121.

48. White, *The Content and the Form* (Baltimore and London: Johns Hopkins University Press, 1987), pp. 1–25.

49. See Inden, *Imagining India* (Oxford and Cambridge, MA: Blackwell, 1990), pp. 85–130.

50. Poliakov, *The Aryan Myth* (New York: Basic Books, 1974).

51. McCutcheon, *Manufacturing Religion: The Discourse on Sui Generis Religion and the Politics of Nostalgia* (New York, Oxford: Oxford University Press, 1997), p. 125. See also Fitzgerald, 'Hinduism and the World Religions Fallacy', *Religion* (1990) 20, pp. 101–118; 'Religious Studies as Cultural Studies: A Philosophical and Anthropological Critique of the Concept of Religion' (1995) *Diskus* 3, 1, pp. 35–47.

52. McCutcheon, *Manufacturing Religion*, p. 3.

53. Ricoeur, *Time and Narrative*, vol. 1 (Chicago and London: Chicago University Press, 1984), p. 3.

54. Ricoeur, 'Life in Quest of Narrative' in Wood (ed.), *On Paul Ricouer, Narrative and Interpretation* (London and New York: Routledge, 1991), p. 25.

55. Ricoeur, *Time and Narrative*, p. 52.

56. Ricoeur, *Time and Narrative*, vol 1., p. 34. For the origins of mimesis see Sorbom, *Mimesis and Art: Studies in the Origin and Early Development of as Aesthetic Vocabulary* (Stockholm: Svenska Bokforlaget, 1966). For mimesis in Western thought the classic is still Auerbach, *Mimesis: The Representation of Reality in Western Literature* (Princeton University Press, 1953). For a critical revision of Auerbach's thesis see also Gebauer, Gunther and Wulf *Mimesis: Art, Culture, Society* (Berkeley, Los Angeles, London: University of California Press, 1995).

57. Ricoeur, *Time and Narrative*, vol. 1, p. 21.

58. Ricoeur contrasts the emplotment (*mythos*) of Aristotle with Augustine's alientation of the soul (*distentio animi*). He eloquently writes 'Augustine groaned under the existential burden of discordance. Aristotle discerns in the poetic act *par excellence* – the composing of the tragic poem – the triumph of concordance over discordance. It goes without saying that it is I, the reader of Augustine and Aristotle, who establishes this relationship between a lived experience where discordance rends concordance and an eminently verbal experience where concordance mends discordance.' *Time and Narrative*, vol. 1, p. 31.

59. Ricoeur, *Time and Narrative*, vol. 1, p. 45.

60. Ricoeur, *Time and Narrative*, vol. 1, p. 55.

61. Ricoeur, *Time and Narrative*, vol. 1, p. 57.

62. Ricoeur, *Time and Narrative*, vol. 1, p. 59.

63. Ricoeur, *Time and Narrative*, vol. 1, p. 60.

64. Ricoeur, *Time and Narrative*, vol. 1, p. 64.

65. Ricoeur, *Time and Narrative*, vol. 1, p. 65.

66. Ricoeur, *Time and Narrative*, vol. 1, p. 64.
67. Ricoeur, *Time and Narrative*, vol. 1, pp. 70–1.
68. Ricoeur, *Time and Narrative*, p. 71; see also 'Life in Quest of Narrative', p. 26.
69. MacIntyre, *After Virtue*, p. 212.
70. Fay, *Contemporary Philosophy of Social Science*, pp. 180–1.
71. Ricoeur, 'Life in Quest of Narrative', p. 32.
72. Chidester, 'Anchoring Religion in the World: A Southern African History of Comparative Religion', *Religion*, vol. 26, 1996, p. 141.
73. Rouse, *Engaging Science*, p. 160.
74. See for example, the work of Guha and his colleagues. Guha and Spivak, (eds) *Selected Subaltern Studies* (Oxford University Press, 1988).
75. Winch, *The Idea of a Social Science and its Relation to Philosophy* (London and Henley: RKP, 1977). For an account of different kinds of relativism see Harre and Krausz *Varieties of Relativism* (Oxford: Blackwell, 1996).
76. Margolis, *The Truth About Relativism* (Oxford and Cambridge, MA: Blackwell, 1991).
77. Gellner, *Postmodernism, Reason and Religion* (Oxford and London: Routledge, 1992).
78. For an argument for the centrality of narrative in the natural sciences see Rouse, *Engaging Science: How to Understand Its Practices Philosophically* (Ithaca and London: Cornell University Press, 1996), pp. 158–78.
79. Margolis writes: 'decisions about the logic of any inquiry are not unconditionally *a priori* to that inquiry, totally unaffected by what we may find to be the structure of a given domain. They are instead internal to and part of the cognitively pertinent characterization of the domain itself.' Margolis, *The Truth About Relativism*, p. 42.
80. Greenblatt, *Renaissance Self-Fashioning: from More to Shakespeare* (University of Chicago Press, 1980), e.g. ch. 1.

Chapter 6

1. Rosaldo, *Culture and Truth: The Remaking of Social Analysis* (London: Routledge, 1993), p. 19.
2. Bakhtin, *Speech Genres and Other Essays* (Austin: University of Texas Press, 1996), p. 114.
3. Rorty, *Philosophy and the Mirror of Nature* (Oxford: Blackwell, 1996 (1980)), pp. 12–13.

4. De Certeau, *Culture in the Plural* (Minneapolis and London: University of Minnesota Press, 1997), p. 123.

5. Bohman, *New Philosophy of Social Science: Problems of Indeterminacy* (Cambridge: Polity Press, 1991), p. 125.

6. Gadamer, *Truth and Method* (London: Sheed & Ward, 1989), p. 383.

7. Grondin puts this well: 'Only in conversation, only in confirmation with another's thought that could also come to dwell within us, can we hope to get beyond the limits of our present horizon.' Grondin, *Introduction to Philosophical Hermeneutics*, (Yale University Press), p. 124.

8. Rosaldo, *Culture and Truth: The Remaking of Social Analysis* (London: Routledge, 1993), p. 19.

9. Rosaldo, *Culture and Truth*, p. 52.

10. Tyler, *The Said and the Unsaid*, (New York: Academic Press, 1978), pp. 90–1.

11. Brown, *Mama Lola: A Voudou Priestess in Brooklyn* (University of California Press, 1991), pp. 14–15.

12. For example, Briggs, *Never in Anger: Portrait of an Eskimo Family* (Cambridge, MA: Harvard University Press, 1970) cited by Rosaldo p. 176. Another example of the refusal to produce an ethnography that reflects a social completeness is Crapanzo, *Tuhami: Portrait of a Moroccan* (Chicago University Press, 1980). See also Clifford and Marcus (eds) *Writing Culture: The Poetics and Politics of Ethnography* (University of California Press, 1986).

13. James Clifford 'On Ethnographic Allegory' in Clifford and Marcus (eds) *Writing Culture*, p. 98–9.

14. Rosaldo, *Culture and Truth*, pp. 9–12.

15. See for example Bainbridge, *The Sociology of Religious Movements* (New York and London: Routledge, 1997).

16. Taylor, *The Ethics of Authenticity* (Harvard University Press, 1991), p. 105–6.

17. Rosaldo, *Culture and Truth*, p. 206–7.

18. For the impact of new technologies in relation to religion see Richard Roberts 'Time, Virtuality and the Goddess' *Cultural Values* vol. 2 nos. 2 and 3 (1998), pp. 270–87.

19. Morson and Emerson (eds) *Rethinking Bakhtin: Extensions and Challenges* (Evanson: Northwestern University Press, 1989), p. 3.

20. On the parallels between Ricoeur and Bakhtin see Gardiner, *The Dialogics of Critique* (London and New York: 1992), pp. 123–36.

21. Thomson, 'Introduction: Bakhtin and Shifting Paradigms', *Critical Studies* vol. 2 no. 1/2 1990, pp. 2–23.

22. See Outhwaite, *Understanding Social Life: The Method Called Verstehen* (London: George Allen & Unwin, 1975), pp. 25–37.

23. Bakhtin, 'K metodologii gumanitarnykh nauk' ('Concerning Methodology in the human sciences') in *Estetika slovesnogo tvorchestva (The Aesthetics of Verbal Creation)*, Moscow: S.G. Bocharov, 1979. Quoted by Tzvetan Todorov, *Mikhail Bakhtin: The Dialogical Principle* (Manchester University Press, 1984), p. 19.

24. Kögler, *The Power of Dialogue*, p. 252.

25. There is large literature on the significance of the body. See for example Turner, *The Body and Society* (Oxford: Blackwell, 1984); Shilling, *The Body and Social Theory* (London, Newbury Park, New Delhi: Sage, 1993); Synnott, *The Social Body* (London and New York: Routledge, 1993). In anthropology very early and significant collection of essays is Blacking (ed.), *The Anthropology of the Body* (London: Academic Press, 1977). For the study of religions see Coakley (ed.), *Religion and the Body* (Cambridge University Press, 1997), Mellor and Shilling, *Reforming the Body Religion: Community and Modernity* (London: Sage, 1997). See also the 4-volumed collection of essays by Feher (ed.) *Fragments for a History of the Body* (New York: Zone, 1989) and the journal *Body and Society* (Sage).

26. Todorov, *Mikhail Bakhtin*, p. 21–2.

27. Bakhtin writes: 'In order to understand, it is immensely important for the person who understands to be *located outside* the object of his or her creative understanding – in time, in space, in culture ... our real exterior can be seen and understood only by other people, because they are located outside us in space and because they are *others*.' Bakhtin, 'Response to a Question from *Novy Mir*,' in *Speech Genres and Other Late Essays* (Austin: University of Texas, 1986), p. 7.

28. Bakhtin, 'The Author and Hero in Aesthetic Activity' in *Art and Answerability: Early Essays by M.M. Bakhtin* (Austin: University of Texas Press, 1990), p. 12.

29. Bakhtin, 'The Author and Hero', p. 14.

30. Bakhtin, 'The Author and Hero', p. 13.

31. Bakhtin quoted in Holquist, *Dialogism*, p. 29. My reading of 'Author and Hero' has been influenced by Holquist's work.

32. Bakhtin, 'The Author and Hero', p. 23.

33. See for example Austin, *How to do Things With Words* (1962); Searle, *Speech Acts: Essays in the Philosophy of Language* (Cambridge University Press, 1969).

34. Bakhtin, 'The Problem of Speech Genres', in *Speech Genres*, p. 69. See also Levinson, *Pragmatics* (Cambridge University Press, 1983), pp. 18–19.

35. Bakhtin, 'The Problem of Speech Genres', p. 91.

36. Voloshinov, *Marxism and the Philosophy of Language* (Cambridge, MA: and London: Harvard University Press, 1986), p. 102. There is

some dispute concerning the authorship of the Bakhtin material. *Marxism and the Philosophy of Language*, for example, was written under the name of V.N. Voloshinov in 1929, but later attributed to Bakhtin. Holquist (*Dialogism: Bakhtin and his World* (London: Routledge, 1990), p. 8) argues that Bakhtin is the sole author of this and other works, though other scholars would wish to distance Bakhtin from the authorship of the texts under the names of Voloshinov and Medvedev (Morson and Emerson (eds) *Rethinking Bakhtin: Extensions and Challenges* (Evanston: Northwestern University Press, 1989)). A third view is that the texts attributed to Voloshinov and Medvedev are collective efforts of the 'Bakhtin school' (Pearce, *Reading Dialogics* (London, New York: Edwin Arnold, 1990, pp. 27–9)). I am assuming the text under the name Voloshinov was written by him.

37. Voloshinov, *Marxism and the Philosophy of Language*, pp. 9–15.
38. Bakhtin, *The Dialogic Imagination: Four Essays*, (Austin: University of Texas Press, 1981), p. 276f.
39. Todorov, *Mikhail Bakhtin: The Dialogical Principle* (Manchester University Press, 1984), p. 60.
40. Kristeva, 'Word, Dialogue and the Novel' in *Desire in Language: A Semiotic Approach to Literature and Art* (Oxford: Blackwell, 1980), p. 66.
41. Bakhtin 'Discourse in the Novel', in Holquist (ed.), *The Dialogic Imagination*, p. 272.
42. Bakhtin 'Discourse in the Novel', p. 273.
43. Saussurre, *A Course in General Linguistics* (London: Fontana, 1974 (1915)).
44. Todorov, *Mikhail Bakhtin*, pp. 42, 57.
45. Voloshinov, *Marxism and the Philosophy of Language*, pp. 58–61, 66–7.
46. Bakhtin, 'Methodology for the Human Sciences', p. 169, in *Speech Genres and Other Late Essays* (Austin: University of Texas Press, 1996).
47. Voloshinov, *Marxism and the Philosophy of Language*, p. 21.
48. See Gardiner et al. (eds) *Bakhtin and the Social Sciences* (London: Sage, 1998).
49. For a succinct overview see Makreel and Owensby 'Wilhelm Dilthey' in Embree et al. *Encyclopedia of Phenomenology* (Dordrecht, Boston, London: Kluwer Academic Publishers, 1997), pp. 143–7.
50. See Pompa, *Vico: A Study of the 'New Science'* (Cambridge University Press, 1990), pp. 159–60.
51. Spiegelberg, *The Phenomenological Movement: Historical Introduction* (3rd edn. Boston, The Hague, Lancaster: Nijhoff, 1984) p. 167.
52. 'the empathic viewing of others is an intuiting', Husserl, *Ideas Pertain-*

ing to a Pure Phenomenology and to a Phenomenological Philosophy,
First Book, (The Hague, Boston, Lancaster: Kluwer Academic Press,
1983), p. 6.

53. Levinas, *The Theory of Intuition in Husserl's Phenomenology* (Evanson: Northwestern University Press, 1995), p. 69ff.

54. Husserl, *Logical Investigations*, p. 327.

55. Husserl, *Cartesian Meditations*, p. 89 'When I, the meditating I, reduce myself to my absolute transcendental ego by phenomenological epoché do I not become *sous ipse*; and do I not remain that, as long as I carry on a constant self-explication under the name of phenomenology? Should not a phenomenology that proposed to solve the problems of Objective being, and to present itself actually as philosophy, be branded therefore as transcendental solipsism?'

56. Husserl, *Cartesian Meditations*, p. 129.

57. Husserl, *Cartesian Meditations*, p. 130.

58. Steinbock, *Home and Beyond: Generative Phenomenology After Husserl* (Evanson: Northwestern University Press, 1995), p. 75.

59. Gadamer, *Truth and Method* (London: Sheed & Ward, 1989), p. 250.

60. Carr, *Time, Narrative and History* (Bloomington: Indiana University Press, 1991), p. 120–22.

61. Steinbock, *Home and Beyond*, e.g. pp. 220–35.

62. Bakhtin, 'The Author and Hero', pp. 25–7.

63. Bakhtin, *Towards a Philosophy of the Act*, p. 15. See Morson and Emerson (eds), *Rethinking Bakhtin: Extensions and Challenges* (Evanson: Northwestern University Press, 1989) 'Introduction', p. 11.

64. Bakhtin, 'The Author and Hero', p. 26.

65. Voloshinov, *Marxism and the Philosophy of Language*, p. 105.

66. Levinas, 'Ethics as First Philosophy', *The Levinas Reader* Sean Hand (ed.) (Oxford and Cambridge: Blackwell, 1989), p. 82.

67. Van der Leeuw, 'Some Recent Achievements of Psychological Research and their Application to History in Particular the History of Religion', in Waardenberg, *Classical Approaches to the Study of Religion* (The Hague: Mouton, 1973), p. 401.

68. Van der Leeuw, in *Classical Approaches*, p. 402.

69. Smart, *Dimensions of the Sacred* (London: Harper Collins, 1996), p. 2.

70. Carr, *Time, Narrative and History* (Bloomington: Indiana University Press, 1986); Lee (ed.), *Life Before Story: Autobiography from a Narrative Perspective* (New York: Praeger, 1994); Sarbin, (ed.) *Narrative Psychology: The Storied Nature of Human Conduct* (New York: Praeger, 1986).

71. Rappaport, *Pigs for the Ancestors* (New Haven: Yale University Press, 1968), pp. 237–8.
72. D'Aquili et al. (eds), *The Spectrum of Ritual: A Biogenetic Analysis* (New York: Columbia University Press, 1979), pp. 12–13.

Chapter 7

1. Husserl, *Cartesian Meditations*, pp. 136–9. See also McIntosh, Donald 'Husserl, Weber, Freud, and the Method of the Human Sciences,' *Philosophy of Social Science*, vol. 27, no. 3, 1997, pp. 328–53.
2. Bowker, *The Sense of God, Sociological, Anthropological and Psychological Approaches to the Origin of the Sense of God* (Oxford: Clarendon Press, 1973), pp. 176–7.
3. On this point see Ricoeur, 'Philosophy and Religious Language', *Journal of Religion*, vol. 54 (1974) pp. 71–85.
4. Rouse, *Engaging Science: How to Understand its Practices Philosophically* (Ithaca and London: Cornell University Press, 1996), p. 166.
5. For a good discussion of this issue see Harré and Krausz, *Varieties of Relativism* (Oxford and Cambridge, MA: Blackwell, 1996), pp. 34–64.
6. Smart, *The Science of Religion and the Sociology of Knowledge: Some Methodological Questions* (Princeton University Press, 1973), p. 54.
7. Davies, *Meister Eckhart, Selected Writings* (Penguin, 1996), pp. xxii–xxiv.
8. Ricoeur, *Time and Narrative*, vol. 3 (University of Chicago Press, 1988), p. 35.
9. Morris, 'Community Beyond Tradition' in Heelas et al. (eds) *Detraditionalization* (Oxford: Blackwell, 1996), p. 225.
10. Morris, 'Community Beyond Tradition', p. 224.
11. Ricoeur, *Time and Narrative*, vol. 3, p. 35.
12. Weber, *Economy and Society: An Outline of Interpretative Sociology*, Roth and Wittich (eds), (New York: Bedminster), pp. 4–5, 22–5.
13. Saussure, *Course in General Linguistics*, p. 129 (quoted in Voloshinov p. 61).
14. Voloshinov, *Marxism and the Philosophy of Language*, pp. 67f.
15. Shlovsky, 'Art as Technique' in Lemon and Reis (eds and trans) *Russian Formalist Criticism: Four Essays* (Lincoln: University of Nebraska Press, 1965). See also Matejka and Pomorska (eds) *Readings in Russian Poetics: Formalist and Structuralist Views* (Cambridge, MA: MIT Press, 1971).
16. For the dialogist criticism of this position see Medvedev, *The Formal Method in Literary Scholarship: A Critical Introduction to Sociological*

Poetics, Wehrle (trs), (Baltimore and London: The Johns Hopkins University Press, 1978), p. 61.

17. Jakobson, Roland 'Closing Statement: Linguistics and Poetics' in Sebeok (ed.) *Style in Language* (Cambridge, Mass: MIT, 1966), p. 358.

18. Morson and Emerson, *Mikhail Bakhtin: Creation of a Prosaics* (Stanford University Press, 1990), p. 128.

19. According to Vygotsky's work – which influenced Bakhtin – a child develops through a number of stages, of particular importance for linguistic development being the moment when a child asks the names for things. At this point development becomes sociohistorical rather than purely biological. Vygotsky, *Thought and Language*, ed. and trs. Alex Kozulin (Cambridge, MA: MIT Press, 1986), p. 94. Quoted in Morson and Emerson, *Mikhail Bakhtin: Creation of a Prosaics* (Stanford University Press, 1990), p. 212. For more recent work on the acquisition of linguistic categories see Atran and Sperber, 'Learning Without Teaching: Its Place in Culture' in Landsman (ed.) *Culture, Schooling and Psychological Development* (Norwood, NJ: Ablex, 1991).

20. Levinson writes: 'deixis concerns the ways in which languages encode or grammatricalize features of the context of utterance or speech event and thus also concerns ways in which the interpretation of utterances depend on the analysis of that context of utterance.' Levinson, *Pragmatics* (Cambridge University Press, 1983), p. 54.

21. Urban, 'The "I" of Discourse' in Benjamin Lee and Greg Urban (eds) *Semiotics, Self and Society* (Berlin, New York: Mouton de Gruyter, 1989).

22. Urban, 'The "I" of Discourse', p. 31.

23. Urban, 'The "I" of Discourse', p. 34.

24. Urban, 'The "I" of Discourse', p. 36.

25. Urban, 'The "I" of Discourse', p. 42.

26. Urban, 'The "I" of Discourse', p. 44–5. For a full ethnography see Urban, *A Discourse-Centred Approach to Culture: Native South American Myths and Rituals* (Austin: University of Texas Press, 1991).

27. Freeman, 'Performing Possession: Ritual and Consciousness in the Teyyam Complex' in Bruckner, Lutze, and Malik (eds) *Flags of Flame; Studies in South Asian Folk Culture* (New Delhi: Manohar Publishers, 1993), pp. 109–38.

28. Silverstein and Urban, 'The Natural History of Discourse', in Silverstein and Urban (eds) *Natural Histories of Discourse* (Chicago and London: University of Chicago Press, 1996), p. 7.

29. Bakhtin, *Problems of Dostoevsky's Poetics* (Minneapolis: University of Minnesota Press, 1984), p. 189.

30. *Jayākhya Saṃhitā* 10. 9, Krishnamacharya (ed.) (Baroda: Gaekwad's Oriental Series, 1931).
31. The use of the optative means that 'he is impelling me to action; he is engaging in an operation which is conducive to my action'. Apadeva, *Mimamsa Nyaya Prakasa*, trs. Franklin Edgerton (New Haven: Harvard University Press, 1929), p. 40.
32. Iser, *The Act of Reading: A Theory of Aesthetic Response* (Baltimore and London: The Johns Hopkins University Press, 1978).
33. Hiltebeitel, *The Cult of Draupadi*, vol. 1, *Mythologies: From Gurukse-tra to Gingee*, (Delhi: MLBD, 1991), p. 139.
34. Freeman, 'Performing Possession: Ritual and Consciousness in the Teyyam Complex', in Bruckner et al. (eds) *Flags of Flame: Studies in South Asian Folk Culture* (New Delhi: Manohar Publishers, 1993).
35. Urban, 'The "I" of Discourse' pp. 38–9. See also Urban, *A Discourse-Centred Approach to Culture: Native South American Myths and Rituals* (Austin: University of Texas Press, 1991).
36. Silverstein and Urban, 'The Natural History of Discourse', p. 1.
37. Ricoeur, 'The Question of the Subject', in *The Conflict of Interpretations*, p. 237.

Chapter 8

1. See Deleuze, *Kant's Critical Philosophy: The Doctrine of the Faculties* (Minneapolis: University of Minnesota Press, 1984 (1963)), chapter 3.
2. Bakhtin, 'The *Bildungsroman* and its Significance in the History of Realism (Towards a Historical Typology of the Novel)' in *Speech Genres and Other Late Essays* (Austin: University of Texas), pp. 10–59; Dumont, *German Ideology From France to Germany and Back* (Chicago and London: University of Chicago Press, 1994), pp. 82–195. See also Bowie, *From Romanticism to Critical Theory: The Philosophy of German Literary Theory* (London and New York: Routledge, 1997).
3. Baudrillard, *Simulations*, (New York: Semiotext(e), 1983), pp. 1–2.
4. Foucault, 'On the Genealogy of Ethics,' in Dreyfus and Rabinow (eds), *Michel Foucault: Beyond Structuralism and Hermeneutics* (University of Chicago Press, 1982), p. 237. On Baudelaire see 'What is Enlightenment?' in Paul Rabinow (ed.) *The Foucault Reader* (Harmondsworth: Penguin, 1984), pp. 41–2.
5. 'My determination of myself is given to me (given as a task – as something yet to be achieved) not in the categories of temporal being, but in the categories of *not-yet-being* ... to be present to myself as someone-yet-to-be' Bakhtin, 'Author and Hero in Aesthetic Activity',

pp. 123–4, *Art and Answerability* (Austin: University of Texas Press, 1990). Meaning in a life therefore becomes aesthetic because it cannot act as a material force (Bakhtin, 'Methodology for the Human Sciences', in *Speech Genres and Other Essays* (Austin: University of Texas Press, 1986), p. 165).

6. In the work of Von Balthasar for example. See Sherry, *Spirit and Beauty, An Introduction to Theological Aesthetics* (Oxford: Clarendon Press, 1992), pp. 17–18.

7. Appadurai (ed.), *The Social Life of Things: Commodities in Cultural Perspective* (Cambridge University Press, 1986); Featherstone, *Consumer Culture and Postmodernism* (London: Sage, 1991). For capitalist resistance to aestheticization and the emphasis on the work ethic see Roberts (ed.), *Religion and the Transformation of Capitalism: Comparative Approaches* (London and New York: Routledge, 1995).

8. Bauman, *Postmodern Ethics* (Oxford and Cambridge, MA: Blackwell, 1993), pp. 33–5.

9. Taylor, *The Ethics of Authenticity*, (Cambridge, MA: and London: Harvard University Press, 1991), p. 29. On the related idea of the 'ethic of humanity' and the idea of 'rights' see Heelas, 'On Things not being Worse, and the Ethic of Humanity', in Heelas et al. (eds) *Detraditionalization* (Oxford and Cambridge, MA: Blackwell, 1996), pp. 200–22.

10. See Lasch, Christopher *The Culture of Narcissism* (London: Abacus, 1980).

11. See Heelas, 'Californian Self Religions and Socializing the Subjective' in Barker (ed.) *New Religious Movements: A Perspective for Understanding Society* (New York: Mellen, 1982), pp. 69–85; Heelas 'Exegesis: Methods and Aims' in Clarke (ed.) *The New Evangelists. Recruitment, Methods and Aims of New Religious Movements* (London: Ethnographica, 1987), pp. 17–41.

12. See Dumont, *Essays on Individualism* (Chicago University Press, 1986), pp. 234–68; Bellamy, *Liberalism and Modern Society* (Cambridge: Polity Press, 1992); Taylor *Sources of the Self: the Making of the Modern Identity* (Cambridge University Press, 1989), ch. 22.

13. Taylor *Sources of the Self: the Making of the Modern Identity* (Cambridge University Press, 1989), part 2.

14. Davies, *Being and Love*, vol. 1 (London: Darton, Longman & Todd, forthcoming).

15. Kant, 'What is Enlightenment?' in Hans Reiss (ed.), *Kant's Political Writings* (Cambridge University Press, 1971), pp. 85–92.

16. Taylor, *The Ethics of Authenticity*, p. 18.

17. 'To let morality out of the stiff armour of the artificially constructed ethical codes (or abandoning the ambition to keep it there), means to *re-personalize it*.' Bauman, *Postmodern Ethics*, p. 34.

18. Taylor, *The Ethics of Authenticity*, p. 23.
19. Rawls, *A Theory of Justice* (Cambridge, MA: Harvard University Press, 1971). For other liberal positions see Dworkin *Taking Rites Seriously* (London: Duckworth, 1977) and Kymlicka, *Liberalism, Community and Culture* (Oxford: The Clarendon Press, 1989).
20. On views of the self in relation to ethics see Margolis, *Life Without Principles* (Oxford: Blackwell, 1996), pp. 19–59. Margolis has put the Kantian universalist claim versus the communitarian, relativist claim in the context of theories of *adequational* and *existential* theories of persons. Adequational theories assume what is objectively true about the world and claim that there is a competence or ability in persons 'adequate' for discerning such objective truths (including morality), in contrast to existentialist theory which does not presume such a rational competence for the discerning of an objective scientific or moral truth.
21. Sandel, *Liberalism and the Limits of Justice* (Cambridge University Press, 1982), p. 181. In this critique of liberalism Sandel shares a platform with MacIntyre. But whereas for MacIntyre ethics needs to be grounded in human nature and to show that some ways of living are right in accordance with the virtues, Sandel wishes to develop an ethics that does not look back to Aristotle, but grounds ethics in contemporary community.
22. Lingis, *The Community of Those Who Have Nothing In Common* (Bloomington and Indianapolis: Indiana University Press, 1994), p. 10.
23. Gardiner, 'Alterity and Ethics', *Theory, Culture and Society*, vol. 13, no. 2, 1996, pp. 121–43.
24. Gardiner, 'Alterity and Ethics', p. 122.
25. Levinas, *Otherwise than Being* (The Hague: Nijhoff, 1981), pp. 119–20.
26. Ricoeur, *Oneself as Another* (Chicago University Press, 1992), pp. 188–9 and 335–41.
27. In this way Bakhtin is close to Gadamer for whom moral knowledge, following Aristotle, is not objective: 'the knower is not standing over against a situation that he merely observes; he is directly confronted with what he sees. It is something that he has to do.' Gadamer, *Truth and Method* (London: Sheed & Ward, 1989), p. 314.
28. Lingis, *The Community of Those Who Have Nothing in Common*, p. 10.
29. See Bourdieu, *Homo Academicus* (Cambridge: Polity Press, 1988) e.g. pp. 73–127.
30. D'Costa, 'The End of "Theology" and "Religious Studies" '. The phenomenological approach is also implicitly questioned by David Ford

'Theology and Religious Studies at the Turn of the Millennium: Reconceiving the Field,' *Teaching Theology and Religious Studies*, vol. 1, 1, 1998, pp. 4–12.

31. Milbank 'The End of Dialogue', p. 190, in D'Costa (ed.), *Christian Uniqueness Reconsidered: The Myth of a Pluralistic Theology of Religions* (New York: Orbis Books, 1990), pp. 174–91.

32. Kögler, *The Power of Dialogue: Critical Hermeneutics after Gadamer and Foucault* (Cambridge, MA: MIT Press, 1996), p. 255.

33. Lingis, *The Community of Those Who Have Nothing in Common*, p. 33.

34. Lingis, *The Community of Those Who Have Nothing in Common*, pp. 24–25.

35. Lingis, *The Community of Those Who Have Nothing in Common*, p. 15.

36. Bauman, *Postmodern Ethics* (Oxford and Cambridge, MA: Blackwell, 1993), p. 8.

37. Bauman, *Postmodern Ethics*, p. 11.

38. e.g. Foucault's *The Order of Things* critiques the 'birth of man' as the privileged, epistemological subject of the human sciences who can rather be understood in terms of language and desire, and whose privileged status has been overthrown by the modern sciences of psychoanalysis and ethnology which question that which 'makes possible knowledge about man' and which deal with what is outside of consciousness in the Western episteme: 'One may say of both of them ... that they dissolve man.' Foucault, *The Order of Things: An Archaeology of the Human Sciences* (London: Routledge, 1989), p. 379. For a useful summary of this position see Best and Kellner, *Postmodern Theory: Critical Interrogations* (London: Macmillan, 1991), pp. 34–75.

39. Touraine, *Critique of Modernity* (Oxford and Cambridge, MA: Blackwell, 1995), pp. 201–32.

40. See Lash, *Sociology of Postmodernism* (London and New York: Routledge, 1990), pp. 61–5.

41. Milbank, *Theology and Social Theory: Beyond Secular Reason* (Oxford: Blackwell, 1990); Ward (ed.) *The Postmodern God: A Theological Reader* (Oxford: Blackwell, 1997).

42. Deleuze, *Difference and Repetition*, trans. by Paul Patton (London: The Athlone Press, 1994), pp. 66, 117–20.

43. Deleuze, *Difference and Repetition*, p. 138.

44. Deleuze, 'Immanence: A Life ... ' *Theory, Culture and Society*, vol. 14, 2, 1997, p. 4.

45. Deleuze and Guattari, *Anti-Oedipus* (Minneapolis: University of Min-

nesota Press, 1983); *A Thousand Plateaus* (Minneapolis: University of Minnesota Press, 1987).

46. Goodchild, 'Deleuzean Ethics', *Theory, Culture and Society*, vol. 14, 2, 1997, pp. 39–50.

47. See for example, Sinfield, *Faultlines: Cultural Materialism and the Politics of Dissident Reading* (Oxford: Clarendon Press, 1992), pp. 29–51.

48. See Goodchild, 'Deleuzean Ethics', *Theory, Culture and Society*, vol. 14, 2, 1997, pp. 39–50.

49. Foucault, 'Politics and Ethics: An Interview' in Rabinow (ed.) *The Foucault Reader* (Harmondsworth: Penguin, 1984), p. 375.

50. See for example Fraser, 'Feminism, Foucault and Deleuze', *Theory, Culture and Society*, vol. 14, 2, 1997, pp. 23–47.

51. Goodchild, 'Deleuzean Ethics', pp. 43–4.

52. Wagner, *The Invention of Culture* (Chicago University Press, 1980).

53. Tyler, 'Post-Modern Ethnography: From Document of the Occult to Occult Document', in Clifford and Marcus, *Writing Culture: The Poetics and Politics of Ethnography* (Berkeley, Los Angeles, London: University of California Press, 1986), p. 123.

54. Heelas et al. (eds), *Detraditionalization*.

55. Tyler, 'Post-Modern Ethnography', p. 126.

56. Brown, *Mama Lola: A Voudou Priestess in Brooklyn* (Berkeley, Los Angeles, Oxford: University of California Press, 1991), p. 14.

57. Métraux, *Voodoo in Haiti* (New York: Schocken Books, 1972).

58. Brown, *Mama Lola*, p. 14.

59. Lingis, *The Community of Those Who Have Nothing in Common*, p. 33.

60. Brown, *Mama Lola*, p. 2.

61. Bahktin, 'Discourse in the Novel' in Holquist (ed.), *The Dialogic Imagination* (Austin: University of Texas Press, 1981), pp. 293–4.

62. Bakhtin interestingly relates trust to aestheticism in that trust and faith produce an aesthetic form or 'concord'. Bakhtin, 'The Author and Hero in Aesthetic Activity', *Art and Answerability*, p. 145.

63. Ricoeur, *Oneself as Another* (University of Chicago Press, 1992), pp. 188–9.

64. Ricoeur, *Oneself as Another*, p. 189.

65. Ricoeur, *Oneself as Another*, p. 193.

66. Ricoeur, *Oneself as Another*, pp. 193–4.

67. Bakhtin, 'Response to a Question from *Novy Mir*' in *Speech Genres and Other Essays* (Austin: University of Texas Press, 1986), p. 7.

68. It is with unfinalizability that Bakhtin introduces the theme of the carnival. Emerson, *The First Hundred Years of Mikhail Bakhtin* (Princeton University Press, 1997), p. 37.

69. See Rehg, *Insight and Solidarity* (Berkeley: University of California Press, 1994) for an overview of Habermas' discourse ethics. See also Bernstein, *Recovering Ethical Life: Jurgen Habermas and the Future of Critical Theory* (London and New York: Routledge, 1995).

70. Benhabib, *Situating the Self: Gender, Community and Postmodernism in Contemporary Ethics* (Cambridge, MA: Polity Press, 1993), pp. 208–9.

71. Bakhtin, 'The Author and Hero', p. 129.

72. Bakhtin, *Problems in Dostoyevsky's Poetics* (Minneapolis and London: University of Minnesota Press, 1984), p. 69.

73. Emerson, *The First Hundred Years of Mikhail Bakhtin*, pp. 155–6.

74. On the notion of narrative identity see Ricoeur, 'Narrative Identity' in Wood (ed.) *On Paul Ricoeur: Narrative and Interpretation* (London: Routledge, 1991), pp. 188–99 and Ricoeur *Oneself as Another* (Chicago and London: University of Chicago Press, 1992) chapters 6 and 7. For a discussion of narrative identity and dialogic identity see de Penter, 'The Dialogics of Narrative Identity' in Bell and Gardiner (eds), *Bakhtin and the Human Sciences* (London, Thousand Oaks, New Delhi: Sage, 1998), pp. 30–48; Hermans and Kempen, *The Dialogical Self: Meaning as Movement* (San Diego: Academic Press, 1993); Sampson, *Celebrating the Other: A Dialogic Account of Human Nature* (Boulder: Westview Press, 1993), pp. 107–9, 111–14, 123–5.

75. Haraway, *Simians, Cyborgs and Women: the Reinvention of Nature* (London: Free Association Books, 1991), p. 196.

76. Benhabib, *Situating the Self*, p. 212.

77. Coakley (ed.), *Religion and the Body* (Cambridge University Press, 1997; King (ed.) *Religion and Gender* (Oxford: Blackwell, 1995).

78. Although too large a subject to engage with here, the importance of the body cannot be underestimated in Bakhtin's work, 'one cannot draw an absolute distinction between body and meaning in the area of culture' ('Response to a Question from *Novy Mir*' in *Speech Genres and Other Essays*, p. 6). See Bakhtin 'The Author and Hero in Aesthetic Activity', pp. 60–1; Hitchcock, 'The Grotesque of the Body Electric' in Bell and Gardiner, *Bakhtin and the Human Sciences* (London, Thousand Oaks, New Delhi: Sage, 1998), pp. 78–94.

Epilogue

1. Nietzsche, *Die Fröhliche Wissenschaft, Werke 2* (Frankfurt, Berlin, Vienna: Ullstein, 1972), no. 125, pp. 126–7.

2. Vattimo, *Beyond Interpretation: The Meaning of Hermeneutics for Philosophy* (Cambridge: Polity Press, 1997), p. 9.

3. D'Costa, 'The End of "Theology" and "Religious Studies" ', *Theology* vol. 94 (1996), pp. 338–51.

4. D'Costa, 'The End of "Theology" and "Religious Studies" ', p. 6. The same point is made by J. Z. Smith ('the academic study of religion is a child of the enlightenment'). Smith, *From Babylon to Jonestown* (Chicago University Press, 1982), p. 104.

5. See Bowker, *Licensed Insanities* (London: Darton, Longman & Todd, 1987), pp. 15–18.

6. This is excellently demonstrated in Freeman's work on Kerala traditions. Freeman, 'Rubies and Coral: The Lapidary Crafting of Language in Kerala', in *Journal of Asian Studies*, vol. 57, 1 (1998), pp. 38–65.

7. See Geuss, *The Idea of a Critical Theory: Habermas and the Frankfurt School* (Cambridge University Press, 1981), pp. 63–9.

8. McCutcheon, 'A Default of Critical Intelligence? The Scholar of Religion as Public Intellectual', *Journal of the American Academy of Religion*, vol. 65, no. 2 (1997), p. 456.

9. Ford, 'Theology and Religious Studies at the Turn of the Millenium: Reconceiving the Field', *Teaching Theology and Religion*, vol. 1, 1, 1998, pp. 4–12.

10. 'The study of religion must attempt to be objectively outlined in a warm way and to follow the logic of the structures it studies'. Smart, *The Science of Religion and the Sociology of Knowledge: Some Methodological Questions* (Princeton University Press, 1973), pp. 37–8.

11. Ford, 'Theology and Religious Studies at the Turn of the Millenium: Reconceiving the Field', p. 5.

12. On this point see Davies and Flood, 'Against Hegemony: Reflexivity and Critique in the Teaching of Theology and Religious Studies' (unpublished).

13. Bowie, 'Trespassing on Sacred Domains: A Feminist Anthropological Approach to Theology and Religious Studies', *Journal of Feminist Studies in Religion*, vol. 13 (1998), pp. 40–62, p. 44.

14. O'Connor, 'The Epistemological Significance of Feminist Research in Religion,' in King (ed.), *Religion and Gender* (Oxford and Cambridge, MA: Blackwell, 1995), p. 46.

15. e.g. Horne and Wussow (eds), *A Dialogue of Feminist Voices: Feminist Literary Theory and Bakhtin* (Minneapolis: Minnesota University Press, 1994); Pearce, *Reading Dialogics* (London: Edwin Arnold, 1994).

16. For an excellent review of gender and religious studies with particular reference to feminism see King, 'Introduction: Gender and the Study of Religion' in King (ed.) *Religion and Gender*, pp. 1–38.

17. Haraway, 'A Cyborg Manifesto' in Haraway, *Simians, Cyborgs and*

Women: the Reinvention of Nature (London: Free Association Books, 1991), p. 154.

18. Haraway, 'A Cyborg Manifesto', p. 181. For the connections between Haraway's vision and Bakhtin see Hitchcock, 'The Grotesque of the Body Electric' in Bell and Gardiner (eds), *Bakhtin and the Human Sciences* (London: Thousand Oaks, New Delhi: Sage, 1998), pp. 78–94.
19. Roberts, 'Time, Virtuality and the Goddess,' *Cultural Values*, vol. 2, nos 2 and 3, (1998), pp. 270–87.
20. Haraway, 'A Cyborg Manifesto', p. 181.
21. Coakley, 'Introduction: Religion and the Body' in Coakley (ed.), *Religion and the Body* (Cambridge University Press, 1997), p. 3.
22. Bhabha, *The Location of Culture* (London and New York: Routledge, 1994), p. 67.
23. Abelove et al. (eds), *Lesbian and Gay Studies Reader* (London: Routledge, 1993), p. xv.
24. Butler, 'Identity and Gender Subordination', p. 21 in Fuss (ed.), *Inside/ Outside: Lesbian Theories, Gay Theories* (London and New York: Routledge, 1992), pp. 13–31.
25. McCutcheon, *Manufacturing Religion: The Discourse on Sui Generis Religion and the Politics of Nostalgia* (Oxford University Press, 1997), p. 22.
26. Noddings, *Caring: A Feminist Approach to Ethics and Moral Education* (Los Angeles: University of California Press, 1984).
27. See Ashcroft, *The Empire Writes Back: Theory and Practice in Postcolonial Literature* (Oxford and Cambridge, MA: Blackwell, 1989); Gates (ed.), *'Race', Writing and Difference* (Chicago University Press, 1985); Moore-Gilbert, *Postcolonial Theory: Contexts, Practices, Politics* (London and New York: Verso, 1997), pp. 5–11.
28. Moore-Gilbert, *Postcolonial Theory: Contexts, Practices*, p. 12.
29. Bhabha, *The Location of Culture*, p. 171.
30. Fanon, *The Wretched of the Earth* (Harmondsworth: Penguin, 1961).
31. Said, *Orientalism* (New York: Pantheon, 1978).
32. Inden, *Imagining India* (Oxford and Cambridge, MA: Blackwell, 1990), pp. 36–48.
33. For example, see Guha and Spivak (eds), *Selected Subaltern Studies* (Oxford University Press, 1988).
34. See Rawlinson, *The Book of Enlightened Masters* (Chicago: Open Court, 1997).
35. See Inden, *Imagining India*, p. 40.
36. Chidester, *Savage Systems: Colonialism and Comparative Religion in Southern Africa* (University of Virginia Press, 1996), pp. 20–9.
37. See Morris 'Community Beyond Tradition', in Heelas et al. (eds)

Detraditionalisation: Critical Reflections on Authority and Identity (Oxford: Blackwell, 1996), pp. 238–45.

38. Smart, 'Discussion' in 'Replies to Don Wiebe in the World Academy of Religion', *Religion*, vol. 23, 1993, p. 93.
39. Bhabha, *The Location of Culture*, p. 170.
40. See, for example, Pollock, 'The Sanskrit Cosmopolis 300–1300: Trans-culturation, Vernacularization, and the Question of Ideology', in Houben (ed.), *Ideology and Status of Sanskrit: Contributions to the History of the Sanskrit Language* (Leiden: Brill, 1996), pp. 197–247.

Bibliography

Abelove, Henry, Michele Aina Barale and David Halpern (eds), *Lesbian and Gay Studies Reader* (London: Routledge, 1993).

Allen, Douglas, 'Recent Defenders of Eliade: A Critical Evaluation', *Religion*, vol. 24 (1995), pp. 333–51.

Alliez, Éric, 'Questionnaire on Deleuze', *Theory, Culture and Society*, vol. 14, 2 (1997), p. 84.

Anderson, Benedict, *Imagined Communities: Reflections on the Origin and Spread of Nationalism* (London and New York: Verso, 1991).

Apadeva, *Mimamsa Nyaya Prakasa*, trs. Franklin Edgerton (New Haven: Harvard University Press, 1929).

Appadurai, A. (ed.), *The Social Life of Things: Commodities in Cultural Perspective* (Cambridge University Press, 1986).

Apel, Karl-Otto, *Understanding and Explanation: A Transcendental-Pragmatic Perspective* (Cambridge, MA: MIT Press, 1984).

Ashcroft, Bill, *The Empire Writes Back: Theory and Practice in Postcolonial Literature* (Oxford and Cambridge, MA: Blackwell, 1989).

Atran, Scott, 'Origin of the Species and Genus Concepts: An Anthropological Perspective', *Journal of the History of Biology*, 1987, vol. 20, pp. 195–279.

—— *Cognitive Foundations of Natural History: Towards an Anthropology of Science* (Cambridge University Press, 1990).

Atran, Scott, and Dan Sperber, 'Learning Without Teaching: Its Place in Culture', in L. Landsman (ed.), *Culture, Schooling and Psychological Development* (Norwood NJ: Ablex, 1990).

Auerbach, Eric, *Mimesis: The Representation of Reality in Western Literature*, trs. Willard Trask (Princeton University Press, 1953).

Austin, J. L., *How to Do Things With Words* (Oxford University Press, 1962).

Badham, Paul, 'John Hick's Global Understanding of Religion' (Tokyo: International Buddhist Study Center, 1992).

282

Bainbridge, W. S., *The Sociology of Religious Movements* (New York and London: Routledge, 1997).

Bakhtin, Mikhail, *The Dialogic Imagination: Four Essays*, ed. M. Holquist, (Austin: University of Texas Press, 1981).

—— *Problems of Dostoevsky's Poetics*, trs. C. Emerson (Minneapolis, London: Minnesota University Press, 1984).

—— *Speech Genres and Other Essays*, trs. Vern W. McGee (Austin: University of Texas Press, 1986).

—— *Art and Answerability: Early Essays by M. M. Bakhtin*, eds M. Holquist and V. Liapunov (Austin: University of Texas Press, 1990).

Barthes, Roland, *Mythologies* (New York: Hill & Wang, 1972).

Baudrillard, Jean, *Simulations* trs. C. Turner (New York: Semiotext(e), 1983).

Bauman, Zygmunt, *Postmodern Ethics* (Oxford and Cambridge, MA: Blackwell, 1993).

Beiser, Fred, *The Fate of Reason: German Philosophy from Kant to Fichte* (Cambridge, MA: and London: Harvard University Press, 1987).

Bell, Michael M. and Michael Gardiner (eds), *Bakhtin and the Human Sciences* (London, Thousand Oaks, New Delhi: Sage, 1998).

Bellamy, Richard, *Liberalism and Modern Society* (Cambridge: Polity Press, 1992).

Benhabib, S., *Situating the Self: Gender, Community and Postmodernism in Contemporary Ethics* (Cambridge: Polity Press, 1992).

Berger, Peter, *The Sacred Canopy: Elements for a Sociological Theory of Religion* (New York: Doubleday, 1967).

—— 'On Phenomenological Research in the Field of Religion', *Encyclopedie Française*, vol. 1957, p. 1932, trs. in J. Waardenburg (ed.) *Classical Approaches to the Study of Religion* (Mouton, The Hague, Paris: Mouton, 1973), p. 665.

Bernstein, J. M., *Recovering Ethical Life: Jurgen Habermas and the Future of Critical Theory* (London and New York: Routledge, 1995).

Bernstein, Richard J., *Beyond Objectivism and Relativism* (University of Pennsylvania Press, 1983).

Best, Steven, and Douglas Kellner, *Postmodern Theory: Critical Interrogations* (London: Macmillan, 1991).

Betz, Hans Dieter, 'Christianity as Religion: Paul's Attempt at Definition in Romans', in Bianchi, Ugo (ed.) *The Notion of 'Religion' in Comparative Research: Selected Proceedings of the XVI IAHR Congress* (Rome: 'L'Erma' di Bretsschneider, 1994), pp. 3–9.

Beyer, S., *Religion and Globalization* (London, Thousand Oaks, New Delhi: Sage, 1994).

Bhabha, Homi, *The Location of Culture* (London and New York: Routledge, 1994).

Bianchi, Ugo (ed.), *The Notion of 'Religion' in Comparative Research: Selected Proceedings of the XVI IAHR Congress* (Rome: 'L'Erma' di Bretschneider, 1994).

Black, Max, 'Metaphor' in Margolis (ed.) *Philosophy Looks at the Arts* (New York: Temple University Press, 1962), pp. 218–35.

Blacking, J. (ed.), *The Anthropology of the Body* (London: Academic Press, 1977).

Blumenberg, Hans, *The Legitimacy of the Modern Age*, trs. Robert M. Wallace (London and Cambridge, MA: MIT Press, 1983).

—— *Work on Myth*, trs. Robert M. Wallace (Cambridge, MA: MIT Press, 1990).

Bock, P. K. (ed.), *Handbook of Psychological Anthropology* (Westport, Conn: Greenwood Press, 1994).

Bohman, James, *New Philosophy of Social Science* (Cambridge: Polity Press, 1991).

Bond, Philip (ed.), *Post-Secular Philosophy* (Oxford: Blackwell, 1998).

Borges, Jorge Luis, *Jorge Luis Borges, Selected Poems 1923–1967* ed. N. T. di Giovanni (London: Allen Lane Penguin, 1972).

Bourdieu, Pierre, *Homo Academicus* trs. Paul Collier (Cambridge: Polity Press, 1988).

—— *Outline of a Theory of Practice*, trs. Richard Nice (Cambridge University Press, 1991).

—— *The Logic of Practice* trs. Richard Nice (Cambridge: Polity Press, 1992).

—— *Sociology in Question* (London, Thousand Oaks, New Delhi: Sage, 1993).

—— *In Other Words: Essays Towards a Reflexive Sociology* trs. Mathew Adamson (Cambridge: Polity Press, 1994).

Bowie, Andrew, *From Romanticism to Critical Theory: The Philosophy of German Literary Theory* (London and New York: Routledge, 1997).

Bowie, Fiona, 'Trespassing on Sacred Domains: A Feminist Anthropological Approach to Theology and Religious Studies', *Journal of Feminist Studies in Religion*, vol. 13, 1998, pp. 40–62.

Bowker, John, *The Sense of God: Sociological, Anthropological and Psychological Approaches to the Origin of the Sense of God* (Oxford University Press, 1973).

—— *Worlds of Faith: Religious Belief and Practice in Britain Today* (London: Ariel, 1983).

—— *Licensed Insanities* (London: Darton, Longman & Todd, 1987).

—— *Is God a Virus? Genes, Culture and Religion* (London: SPCK, 1995).

Boyer, Pascal, *The Naturalness of Religious Ideas: A Cognitive Theory of Religion* (Berkeley, Los Angeles, London: University of California Press, 1994).

Boyer, Pascal (ed.), *Cognitive Aspects of Religious Symbolism* (Cambridge University Press, 1993).

Brown, Karen, *Mama Lola: A Voudou Priestess in Brooklyn* (University of California Press, 1991).

Browning, Don S. and Francis Schussler Fiorenza (eds), *Habermas, Modernity and Public Theology* (New York: Crossroad, 1992).

Brunner, Hélène, 'Le Sādhaka, personnage oubliee dans l'Inde du Sud,' *Journal Asiatique* (1975), pp. 411–43.

Buckley, R. Philip, 'Edmund Husserl' in Embree et al. (eds) *The Encyclopedia of Phenomenology* (Dordrecht, Boston, London: Kluwer Academic Publishers, 1997).

Burroughs, William, *Naked Lunch* (London: Paladin, 1992 (1959)).

—— *Cities of the Red Night*, trilogy (London: Paladin, 1981,1983, 1987).

Callinicos, Alex, *Theories and Narratives: Reflections on the Philosophy of History* (Cambridge: Polity Press, 1995).

Camus, Albert, *The Outsider*, trs. Stuart Gilbert (Penguin, 1961).

Capps, Walter, 'On Religious Studies, In Lieu of an Overview' *Journal of the American Academy of Religion*, 42 (1974), pp. 727–33.

—— *Religious Studies: the Making of a Discipline* (Minneapolis: Fortress Press, 1995).

Cassirer, E., *The Philosophy of Symbolic Forms*, vol. 2 (Yale University Press, 1955).

Casson, R. W., *Language, Culture and Cognition* (New York: Macmillan, 1981).

—— 'Cognitive Anthropology' in Philip K. Bock (ed.), *Handbook of Psychological Anthropology* (Westport: Greenwood Press, 1994).

Castoriadis, C., *The Imaginary Institution of Society*, trs. Kathleen Blamey (Cambridge: Polity Press, 1987).

Carr, D., *Phenomenology and the Problem of History* (Evanston: Northwestern University Press, 1974).

—— *Time, Narrative and History* (New York: Columbia University Press, 1986).

Chidester, David, *Savage Systems: Colonialism and Comparative Religion in Southern Africa* (University of Virginia Press, 1996).

—— 'Anchoring Religion in the World: A Southern African History of Comparative Religion', *Religion*, vol. 26 (1996), pp. 141–60.

Clarke, P. and P. Byrne, *Religion Defined and Explained* (London: Macmillan, 1993).

Clayton, John, 'Thomas Jefferson and the Study of Religion' (inaugural lecture, Lancaster University, 1992).

Clifford, James, and Marcus, George E. (eds), *Writing Culture: The Poetics and Politics of Ethnography* (Berkeley and Los Angeles: University of California Press, 1986).

Coakley, S. (ed.), *Religion and the Body* (Cambridge University Press, 1997).

Code, Lorraine, *Rhetorical Spaces: Essays on Gendered Locations* (London: Routledge, 1995).

Cohen, Werner, 'What is Religion? An Analysis for Cross-Cultural Comparisons', *Journal of Christian Education*, vol. 7 (1964), pp. 116–38.

—— ' "Religion" in Non-Western Cultures?' *American Anthropologist*, vol. 69 (1967), 1 pp. 73–6.

Colby, B., 'Ethnographic Semantics: A Preliminary Survey', *American Anthropology* (1966), vol. 7, pp. 3–32.

Crapanzo, V., *Tuhami: Portrait of a Moroccan* (Chicago University Press, 1980).

Critchley, Simon, *Very Little … Almost Nothing: Death, Philosophy, Literature* (London and New York: Routledge, 1997).

Cumpsty, J., *Religion as Belonging: A General Theory of Religion* (London: University of America Press, 1991).

D'Aquili, G. Eugene et al. (eds) *The Spectrum of Ritual: A Biogenetic Analysis* (New York: Columbia University Press, 1979).

Dallmayr, Fred R. and Thomas A. McCarthy (eds) *Understanding and Social Inquiry* (Notre Dame University Press, 1977).

Davies, Gregory W., 'Theology and Religious Studies in the University: Some Ambiguities Revisited', *Religion* 26, 1996, pp. 49–68.

Davies, Oliver, *Meister Eckhart, Selected Writings* (Penguin, 1996).

—— 'Culture and Spirituality' (Oxford: Westminster College, 1996).

—— *Being and Love*, vol. 1 (London: T. & T. Clark, forthcoming).

Davies, Oliver, and Gavin Flood, 'The Other Tiger: Reflections on Method in Theology and Religious Studies' (unpublished).

Dawkins, Richard, *The Selfish Gene* (New York: Oxford University Press, 1976).

Dawson, Lorne, 'On Reference to the Transcendent in the Scientific Study of Religion: A Qualified Idealist Proposal', *Religion* (1987), vol. 17, pp. 227–50.

—— *Reason, Freedom and Religion: Closing the Gap Between the Humanities and Scientific Study of Religion*, Toronto Studies in Religion (New York: Peter Lang, 1988).

—— '*Sui Generis* Phenomena and Disciplinary Axioms: Rethinking Pals Proposal', *Religion* (1990) vol. 20, pp. 38–51.

—— 'On Reducing Reductionism in the Academic Study of Religion: Dippman's Spurious Distinction', *Method and Theory in the Study of Religion*, vol. 5, 1, 1993, pp. 27–45, p. 43.

De Certeau, Michel, *The Writing of History*, trs. Tom Conley (New York: Columbia University Press, 1988).

286

—— *The Mystic Fable* 1 *The Sixteenth and Seventeenth Centuries*, trs. M. B. Smith (Chicago University Press, 1992).

—— *Culture in the Plural*, ed. Luce Giard, trs. Tom Conley (Minneapolis and London: University of Minnesota Press, 1997).

D'Costa, Gavin, 'The End of "Theology" and "Religious Studies" ', *Modern Theology*, vol. 94 (1996), pp. 338–51.

D'Costa, Gavin (ed.), *Christian Uniqueness Reconsidered: The Myth of a Pluralist Theology of Religions* (New York: Orbis, 1990).

Deleuze, Gilles, *Kant's Critical Philosophy: The Doctrine of the Faculties*, trs. Hugh Tomlinsion and Barbara Haberrjam (Minneapolis: University of Minnesota Press, 1984 (1963)).

—— *Difference and Repetition*, trs. Paul Patton (London: The Athlone Press, 1994).

—— 'Immanence: A Life . . . ' *Theory, Culture and Society*, vol. 14, 2, 1997, p. 4.

Deleuze, Gilles, and Felix Guattari, *Anti-Oedipus*, trs. Paul Patton (Minneapolis: University of Minnesota Press, 1983); *A Thousand Plateaus* (Minneapolis: University of Minnesota Press, 1987).

Derrida, Jacques, *Speech and Phenomena*, trs. David Allision (Evanson, IL: Northwestern University Press, 1973).

—— *Of Grammatology*, trs. Gayatri Spivak (Baltimore and London: Johns Hopkins University Press, 1976).

—— *Writing and Difference*, trs. Alan Bass (London: Routledge, 1978).

Despland, Michel, *La religion en occident: evolution des idées et du vecu* (Montreal: Editions Fidee, 1979).

Despland, Michel, and Gerard Vallee (eds), *Religion in History: the Word, the Idea, the Reality* (Waterloo, Ontario: Wilfred Laurier University Press, 1992).

Dews, Peter, *Logics of Disintegration: Post-Structuralist Thought and the Claims of Critical Theory* (London: Verso, 1987).

Dhavamony, Mariasusai, *The Phenomenology of Religion* (Rome: Gregorian University Press, 1973).

Dijk, Teun van (ed.), *Discourse Studies: A Multidisciplinary Approach*, 2 vols. (London, Thousand Oaks, New Delhi: Sage, 1997).

Dixon, K., *The Sociology of Belief: Fallacy and Foundation* (London: RKP, 1980).

Doty, W. G., *Mythography: The Study of Myths and Rituals* (Tuscaloosa: University of Alabama Press, 1986).

Dreyfus, Hubert L. and Paul Rabinow (eds), *Michel Foucault: Beyond Structuralism and Hermeneutics* (University of Chicago Press, 1982).

Drummond, R. H., 'Christian Theology and the History of Religions', *Journal of Ecumenical Studies*, vol. 12 (1975), pp. 389–405.

Dumont, Louis, *Essays on Individualism* (Chicago University Press, 1986).

—— *German Ideology From France to Germany and Back* (Chicago and London: University of Chicago Press, 1994).

Dundas, P., *The Jains* (London and New York: Routledge, 1992).

Dworkin, Ronald, *Taking Rites Seriously* (London: Duckworth, 1977).

Ebeling, Gerhard, *Introduction to a Theological Theory of Language* (London: Collins, 1973).

Eco, U., *A Theory of Semiotics* (Bloomington: Indiana University Press, 1976).

Edsman, Carl-Martin, 'Theology or Religious Studies?', *Religion*, 4 (1974), pp. 59–74.

Eliade, Mircea, *Patterns in Comparative Religion* (Cleveland: Meridian Books, 1963 (1958)).

—— *The Quest* (University of Chicago Press, 1969).

—— *The Myth of the Eternal Return* (Princeton: Bollingen, 1971).

Embree, Lester, 'The Phenomenology of Representational Awareness', *Human Studies*, vol. 15 (1992), pp. 301–14.

Embree, Lester, et al. (eds) *The Encyclopedia of Phenomenology* (Dordrecht, Boston, London: Kluwer Academic Publishers, 1997).

Emerson, Caryl, *The First Hundred Years of Mikhail Bakhtin* (Princeton University Press, 1997).

Evans, J. Claude, 'Phenomenological Deconstruction: Husserl's Method of Abbau', *Journal of the British Society for Phenomenology*, 21 (1990), pp. 14–25.

—— *Strategies of Deconstruction: Derrida and the Myth of the Voice* (Minneapolis: University of Minnesota Press, 1991).

Evans, J. Claude and Leonard Lawlor, 'Jaques Derrida' in Embree at al. (eds), *Encyclopedia of Phenomenology* (Dordrecht, Boston, London: Kluwer Academic Publishers, 1997), pp. 141–3.

Evans-Prichard, E., *The Institutions of Primitive Society* (Oxford: Blackwell, 1954).

Fanon, Franz, *The Wretched of the Earth* (Harmondsworth: Penguin, 1961).

Fay, Brian, *Changing Social Science* (Albany: Suny Press, 1983).

—— *Contemporary Philosophy of Social Science* (Oxford: Blackwell, 1996).

Featherstone, Mike, *Consumer Culture and Postmodernism* (London, Thousand Oaks, New Delhi: Sage, 1991).

—— *Undoing Culture: Globalization, Postmodernism and Identity* (London, Thousand Oaks, New Delhi: Sage, 1995).

Feher, Michel (ed.), *Fragments for a History of the Body*, 4 parts (New York: Zone, 1989).

Feil, Ernst, 'From the Classical *Religio* to the Modern *religion*: Elements of a Transformation between 1550 and 1650', in Despland, Michel and Gerard

Vallee (eds) *Religion in History: the Word, the Idea, the Reality* (Waterloo, Ontario: Wilfred Laurier University Press, 1992).

Ferré, F., *Language, Logic and God* (London: Eyre & Spottiswoode, 1962).

Feyerabend, Paul, *Against Method: Outline of an Anarchistic Theory of Knowledge* (London: NLB, 1975).

Fichte, J., *The Vocation of Man* (Indianapolis: Hackett, 1987).

Fitzgerald, Tim, 'Hinduism and the World Religion Fallacy', *Religion* (1990), vol. 20, pp. 101–18.

—— 'Religious Studies as Cultural Studies: A Philosophical and Anthropological Critique of the Category of Religion', *Diskus* (1995) 3, 1, pp. 35–47.

Flood, Gavin, *An Introduction to Hinduism* (Cambridge University Press, 1996).

Ford, David, 'Theology and Religious Studies at the Turn of the Millennium: Reconceiving the Field', *Teaching Theology and Religion* (1998), vol. 1 (1) pp. 4–12.

Foucault, M., *The Order of Things: An Archaeology of the Human Sciences* (London: Routledge, 1989).

Fraser, Mariam, 'Feminism, Foucault and Deleuze', *Theory, Culture and Society*, vol. 14, 2, (1997), pp. 23–47.

Freeman, Rich, 'Performing Possession: Ritual and Consciousness in the Teyyam Complex', in H. Bruckner, L. Lutze and A. Malik (eds) *Flags of Flame; Studies in South Asian Folk Culture* (New Delhi: Manohar Publishers, 1993).

—— 'Rubies and Coral: The Lapidary Crafting of Language in Kerala', in *The Journal of Asian Studies*, vol. 57 (1998), pp. 38–65.

Freidman, Jonathan, *Cultural Identity and Global Process* (London, Thousand Oaks, New Delhi: Sage, 1994).

Fuss, Diana (ed.), *Inside/Outside: Lesbian Theories, Gay Theories* (London and New York: Routledge, 1992).

Gadamer, Hans Georg, *Truth and Method* (London: Sheed & Ward, 1989).

Gardiner, M., *The Dialogics of Critique* (London and New York: Routledge, 1992).

—— 'Alterity and Ethics', *Theory, Culture and Society*, vol. 13, 2 (1996), pp. 121–43.

Gates, Henry L. (ed.), *'Race', Writing and Difference* (Chicago University Press, 1985).

Gebauer, Gunther, and Christoph Wulf, *Mimesis: Art, Culture, Society* (Berkeley, Los Angeles, London: University of California Press, 1995).

Geertz, A., *The Invention of Prophecy: Continuity and Meaning in Hopi Religion* (Berkeley: University of California Press, 1994).

Geertz, Clifford, *The Interpretation of Cultures* (London: Fontana Press, 1993).

Gellner, E., *Postmodernism, Reason and Religion* (Oxford and London: Routledge, 1992).

Gennette, G., *Narrative Discourse* (Oxford: Blackwell, 1980).

Geuss, Raymond, *The Idea of a Critical Theory: Habermas and the Frankfurt School* (Cambridge University Press, 1981).

Giddens, Anthony, *New Rules of Sociological Method* (Cambridge: Polity Press, 1993 (1976)).

Goodchild, 'Deleuzean Ethics', *Theory, Culture and Society*, vol. 14, 2, 1997, pp. 39–50.

Green, Garett, 'Challenging the Religious Studies Canon: Karl Barth's Theory of Religion', *Journal of Religion*, vol. 75, 1995, pp. 473–86.

Greenblatt, S., *Renaissance Self-Fashioning: from More to Shakespeare* (University of Chicago Press, 1980).

Griffin, D. R., *God and Religion in the Postmodern World: Essays in Postmodern Theology* (Albany: Suny Press, 1989).

Grondin, Jean, *Introduction to Philosophical Hermeneutics*, trs. Joel Weinsheimer (Yale University Press, 1994).

Guha, R., and Spivak, G. C. (eds) *Selected Subaltern Studies* (Oxford University Press, 1988).

Habermas, Jurgen, 'Analytische Wissenschaftstheorie und Dialektik', in *Zeugnisse: Theodor W. Adorno zum sechzigsten Geburstag* (Frankfurt: Suhrkamp, 1963), pp. 500–01.

—— *The Philosophical Discourse of Modernity*, trs. Frederick Lawrence (Cambridge: Polity Press, 1985).

—— *Knowledge and Human Interests*, trs. Jeremy J. Shapiro (Cambridge: Polity Press, 1987).

—— *On the Logic of the Social Sciences*, trs. S. W. Nicholson and J. A. Stark (Cambridge: Polity Press, 1988).

Halbfass, Wilhelm, *India and Europe* (Albany: Suny Press, 1988).

Hannerz, Ulf, *Transnational Connections: Culture, People, Places* (London and New York: Routledge, 1996).

Haraway, Donna, *Simians, Cyborgs and Women: the Reinvention of Nature* (London: Free Association Books, 1991).

Harré, Rom, and Michael Krausz, *Varieties of Relativism* (Oxford: Blackwell, 1996).

Harré, R., and Secord, P. F., *The Explanation of Social Behaviour* (Oxford: Blackwell, 1972).

Harrison, Peter, *'Religion' and the Religions in the English Enlightenment* (Cambridge University Press 1990).

Hauerwas, Stanley, *Dispatches from the Front: Theological Engagements with the Secular* (Durham, NC: Duke University Press, 1994).

Hauerwas, S., and William Willimon, *Resident Aliens: A Provocative Chris-*

tian Assessment of Culture and Ministry for People Who Know That Something Is Wrong (Nashville: Abingdon, 1989).

Hebblethwaite, Brian, *The Problems of Theology* (Cambridge University Press, 1980).

Heelas, Paul, 'Californian Self Religions and Socializing the Subjective', in Barker (ed.) *New Religious Movements: A Perspective for Understanding Society* (New York: Mellen, 1982), pp. 69–85.

—— 'Exegesis: Methods and Aims' in Clarke (ed.) *The New Evangelists. Recruitment, Methods and Aims of New Religious Movements* (London: Ethnographica, 1987), pp. 17–41.

—— *The New Age* (London: Routledge, 1997).

Heelas, Paul (ed.), *Religion, Modernity and Postmodernity* (Oxford: Blackwell, 1998).

Heelas, P., Scott Lash, and Paul Morris (eds), *Detraditionalization* (Oxford: Blackwell, 1996).

Heidegger, M., *Being and Time* trs. J. Macquarrie and E. Robinson (Oxford: Blackwell, 1962).

Held, David, and J. B. Thompson (eds), *Social Theory of Modern Societies: Anthony Giddens and his Critics* (Cambridge University Press, 1989).

Hempel, Carl, 'Reasons and Covering Laws in Historical Explanation', in Sidney Hook (ed.), *Philosophy and History* (New York University Press, 1963), pp. 143–63.

—— *Aspects of Scientific Explanation and Other Essays in the Philosophy of Science* (New York: Free Press, 1965).

—— *Philosophy of Natural Science* (Englewood Cliffs: Prentice Hall, 1966).

Hermans, Hubert J. M., and Harry J. G. Kempen, *The Dialogical Self: Meaning as Movement* (San Diego: Academic Press, 1993).

Hick, John, *An Interpretation of Religion: Human Responses to the Transcendent* (London: Macmillan, 1989).

Hiltebeitel, Alf, *The Cult of Draupadi*, vol. 1, *Mythologies: From Guruksetra to Gingee* (Delhi: MLBD, 1991).

Hockey, James, and A. Dawson (eds), *After Writing Culture* (London: Routledge, 1997).

Holquist, M., *Dialogism: Bakhtin and his World* (London: Routledge, 1990).

Horne, Karen, and Helen Wussow (eds), *A Dialogue of Feminist Voices: Feminist Literary Theory and Bakhtin* (Minneapolis: Minnesota University Press, 1994).

Hoy, David C. and Thomas McCarthy, *Critical Theory* (Oxford and Cambridge, MA: Blackwell, 1994).

Hufford, David, 'The Scholarly Voice and the Personal Voice: Reflexivity in Belief Studies', *Western Folklore*, vol. 54 (1995) pp. 57–76.

Husserl, Edmund, *Ideas Pertaining to a Pure Phenomenology and to a Phenomenological Philosophy*, trs. W. Boyce Gibson (Boston, The Hague, Lancaster: Nijhoff, 1983).

—— *Cartesian Meditations. An Introduction to Phenomenology*, trs. Dorion Cairns (Dordrecht, Boston and London: Kluwer Academic Publishers, 1993 (1950)).

—— *The Crisis of European Sciences and Transcendental Phenomenology*, trs. David Carr (Evanston: Northwestern University Press, 1970).

Idinopulos, Thomas A. and Edward Yonan (eds) *Religion and Reductionism: Essays on Eliade, Segal, and the Challenge of the Social Sciences for the Study of Religion* (Leiden, New York, Cologne: Brill, 1994).

Inden, R., *Imagining India* (Oxford and Cambridge, MA: Blackwell, 1990).

Inglis, Fred, *Cultural Studies* (Oxford and Cambridge, MA: Blackwell, 1993).

Irmscher, Johannes, 'Der Terminus *Religio* und Seine Antiken Entsprechnungen Im Philologischen und Religionsgeschechtlichen Vergleich', in Bianchi (ed.), *The Notion of 'Religion' in Comparative Research: Selected Proceedings of the XVI IAHR Congress* (Rome: 'L'Erma' di Bretschneider, 1994), pp. 63–73.

Iser, W., *The Act of Reading: A Theory of Aesthetic Response* (Baltimore and London: The Johns Hopkins University Press, 1978).

Isichei, Elizabeth, 'Some Ambiguities in the Academic Study of Religion', *Religion*, vol. 23 (1993), pp. 379–90.

Jaffrelot, Christophe, *The Hindu Nationalist Movement and Indian Politics, 1925 to the 1990s*, trs. C. Hurst & Co. (London: Hurst & Co., 1996).

James, George A., 'Phenomenology and the Study of Religion', *Journal of Religion*, vol. 65, no. 3 (1985).

—— 'Phenomenology and the Study of Religion: The Archaeology of an Approach', *The Journal of Religion*, vol. 65, 3, (1985), pp. 311–35.

Janet, W. D. (ed.), *Directions in Cognitive Anthropology*, (Urbana, IL: University of Illinois Press, 1985).

Jenkins, R., 'Pierre Bourdieu and the Reproduction of Determinism', *Sociology*, vol. 16, 1982, pp. 270–81.

Jenks, Chris, *Culture* (London and New York: Routledge, 1993).

Jensen, Jeppe Sinding, 'Is a Phenomenology of Religion Possible?', *Method and Theory in the Study of Religion*, vol. 5, 2, (1993), pp. 109–33.

John, Lee, D. (ed.), *Life Before Story: Autobiography from a Narrative Perspective* (New York: Praeger, 1994).

Kant, E., 'What is Enlightenment?', in Hans Reiss (ed.), H. B. Nisbett (trs.) *Kant's Political Writings* (Cambridge University Press, 1971).

Keat, R. and J. Urry, *Social Theory as Science* (London: RKP, 1975).

Kelkel, Arion L., 'Language in Husserl', L. Embree, et al. (eds) *Encyclopedia of Phenomenology* (Dordrecht, Boston, London: Kluwer Academic Publishers, 1997).

King, Ursula (ed.), *Turning Points in Religious Studies. Essays in Honour of Geoffrey Parrinder* (Edinburgh: T. & T. Clark, 1990).

—— *Religion and Gender* (Oxford: Blackwell, 1995).

Kitagawa, J. M. 'Foreword', Eliade, M. (ed.), *Encyclopedia of Religion* vol. 1 (New York: Macmillan, 1987).

Kockelmans, J. J., *Edmund Husserl's Phenomenology* (West Lafayette: Purdue University Press, 1994).

Kögler, Hans Herbert, *The Power of Dialogue: Critical Hermeneutics After Gadamer and Foucault*, trs. Paul Hendrickson (Cambridge, MA: London: MIT Press, 1996).

Kolakowski, Lesek, *Positivist Philosophy* (Penguin, 1972).

—— *Religion* (Glasgow: Fontana, 1982).

Krishnamacharya, E. (ed.), *Jayākhya Saṃhitā* (Baroda: Gaekwad's Oriental Series, 1931).

Kristeva, Julia, *Desire in Language: A Semiotic Approach to Literature and Art* (Oxford: Blackwell, 1980).

—— *In the Beginning Was Love* (New York: Columbia University Press, 1988).

Kuhn, T., *The Structure of Scientific Revolutions* (University of Chicago Press, 2nd edn. 1975).

Kymlicka, Will, *Liberalism, Community and Culture* (Oxford: The Clarendon Press, 1989).

La Barre, Weston, *The Ghost Dance* (New York: Dell Publications, 1970).

Lakatos, Imre, 'Falsification and the Methodology of Scientific Research Programmes', in Lakatos and Musgrave, A. (eds), *Criticism and the Growth of Knowledge* (Cambridge University Press, 1970).

Lakoff, George, *Women, Fire and Dangerous Things: What Categories Reveal About the Mind* (Chicago University Press, 1987).

Lasch, Christopher, *The Culture of Narcissism* (London: Abacus, 1980).

Lash, Nicholas, *The Beginning and the End of 'Religion'* (Cambridge University Press, 1996).

Lash, Scott, *Sociology of Postmodernism* (London and New York: Routledge, 1990).

Laudan, Larry, *Science and Relativism* (Chicago University Press, 1990).

Lawlor, Leonard, 'Navigating a Passage: Deconstruction as Phenomenology', *Diacritics*, vol. 23 (1993), pp. 3–15.

Lawson, E. Thomas, and Robert M. McCauley, *Rethinking Religion: Connecting Cognition and Culture* (Cambridge University Press, 1990).

Lessing, Gotthold, *Laokoon, an Essay on the Limits of Painting and Poetry* (Baltimore and London: Johns Hopkins University Press, 1984 (1766)).

Levi-Strauss, Claude, *Structural Anthropology* (New York: Basic Books, 1963).

—— *The Raw and the Cooked*, trs. J. and D. Weightman (Penguin, 1992 (1964)).

Levin, David M., *The Body's Recollection of Being: Phenomenological Psychology and the Deconstruction of Nihilism* (London and Boston: RKP, 1985).

Levinas, Emmanuel, 'Ethics as First Philosophy', *The Levinas Reader*, Sean Hand (ed.) (Oxford and Cambridge: Blackwell, 1989).

—— *The Theory of Intuition in Husserl's Phenomenology*, trs. A. Orianne (Evanston: Northwestern University Press, 1995).

—— *Otherwise than Being or Beyond Essence*, trs. Alphonso Lingis (The Hague: Nijhoff, 1981).

—— *Totality and Infinity: An Essay on Exteriority*, trs. Alphonso Lingis (Pittsburgh: Duquesne University, 1969).

Levinson, Stephen C., *Pragmatics* (Cambridge University Press, 1983).

Lindbeck, George, *The Nature of Doctrine: Religion and Theology in a Postliberal Age* (London: SPCK, 1984).

Lingis, Alphonso, *The Community of Those Who Have Nothing in Common* (Bloomington and Indianapolis: Indianna University Press, 1994).

Luckman, T., *The Invisible Religion: the Problem of Religion in Modern Society* (New York: Macmillan, 1967).

Lyotard, Jean-Francois, *Phenomenology*, trs. Brian Beakley (Albany: Suny Press, 1991).

MacIntyre, A., 'Epistemological Crises, Dramatic Narrative, and the Philosophy of Science', *The Monist*, 60 (1977), pp. 453–71. Reprinted in Appleby et al. (eds) *Knowledge and Postmodernism in Historical Perspective* (New York and London: Routledge, 1996).

—— *After Virtue: A Study in Moral Theory* (London: Duckworth, 1985).

Makreel, Rudolf A., and Jacob Owensby, 'Wilhelm Dilthey', in Embree et al. (eds) *The Encyclopedia of Phenomenology*, pp. 143–7.

Margolis, Joseph, *The Truth About Relativism* (Oxford and Cambridge, MA: Blackwell, 1991).

—— *Life Without Principles* (Oxford: Blackwell, 1996).

Marion, Jean-Luc, *God Without Being* (University of Chicago Press, 1991).

Marsden, George, *The Outrageous Idea of Christian Scholarship* (Oxford University Press, 1997).

Matejka, L., and K. Pomorska (eds), *Readings in Russian Poetics: Formalist and Structuralist Views* (Cambridge, MA: MIT Press, 1971).

McCutcehon, Russel, 'The Myth of the Apolitical Scholar: The Life and Woks of Mircea Eliade', *Queens Quarterly*, vol. 100, no. 3 (1993), pp. 642–63.

—— 'The Category "Religion" in Recent Publications', *Numen* (1995), vol. 42, pp. 284–309.

—— *Manufacturing Religion: The Discourse on Sui Generis Religion and the Politics of Nostalgia* (New York, Oxford: Oxford University Press, 1997).

—— 'A Default of Critical Intelligence? The Scholar of Religion as Public Intellectual', *Journal of the American Academy of Religion*, vol. 65, no. 2 (1997), pp. 443–68.

McGinn, Bernard, *The Presence of God: A History of Western Christian Mysticism*, 1 *The Foundations of Mysticism* (London: SCM Press, 1992).

McIntosh, Donald, 'Husserl, Weber, Freud, and the Method of the Human Sciences', *Philosophy of Social Science*, vol. 27, no. 3, 1997, pp. 328–53.

Medvedev, P. N., *The Formal Method in Literary Scholarship: A Critical Introduction to Sociological Poetics*, trs. Albert Wehrle (Baltimore and London: The Johns Hopkins University Press, 1978).

Mellor, P., and C. Shilling, *Reforming the Body Religion: Community and Modernity* (London, Thousand Oaks, New Delhi: Sage, 1997).

Métraux, A., *Voodoo in Haiti* (New York: Schocken Books, 1972).

Milbank, John, *Theology and Social Theory: Beyond Secular Reason* (Oxford: Blackwell, 1990).

—— *The Word Made Strange: Theology, Language, Culture* (Oxford: Blackwell, 1997).

Milner, Murray, *Status and Sacredness: A General Theory of Status Relations and an Analysis of Indian Culture* (New York, Oxford: Oxford University Press, 1994).

Mink, L., *Historical Understanding* (Ithaca: Cornell University Press, 1987).

Mohanty, J. R., *Edmund Husserl's Theory of Meaning* (The Hague: Martinus Nijhoff, 1976).

—— *Phenomenology: Between Essentialism and Transcendental Philosophy* (Evanston: Northwestern University Press, 1997).

Moi, Toril (ed.), *The Kristeva Reader* (Oxford: Blackwell, 1986).

Moore-Gilbert, Bart, *Postcolonial Theory: Contexts, Practices, Politics* (London and New York: Verso, 1997).

Morrow, R. A., with David D. Brown, *Critical Theory and Methodology* (London, Thousand Oaks, New Delhi: Sage, 1994).

Morson, Gary S., and Caryl Emerson, *Mikhail Bakhtin: Creation of a Prosaics* (Stanford University Press, 1990).

Morson, Gary S., and Caryl Emerson (eds) *Rethinking Bakhtin: Extensions and Challenges* (Evanston: Northwestern University Press, 1989).

Müller, Max, *Chips from a German Workshop*, vol. 1, *Essays on the Science of Religion* (London: Longman, Green & Co., 1867).

Müller, Max, *Introduction to the Science of Religion: Four Lectures Delivered at the Royal Institution with two Essays on False Analogies and the Philosophy of Mythology* (London: Longman, Green & Co., 1873).

Mumby, D. K., *Communication and Power in Organizations: Discourse, Ideology and Domination* (Norwood, NJ: Ablex, 1988).

Mumme, Patricia, 'Haunted by Sankara's Ghost: The Srivaisnava Interpretation of Bhagavad Gita 18.66', in Timm (ed.), *Texts in Context: Traditional Hermeneutics in South Asia* (Albany: Suny Press, 1992), pp. 69–84.

Murphy, T. '*Wesen und Erscheinung* in the History of the Study of Religion: A Post-structuralist Perspective', *Method and Theory in the Study of Religion*, vol. 6 (1994), pp. 119–46.

Nagel, T., *The View from Nowhere* (Oxford University Press, 1986).

Nietzsche, F., *Die Fröhliche Wissenschaft, Werke 2* (Frankfurt, Berlin, Vienna: Ullstein, 1972).

Noddings, Nel, *Caring: A Feminist Approach to Ethics and Moral Education* (Los Angeles: University of California Press, 1984).

Obeyesekere, Gananath, *Medusa's Hair: Essays on Personal Symbols and Religious Experience* (Chicago and London: Chicago University Press, 1981).

O'Connor, June, 'The Epistemological Significance of Feminist Research in Religion', in Ursula King (ed.), *Religion and Gender*, (Oxford: Blackwell, 1995).

Otto, Rudolf, *The Idea of the Holy*, trs. John Harvey (Oxford University Press, 1982 (1923)).

Outhwaite, W., *Understanding Social Life: The Method Called Verstehen* (London: George Allen & Unwin, 1975).

Paden, William E., *Interpreting the Sacred: Ways of Viewing Religion* (Boston: Beacon, 1992).

Pals, Daniel, 'Reductionism and Belief: An Appraisal of Recent Attacks on the Doctrine of Irreducible Religions', *Journal of Religion* (1986), vol. 66, pp. 18–36.

—— 'Is Religion a *Sui Generis* Phenomenon?', *Journal of the American Academy of Religion* (1987), vol. 55, pp. 259–82.

—— 'Autonomy, Legitimacy and the Study of Religion', *Religion* (1990), vol. 20, pp. 1–16.

—— 'Autonomy Revisited: A Rejoinder to Its Critics', *Religion* (1990), vol. 20, pp. 30–37.

—— 'Explanation, Social Science, and the Study of Religion: A Response to Segal with Comment on the Zygon exchange', *Zygon, Journal of Religion and Science* (1992), vol. 27, no. 1, pp. 89–105.

Parsons, Talcott, 'Religion in a Modern Pluralist Society', *Review of Religious Research*, vol. 7 (1966), pp. 125–46.

Paul Ellen Frankel, Fred D. Miller, and Jeffrey Paul (eds) *The Communitarian Challenge to Liberalism* (Cambridge University Press, 1997).

Peacocke, A. (ed.), *Reductionism in Academic Disciplines* (Worcester: Billing & Son, 1985).

Pearce, Lynne, *Reading Dialogics* (London, New York: Edward Arnold, 1990).

Penner, Hans, *Impasse and Resolution: A Critique of the Study of Religion*, Toronto Studies in Religion, vol. 8 (New York: Peter Lang, 1989).

Penner, Hans H., and E. A. Yonan, 'Is a Science of Religion Possible?', *Journal of Religion*, vol. 52 (1972), pp. 107–33.

Peukert, Helmut, 'Enlightenment and Theology as Unfinished Projects', in Don S. Browning and Francis Schussler Fiorenza (eds) *Habermas, Modernity and Public Theology* (New York: Crossroad, 1992).

Piatigorsky, A., *Mythological Deliberations: Lectures on the Phenomenology of Myth* (London: SOAS, 1993).

Pickstock, C., *After Writing: On the Liturgical Consummation of Philosophy* (Oxford: Blackwell, 1998).

Poliakov, L., *The Aryan Myth* (New York: Basic Books, 1974).

Pollock, Sheldon, 'The Sanskrit Cosmopolis 300–1300: Transculturation, Vernacularization, and the Question of Ideology', in Jan E. M. Houben (ed.), *Ideology and Status of Sanskrit: Contributions to the History of the Sanskrit Language* (Leiden: Brill, 1996), pp. 197–247.

Pompa, Leon, *Vico: A Study of the 'New Science'* (Cambridge University Press, 1990).

Preus, S., *Explaining Religion: Criticism and Theory from Bodin to Freud* (New Haven and London: Yale University Press, 1987).

Pye, Michael, 'The Notion of Religion in Comparative Research', *Selected Proceedings of the XVI IAHR Congress*, (1994), pp. 115–22.

Rabinow, Paul (ed.) *The Foucault Reader* (Harmondsworth: Penguin, 1984).

Rappaport, Roy, *Pigs for the Ancestors* (New Haven: Yale University Press, 1968).

Rao, V. N., *Siva's Warriors: the Basava Purana of Palkuriki Somanatha* (Princeton University Press, 1990).

Rawlinson, Andrew, *The Book of Enlightened Masters* (Chicago: Open Court, 1997).

Rawls, J. *A Theory of Justice* (Cambridge, MA: Harvard University Press, 1971).

Rehg, William, *Insight and Solidarity* (Berkeley: University of California Press, 1994).

Rennie, Bryan, *Reconstructing Eliade: Making Sense of Religion* (Albany: Suny Press, 1996).

Rickert, H., *The Limits of Concept Formation in Natural Science: A Logical Introduction to the Historical Sciences*, trs. Guy Oakes (Cambridge University Press, 1986).

Ricoeur, Paul, *The Conflict of Interpretations: Essays in Hermeneutics*, Don Ihde (ed.), (Evanston: Northwestern University Press, 1974).

—— 'Philosophy and Religious Language', *Journal of Religion*, vol. 54 (1974), pp. 71–85.

—— *Hermeneutics and the Human Sciences*, trs. John Thompson (Cambridge University Press, 1981).

—— *Time and Narrative*, 3 vols, trs. Kathleen McLaughlin and David Pellauer (Chicago University Press, 1984, 1985, 1988).

—— 'Life in Quest of Narrative', in Wood, D. (ed.), *On Paul Ricouer, Narrative and Interpretation* (London and New York: Routledge, 1991).

—— *Oneself as Another*, trs. Kathleen Blamey (Chicago University Press, 1992).

Ritzer, George (ed.), *Metatheorizing* (London, Thousand Oaks, New Delhi: Sage, 1992).

Roberts, Richard, 'Interpretations of Resurgent Religion', *Theory, Culture and Society*, vol. 13, 1, 1996, p. 137.

—— 'The Construals of "Europe": Religion, Theology and the Problematics of Modernity', in Heelas (ed.), *Religion, Modernity and Postmodernity* (Oxford: Blackwell, 1998), pp. 186–217.

—— 'Time, Virtuality and the Goddess', *Cultural Values*, vol. 2, nos 2 and 3, (1998), pp. 270–87.

Roberts, R. (ed.), *Religion and the Transformation of Capitalism: Comparative Approaches* (London and New York: Routledge, 1995).

Robertson, R., *Globalization* (London: Sage, 1992).

Rockmore, Thomas, 'Fichte, Husserl and Philosophical Science', *International Philosophical Quarterly*, vol. 19 (1979), pp. 15–27.

Rorty, R., *Philosophy and the Mirror of Nature* (Oxford and Cambridge, MA: Blackwell, 1980).

Rosaldo, R., *Culture and Truth: The Remaking of Social Analysis* (London: Routledge, 1993).

Rosch, E., 'Human Categorisation', in N. Warren (ed.), *Studies in Cross-Cultural Psychology* (London: Academic Press, 1978).

Rouse, Joseph, *Engaging Science: How to Understand Its Practices Philosophically* (Ithaca and London: Cornell University Press, 1996).

Rudolf, Kurt, 'Inwieweit ist der Begriff "Religion" Eurozentrisch?' in Bianchi, Ugo (ed.), *The Notion of 'Religion' in Comparative Research: Selected Proceedings of the XVI IAHR Congress* (Rome: 'L'Erma' di Bretschneider, 1994), pp. 131–9.

Rumsey, Alan, 'Wording, Meaning and Linguistic Ideology', *American Anthropologist*, 92 (1990), pp. 346–61.

Ryba, T., *The Essence of Phenomenology and its Meaning for the Scientific Study of Religion* (New York: Peter Lang, 1991).

Said, Edward, *Orientalism* (New York: Pantheon, 1978).

Saler, Benson, *Conceptualising Religion: Immanent Anthropologists, Transcendent Natives and Unbounded Categories* (Leiden: Brill, 1993).

Sampson, Edward E., *Celebrating the Other: A Dialogic Account of Human Nature* (Boulder: Westview Press, 1993).

Samuel, G., *Mind, Body and Culture: Anthropology and the Biological Interface* (Cambridge University Press, 1990).

Sandel, Michael J., *Liberalism and the Limits of Justice* (Cambridge University Press, 1982).

Sandywell, Barry, *Logological Investigations*, 3 vols. (London: Routledge, 1996).

Sarbin, T. (ed.), *Narrative Psychology: The Storied Nature of Human Conduct* (New York: Praeger, 1986).

Saussurre, Ferdinand de, *A Course in General Linguistics* (London: Fontana, 1974 (1915)).

Searle, John R., *Speech Acts: Essays in the Philosophy of Language* (Cambridge University Press, 1969).

Sebeok, T. A. (ed.), *Style in Language* (Cambridge, Mass: MIT, 1966.

Seebohm, Thomas M., 'Johann Gottlieb Fichte', in Embree et al. (eds), *The Encyclopedia of Phenomenology* (Dordrecht, Boston, London: Kluwer Academic Publishers, 1997), pp. 223–6.

Segal, Robert, 'In Defense of Reductionism', *Journal of the American Academy of Religion* (1983), vol. 51, pp. 97–124.

—— *Religion and the Social Sciences: Essays on the Confrontation* (Atlanta: Scholars Press, 1989).

—— *Explaining and Interpreting Religion, Essays on the Issue* (New York: Peter Lang, 1992).

Scheler, Max, *On the Eternal in Man* (London: SCM Press, 1960 (1922)).

Schutz, Alfred, *The Phenomenology of the Social World* (London: Heinemann, 1972).

Shapin, Steven, *A Social History of Truth: Civility and Science in Seventeenth-Century England* (University of Chicago Press, 1994).

Sharpe, Eric, *Comparative Religion: A History* (London: Duckworth, 1975).

—— *Understanding Religion* (London: Duckworth, 1983).

Shepherd, John, 'Debating Point (4): Phenomenological Perspectivalism', *British Association for the Study of Religions Bulletin*, no. 71, March 1994.

Sherry, Patrick, *Spirit and Beauty, An Introduction to Theological Aesthetics* (Oxford: Clarendon Press, 1992).

Shilling, Chris, *The Body and Social Theory* (London, Newbury Park, New Delhi: Sage, 1993).

Shlovsky, V., 'Art as Technique' in L. T. Lemon and Marion Reis (eds)

Russian Formalist Criticism: Four Essays (Lincoln: University of Nebraska Press, 1965).

Silverstein, M., and Greg Urban (eds) *Natural Histories of Discourse* (Chicago and London: University of Chicago Press, 1996).

Sinfield, Alan, *Faultlines: Cultural Materialism and the Politics of Dissident Reading* (Oxford: Clarendon Press, 1992).

Smart, Ninian, *Reasons and Faiths* (London: SPCK, 1958).

—— *The Science of Religion and the Sociology of Knowledge* (Princeton University Press, 1973).

—— *The Religious Experience of Mankind* (New York: Fontana, 1969).

—— 'Discussion', in 'Replies to Don Wiebe in the World Academy of Religion', *Religion*, vol. 23, 1993, p. 93.

—— 'Religious Studies and Theology', in *The Council of Societies for the Study of Religion Bulletin*, vol. 26, 3, 1997, pp. 66–8.

Smith, J. Z., *Imagining Religion, from Babylon to Jonestown* (University of Chicago Press, 1982).

Smith, W. Cantwell, *The Meaning and End of Religion* (New York: Macmillan, 1962).

Sontheimer, G-D., and Herman Kulke (eds), *Hinduism Reconsidered*, 2nd edn. (Delhi: Manonhar, 1997).

Sorbom, Goran, *Mimesis and Art: Studies in the Origin and Early Development of an Aesthetic Vocabulary* (Stockholm: Svenska Bokforlaget, 1966).

Sosa, E. (ed.), *Causation and Conditionals* (Oxford University Press, 1975).

Soskice, Janet, *Metaphor and Religious Language* (Oxford: Clarendon Press, 1989).

Sperber, Dan, *Rethinking Symbolism* (Cambridge University Press, 1975).

Spiegelberg, H., *The Phenomenological Movement: An Historical Introduction* (The Hague, Boston, Lancaster: Martinus Nijhoff, 1984 (1960)).

Spiro, M., 'Religion: Some Problems of Definition and Explanation', in Banton, M. (ed.), *Anthropological Approaches to the Study of Religion* (London: Tavistock, 1978 (1966)).

Staal, Frits, *Rules Without Meaning: Ritual, Mantras and the Human Sciences* (New York: Peter Lang, 1989).

Stark, R., and Bainbridge, W. S., *A Theory of Religion* (New York: Peter Lang, 1987).

Steinbock, A. J., *Home and Beyond, Generative Phenomenology After Husserl* (Evanston: Northwestern University Press, 1995).

Stinchcombe, A. L., 'The Origins of Sociology as a Discipline', *Acta Sociologica* 1984, vol. 27, pp. 51–61.

Stone, Jon R. (ed.), *The Craft of Religious Studies* (New York: St Martin's Press, 1997).

Strenski, Ivan, *Religion in Relation: Method, Application, and Moral Location* (Columbia: University of South Carolina Press, 1993).

Synnott, Anthony, *The Social Body* (London and New York: Routledge, 1993).

Taylor, Charles, 'Interpretation and the Sciences of Man', in *Philosophy and the Human Sciences: Philosophical Papers 2* (Cambridge University Press, 1985).

—— *Sources of the Self* (Cambridge University Press, 1989).

—— *The Ethics of Authenticity* (Harvard University Press, 1991).

Taylor, Mark, *Erring: A Postmodern A/theology* (University of Chicago Press, 1984).

Taylor, Mark (ed.), *Critical Terms for Religious Studies* (University of Chicago Press, 1998).

Taylor, S., *The Said and the Unsaid* (New York: Academic Press, 1978).

Thompson, John B., *Critical Hermeneutics: A Study in the Thought of Paul Ricouer and Jürgen Habermas* (Cambridge University Press, 1981).

Thomson, Clive, 'Introduction: Bakhtin and Shifting Paradigms', *Critical Studies*, vol. 2 no. 1/2 (1990), pp. 2–23.

Tilley, Terrence W., *Postmodern Theologies: The Challenge of Religious Diversity* (New York: Orbis Books, 1996).

Todorov, Tzvetan, *Mikhail Bakhtin: The Dialogical Principle* (Manchester University Press, 1984).

Touraine, A., *Critique of Modernity*, trs. David Macey (Oxford and Cambridge, MA: Blackwell, 1995).

Tracy, David, *The Analogical Imagination: Christian Theology and the Culture of Pluralism* (London: SCM, 1981).

Turner, Bryan S., *The Body and Society* (Oxford: Blackwell, 1984).

—— *Orientalism, Postmodernism and Globalism* (London: Routledge, 1994).

Tyler, S. A. (ed.), *Cognitive Anthropology* (New York: Holt, Rinehart & Winston, 1969).

Urban, Greg, 'The "I" of Discourse', in Benjamin Lee and Greg Urban (eds), *Semiotics, Self and Society* (Berlin, New York: Mouton de Gruyter, 1989).

—— *A Discourse-Centred Approach to Culture: Native South American Myths and Rituals* (Austin: University of Texas Press, 1991).

Van der Leeuw, G., *Religion in Essence and Manifestation* (New York: Harper Tourchbooks, 1973).

Vattimo, Gianni, *Beyond Interpretation: The Meaning of Hermeneutics for Philosophy*, trs. David Webb (Cambridge: Polity Press, 1997).

—— *The End of Modernity*, trs. John R. Snyder (Cambridge: Polity Press, 1988).

Vico, G., *The New Science*, Bergin, T. G., and M. H. Fisch (eds), (Ithaca and London: Cornell University Press, 1968).

Voloshinov, V. N., *Marxism and the Philosophy of Language*, trs. L. Matejka and I. R. Titunik (Cambridge, MA: and London: Harvard University Press, 1986).

Vygotsky, Lev S., *Thought and Language*, Alex Kozulin (ed.), (Cambridge, MA: MIT Press, 1986).

Waardenburg, J. (ed.), *Classical Approaches to the Study of Religion*, vol. 1 (The Hague, Paris: Mouton, 1973).

Wach, Joachim, *Types of Religious Experience, Christian and Non-Christian* (Chicago: University of Chicago Press, 1951).

Wagner, Roy, *The Invention of Culture* (Chicago University Press, 1980).

Walzer, Michael, 'The Communitarian Critique of Liberalism', *Political Theory*, vol. 18 (1990), pp. 6–23.

Ward, G. (ed.), *The Postmodern God: A Theological Reader* (Oxford: Blackwell, 1997).

Ward, G., 'Kenosis and Naming: Beyond Analogy and Towards Allegoria Amoris' in Heelas (ed.), *Religion, Modernity and Postmodernity* (Oxford: Blackwell, 1998), pp. 233–57.

Warnke, Marina, *Gadamer: Hermeneutics, Tradition and Reason* (Cambridge: Polity Press, 1987).

Wax, Murray L., 'Religion as Universal: Tribulations of an Anthropological Enterprise', *Zygon* (1984), vol. 19, 1, pp. 5–20.

Weber, Max, *The Methodology of the Social Sciences* (New York: Free Press, 1949).

—— *Economy and Society: An Outline of Interpretative Sociology*, eds G. Roth and C. Wittich (Berkeley: University of California Press, 1978).

Whaling, Frank (ed.), *Contemporary Approaches to the Study of Religion* (Berlin, New York, Amsterdam: Mouton, 1984).

White, Hayden, *Metahistory* (Baltimore and London: Johns Hopkins University Press, 1973).

—— *Tropics of Discourse* (Baltimore and London: Johns Hopkins University Press, 1978).

—— *The Content and the Form* (Baltimore and London: Johns Hopkins University Press, 1987).

Whorf, Bejamin Lee, 'The Relation of Habitual Thought to Behaviour and Language', pp. 148–9 in *Language, Thought and Reality* (Cambridge, MA: MIT Press, 1956), pp. 134–59.

Wiebe, Donald, *Religion and Truth: Towards an Alternative Paradigm for the Study of Religion* (The Hague: Mouton, 1981).

—— 'Theory in the Study of Religion', *Religion* 13 (1983), pp. 283–309.

—— 'Beyond the Sceptic and the Devotee: Reductionism in the Scientific

Study of Religion', *Journal of the American Academy of Religion* (1984), vol. 52, pp. 156–65.

—— 'The Failure of Nerve in the Academic Study of Religion', *Studies in Religion/Sciences Religieuses* 13/ 4 (1984), pp. 401–22.

—— 'A Positive Episteme for the Study of Religion', *The Scottish Journal of Religious Studies*, 6 (1985), pp. 78–95.

—— 'Why the Academic Study of Religion? Motive and Method in the Study of Religion', *Religious Studies* (1988), vol. 24, pp. 403–13.

—— 'Disciplinary Axioms, Boundary Conditions and the Academic Study of Religion: Comments on Pals and Dawson', *Religion* (1990), vol. 20, pp. 17–29.

Wilson, Brian, 'Aspects of Secularisation in the West', *Japanese Journal of Religious Studies*, vol. 3, 1976, pp. 259–76.

Wilson, E., *On Human Nature* (Harvard University Press, 1978).

Winch, P., *The Idea of a Social Science and its Relation to Philosophy* (London: RKP, 1977 (1958)).

Wood, D. (ed.), *On Paul Ricoeur, Narrative and Interpretation* (London and New York: Routledge, 1991).

Woolgar, S. (ed.), *Knowledge and Reflexivity: New Frontiers in the Sociology of Knowledge* (London: Sage, 1991).

Yonan, E., 'Is a Science of Religion Possible?', *Journal of Religion*, vol. 52, 1972, pp. 107–33.

Index